The Dynamics of Violence
in Central Africa

OTHER BOOKS BY RENÉ LEMARCHAND

Political Awakening in the Congo
Rwanda and Burundi
African Kingships in Perspective (*editor*)
American Policy in Southern Africa: The Stakes and the Stance (*editor*)
Political Clientelism, Patronage and Development (*coeditor with
    S. N. Eisenstadt*)
The Green and the Black: Qadhafi's Policies in Africa (*editor*)
Burundi: Ethnic Conflict and Genocide

The Dynamics of Violence in Central Africa

RENÉ LEMARCHAND

PENN

University of Pennsylvania Press

Philadelphia

National and Ethnic Conflict in the 21st Century

Copyright © 2009 University of Pennsylvania Press

All rights reserved. Except for brief quotations used for purposes of review or scholarly citation, none of this book may be reproduced in any form by any means without written permission from the publisher.

Published by
University of Pennsylvania Press
Philadelphia, Pennsylvania 19104-4112

Printed in the United States of America on acid-free paper

10 9 8 7 6 5 4 3 2

Library of Congress Cataloging-in-Publication Data

Lemarchand, René.

   The dynamics of violence in central Africa / René Lemarchand.
     p. cm. — (National and ethnic conflict in the twenty-first century)
   Includes bibliographical references and index.
   ISBN 978-0-8122-4120-4 (alk. paper)
   1. Africa, Central—Politics and government—1960– 2. Africa, Central—Economic conditions—1960– 3. Africa, Central—Ethnic relations—Political aspects. 4. Political violence—Great Lakes Region (Africa) 5. Geopolitics—Great Lakes Region (Africa) 6. Genocide—Great Lakes Region (Africa) I. Title.
DT352.8.L46 2008
967.03—dc22
                                              2008018612

In memory of Lando Ndasingwa, a man of rare integrity and a friend of many years, savagely murdered in Kigali on the first day of the Rwanda bloodbath, April 7, 1994, along with his Canadian wife and two children

Contents

Preface   ix

PART I. THE REGIONAL CONTEXT

Chapter 1. The Geopolitics of the Great Lakes Region   3

Chapter 2. The Road to Hell   30

PART II. RWANDA AND BURUNDI: THE GENOCIDAL TWINS

Comparative Perspectives

Chapter 3. Ethnicity as Myth   49

Chapter 4. Genocide in the Great Lakes: Which Genocide? Whose Genocide?   69

Rwanda

Chapter 5. The Rationality of Genocide   79

Chapter 6. Hate Crimes   88

Chapter 7. The Politics of Memory   99

Chapter 8. Rwanda and the Holocaust Reconsidered   109

Burundi

Chapter 9. Burundi 1972: A Forgotten Genocide   129

Chapter 10. Burundi at the Crossroads   141

Chapter 11. Burundi's Endangered Transition   158

PART III. THE DEMOCRATIC REPUBLIC OF THE CONGO: FROM FAILED STATE TO FRAGILE TRANSITION

Chapter 12. A Blocked Transition: Zaire in 1993   191

Chapter 13. Ethnic Violence, Public Policies, and Social Capital in North Kivu   205

Chapter 14. The DRC: From Failure to Potential Reconstruction   216

Chapter 15. The Tunnel at the End of the Light   249

Chapter 16. From Kabila to Kabila: What Else Is New?   260

Notes   281

Index   313

Acknowledgments   325

Preface

The one duty we owe to history is to rewrite it.
—Oscar Wilde

The Great Lakes region matters. It matters because of its vast territorial expanse and the many borders it shares with neighboring states, and the ever-present danger of violence spilling across boundaries. It matters because the Congo's huge mineral wealth translates into a uniquely favorable potential for economic development. While claiming the largest deposits of copper, cobalt, diamonds and gold anywhere in the continent—it is not for nothing that the Belgians called it a "geological scandal"—more than 60 percent of its population lives below the poverty line. More importantly, it matters because of the appalling bloodshed it continues to experience. Public revulsion over the Rwanda genocide has all but overshadowed the far greater scale of the human losses suffered in eastern Congo. The death toll between 1998 and 2004 was estimated to be nearly 4 million.[1] If one adds the killings in Rwanda and Burundi since 1994, one reaches the staggering figure of approximately 5.5 million. To this day as many as 38,000 die every month of war-related causes. In many parts of the country, rape has become the weapon of choice of militias. The unspeakable has become commonplace. This in itself is a sufficient reason to devote serious attention to an area that is all too often dismissed as a latter-day version of the Heart of Darkness, entirely beyond redemption.

At the root of the misconceptions and prejudices that figure so prominently in the media coverage of Central Africa lies an abysmal ignorance of its past and recent history.[2] My aim here is not only to challenge many such received ideas but also, by the same token, to deepen the understanding of the region by offering comparative insights into the dynamics of violence in each of the three states around which these essays are constructed (Rwanda, Burundi, and the Democratic Republic of the Congo [DRC]).

Viewing their agonies in isolation from each other reveals only a fraction of the regional forces at work behind the surge of ethnic strife. Just as the shock waves of the Rwanda bloodbath have sent violent tremors to neighboring states, its seemingly ineluctable advent is inseparable from the long-term processes of change that have taken place in the region. Only through a regional lens can one bring into focus the violent patterns of interaction that form the essential backdrop to the spread of bloodshed within and across boundaries.

Part I of the book ("The Regional Context") is an attempt to set the political trajectories of each state in a wider perspective. After looking at the geopolitical setting (Chapter 1)—so as to make more legible the region's complex social configurations, recasting of identities, and spatial fall-out—we turn to more specific dimensions of analysis (Chapter 2). Here the emphasis is on processes of exclusion, marginalization, and political mobilization as vectors of conflict. In the light of the empirical evidence, I suggest a critical reconsideration of the more fashionable explanatory models that have gained currency among contemporary social scientists, from Samuel Huntington to Paul Collier.

This broad sketch is meant as a backdrop for a more sustained examination of the politics of mass violence in Rwanda, Burundi, and the DRC. Part II ("Rwanda and Burundi: The Genocidal Twins") is an attempt to set the historical roots and circumstances of genocidal killings in Rwanda and Burundi in a comparative perspective. Ultimately the aim is to analyze the reciprocal impact of one upon the other. Sometimes referred to as the "false twins," the phrase also applies to their experience of genocide. Although the 1972 carnage in Burundi never reached the magnitude of its 1994 counterpart in Rwanda, and the bulk of the victims were Hutu, this should not obscure the similarities in the dynamics of the killings in each state and how the Burundi carnage has reverberated upon Rwanda.

Behind these horror stories lies a sociological puzzle, which for the sake of clarity, requires a brief historical digression. Although Rwanda and Burundi have more in common than any other two states in the continent in terms of size, ethnic maps, language, and culture, they crossed the threshold of independence under radically different circumstances, one (Rwanda) ending up as a republic under Hutu hegemony, the other (Burundi) as a constitutional monarchy under the rule of the Tutsi minority. Not until 1965 did the army abolish the monarchy. And although both experienced genocide, Rwanda today has emerged as a thinly disguised Tutsi dictatorship, with Burundi, on the other hand, painstakingly charting a new course toward a multi-party and multi-ethnic democracy. Seldom anywhere have Sigmund Freud's reflections on "the narcissism of minor differences"[3] received a more dramatic confirmation: nowhere in Africa has fratricidal strife torn apart communities as nearly identical as between Hutu and Tutsi.

The key to the puzzle lies in history. For all their similarities, traditional Burundi was far from being a carbon copy of Rwanda. In neither state is ethnic conflict reducible to age-old enmities, yet the Hutu-Tutsi split was far more pronounced, and therefore more potentially menacing, in Rwanda, where the "premise of inequality"—greatly reinforced by the legacy of colonial rule—emerged as the central axis around which Hutu-Tutsi relations revolved. Burundi society, by contrast, was significantly more complicated and therefore more flexible. Typically, at first the focus of conflict had little to do with Hutu and Tutsi, involving instead political rivalries between the representatives of dynastic factions, known as the Bezi and Batare. The years following independence saw a drastic transformation of the parameters of conflict, where the Rwanda model took on the quality of a self-fulfilling prophecy. As many Hutu elites increasingly came to look to Rwanda as the exemplary polity, growing fears spread in Burundi's Tutsi population of an impending Rwanda-like revolution. Unless Hutu claims to power were resisted, they would share the fate of their Rwandan kinsmen. This meant a more or less systematic exclusion of Hutu elements from positions of authority. Exclusion led to insurrection, and insurrection to repression, culminating in 1972 with what must be described as the first recorded genocide in independent Africa.

The centrality of myth-making as a key element behind conflicting identities is the subject of Chapter 3, with particular emphasis on the case of Rwanda. Here the discussion finds a convenient point of entry in John Lonsdale's concept of "moral ethnicity" (evolving into a singularly immoral definition of the Tutsi "other"), as well as in Terence Ranger's seminal insights into the different "imaginations" involved in the historical process of redefining social entities. The parallel agonies of the two states are the subject of Chapter 4, which also tries to bring out the relevance of the killings in Burundi to an understanding of the Rwanda tragedy.

Chapters 5 to 8 explore the multiple dimensions of the Rwanda genocide. Chapter 5 looks at the perverse "rationality" of mass murder and shows the fallacy behind the all-too-prevalent notion of a spontaneous, uncontrollable outburst of collective ethnic hatred; Chapter 6 is about the danger of reducing the horrors of mass crimes to a story of good and evil; Chapter 7 probes the politics of memory in contemporary Rwanda and leans heavily on Paul Ricoeur's analytic categories to describe the ways in which ethnic memory is manipulated by the Kagame government; Chapter 8 is an attempt to bring out the singularity of the Rwandan bloodbath and in so doing warns against the all-too-frequent tendency to draw an uncritical parallel between the Holocaust and Rwanda.

Not only is the analogy with the Holocaust misleading on historical grounds (Jews never invaded Germany with the assistance of a neighboring state for the purpose of bringing down the government); it suggests a way of apportioning responsibility that can lead only to the gravest of misunderstandings. Drawing the line between the good guys and the bad guys is easy enough in the case of Nazi Germany; in Rwanda the distinction is far more problematic, if only because it defies the simplistic equation between Hutu murderers and Tutsi victims. This inherently complex dimension is one that is systematically shoved under the rug in official Rwandan historiography. The watchword in Rwanda today, symbolized by the moving memorial to Tutsi victims, is "Never forget!"—but there is an unspoken subtext: "Never remember!" Never remember the 1972 genocide of Hutu in Burundi, the massacre of Hutu refugees in eastern Congo, or the systematic elimination of Hutu civilians during and after the 1990 invasion of Rwanda by Kagame's soldiers. Above all, never remember Kagame's onus of responsibility in the shooting down of the plane carrying the presidents of Rwanda and Burundi to Kigali, the detonator that ignited the genocide. His involvement in the crash is convincingly demonstrated in Lieutenant Abdul Joshua Ruzibiza's autobiographical narrative while serving in Kagame's Rwanda Patriotic Front (RPF),[4] as well as in the judicial investigation of French magistrate Jean-Louis Bruguière. I have no hesitation to concede that the analysis in Chapters 5 to 8 would have been significantly enriched had I had access to these vitally important sources.

The Burundi genocide—a largely forgotten drama, yet still poignantly relevant to an understanding of the contemporary political scene—is dealt with in Chapter 9. Whereas Chapter 10 turns the spotlight on the state of play on the eve of the transition to democracy, Chapter 11 looks at Burundi's "endangered transition" in the wake of the 2005 elections.

Part III (on the Democratic Republic of the Congo) is a somewhat impressionistic and largely retrospective portrayal of the forces that have made the former Belgian colony one of the most violent areas on the continent. It looks at the multiple crises that have engulfed the Congo in a time-space perspective. Chapter 12 is excerpted from my 1993 USAID report, at a time when Mobutu stood as the arch-villain in blocking the country's transition to democracy. I include it because it captures some of the problems which continue to beset the country after its first multiparty elections in thirty years. Looking back to my diagnosis there of Zairian ailments—a weak civil society, the omnipresent threat of insecurity, the appalling lack of cohesion and professionalism of the army, an economy in shambles—the continuing threats they pose to the resurrection of the Congolese body politic are hard to escape. Chapter 13—first presented at a 1999 conference on the theme of social capital at the University of Antwerp—uses Robert Putnam's civil society lens to delve into the complex interconnections between ethnic violence, public policies and social capital in the Kivu region, one of the most potentially unstable arenas anywhere in the DRC, along with Ituri. Chapter 14 is a broad-gauged analysis of the Congo as a failed state and of the persistent hurdles that stand in the way of a reconstructed state system. The title of Chapter 15 captures the gist of the argument: the "tunnel at the end of the light" metaphor is enough to disabuse the reader of the notion that elections can serve as a panacea to resolve the country's enduring ills, ranging from residual pockets of insurgency to rampant corruption, widespread poverty, and persistent indiscipline and chronic defections within the armed forces, not to mention the ever-present threat of armed intervention from Rwanda.

The concluding chapter ("From Kabila to Kabila: What Else Is New?") is a reflection on the lessons to be drawn from the Congo's first multiparty poll in forty years (held at a cost of over half a billion dollars to the international community). While reiterating the well-worn cliché about elections not being a guarantee of future stability, or a substitute for a functioning state, it tries to assess the historic legacy of the Mobutist state and that of his successor, the despotic buffoon whose son is now in charge of charting a new course toward peace and democracy. Although there can be no question about the significance of the changes that have occurred since the death of Kabila *père*, today the Congo remains dangerously vulnerable to the ills inherited from Mobutu's thirty-year dictatorship.

Attempts to sketch future trends are not without risks: the newly emergent institutions are conspicuously weak, the concatenation of forces on the ground in a state of flux, and leadership patterns at the provincial levels all but impossible to pin down. Nonetheless, some plausible scenarios come to mind. The most obvious relates to the continuing impact of outside forces on the salience and direction of domestic conflict. In the past the sheltering of opposition movements from Rwanda, Burundi, and Uganda have raised major security concerns among their respective governments and have served as a pretext for armed incursions. In recent times the stakes have become more complicated, with access to mineral wealth looming increasingly large on the agenda of Rwanda and Uganda, and the many connecting links between eastern Congo and its neighbors portend continuing conflict.

The likelihood of what Samuel Huntington calls "within-state fault line conflicts"[5] acting as a catalyst for interstate confrontations is not to be discounted. The mutual distrust between the self-styled *indigènes* or "native sons" in North and South Kivu, and the Kinyarwanda-speaking *allogènes*, will not go away any time soon,[6] any more than the bitter enmities between remnants of the Hutu genocidaires and the Tutsi communities indigenous to eastern DRC. The conflict lies at the heart of the tensions that brought Rwanda and the DRC to the brink of war in late 2004. It could resurface at any time in the future.

How such conflicts might play themselves out on the ground is an open question. The gravest danger would arise from the simultaneity of violent insurrections in both east and west, as happened in the wake of the transition to multiparty democracy, thus confronting the fledgling Congolese armed forces with an unmanageable challenge. But by far the worse-case scenario is one where the army might dissolve in the midst of factional rivalries, leaving the government in a state of utter impotence in the face of widespread outbreaks of violence. Granted that the main guarantee of future stability lies in the presence of the Mission de l'Organisation des Nations Unies du Congo (MONUC) peacekeepers, when one considers the costs of its operation and the less than cooperative attitude of the Congolese government, one wonders how much longer the MONUC can be relied on to help maintain a modicum of peace and stability. Even in the best of circumstances, its past performance raises serious doubts as to whether it will be equal to the task.

Just as debatable is whether the long-awaited transition to democracy can do more than provide a constitutional fig leaf to conceal the nakedness of a party-dominated, clientelist polity. Even at this early stage, there are ample signs that Kabila *fils* is unlikely to distance himself from the authoritarian style of his predecessor. The legitimate political opposition has been either forced into submission, bought off, or reduced to a marginal position. The army, meanwhile, will remain the Achilles' heel of the regime. Its restructuring is still at an incipient stage. Its nuisance capacity is not the least of the problems inherited from the Mobutist past. In this, as in many other ways, the DRC bears testimony to the many wounds inflicted upon its people by its rulers with the help of its neighbors.

The Congo's supreme anomaly—a country of immense wealth home to one of the continent's poorest populations—will continue to shock, intrigue, or infuriate observers and political actors alike for many years to come. Yoked together by an accident of history, the three states of the former Belgian Africa are each engaged in a process of self-reinvention, each trying to shape its future in defiance of its past. Whether the legacy of their recent agonies can be set aside for the sake of a more promising destiny is impossible to tell. That they will continue to influence each

Chapter 1
The Geopolitics of the Great Lakes Region

In common usage the Great Lakes region refers to Central Africa's Great Rift valley, stretching on a north-south axis along the Congo-Nile crest, from Lake Tanganyika in the south to Lake Edward and the legendary Mountains of the Moon in the north. But where exactly does it begin, and where does it end? Should it include western Tanzania and southwestern Sudan? Should the Maniema and north Katanga be factored in as well? The answers are anything but straightforward. There is general agreement, however, that a minimal definition should include Rwanda, Burundi, eastern Congo, and southwestern Uganda as the core area of what once was called the "interlacustrine" zone of the continent, covering an estimated 300,000 square miles. This is the sense in which we shall use the phrase.

The interlacustrine metaphor, though still fashionable among geographers, suggests too much in the way of uniformity and too little about the diversity of peoples, cultures, and subregions subsumed under this label.[1] There is a fundamental truth in the observation that "the extent to which people are attached to their native turf (*terroir d'origine*) is still highly developed among the people of the Great Lakes."[2] To this day, group loyalties continue to cluster around precolonial *terroirs*. Whereas many readily identify with places like Nduga, Kiga, Bwisha, Bwito, Masisi, Rutshuru, Beni-Butembo, to name only a few, nowhere among Africans is the Great Lakes referent perceived as a meaningful identity marker. The phrase, as Jean-Pierre Chrétien reminds us, is evocative of "the German tradition of a *Volkgeist*, as if a kind of common soul had emerged from the proximity of these lakes."[3] Though encompassing many of the shared cultural traits identified by the French historian—a high population density, the agropastoral tandem, the heritage of kingship, a tendency for outsiders to look at these societies through the lens of race, and so forth—in the end, he adds that what links these peoples and cultures together is "a kind of connivance born of multiple confrontations and countless encounters."[4] Since these words were written (1986), most of these encounters have been extremely bloody and their after-effects, devastating.

At the root of these confrontations lies an array of forces and circumstances of enormous complexity. Most are the product of human decisions made during the colonial and postcolonial eras, but these must be seen in the perspective of the drastic changes that have taken place in the regional environment. Politics and geography intersect in different ways at different points in time, but the key variables remain the same. The potential for conflict is inscribed in the discontinuities in population densities, the availability of land, the cultural fault lines discernible in different language patterns, modes of social organization, and ecological circumstances. None of the above were fixed from time immemorial. As has been noted time and again, most recently by Michael Mann, modernity has gone hand in hand with eruptions of ethnic violence.[5] Societies that were once held together by hierarchies of birth, rank, and privilege have been subjected to profound disruptions of their social fabric, ushering in "masterless men,"[6] marginalized youth, and warlords in search of gold, diamonds, and coltan. Today's demographic explosion in Rwanda, resulting in a population density of 300 per square kilometer, is without parallel elsewhere, causing a drastic shrinking of cultivable land; areas where land hunger was almost unknown at the inception of colonial rule (as in Rutshuru and Masisi) are now saturated; deforestation has denuded large tracts of land, accelerating soil erosion and reducing crop cultivation;[7] almost everywhere wildlife is fast disappearing, most notably hippos, elephants, and mountain gorillas, with profoundly negative effects on the region's ecosystem.[8] Once described as a tourist paradise,[9] today's Great Lakes region shows many of the symptoms of a Hobbesian universe.

Convenient though it is to speak of the crisis in the Great Lakes in the singular, it makes more sense to think in terms of a multiplicity of crises, which, though historically distinct and occurring in specific national contexts, have set off violent chain reactions in neighboring states. The Hutu revolution (1959–62) in Rwanda was one such crisis. Another was the 1994 genocide. Both have sent shock waves through the region the first creating the conditions of a "partial genocide" of Hutu in Burundi in 1972, the second unleashing ethnic cleansing, population displacements, and civil war through many parts of the Congo, resulting in human losses far greater than in either Burundi in 1972 or Rwanda in 1994. To these we shall return in a moment, but before going any further, a note of caution is in order about some of the misconceptions surrounding the region's recent agonies.

Challenging Received Ideas

The belief that nowhere in the continent has violence taken a heavier toll than in Rwanda, with nearly a million deaths, overwhelmingly Tutsi, is one of the most persistent and persistently misleading ideas about the region. It may come as a surprise, therefore, that four times as many people have died in eastern Congo between 1998 and 2006. Although the exact number will never be known, a recent survey by the International Rescue Committee (IRC) shows that nearly four million people were killed from war-related causes in the Democratic Republic of the Congo (DRC) since 1998, "the largest documented death toll in a conflict since World War II."[10] Citing the IRC survey, the British medical journal *The Lancet* recently drew the right conclusion: "It is a sad indictment of us all that seven years into this crisis ignorance about its scale and impact is almost universal, and that international engagement remains completely out of proportion to humanitarian need."[11]

Ignorance in this case is largely a reflection of public indifference in the face of a situation that, however unfortunate, is generally seen by outside observers as African-made, rooted in the incorrigible greed of rival warlords and therefore, the responsibility of Africans. But this is only partially true. This is how a British journalist sees the other side of the coin in his coverage of "the most savage war in the world": "it is also the story of a trail of blood that leads directly to you: to your remote control, to your mobile phone, to your laptop and to your diamond necklace . . . it is a battle for the metals that make our technological society vibrate and ring and bling."[12] Western economic interests are indeed deeply involved in the conflict through their participation, direct or indirect, in the illicit trade in arms and mineral resources. Both span a wide network of companies, brokers, money changers, and facilitators. European companies—Belgian (Cogecom), Swiss (Finmining, Raremet), German (Masingiro), Dutch (Chemie Pharmacie)—figure prominently in the war economy of the region, a fact conclusively demonstrated by several outstanding investigative reports.[13] Among various forms of the involvement of the United States, passing reference must be made to the joint venture between the American corporation Trinitech and the Dutch firm Chemie Pharmacie, in which the U.S. embassy in Kigali may have played a "facilitating" role. As reported by one well-informed observer, "the economic section of the U.S. embassy in Kigali has been extremely active at the beginning of the war in helping establish joint ventures to exploit coltan," a fact carefully expunged from all official reports, leaving only Africans to be incriminated.[14] Though seldom brought into the public domain, the share of responsibility of Western corporate interests in supporting a war economy that has resulted in the deaths of millions, cannot be ignored.

Frequent reference to confrontations among warring factions as a "resource war" points to yet another misconception, for which Paul Collier deserves full credit.[15] This is not to imply that "greed" is not a factor in *sustaining* the bloodshed; the point rather is that it never played the

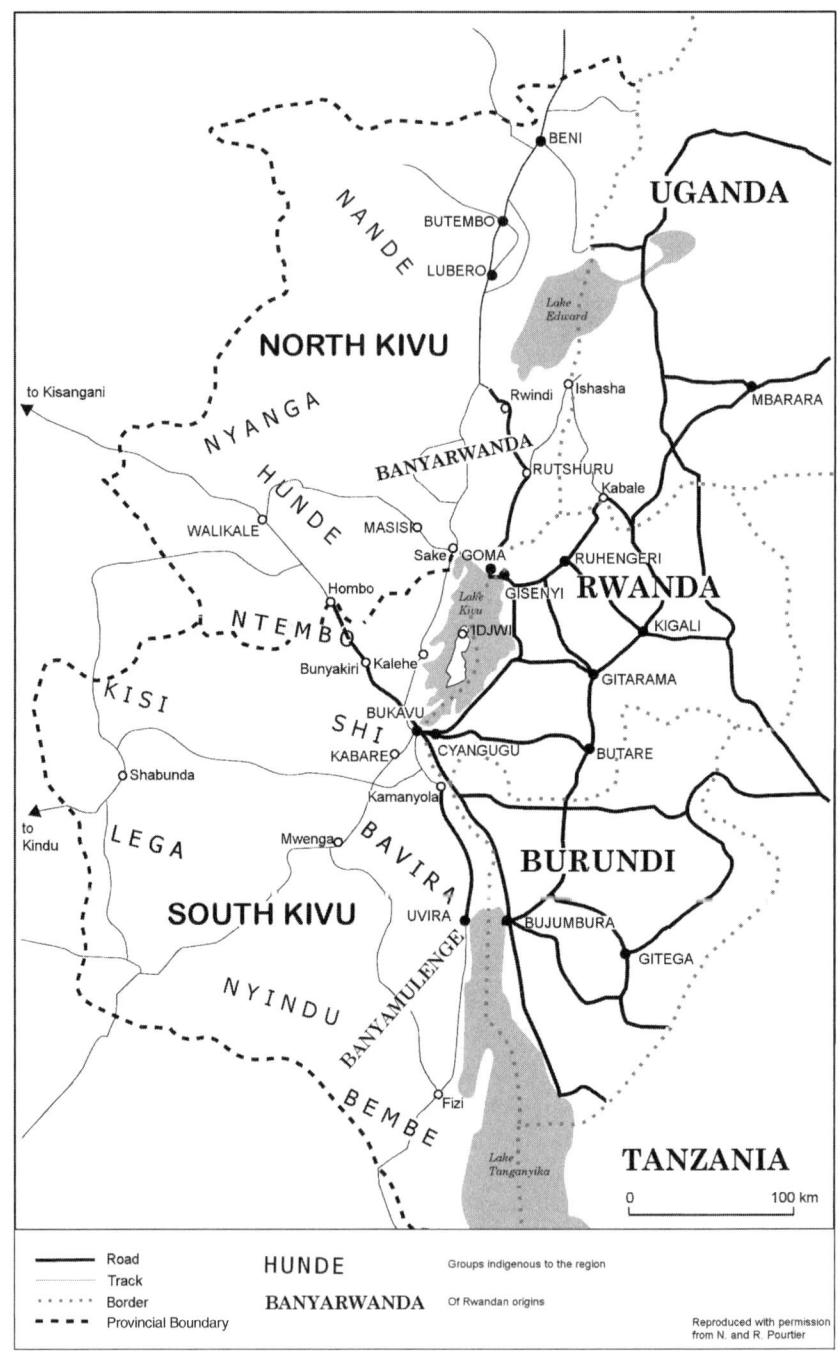

Map 1. Ethnic map of North and South Kivu. Reproduced from Roland Pourtier, "Cong-Zaire-Congo: Un itinéraire géoplitque au coeur de l'Afrique," *Hérodote,* nos. 86/87 (1997): 22, by permission of the author.

central role that Collier would like us to believe in setting in motion the infernal machine leading to interethnic and interstate violence. As recent academic research has shown, instead of invoking the logic of self-serving enrichment, the denial of economic opportunities, more often than not as a result of political exclusion, emerges as the critical factor in the etiology of conflict.[16] The basic distinction here is between exclusion as the initial motive and greed as a propelling force at a later stage of intergroup violence. The passage from exclusion to greed is not automatic; it implies major changes in the regional field of politics that also point to basic shifts in identity patterns.

Deconstructing Social Identities

Tempting as it is to view ethnic diversity as the central determinant of violent behavior in the region, the evidence shows otherwise. To the extent that it does provide a meaningful point of reference, ethnicity is not a throwback to primeval enmities. Whether socially constructed, manipulated, invented, or mobilized, it is a recent phenomenon, even when its roots are sometimes traceable to precolonial times (as in the case of the Banyamulenge). Its contours, moreover, are constantly shifting, as are the human targets against which it is directed. Communities seen as allies one day are viewed as enemies the next. New coalitions are built for short-term advantage, only to dissolve into warring factions when new options suddenly emerge. In this highly fluid political field, conflict is not reducible to any single identity marker. It is better conceptualized as involving different social boundaries, activated at different points in time, in response to changing political stakes.

Hutu versus Tutsi: The Reductionist Trap

No serious analyst of the recent history of the Great Lakes would deny the central significance of the Rwanda genocide on the polarization of Hutu-Tutsi identities throughout the region. Nonetheless, to reduce every conflict at every stage of its evolution to a straight Hutu-Tutsi confrontation is unconvincing. Such a dualism overlooks the presence of alternative forms of identification and wrongly assumes the salience of the Hutu-Tutsi dichotomy to be a permanent feature of the political landscape.

The danger of Hutu-Tutsi reductionism is all the more evident when one considers the ethnographic composition of the region. Rwanda and Burundi, after all, are not the only countries whose ethnic maps reveal the existence of Hutu and Tutsi. Kinyarwanda or Kirundi-speaking people also are found in eastern Congo, southern Uganda, and western

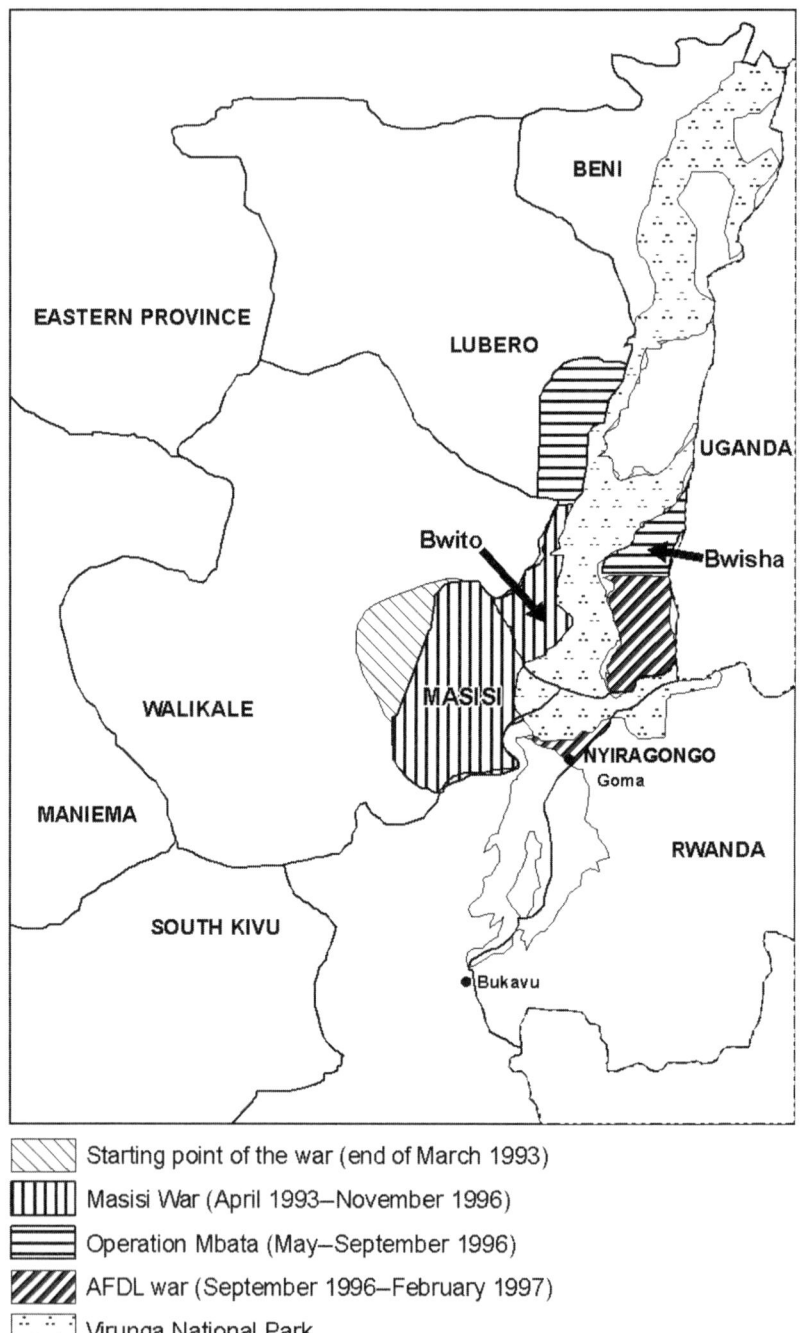

Map 2. Areas of confrontation in North Kivu. Reproduced from F. Reyntjens and S. Marysse, eds., *L'Afriquw des Grands Lacs: Annuaire 2005–2006* (Paris: L'Harmattan, 2006), p. 37, by permission of the editors.

Tanzania. According to the best estimates, the region claims roughly twelve million people speaking Kinyarwanda, and nearly twenty million if Kirundi, a language closely related to Kinyarwanda, is included. Although many migrated from Rwanda and Burundi to neighboring states during and after the colonial period, the presence of Hutu and Tutsi in eastern Congo reaches back to precolonial times. What needs to be underscored is that migrations from Rwanda or Burundi did not occur only one time but were staggered through the centuries. Length of residence, ecology, and history have shaped identities in ways that defy simple categorizations such as Hutu and Tutsi. It is with reason, therefore, that some analysts, in coming to grips with the politics of North Kivu, insist on drawing distinctions between the Hutu from Bwisha, those from Rutshuru, and those from Masisi and Kalehe.[17]

Such nuances went largely unnoticed by Belgian civil servants. In its effort to make more "legible," the complex ethnic configurations of the region, the colonial state contributed significantly to formalizing and legitimizing the Hutu-Tutsi polarity. Thus the 1959 census figures for what was then the Kivu region (now divided into North and South Kivu and Maniema) designate, oddly enough, as "Bantous Hamites" and "Hamites," respectively, the 184,089 Hutu and 53,233 Tutsi registered, thus making the "Banyarwanda" the third-largest group after the Banande (390,704) and the Bashi (382, 572).[18] Time and again historians have drawn attention to the perverse effects of the colonizer's recourse to Hamitic and Bantu labels, as if to impose its own normative construction on Hutu and Tutsi.[19] Equally striking is the phenomenon described by James Scott in *Seeing Like a State*, namely, "the state's attempt to make a society legible, to arrange the population in ways that simplified the classic state functions." These state simplifications, he adds, "did not successfully represent the actual activity of the society they depicted, nor were they intended to . . . they were maps that, when allied with state power, would enable much of the reality they depicted to be remade."[20]

Nonetheless, such attempts at remaking social realities did not obliterate all distinctions within Hutu and Tutsi. Nor did they erase the persistent tension between them, on the one hand, and the so-called "native" Congolese on the other. Many Kinyarwanda speakers, Hutu and Tutsi, trace their families' origins to precolonial times and have every right to claim the status of Congolese citizens. This is certainly true of the Banyamulenge ("the people from Mulenge") established in the high plateau area of South Kivu since the nineteenth century if not earlier,[21] and of the Hutu of Bwisha, many of whom lived in this area long before the onset of colonial rule, whereas others came as agricultural laborers from Rwanda in the 1930s to supply the European plantocracy of North Kivu with cheap labor. In short, as social categories, the terms "Hutu"

The Case of the Banyamulenge

A rather unique case of ethnogenesis, the Banyamulenge are a perfect example of how geography, history, and politics combine to create a new set of identities within the larger Banyarwanda cultural frame.[22] Heavily concentrated on the high-lying plateau of the Itombwe region of South Kivu, estimates of their numerical importance vary wildly. The figure of 400,000 cited by the late Joseph Muembo is grossly inflated.[23] A more reliable figure would be between 50,000 and 70,000. Their name derives from the locality (Mulenge) whence they are said to originate. The term, however, has been the source of much controversy because it became increasingly used in the late 1990s as an omnibus label to designate all Tutsi living in North and South Kivu. It came into usage in 1976 as a result of the efforts of the late Gisaro Muhoza, a member of parliament from South Kivu, to regroup the Banyamulenge populations of Mwenga, Fizi, and Uvira territories into a single administrative entity. Although his initiative failed, the name stuck, and by 1996 it was often used by ethnic Tutsi and Congolese to designate all Tutsi residents of North and South Kivu.

Though much of their history is shrouded in mystery, most historians would agree that the Banyamulenge are descendants of Tutsi pastoralists who migrated from Rwanda some time in the nineteenth century, long before the advent of colonial rule (a fact vehemently contested, however, by many Congolese intellectuals). They are culturally and socially distinct from the long-established ethnic Tutsi of North Kivu and the Tutsi refugees of the 1959–62 Rwanda revolution. Many do not speak Kinyarwanda, and those who do, speak it differently. Their political awakening can be traced back to the eastern Congo rebellion of 1964–65. Many initially joined the insurgency, only to switch sides when they saw their cattle being slaughtered to feed the insurgents. Their contribution to the counterinsurgency did not go unnoticed in Kinshasa. Many were rewarded with lucrative positions in the provincial capital, and more and more of their children flocked to missionary schools. From a primarily rural, isolated, backward community, the Banyamulenge would soon become increasingly aware of themselves as a political force.

It is impossible to tell how many joined the Rwanda Patriotic Front (RPF) in the 1990s. What is beyond doubt is that they formed the bulk of Kabila's Alliance des Forces Démocratiques pour la Libération du Congo (AFDL) in 1996 and after the fall of Bukavu, they filled most of the administrative positions vacated by the Congolese, some of whom were ardent Mobutists. Equally clear is that they suffered very heavy losses during the anti-Mobutist crusade, as well as during the 1998 crisis when many were massacred by Kabila's supporters in Kinshasa and Lubumbashi. It was said that in the late 1990s, Bukavu claimed a larger number of Banyamulenge widows than any other town in the region.

The creation in mid-1998 of the Rassemblement Congolais pour la Démocratie (RCD), under Rwandan sponsorship, was meant to provide the Banyamulenge with a vehicle for the defense of their interests—and of anyone else's who cared to join—but as it evolved into an instrument for the defense of Rwandan interests in eastern Congo, many felt aggrieved and alienated. The feeling that they have been "instrumentalized" by Kagame is shared widely among them. As we shall see, this sense of grievance against Rwanda is in large part responsible for the internal strains and divisions suffered by the community. All this, however, does not detract from the fact that as a group, the Banyamulenge are profoundly aware of their cultural distinctiveness. Few people have been dealt a harsher blow by history: many argue, with justice, that they have been twice victimized; first by Kagame, who used them as cannon fodder for the defense of Rwanda's strategic interests; and then by Congolese extremists, as happened in Bukavu in June 2004 when in the wake of an abortive Banyamulenge-led coup, hundreds perished. Today Bukavu is virtually "free" of Banyamulenge.

OTHERNESS

What defines the "other" as an ally or an enemy? Several objective criteria come to mind: language (e.g., "Rwandophones" or Kinyawanda speakers), country of origin ("Banyarwanda"), place of settlement ("Banyamulenge," the people of Mulenge), ethnicity (Hutu and Tutsi), to which must be added *morphologie*, or body maps, a reference that increasingly crops up in newspaper articles in Goma and Bukavu. None of the above, however, tells us why one set of criteria should be more relevant than another at any given time: why, for example, Hutu and Tutsi generally were lumped together as the embodiment of a "Banyarwanda" menace from 1963 until 1994, when the label quickly dissolved into Hutu-Tutsi enmities; or why the term Banyamulenge, as distinct from Tutsi, carried such threatening overtones among other communities from 1996 onward.

Otherness has less to do with objective identity markers than with the perceived threats posed by one community to another. Whether real or imaginary, such threats do not materialize out of thin air. They are intimately related to changes in the national and regional political environments. Political murder (Ndadaye in 1993), genocide (Rwanda in 1994), refugee flows (predominantly Tutsi in 1959–63, Hutu in 1994), ethnic cleansing (of Hutu refugees in eastern Congo in 1996–97), and the approach of elections (2005–6)—these, as we shall see, are the events and circumstances that have crystallized group identities.

Several phases can be identified in the redefinition of group identities:

1. From the so-called "Kanyarwanda war" in 1963 until 1994, the tendency among "native" Congolese was to view all Banyarwanda living in eastern Congo as the incarnation of a multifaceted menace.
2. After the Rwanda bloodbath, the Hutu-Tutsi conflict metastasized through much of North and South Kivu, causing untold casualties among long-time Tutsi residents and set the stage for the 1996 Rwandan-led and Rwandan-inspired invasion of the Congo by the Alliance des Forces Démocratiques pour la Libération du Congo (AFDL).[24] From then on, the Hutu-Tutsi frame of reference became the dominant identity marker and a powerful tool of propaganda for extremists at both ends of the ethnic spectrum.[25]
3. Yet by 1998, with the second Congo war, as an ever greater number of actors comes into view, the political equations became more complicated, and the straight Hutu-Tutsi cleavage frame somewhat less relevant. A more complex cognitive map emerged causing Hutu and Tutsi to fragment into factions, and enter new patterns of alliances at home and abroad.
4. Not the least intriguing of the mutations undergone by the regional identity prism is the emergence in recent times of language as the principal yardstick for lumping together Hutu and Tutsi under the "Rwandophone" label, a strategy clearly inspired by the provincial authorities of North Kivu to expand their grassroots constituency on the eve of elections.

To grasp the significance of these episodes, something must be said of the long-term social and economic forces that have reshaped regional identities.

Multilayered Conflicts

The theme of exclusion runs like a red skein through the history of the Great Lakes. It lies at the heart of the 1959–62 Hutu revolution in Rwanda; thirty years later it served as the propelling force behind the 1990 invasion of Rwanda by the Rwanda Patriotic Front (RPF).[26] Barely concealed by the ban on ethnic labels, ethnic discrimination has since emerged as the hallmark of the Kagame regime, to an extent unprecedented in the history of Rwanda. Burundi is another case in point: political exclusion is the obvious explanation behind the Hutu insurrection of 1972, in turn leading to the first genocide recorded in the annals of the Great Lakes.[27] Nor is eastern Congo an exception. Where it does stand as a special case is that the groups targeted for political exclusion are not always the same as those affected by economic and social discrimination. In the 1970s and 1980s, the former were generally of Rwandan origins,[28] whether Hutu or Tutsi; the latter included those "native" Congolese communities who insistently denounced the "Banyarwanda" as the main source of economic oppression. Out of this situation has emerged a rich potential for intergroup violence.

The Threat of Banyarwanda Domination: "Kanyarwanda," 1963–66

The little-known "Kanyarwanda war" was the first public display of anti-Tutsi sentiment in post-independence Zaire. It lasted from 1963 to 1966 and resulted in large-scale massacres of Hutu and Tutsi. Its focus was the newly created "provincette" of North Kivu, one of the three entities that once formed Kivu province. The decision to carve smaller entities out of the pre-existing province was in large part inspired by the growing fears of Congolese "tribes," notably the Hunde, that the Banyarwanda were about to tighten their grip on provincial institutions and thus threaten the autonomy of their ethnic neighbors. The geographical focus of the anti-Banyarwanda revolt was Masisi, and it involved, in essence, an alliance of Hunde and Nande elements against Hutu and Tutsi, with the Bashi generally supportive of the Banyarwanda. One of the first moves of the Hunde insurgents, according to one observer, was to reduce to ashes the local administrative archives so as to prevent the identification of the Banyarwanda otherwise than as refugees or foreigners.[29] That the insurrection should have had its point of ignition in Masisi—where large tracts of land had long been appropriated by Banyarwanda elements—is no less significant than the burning of provincial archives: in whipping up anti-Banyarwanda feelings, the Kanyarwanda uprising was meant to call into question their claims to the land, as well as their citizenship, as much as their dominant position at the provincial level.

The Land Problem

Thirty years after the Kanyarwanda war, Masisi would flare up again in an orgy of anti-Banyarwanda violence. In March 1993, like a bolt out of the blue, armed groups of Nande, Hunde, and Nyanga youth suddenly turned against all Banyarwanda in sight. The intervention of Mobutu's army, code-named Operation Mbata, though intended to restore order, in fact generated further violence. From May to September 1996, Zairian troops lived up to their reputation as a rabble, plundering much of the rural areas south of Bwisha, along the Rwandan border.[30] By the time violence died down, an estimated 14,000 people had been killed, most of them Banyarwanda. Although the precipitating factors remain unclear,[31] there can be little doubt that the underlying causes of the insurrection lay in the growing scarcity of land, which drove the local peasant communities to the edge of starvation. For this situation the insurgents did not hesitate to hold the Banyarwanda responsible.

One need not go too far back into the past to realize that the colonial state also bears much of the blame. The story has been told many times of how, in the 1930s, Belgian authorities embarked on a vast resettlement scheme designed to encourage the influx of Banyarwanda (essentially Hutu) from Rwanda to North Kivu, the aim being to provide Belgian planters with a cheap labor force and create an outlet for the growing population pressure in Rwanda.[32] What is not always realized is that this sudden influx of immigrants played havoc with the traditional organization of the host communities, most notably the Hunde. Not content to expel many Hunde clans from their traditional homelands, the Belgian authorities proceeded to create a Banyarwanda chiefdom in the heart of Hunde domains, the so-called Gishari enclave (Bwisha), headed by a Tutsi chief.[33] The Gishari take-over was only the thin edge of the wedge. By 1959 in Rutshuru, the Hutu and Tutsi were ten times as numerous as the indigenous Hunde population (10,193); in Masisi almost two thirds of the population were immigrants from Rwanda.[34]

Unlike the early migrant laborers who settled in Bwisha and Masisi under the wing of the Mission Immigration Banyarwanda (MIB), the "fifty-niners", so-called because they fled Rwanda during the revolution of 1959–62, were overwhelmingly Tutsi; they were incomparably better off in terms of material wealth and education than their Hutu predecessors; and they could count on the unfailing support of a leading émigré figure, Barthélemy Bisengimana, who by 1970 wielded considerable power as Mobutu's chief of staff. What Bisengimana could not achieve, bribery usually did. Bribing the local authorities to acquire land became standard practice.

The result has been to set in motion a massive process of land alienation. The extent of the holdings acquired by wealthy Tutsi speaks for itself: Kasungu received 10,000 hectares, Ngizayo 2,000, Bisengimana himself received one of the biggest ranches in the region, over 5,000 hectares.[35] The expropriation of native lands was further facilitated by the Bakajika law of 1966, which converted all public land into the domain of the state, followed by the Zairianization measures of 1973. Instrumental as it was in operating massive land transfers into Tutsi hands, the effects of "étatisation-cum-zairianization" were by no means limited to North Kivu. At the root of the Hema-Lendu conflict in Ituri lies a very similar phenomenon. As Thierry Vircoulon has shown, the accumulation of land in Hema hands, with the Lendu often reduced to the status of day laborers, occurred largely at the expense of the Lendu communities, who, like many Hunde and Nyanga in North Kivu, eventually found themselves facing a subsistence crisis.[36]

While exacerbating anti-Banyarwanda sentiment, land expropriation has had a profoundly disruptive impact on indigenous societies. This is a point of crucial significance to an understanding of the next phase in the regional dynamics of violence. As Vlassenroot has convincingly argued, the cumulative effects of the repeated violations of customary land rights, the break-up of patron-client ties, and the erosion of chiefly authority have created a critical mass of marginalized youth, many of whom later joined the warlords.[37] And just as the warlords can be seen as surrogate patrons for their deracinated followers, fighting for gold and diamonds and coltan is perhaps best understood, in David Keen's words, as "a way of creating an alternative system of profit, power and even protection."[38]

Another consequence of the land issue has been to give added urgency to the citizenship problem. The land problem and the nationality problem are but two sides of the same coin. Access to land presupposes access to citizenship; withdrawal of citizenship rights from the Banyarwanda meant the end of their security in land rights. But it would also mean, for many, the end of their physical security as residents of eastern Congo.

THE NATIONALITY QUESTION

A turning point in relations between immigrant and indigenous communities came in 1981, with the adoption of a new nationality law. By a stroke of the pen the Legislative Council repealed the 1972 law that gave citizenship rights to "persons originating from Rwanda-Urundi who were residents of the Kivu before January 1, 1950," and instead adopted the notoriously restrictive *ordonnance-loi* of March 28, 1981, which stipulated that citizenship could only be conferred on persons "who could show that one of their ancestors was a member of a tribe or part of a tribe established in the Congo prior to October 18, 1908," when the Congo formally became a Belgian colony.[39] The dismissal of Bisengimana in 1977, for reasons that remain unclear, thus paved the way for the virtual denial of citizenship rights to all Banyarwanda, irrespective of their date of arrival.

Although the 1981 law was never implemented, it nevertheless provided official justification for further discriminatory moves. Candidates suspected of "foreign" origins were systematically prevented from running during the 1982 and 1987 elections on grounds of "dubious nationality." Despite great hopes among the Banyarwanda that the National Conference (1991) would resolve the nationality issue to their satisfaction, this was not to be the case. The party delegations representing their interests were refused admission to the conference. Civil society delegates did not fare much better. Given their well-established claims to citizenship, the Banyamulenge of South Kivu were especially resentful of such exclusionary measures. After the candidacies of two leading Banyamulenge were declared invalid in 1987, their constituents destroyed the ballot boxes. Many were arrested. When in October 1993 the news reached South Kivu that the newly elected Hutu president of Burundi, President Ndadaye, had been killed by Tutsi officers, several Banyamulenge were stoned to death in the streets of Uvira.[40]

The worst was yet to come. While the victory of the FPR in Kigali was greeted with mixed feelings in eastern Congo, the report of the so-called Vangu commission—a parliamentary commission charged with investigating the identity of the refugee populations—declared the Banyamulenge "foreign migrants" ("*immigrés étrangers*"). On the basis of this palpable absurdity, the transitional parliament adopted a resolution on April 28, 1995 demanding the repatriation to their countries of origin of "all Rwanda and Burundi refugees and immigrants, without condition and without delay," including the Banyamulenge, henceforth categorized as foreigners.[41] From then on, the Banyamulenge came to be seen increasingly as Rwandan Tutsi in disguise. As the weekly paper *Munanira*, published in Uvira, commented, "this sly Zairwa [*sic*] is but a Rwandan whose morphology and ideology is identical to that of Paul Kagame. The Banyamulenge are quite simply, Tutsi, and Rwandans at that."[42]

As happened elsewhere in the history of the Great Lakes, the stage was set for a self-fulfilling prophecy—grounded in self-protection—that inevitably led the Banyamulenge to become Kigali's staunchest allies during the AFDL rebellion leading to the undoing of the Mobutist dictatorship.

Interlocking Crises

As the history of the region makes clear, its social upheavals are closely interconnected. An obvious example is the murderous, cross-border tit-for-tat behind the ethnic crises in Rwanda and Burundi: the Hutu revolution in Rwanda generated a powerful backlash in Burundi, steadily raising the ethnic temperature until some 200,000 Hutu were killed by Tutsi in 1972, in what can legitimately be called a partial genocide. In Rwanda, the blow-back effect of the Burundi carnage took the form of violent anti-Tutsi pogroms, which paved the way for the rise to power of Juvénal Habyarimana in 1973. We also noted how in Uvira the news of Ndadaye's death triggered a brutal retaliation against Banyamulenge civilians. It is in Rwanda, however, that Ndadaye's assassination had its most dramatic impact as it ushered an immediate and drastic radicalization of anti-Tutsi sentiment, via the "Hutu Power" faction, that played directly into the hands of the génocidaires.

None of the above, however, carried consequences as devastating and wide-ranging as the 1994 genocide. The fallout has been little short of seismic. The litany of cataclysms is all too familiar: over a million Hutu refugees pouring across the border into Rwanda, creating chaos and penury in many parts of North and South Kivu; repeated cross-border raids into Rwanda by remnants of the Forces Armées Rwandaises (FAR) and *interahamwe* ("those who stand together"), accompanied in parts of North Kivu by wholesale massacres of ethnic Tutsi, causing many to seek refuge in Rwanda; growing evidence of humanitarian aid diverted to extremist hands and of Mobutu's military assistance to the Hutu refugee leaders. All of which raised deep anxieties among Rwanda's new leaders.

The critical turning points came in 1996 and 1998.[43] The destruction of the refugee camps in October 1996, followed by the killing of tens of thousands of civilian refugees by units of the Rwanda Patriotic Front (RPF; now known as the Rwanda Defense Forces [RDF]), was only the first stage of a grand politicomilitary strategy aimed at the overthrow of the Mobutist dictatorship and its replacement by a Tutsi-led protectorate. The 1997 war, nominally fought by Laurent Kabila's AFDL, with critical support from Rwanda, Uganda, and Angola, successfully achieved each of these objectives. As Kinshasa fell to the AFDL "rebels," Kabila emerged as the ideal candidate to play the role of a compliant head of state—which he did until August 1998—when he turned against the kingmakers, thus triggering the second Congo war.

Rather than retelling the story of the 1998 crisis, let us at this point shift our focus and consider the case of RCD Commander Laurent Nkunda: his trajectory is illustrative of a range of experiences that help uncover the links between certain crucial episodes in the history of the region.

Agency: A Spoiler Named Nkunda

Commander Laurent Nkunda's main claim to fame is to be among the most persistent "spoilers" of the precarious peace that loomed on the Kivu horizon after the 2002 Global and Inclusive Agreement.[44] He has fought in two theaters, in Rwanda and in the Congo, and is responsible for the deaths of hundreds of Congolese—and indirectly, of the many Banyamulenge murdered in Gatumba (Burundi) in August 2004.

A reliable source describes him as "the son of a Tutsi cattle herder in Masisi," who spent time "teaching in a local school before joining the RPF in the early 1990s."[45] Although there is every reason to believe that he must have fought in Rwanda during the civil war, exactly where and in what capacity remains unknown. He eventually surfaced in eastern Congo as a member of the AFDL and after 1998, joined the RCD, "where he was an intelligence officer and held various key positions in the military leadership."

His reputation for brutality is well established. So is his role in organizing the bloody repression of the Kisangani mutiny in May 2002. When a group of soldiers and police officers of the DRC mutinied against their RCD officers, Nkunda was serving as commander of the seventh brigade in Goma after completing a military training program at Gabiro in Rwanda. Along with several Kinyarwanda-speaking officers, including the notorious Gabriel Amisi, and 120 troops, Nkunda was sent to Kisangani to restore peace and order. He did so with exemplary cruelty, carrying out scores of summary executions. According to Human Rights Watch, "RCD officers had been responsible for the deaths of more than 160 persons."[46]

After the installation of the transitional government in 2003, he was appointed regional military commander of Kasai Oriental. He declined the offer, however, "saying that it would not be safe for him to travel to Kinshasa and Mbuji-Mayi." He resigned his position in the Forces Armées de la République Démocratique du Congo (FARDC), presumably to make himself available for other missions. One such mission occurred in May 2004, in Bukavu, when a Banyamulenge colonel, Jules Mutebutsi, also trained in Rwanda and subsequently integrated into the FARDC, mutinied against his commanding officer (General Mbudja Mabe, commander of the tenth military region) and seized control of the provincial capital of South Kivu. It was Nkunda, however, who provided the much needed military assistance to overcome the resistance of the FARDC. Although the mutiny proved short-lived, more enduring were its aftereffects. After the army retook control of the city, scores of Banyamulenge were killed by mobs of enraged Congolese, while thousands found refuge in the Gatumba refugee camp in Burundi. It was in Gatumba, in August of the same year, that over a hundred perished at the hands of Hutu extremists affiliated with the Burundi-based Forces Nationales de Libération (FNL) and Mai-Mai elements from the DRC.

Determined to live up to his reputation, Nkunda's next port of call was Kanyabonga, near the border with Rwanda, where in December 2004 he took on several units of the FARDC, presumably with logistical assistance from the Rwandan army, bringing relations between Rwanda and the DRC near the breaking point. More recently, in January 2006, Commander Nkunda made another show of military prowess when he attacked the town of Rutshuru, causing the displacement of tens of thousands of panic-stricken villagers.

One hesitates to make too much of the Nkunda vignette, but it is emblematic of how at certain critical junctures, the choices made by individual actors have triggered one crisis after another. Once this is said, the regional context in which decisions were made is no less worthy of attention.

CROSSBORDER TIES: THE KIN COUNTRY SYNDROME

What Huntington refers to as the "kin country syndrome"[47]—where communities sharing similar cultural ties are mobilized across national boundaries, in support of, or against, a government—draws attention to an obvious dimension of the Great Lakes crises. Although the phenomenon is not unique to the region, in no other part of the continent has it played a more decisive role in projecting ethnic hatreds from one national arena to another.

Kin country rallying was indeed a critical vector in the diffusion of ethnic enmities from Rwanda into Burundi in the early 1960s and back from Burundi into Rwanda in 1973. So, also, among ethnic Tutsi in eastern Congo during the early stages of the civil war in Rwanda, when hundreds were recruited into the ranks of the FPR. And when they found themselves in the crosshairs of Congolese and refugee extremists in 1996, Rwanda did not hesitate to reciprocate the favor. While the FPR acted as the senior partner, many Banyamulenge served as auxiliaries in the destruction of the refugee camps and in subsequent "cleansing" operations. Much the same coalescence of ethnic affinities presided over the emergence of the solidly Hutu Forces Démocratique pour la Libération du Rwanda (FDLR) in eastern Congo, notwithstanding the bitter rivalries currently tearing its leadership.[48]

Again, consider the case of the Nande of North Kivu (known as Bakonjo in Uganda): for years Nande involvement in the wide-ranging trade networks, linking their core area of Butembo-Beni to East Africa and beyond, helped strengthen Nande-Bakonjo ties, but the connection became politically significant in the 1990s when, in his effort to weaken the Museveni regime, Mobutu did everything he could to bolster the Bakonjo-led National Army for the Liberation of Uganda (NALU), a move which elicited a fair degree of sympathy among the Nande.[49] Parts of North Kivu became a privileged sanctuary for NALU militants. According to one observer, armed with weapons sent from Kinshasa and Khartoum, on November 13 they launched a major offensive against Uganda, which temporarily brought under NALU its control much of the Kasese district and the town of Mbarara.[50]

Such "fault line conflicts," Huntington notes, "tend to be vicious and bloody, since fundamental issues of identity are at stake. In addition, they tend to be lengthy; they may be interrupted by truces or agreements but these tend to break down and the conflict is resumed."[51]

REFUGEE FLOWS

In the absence of massive outpourings of Hutu refugees to neighboring states—with vivid memories of the violence they experienced or inflicted—it is a question whether kinship ties could have been mobilized so quickly and so effectively, and whether the security concerns of neighboring states would have assumed the same urgency. Much of the history of the region is indeed reducible to the transformation of refugee-generating conflict into conflict-generating refugees, or as Myron Weiner puts it, "conflicts create refugees, but refugees also create conflicts."[52] From the days of the Hutu revolution in Rwanda to the invasion of the "refugee warriors" from Uganda in 1994, from the huge exodus of Hutu from Burundi in 1972 to the "cleansing" of Hutu refugee camps in 1996–97, the pattern that emerges again and again is one in which refugee populations serve as the vehicles through which ethnic identities are mobilized and manipulated, host communities preyed upon, and external resources extracted. The net result, as one observer noted, has been to "create domestic instability, generate interstate tension and threaten international security."[53]

The view that "refugees are potentially a tool in interstate conflicts"[54] is nowhere more cruelly demonstrated than by the fate that befell the Hutu refugees—numbering over a million. Manipulated by their own leaders, as well as by Mobutu and ultimately by Laurent Kabila, they paid a heavy price in the retribution visited upon them by the FPR. Beatrice Umutesi's searing account of her grueling trek across two thousand miles bears testimony to the refugee's agonies in the course of the relentless manhunt conducted by the Rwandan army assisted by AFDL units.[55] There is no need to speak of a "humanitarian hysteria"[56] to describe the concern of the international community in order to recognize the self-destructive consequences of the disastrous policies pursued by Hutu extremists and their Zairian allies. There can be no denying that Hutu leaders did organize armed raids into Rwanda. Nor is there any doubt about the diverting of humanitarian aid, presumably to use it as a bargaining chip with civilian refugees, or about Mobutu's role in arming refugee factions. Just how serious were the risks thus posed to the host country became clear after the Rwandan military began a series of attacks against the camps on October 18, 1996.

Arming refugees is one thing; disarming them is a far more difficult undertaking. Thus, if Laurent Kabila found it expedient in 1998 to arm Hutu refugees in his campaign against the Rwanda-backed RCD, disarming them after they have outlived their strategic usefulness was only one of the many headaches facing his son on the eve of multi-party elections.

As the foregoing suggests, strategies based on a calculus of short-term advantages may entail heavy costs a few years down the road. Similarly, alliances that seem perfectly logical one day may turn out to be utterly counterproductive the next. Kagame's experience with his less than obedient AFDL ally is just one example of the inherent fickleness of political clients.

A Fluid Landscape

The 1997 anti-Mobutist crusade did little more than replace one dictatorship with another. The 1998 war, on the other hand, marks a sharp break in the region's history. It ushered in one of the bloodiest wars recorded in recent times, the effects of which are still tragically visible in many parts of the country. Much of this violence, however, has gone unreported. It unfolds not along a well delineated battle line but in oil-slick patterns in separate provincial and subprovincial arenas. Each episode has its own logic, each its own set of actors. And each is in some measure traceable to the reversal of alliances that followed in the wake of Kabila's decision to challenge the overrule of his Tutsi "protectors."

SWITCHING SIDES

How the Kigali-sponsored attack against the refugee camps morphed into a full-scale, externally supported invasion aimed at the overthrow of Mobutu is beyond the scope of this discussion.[57] Suffice it to note that the AFDL could not have reached Kinshasa with such speed and relative ease without the critical support it received from Rwanda, Uganda, and Angola. Their shared dislike of Mobutu, based on a realistic assessment of their respective interests, proved a fragile glue in the face of the new challenges raised by Kabila's revolt. Thus, if Angola remained Kinshasa's most trusted ally and would soon be joined by Zimbabwe—whose mercenary motives are well established—Rwanda and Uganda needed little prodding to turn against their renegade client. And whereas Burundi displayed, in Lanotte's felicitous phrasing, a "tolerant complicity" in the fight against Kabila,[58] eventually Namibia, the Sudan, and Chad all joined Luanda in giving their half-hearted support to Kinshasa.

Basically, the old axiom according to which "the enemy of my enemy is my friend, and the friend of my enemy is my enemy" provides the essential logic behind the making and unmaking of alliances during the 1997 and 1998 wars.[59] This applies to interstate as well as domestic alliances. In each case, the pattern is one in which friends and enemies reverse roles in response to their changing perceptions of the other's motives. What Rwanda and Uganda saw as a betrayal, Angola perceived as a legitimate move. Uganda's support of the Sudan People's Liberation Army (SPLA) made it a matter of realpolitik for Khartoum to join hands with Kinshasa. In sending 2,000 troops to battle against Jean-Pierre Bemba's Mouvement de Libération du Congo (MLC), Chad felt obligated to heed Khartoum's prodding (until the cost in human losses proved too onerous) in recognition of Sudan's past support to Idriss Déby.

Of the many alliances of convenience formed during the first and second Congo wars, none seemed more durable than the one between Rwanda and Uganda. Both viewed Mobutu with equal distaste, and both saw treasonable behavior in Kabila's volte-face. Yet by late 1999, the alliance had all but disintegrated. The bitter infighting that erupted in Kisangani in 1999, 2000, and 2001 over access to the rich mineral deposits of Bafwasende and other localities did more than spell the end of a friendly relationship. It brought the former allies to the brink of a full-scale war.

Much the same switching of partnerships can be seen at the domestic level. As long as he owed fealty to his Rwandan patrons, Kabila thought nothing of covering up the murder of Hutu refugees; nor did he shrink from blocking the work of the UN forensic investigation team in 1997, even demanding the sacking of its president, Roberto Garreton, "after he produced a preliminary sixteen-page report that identified forty sites where Kabila's AFDL was suspected of having committed atrocities."[60] A year later, however, those refugee leaders who managed to survive the carnage had become Kabila's best friends in his fight against Rwandan "rebels."

The mixed fortunes of the RCD are another case in point. Despite or because of its murky origins—having been conceived, created, nurtured, and supported by Kigali to defend its interests in eastern Congo—the RCD today is a weak version of its former self. In addition to its core constituency, made up of Banyamulenge,[61] it was able at first to recruit a number of influential politicians of different ethnic and provincial origins. Many have since left the movement. The old-guard Mobutists, Lunda Bululu, Lambert Mende, and Alexis Thambwe have joined other parties; Arthur Zaidi Ngoma has founded his own political formation (Camp de la Patrie), and so has Mbusa Nyamwezi (Forces du Renouveau); Wamba dia Wamba—whose early defection led to the first of many

RCD clones, the so-called RCD-Kisangani, as distinct from the RCD-Goma—has resumed his academic career after a calamitous series of setbacks. What is left of the party is something of an empty shell, with its formal head, Azarias Ruberwa, in Kinshasa, desperately trying to stem the tide of dissidence.

Of the many defections suffered by the RDC, perhaps the least expected was initiated by a leading Banyamulenge personality, Manasse Ruhimbika. His short-lived Forces Républicaines Fédéralistes (FRF) made plain the lack of internal cohesion among the Banyamulenge and the growing resentment harbored by many, including Ruhimbika, over Rwanda's dominance of the RCD. The FRF break-away was only the harbinger of a far more serious split, which by 2002 had turned into a full-scale rebellion against the RCD. Led by a former RCD commander, Patrick Masunzu, the insurrection quickly spread through the Itombwe plateau, the traditional homeland of the Banyamulenge, and for a while reportedly coalesced with the FDLR and Mai-Mai elements. Masunzu's forces fought pitched battles against RCD troops, resulting in heavy losses on both sides, and some 40,000 displaced.[62] Reflecting on the lessons of the insurrection, one observer commented, "Banyamulege opinion is now profoundly divided. Some still back the RCD; many feel it has abandoned their interests."[63] This is as true today as it was in 2003.

Thus, if fragmentation is indeed the most salient characteristic of Congolese politics, this is in part due to the persistence of highly divisive issues, having to do with disagreements over the extent and legitimacy of the Rwandan connection, the sharing of resources among allies, the choice of tactical alliances, and so forth. But this is only one aspect of a more complicated reality.

PATTERNS OF FRAGMENTATION

The political vacuum created by the sudden collapse of the Mobutist state must be seen as a key factor in the rapid fragmentation of the political arena. On the debris of the state, overnight a host of civil society organizations and militias mushroomed, of which the Mai-Mai militias are the most notorious for their propensity to fragment and proliferate. Pinning them down long enough to analyze their contours is not easy. Nonetheless, the political dynamic behind the surge of armed factions seems reasonably clear.[64]

Unlike what can observed in the case of the RCD, where fragmentation starts at the top, the efflorescence of Mai-Mai factions is a locally rooted phenomenon. It stems in part from the Mobutist legacy of playing one ethnic community off against another—sometimes referred to as the "géopolitique" argument—and in part from the persistence over time—through youth groups, civil society organizations, and church groups[65]—of recruitment strategies based on ethnoregional ties. Describing the state of the play in South Kivu in 2000, Ruhimbika notes that "there are five major Mai-Mai axes which reflect local ethnic configurations": the Fizi axis (Dunia), the Uvira axis (Bidalira), the Kizuka high plateau area (Mulemera), the Ruzizi axis (controlled by Hutu militias), and the Lubumba axis (also controlled by Bidalira).[66] Although the ethno-regional dimension is a common characteristic of most Mai-Mai factions, their members, as Ruhimbika's description suggests, come from different horizons: some, like "the old general Louis Bidalira," are veterans of the 1964 Simba rebellion in eastern Congo; others are Hutu refugees from Burundi, as in the Ruzizi valley; and others are recycled *interahamwe* or their offspring. Viewed from a broader perspective, however, the Mai-Mai can best be seen as the political manifestation of the social exclusion affecting a growing number of marginalized youth. As Vlassenroot and Van Acker perceptively note, "the formation of the Mai-Mai must be understood as a social process which creates its own rationality, it is dictated by their rejection of the institutional order, and shaped by an environment which offers ample opportunities for creating and exploiting illicit trade networks and invites warlord types of activities."[67]

In their early phase of development, the Mai-Mai were not so much motivated by greed as by the need to protect their communities against the threats posed by newcomers; first the Hutu refugees in 1994 and then, the Tutsi after the AFDL insurrection. Beginning in early 1997, after the assassination of a leading Mai-Mai personality, the main thrust of their activities was directed against the Rwandan occupying forces and their local allies. By the late 1990s, however, access to mineral wealth loomed increasingly large on their agenda. In a pattern that has repeated itself again and again, the quest for gold and diamonds has gone hand in hand with the procurement of weapons. The picture drawn by Vlassenroot and Van Acker in 2001 is still relevant today: "Since the militia leaders control the bulk of economic activities in the mineral-rich areas, the Mai-Mai, along with the *interahamwe* and FDD, have created their own war economy and are riding a wave of prosperity, which in turn brought about a decline in security in the mining districts."[68] The shift from "protection" to "greed" has been accompanied by a proliferation of armed factions, including Mai-Mai, in what looks increasingly like a free-for-all competition for loot.

An extreme but not untypical case is that of Ituri: since 2003, no fewer than eight armed factions have been involved in the scramble for gold and diamonds. Closer scrutiny suggests that greed was not the only motive behind this situation of intense competitiveness. In the words of one non-governmental organization (NGO) report, "the conflict which was over land at the beginning, has taken on multiple dimensions. Ethnicity is not a sufficient point of reference to understand what is going on in Ituri. Perpetrators of violence are at once and the same time ethnically based politico-military groups (UPC, PUSIC, FNI and FRPI), heterogeneous armed groups (FAPC and FPDC) and states (Uganda, Rwanda and RDC). The facts also demonstrate that the motives for confrontation are not always dictated by ethnic hatred, but by other considerations having to do with efforts at political positioning, the quest for material gain, the struggle for local, national or sub-regional leadership."[69]

The story of how the original RCD broke into warring factions reveals much the same plurality of motives, albeit with ethnic and sub-ethnic cleavages looming increasingly large as a source of division. Personal and political grudges were certainly instrumental in causing Wamba-dia-Wamba's decision to form his own party in Kisangani (RCD-K), but the choice of Kisangani was not made at random. The prospects of easy access to the area's rich mineral deposits were just as crucial for the dissident leader as they were, a few months later, in triggering the violent confrontation between Rwanda and Uganda, at which point he had few other options than to move to Bunia, the capital of Ituri. This is where the seeds of his undoing were sown. Quite aside from the greed factor, in the context of a growing ethnic polarization between Hema and Lendu, his decision to side with the Lendu immediately sealed a Nande-Hema alliance against him, bringing together Mbusa Nyamesi (Nande) and Tibasima (Hema) as the key players, identified with the RDC-Mouvement de Libération (RCD-ML). With Uganda firmly behind the Hema, Wamba eventually bowed to Museveni's pressure to leave Bunia, thus paving the way for the next round, between Nande and Hema. Eventually the Hema-Gegere group decided to break away from the RCD-ML in hopes of getting the exclusive benefit of the Kilo-Moto gold mines and under the leadership of Thomas Lubanga, formed the Union des Populations Congolaises (UPC). In time, however, intra-Hema rivalries would prompt the culturally distinct southern Hema to set up their own group, the Parti pour l'Unité et la Sauvegarde de l'Intégrité du Congo (PUSIC), led by chief Kahwa, whereas the northern Gegere-Hema remained under Lubanga's wing. Meanwhile, unable to hold his ground against the Hema's UPC, Nyamwesi retired to his solidly Nande fiefdom of Beni-Butambo, while Ituri sank inexorably into an ever more bloody factional strife. Ethnicity, greed, and political ambitions were all involved, though not always in equal proportion, in the unraveling of the original RCD.

And so were external actors, most notably Uganda and Rwanda. A detailed discussion of their involvement in Ituri politics would take us too far afield. Suffice it to note that both share a large part of responsibility in the factional strife that engulfed a large section of the province. First, by supporting the Hema against the Lendu, then switching sides while Rwanda threw its weight around the Hema, Uganda has played a major role in intensifying the conflict. And the same applies to Rwanda, even though Kigali made every effort to create the illusion that assistance to UPC was the initiative of the RCD-Goma. In truth, the UPC entered into an alliance with the RCD-Goma in January 2003, which provided for political and military assistance, but as early as June 2002, Rwanda was already delivering large quantities of arms and ammunition to the UPC. In trying to grasp the dynamic of violence in eastern Congo, one is reminded of Tilly's pithy formula, "someone who produces both the danger and, at a price, the shield against it, is a racketeer."[70] Nurtured by foreign patrons, and relayed by local warlords, the racketeering shows no sign of coming to an end any time soon.

The Rwandan Menace

In terms of size and potential wealth, there is no greater contrast than between minute, overpopulated, resource-poor Rwanda and its "scandalously" well-endowed, giant neighbor to the west; the anomaly lies in the overwhelming military superiority of Rwanda's RDF, one of the most experienced, disciplined, and efficient armed forces in the region.

The threats posed by Rwanda to its Congolese neighbor were cruelly revealed during the 1997 and 1998 wars, and by the repeated forays of the RDF into the DRC from 1998 to 2002, as far south into the interior as north Katanga and Kasai and Beni-Butembo in the north. Following the 2002 Pretoria accords, the bulk of Rwanda's army formally withdrew from the DRC; nonetheless, writes Reyntjens, "[it] later maintained a covert presence both directly and indirectly through its proxy, the RCD-Goma."[71] Just how serious is the challenge of its proxy was made clear during the May 2004 offensive on Bukavu, the border attacks on Kanyabonga in December 2004 and in Rutshuru in January 2006.

Ironically, Rwanda was the first to feel threatened by the presence of armed Hutu refugees in eastern Congo; its security concerns made it mandatory to "neutralize" the camps from which originated the raids against its national territory. Expansion quickly followed preemption and with the power vacuum created by the fall of the Mobutist state, the need to fill it with trustworthy allies backed by effective military force became all the more urgent. This is where a radical shift occurred in Rwanda's policy goals. Security meant, in essence, continuing access to mineral resources, not only to reward local allies but to strengthen its military establishment. No longer is Rwanda's security imperiled by Hutu rebels but, if anything, by rebels within its own military establishment. This is not to underestimate the nuisance potential of the radical, Hutu-led Forces Démocratiques pour la Libération du Rwanda (FDLR), consisting mainly of remnants of the *interahamwe* and ex-FAR. Although these constitute a clear and present danger to the civilian populations of North and South Kivu and parts of Maniema, Rwanda's allegation that they pose a mortal threat to its security is vastly exaggerated; nonetheless, the FDLR offer a convenient pretext for Kigali's military incursions into North Kivu. The FDLR are no match for an estimated 70,000 men under arms and a sophisticated military arsenal, consisting of armored personnel carriers (APCs), tanks, and helicopters. Even though it is not immediately threatened by rebel forces, Rwanda's maintenance of its armed forces is heavily dependent on free access to its neighbor's wealth.

Exactly how much of the mineral pie goes to Rwanda and how much to its local allies is impossible to tell because of the secrecy surrounding these transactions and the number of intermediaries and joint ventures involved. A rough indication of the profits going to the RCD was disclosed by Adolphe Onusumba, a key RCD figure, who is reported to have declared in 2000, "We raise more or less $200,000 per month from diamonds. . . . Coltan gives us more: a million dollars a month."[72] This is probably a fraction of the overall profits going into Rwandan pockets.[73] Whether or how far discords over the sharing of the Congo's wealth have contributed to the RCD's declining fortunes is moot. What is beyond doubt is that the RCD is no longer Kagame's most dependable ally in eastern DRC. In the words of one observer, "the Rwandan government has progressively relegated the national RCD leadership to a secondary tool of influence in Kinshasa and focused instead on creating and strengthening autonomous power bases in areas of the DRC it considers to be within its sphere of influence."[74]

Rwanda's principal ally in eastern DRC is the multifaceted NGO Tous pour la Paix et le Développement (TPD), headed until 2000 by the all-powerful North Kivu governor, Eugene Serufuli Ngayabaseka. It was founded in 1998, ostensibly "to assist Congolese refugees in Rwanda to return to the DRC,"[75] meaning essentially those Tutsi elements indigenous to North Kivu who fled the violence in 1995 and 1996. Of far greater significance, however, are TPD's "latent" functions. Its aims are to expand and strengthen Kigali's grassroots "constituencies" politically, militarily, and economically. This is how Dennis Tull describes its activities: "[to help] the RCD establish a strong power base on both an elite level as well as on the ground by forging close links between Kigali, the RCD and a Banyarwanda group consisting of rich landowners and repatriates in North Kivu . . . to address Rwanda's security concerns by reinforcing military recruitment among the Banyarwanda repatriates . . . thirdly, by supposedly promoting humanitarian concerns, the repatriation network might have tapped resources provided by international agencies, thus contributing to the financing of this alliance."[76] The emphasis placed on the recruitment of Hutu participants in the TPD is the most arresting—and potentially risky—aspect of Kigali's new strategy.

That Serufuli happens to be a Hutu, and a Hutu from Rutshuru at that, is of course indicative of the new course being charted by Kigali. No longer is the aim to assemble a group of potential supporters from various ethnic and regional horizons around a core of Banyamulenge faithful, as was the case during the early years of the RCD, but to reach out to Hutu elements indigenous to North Kivu. In a fascinating exploration of the TPD's historical antecedents, Bucyalime Mararo shows its curious pedigree, traceable to the pro-Hutu Mutuelle agricole des Virunga (MAGRIVI) and the more "ecumenical" Mutuelle UMOJA. TPD, in short, has deep roots in the social landscape of the region. In one significant respect, its settlement policies are ominously reminiscent of the colonial era, when Hutu migrants gradually pushed the Hunde out of their traditional domains in Masisi, thus creating lasting enmities between them. As Hutu chiefs are once again replacing Hunde authorities, and appropriating their landholdings, the stage is set for a renewal of tension.[77] Whether their shared awareness of being up against a common ethnic enemy can help forge closer ties between Hutu and Tutsi remains to be seen.

In brief, in the short term, the menace posed by Rwanda's new course lies in the challenge it poses to the transition to multiparty democracy. It stems from the support network put in place on behalf of its client faction and the possibility that should the RCD lose the electoral battle, the patron state would not hesitate to use bullets against ballots, directly or indirectly. In the longer term, the threat is economic because the continuing siphoning off of minerals inevitably translates into huge opportunity costs for the Congolese people. However, the political and economic sides of the coin are intimately related. Only by nurturing and manipulating a vast array of vested interests among the host communities of eastern Congo can Rwanda hope to meet the twin challenges of its foreign policy, namely, make eastern Congo safe for ethnic Tutsi and extract the resources needed to meet the demands of its formidable military establishment.

Looking back at the violence that has swept across the Great Lakes, future historians will ponder the analogy with the Thirty Years War. In both instances, we are dealing not with one war but an aggregation of wars; in each instance the logic of the unforeseen lies at the root of the endless and violent episodes generated by the initial event; and ultimately, leaving behind nothing but waste and destruction in its wake.

This is how C. V. Wedgewood, in her classic account, summed up the chaos and bloodshed unleashed through Europe from 1618 to 1648: "Morally subversive, economically destructive, socially degrading, confused in its causes, devious in its results, it is the outstanding example in European history of meaningless conflict."[78]

What better epitaph for a conflict that has taken four million lives—and nearly six, when the losses in Rwanda and Burundi, are added to the toll—displaced hundreds of thousands, raised ethnic hatreds to unprecedented levels, and made a wasteland of many parts of the environment?

Chapter 2
The Road to Hell

If the fate of the African continent evokes hopelessness, nowhere is this sense of despair more evident than in former Belgian Africa. No other region has experienced a more deadly combination of external aggression, foreign-linked factionalism, interstate violence, factional strife, and ethnic rivalries. Nowhere else in Africa has genocide exacted a more horrendous price in human lives lost, economic and financial resources squandered, and developmental opportunities wasted. The scale of the disaster is in sharp contrast with the polite indifference of the international community in the face of this unprecedented human tragedy. What has been called Africa's first world war has yet to attract the world's attention.

The marginal ranking of Africa in the scale of international priorities is one obvious explanation for this generalized lack of interest in the Great Lakes crisis. Another is the sheer complexity of the forces involved. When one considers the multiplicity of political actors—domestic and foreign—the fluidity of factional alliances, the spillover of ethnic violence across boundaries, and the extreme fragmentation of political arenas, it is easy to see why the international community should have second thoughts about the wisdom of a concerted peace initiative. No other crisis on the continent seems more resistant to conflict resolution.

Adding to the confusion is the plethora of competing explanatory models that come to mind. How much credence should one give to Paul Collier's recent thesis that "it is the feasibility of predation which determines the risk of conflict"?[1] Is the crisis in the Great Lakes an extreme example of the "criminalization of the state"?[2] Or should one turn instead to Jeffrey Herbst's demographic argument and look for evidence of low population density, combined with the weakness of state boundaries, as an explanation for Kabila's inability to effectively broadcast the power of the Congo state?[3] If Samuel Huntington's "clash of civilizations" model hardly applies, what of his contention that the "kin country syndrome" is the key to an understanding of regional instability?[4] To these questions we shall return.

This chapter offers a different prism to view the roots of the crisis. The key concept around which much of this discussion revolves is that of exclusion. Political, economic, and social exclusion are seen as the principal dimensions that must be explored if we are to grasp the dynamics of domestic and inter-state violence in the Great Lakes. This is not meant to minimize the significance of external aggression. The capacity of Rwanda and Uganda to effectively project their military force into eastern Congo, albeit with mixed results for both, is unquestionably a major contributory factor to regional instability. External intervention, however, must be seen in the broader historical context of the forces that have shaped the tragic destinies of former Belgian Africa. Briefly stated, the central pattern that recurs time and again is one in which ethnic polarization paves the way for political exclusion, exclusion eventually leading to insurrection, insurrection to repression, and repression to massive flows of refugees and internally displaced persons, which in turn become the vectors of further instability. The involvement of external actors, as we shall see, is inseparable from the perceived threats posed by mobilized refugee diasporas to their countries of origin, as well as to specific communities within the host country.

Historical Backdrop

Let us begin with a brief reminder of basic historical facts.

RANKED SOCIETIES, EXCLUSION, AND INSURRECTION

In the context of ranked societies like Rwanda and Burundi, where a two-tier structure of ethnic domination tended to vest power and privilege in the hands of the Tutsi minority, political exclusion was the rule for roughly 80 per cent of the population, consisting essentially of Hutu peasants. In Rwanda, the Hutu revolution of 1959–62—powerfully assisted if not engineered by the Belgian authorities—brought to a close the era of Tutsi hegemony.[5] While opening the way for the enthronement of the representatives of the Hutu, an estimated 200,000 Tutsi were forced into exile in neighbouring and other countries between 1959 and 1963—approximately 70,000 to Uganda, 25,000 to the Congo and 50,000 to Burundi.[6]

In Burundi, by contrast, where the "premise of inequality" was far less institutionalized and social relations more complex, ethnic polarization proceeded at a slower pace, allowing the Tutsi elites to consolidate their grip on the government and the army long before they faced the challenge of a servile insurrection. Every attempt made by Hutu leaders to overthrow the government—in 1965, 1969, and 1972—ended in dismal failure, each time resulting in extremely brutal repression, culminating in 1972 with the genocidal massacre of anywhere from 100,000 to 200,000

Hutu.[7] Not until 1993, with the election of a Hutu to the presidency, Melchior Ndadaye, were the Hutu given to believe that they would soon control their political destinies, only to be robbed of this opportunity on October 21, when a radical faction within the all-Tutsi army killed the newly elected president, the speaker, and deputy-speaker of the National Assembly and overthrew the government. Six months later, after three and a half years of bitter civil war, opposing the predominantly Tutsi troops of the RPF against the FAR, Rwanda became the scene of one of the biggest genocides of the last century: between 600,000 and 800,000 people, mostly Tutsi, were sent to their graves by Hutu militias (*interahamwe*) and army men.[8]

THE BANYARWANDA OF EASTERN CONGO

Until then, the principal victims of political exclusion were the Tutsi of Rwanda and the Hutu of Burundi. Their closest analogs in eastern Congo were the "Banyarwanda," a label that belies the diversity of their ethnic and regional origins.[9] Included under that rubric are three distinctive communities: (a) Hutu and Tutsi who had settled in the Kivu region long before the advent of colonial rule, including a group of ethnic Tutsi indigenous to south Kivu (located in the Mulenge region) known as Banyamulenge; (b) descendants of migrant workers, mostly Hutu, brought in from Rwanda in the 1930s and 1940s under the auspices of the colonial state; (c) tens of thousands of Tutsi refugees who fled Rwanda in the wake of the 1959 Hutu revolution, and hence referred to as fifty-niners.

By 1981, following the promulgation of a retroactive nationality law, the Banyarwanda were for all intents and purposes denied citizenship because none could possibly meet the legal requirement of proof of ancestral residence before October 18, 1908, when the Congo Free State formally became a Belgian colony. By 1990, at the time of the RPF invasion of Rwanda, Banyarwanda resentment of Mobutu's exclusionary policies were matched by their growing sympathy for the cause of the RPF. Many did in fact join the ranks of the RPF and fought alongside their Ugandan kinsmen. By then both groups shared the deepest anxieties about their future in their respective countries of asylum. They would soon become critically important actors in the regional political equation.[10]

The devastating ripple effects of the Rwanda cataclysm were felt immediately in eastern Congo. The sudden influx of over a million Hutu refugees across the border, accompanied by the fleeing remnants of the FAR and *interahamwe*, brought a major environmental and human disaster to the region, while at the same time triggering a drastic reordering of ethnic loyalties. Almost overnight the Banyarwanda community split into warring factions, pitting Hutu against Tutsi.[11] Meanwhile, in the interstices of the Hutu-Tutsi tug-of-war, emerged a shadowy constellation of armed factions, the Mai-Mai. Drawn from ethnic groups indigenous to the region—Hunde, Nande, Nyanga, Bashi, and so forth—to this day, the Mai-Mai are notorious for the fickleness of their political loyalties, the fluidity of their political alignments, and their addiction to violence. Swiftly responding to changing circumstances, they first turned against Hutu elements, then against local Tutsi, and ultimately against the Rwandan invaders and their Congolese allies.

1996: The Turning of the Tide

The destruction of the refugee camps by units of the Rwandan Patriotic Army (RPA), in October 1996, marks a turning point in the tortured history of the region. It signals the meteoric rise to power of Laurent-Desiré Kabila as the deus ex machina imposed by Museveni upon Kagame to lead the anti-Mobutist crusade under the banner of the AFDL. While the AFDL and its Rwandan allies fought their way to Kinshasa, forcing Mobutu to throw in the sponge in May 1997, the shooting up of the camps released a huge flow of refugees across the Congo, fleeing the RPA's search-and-destroy operations. The attack on the camps also marks the entry of new international actors in the Congolese arena, most notably Rwanda and Uganda. For a brief moment, the surge of popular enthusiasm caused by the overthrow of the Mobutist dictatorship seemed to submerge factional and ethnic divisions—but only for a while. With a substantial presence of Rwandans on the ground acting in military and administrative capacities, anti-Tutsi feelings rapidly spread among a broad spectrum of the Congolese population in North and South Kivu, in the Katanga, as well as in the capital city. Unable or unwilling to discriminate between Rwandan Tutsi, on the one hand, and Banyamulenge and fifty-niners on the other, for the self-styled "Congolais authentiques," anyone with the looks of a Tutsi would be fair game when push came to shove in July 1998.

1998: The Turning of the Tables

The next and most critical stage in the Great Lakes saga came in August 1998 when, sensing the liabilities involved in his dependency on Tutsi "advisors," the new king of the Congo took the fateful step of turning against the kingmakers, thus paving the way for a replay of 1996. Yet the state of the play on the ground was now very different from the quasi-unanimous crusade of 1996. As 1998 drew to a close, no fewer than six African armies were involved, albeit to a greater or lesser extent, on the side of Kabila (Angola, Namibia, Zimbabwe, Chad, Congo Brazzaville, and the Sudan). Against this formidable coalition stood the fragile alliance of Rwanda and Uganda and their Congolese client faction, the Rassemblement Congolais pour la Démocratie (RCD), soon to break up into two rival groups, while a third rebel faction emerged in northern Congo, Jean-Pierre Bemba's MLC.

The 1998 crisis brought to light an immediate hardening of anti-Tutsi sentiment throughout the Congo, and particularly in North and South Kivu, where it was now the turn of the Congolese "autochtons" (i.e., non-Banyarwanda) to pay the price of exclusion. Denied all possibility of political participation, economically exploited by Rwandan interlopers, and trampled underfoot by foreign occupying forces, their most salient common characteristic is their visceral hatred of all Tutsi, whether of Rwandan or Congolese origins. Little wonder that today the Mai-Mai are increasingly training their gun sights on RPA units operating in the Kivu—and in the process, unleashing a terrible retribution upon civilian populations—as well as on the Banyamulenge, even though the latter fully qualify as "autochtons." Evidently, their deep historic roots in South Kivu do not exonerate them of the suspicion of being in league with the Kagame government. The truth is that the Banyamulenge and the ethnic Tutsi, in general, are anything but united in their attitude toward Kigali. Many Banyamulenge resent the fact that they have been instrumentalized by Kagame, that they have become mere pawns in the regional poker game. Most of them, however, privately admit that Rwanda's military presence in eastern Congo is their sole protection against another genocidal carnage.

To sum up: exclusion does not just suddenly materialize out of the primeval fissures of the plural society; its roots are traceable to the rapid mobilization of ethnic identities unleashed by the democratization of societies built on the "premise of inequality" and to the profoundly discriminatory implications of public policies directed against specific ethnic communities. In all three states, however, refugee flows were the crucial factor behind the rapid polarization of ethnic feelings in the host countries. Everywhere, refugee-generating violence has produced violence-generating refugee flows.

Dimensions of Exclusion

In the context of this discussion, political exclusion means the denial of political rights to specific ethnic or ethnoregional communities, most notably the right to vote, organize political parties, freely contest elections, and thus become full participants in the political life of their country. Obvious cases are the Tutsi in post-revolutionary Rwanda and the Hutu in Burundi until the 1993 aborted transition to multiparty democracy (some might argue that relatively little changed since then), to which must be added the Banyarwanda of eastern Congo, after being disenfranchised by the 1981 nationality law, as well as the Tutsi refugee diaspora of Uganda, for whom naturalization was never envisaged. Admittedly, political exclusion is a relative concept, both in terms of the range of disabilities suffered by the excluded communities, and the context in which it occurs. It is easy to see why, for example, in the context of Mobutu's dictatorship, the withdrawal of citizenship rights from the Banyarwanda did not produce the same violent reaction as the refusal of the Burundi authority to recognize the victory of the Hutu at the polls in 1965. Again, it is one thing for a minority to be politically excluded and quite another for a group representing 80 percent of the population to be reduced to a silent majority, as is clearly the case today for the Hutu of Rwanda.

Economic exclusion, on the other hand, refers first and foremost to the denial of traditional rights to land. Given that land is the principal economic resource of peasant communities, denial of access to land use inevitably implies economic impoverishment or worse. Here again contextual factors are important. Although rising population densities and environmental degradation are everywhere a fundamental aspect of the land problem, nowhere is the problem more acute than where land has been redistributed to meet the needs of machine politics (as in pregenocide Rwanda), or reallocated to new claimants (as happened in North Kivu in the 1970s when tens of thousands of acres of land were bought off by Tutsi fifty-niners), or where rural insecurity becomes a pretext for massive population transfers in regroupment camps (as in Burundi and northern Rwanda).

Social exclusion goes hand in hand with the erosion of traditional social networks and the collapse of the safety nets that once supported the traditional social order of peasant communities. The result is a growing marginalization of rural youth. Deprived of the minimal economic security and coping mechanisms built into the customary social nets, yet denied the opportunity to make their mark in life through alternative channels, their life chances are almost nil.

To be sure, political exclusion does not always imply economic exclusion. If there is little doubt that the 1959 Hutu revolution in Rwanda received its impetus from the political exclusion of Western-educated Hutu elites, it is equally clear that economic exclusion had relatively little to do with the Hutu-Tutsi conflict. One might even argue that in some instances, withdrawal of political rights translates into rising levels of economic achievement for the excluded community, as shown by the large number of relatively well-to-do Tutsi entrepreneurs in pregenocide Rwanda. Nonetheless, processes of political, economic, and social exclusion are closely interconnected: just as refugee diasporas have exacerbated the problem of natural resource scarcities in the host countries, most conspicuously in eastern Congo and to a lesser extent in Uganda, the resultant shrinkage of land capable of cultivation, along with the dislocation of traditional social networks, must be seen as major contributory factors to the marginalization of youth and the rise of armed militias. The cumulative effect of these phenomena is nowhere more potentially disruptive than where specific ethnic communities bear the full brunt of economic and social exclusion.

Refugee flows provide the conceptual link among all three forms of exclusion. Not that refugees are always on the losing side economically, although in most cases they are. The more important point is that the side effects of large numbers of refugees moving into any given country of asylum translates into severe economic and social hardships for the host society. Rising commodity prices, the rapid depletion of environmental resources, and the frequency of petty crimes within and outside the camps, not to mention the systematic raiding of cattle, crops, and vehicles (as happened in eastern Congo in 1994), are all part of the catalogue of deprivations inflicted on the host communities. In such circumstances, refugees become an easy target for politicians eager to translate diffuse grievances into political capital. In different circumstances, however, they also can be mobilized by opposition groups to strengthen their hand against domestic foes, as indeed happened in Uganda in the 1980s and in Burundi in the 1960s. Refugee populations, in short, have served as a major political resource, either as foil or as a source of support.

The Politics of Mobilized Diasporas

Since 1959 the multiplicity of crises experienced by Rwanda and Burundi have generated four major refugee flows: (a) between 1959 and 1963 an estimated 150,000 Tutsis fled Rwanda in the wake of the Hutu revolution, the majority seeking asylum in Uganda, Burundi, and eastern Congo; (b) the second major exodus involved approximately 300,000 Hutu from Burundi fleeing the 1972 genocidal massacres of Hutu by the Tutsi-dominated army, most of them headed for Tanzania and Rwanda; (c) the next wave of Hutu refugees from Burundi, numbering perhaps as many as 400,000, of whom more than half ended up in Rwanda, followed the reciprocal massacres of Tutsi and Hutu, triggered by the assassination of President-elect Melchior Ndadaye on October 21, 1993, adding tens of thousands to the refugee camps in Tanzania, Rwanda, and South

Kivu; (d) in 1994, the fourth and largest outpouring of refugees involved approximately two million Hutu from Rwanda fleeing the avenging arm of the FPR. Over a million settled in eastern Congo, the rest in Tanzania.

All of the above qualify as mobilized diasporas, in that they shared specific political objectives, were politically organized, and made a sustained effort to consolidate their grip on the refugee population. This is still the case for the Hutu diaspora from Burundi and what little is left of its counterpart from Rwanda. Ultimately, their overriding goal was to return to their homeland as citizens, by force if necessary. So far only the Tutsi refugees, under the banner of the FPR, after thirty-five years of exile were able to do so.

But if the saga of the Tutsi diaspora is a success story of sorts—but at what price!—its early history is a tale of consistent failure—political and military—causing enormous bloodshed inside Rwanda, a situation for which there are tragic recent parallels among the Hutu diasporas from Burundi and Rwanda.

Refugees are first and foremost an object of humanitarian concern; only at a later stage, after metamorphosing into a mobilized diaspora, do they emerge as a source of political concern for domestic, regional, and international actors. The obstacles in the way of effective political mobilization cover a wide gamut: the material and emotional costs of uprootedness, the geographical dispersal of the camps, the inadequacy of communication facilities, factional rivalries, and the constraints on political activities imposed by the host country are the usual handicaps faced by refugee diasporas. These disabilities vary enormously over time, however, and from one setting to another. The single most important conditioning factor, however, lies in the receptivity of the host country to the political goals and organizational efforts of refugee communities.

THE FIFTY-NINERS IN EASTERN CONGO: INYENZI AND MULELISTES

A brief comparative glance at the record of the first Tutsi diaspora, in the early sixties (the fifty-niners), with that of the second generation of refugee warriors in the 1990s, is instructive in this regard.[12] Even more revealing is the comparison with the Hutu diasporas.

Organizational strength, internal cohesion, leadership skills, and the ability to draw maximum tactical advantage from the domestic politics of the host country; these are the key ingredients that spell the difference between success and failure. On each count, the record of the Tutsi fifty-niners can only be described as dismal. Though formally affiliated with the monarchist Union Nationale Rwandaise (UNAR), the party virtually disintegrated after its leadership was forced into exile. While some Unaristes joined hands with the Muleliste rebellion in eastern Congo in 1964–65, a small group went to Communist China for military training; others, labeled *inyenzi* ("cockroaches") by the new Rwanda government, opted for a "direct action" strategy and proceeded to launch armed raids from Burundi, the Congo, and Uganda, only to be repulsed—at great cost to themselves and Tutsi civilians inside Rwanda—by the Rwandan National Guard and their Belgian advisers.[13] Despite substantial support from a group of radical Tutsi politicians in Bujumbura (but not from the Crown), they never were able to translate this informal alliance into an effective military posture. In eastern Congo, their tactical alliance with the Banyamulenge of South Kivu proved short-lived; the Banyamulenge rapidly switched sides after the setbacks inflicted to the Mulelistes by the Armée Nationale Congolaise (ANC). Even more damaging to their ultimate goals was their international image as crypto-communists in league with Communist China.

THE SECOND-GENERATION TUTSI DIASPORA: UGANDA

The second generation of Tutsi exiles drew important lessons from their elders' inability to get their act together. None were more aware of the necessity to clean up their act than the Ugandan exiles who provided the spearhead of the military crusade that ultimately led to the capture of power in Kigali in July 1994. Though space limitations do not permit a full discussion of their troubled history, most observers would agree that the key to their success lies as much in their organizational skills as in their ability to make the most of the opportunities offered by the rise in 1981 of the anti-Obote guerrilla movement headed by Yoweri Museveni, the National Resistance Army (NRA).[14]

Already in the 1970s, the Rwandan Alliance for National Unity (RANU) provided a coherent organizational frame for mobilizing support within and outside Uganda: collecting funds, coordinating cultural activities, reaching out to the international community, and lobbying for the right to return to Rwanda. Between 1981 and 1986, when the NRA seized power in Kampala, a solid phalanx of second generation fifty-niners joined Museveni's movement, fought pitched battles in the Luwero triangle at a cost of 60,000 killed in action, and ultimately gained strategic access to Museveni's security apparatus when two of their officers, Fred Rwigema and Paul Kagame, respectively, rose to the positions of Deputy Minister of Defence and Deputy Chief of Military Intelligence.

Meanwhile a series of initiatives from Tutsi exiles in Uganda and the United States led to the birth, in 1987, of the RPF and the tacit endorsement by many of its leaders of the military option of a return by force. By the eve of October 1, 1990 and the attack on Rwanda, the RPF had grown into a powerful politicomilitary organization, combining political mobilization and military training with wide-ranging lobbying activities in the United States and Europe. By then, its recruitment net extended to Tutsi exile communities in Burundi, Kenya, Tanzania, and eastern Congo, infusing further strength into its ranks. Only after its capture of power on July 4, 1994, did the RPA develop into a formidable military machine, capable of effectively projecting its muscle into eastern Congo and beyond.

THE HUTU DIASPORAS

If the destinies of the RPF were served by exceptionally good fortune, the same cannot be said of the Burundi Hutu diasporas. Although the 1972 diaspora gave birth to the Parti de la Libération du Peuple Hutu (Palipehutu) in the Mishamo refugee camp in Tanzania in 1980, at no time was the party able to aggregate a range of political and military resources comparable to the RPF; its leadership never was able to match the organizational and strategic talent of a Rwigema or a Paul Kagame, let alone the latter's diplomatic skill in reaching out to external actors.

At no time was the party able to capitalize on anything like the extraordinary good luck of the FPR in Uganda in the early 1980s. Burundi exiles are notorious for their lack of internal cohesion.[15] Their history is one of incessant splits, whether in Europe, in Rwanda, or in Tanzania. Their fissiparous characteristics became even more evident after the 1993 exodus and the emergence of several military wings of rival parties, the Front de Libération National (Frolina), the Forces pour la Défense de la Démocratie (FDD), and the division of the Palipehutu into three separate factions. Though some are said to draw benefits from the smuggling networks in Kigoma, and more recently from the shipment of arms from Zimbabwe and Kinshasa, their resource base is hopelessly inadequate for the task at hand: "All of the rebel groups (in Tanzania) complain of the lack of funding, arms and other resources necessary to carry out a sustained military campaign in Burundi."[16] Again, compared to the RPF's ability to draw international support (most notably from the U.S. Committee for Refugees in Washington) and visibility, the performance of the refugee factions on that score is less than impressive. "The main complaint of the rebels," notes a recent International Crisis Group report, "is the lack of international support. As one rebel leader said: 'we don't have anyone to support us the way the Banyamulenge are supported by Rwanda and Uganda.'"[17]

The case of the 1994 refugees from Rwanda is unlike any other in terms of the magnitude of the human flow, the volume of weaponry transferred, the tightness of the political and military encadrement, the extensive support it received from the Mobutist state, its devastating impact on the natural environment, its catalytic effect on ethnic loyalties, the questions its raises about the political implications of humanitarian aid, and last but not least, the ultimate tragedy they suffered at the hands of the RPA. To review each of these dimensions would take us too far afield. Suffice to note that the seriousness of the threats posed to the new Rwandan state was without parallel in the history of mobilized diasporas. Exceptional circumstances called for exceptional measures. However, the destruction of the camps in October 1996 by the RPA was part of a wider underlying design, namely, not just to "secure" Rwanda's western border but to (a) to extend the search-and-destroy operations to the campsites in South Kivu and in so doing, deal a crippling blow to the refugee populations sheltering extremists (b) deny Uganda's armed opposition movements (notably Tabliq and the West Nile Liberation Front) access to safe havens in the Congo, and (c) pave the way for Kabila's "second coming." On each count the Kagame strategy succeeded beyond all expectations, at least in the short run. From a wider perspective and with the benefit of hindsight, it is clear that the ultimate goal of the operation—making the Congo safe for Rwanda—has fallen somewhat short of the master planners' expectations.

The Tools of Political Mobilization

As this discussion makes clear, contextual variables are of critical importance in explaining the success or failure of mobilized diasporas. Nonetheless, agency also matters. Context alone is not enough to explain the different tools and techniques that enter into processes of mobilization: ranging from coercion to ideological manipulation, from rumor mongering to arms smuggling, from practices and attitudes borrowed from the world of the invisible, and to the use and misuse of information designed to raise the political awareness of the rank and file. Not all of these are productive of success.

Coercive mobilization by some factions of the Hutu diaspora has often had the opposite effect of what was intended, causing tremendous disaffection among civilians and bitter rivalries among exile factions. What some factions view as legitimate means of ideological mobilization—such as the diffusion of historical narratives designed to demonize the Tutsi enemy, a favorite Palipehutiste technique—others tend to reject. Recourse to magic looms large in the arsenal of Congolese factions, notably among the Mai-Mai and the RCD, sometimes with disastrous consequences for the families and communities to whom, wrongly or rightly, magic powers have been attributed. Next to the availability of funding and weapons, information (or misinformation) is of critical importance. On that score, the performance of the Tutsi diaspora in Uganda ranks far above its Hutu counterparts.

Quite aside from its efficiency in collecting funds from exile Tutsi communities and gaining a privileged access to NRA equipment, compared to Hutu refugee movements, the Uganda exiles have been remarkably adept at mobilizing support through their skillful manipulation of information. This fact goes far in explaining its capacity to sway international public opinion long after the diaspora had become a nation.

Another Look at Theory

What new light do the theories mentioned earlier shed on the dynamics of ethnoregional conflict in the Great Lakes? The answer, in part, depends on how they "fit" into any particular aspect of the crisis.

Let us begin with Huntington. The whole drift of our argument, centered on the concept of exclusion, can be read as a refutation of the "clash of civilization" thesis; by the same token, his discussion of the "kin country syndrome" is of direct relevance to an understanding of the patterns of ethnic mobilization unleashed by refugee diasporas. As our previous discussion makes clear, where ethnic fault lines cut across national boundaries, conflict tends to spill over from one national arena to the next, transforming kin solidarities into a powerful vector of transnational violence. An action-reaction pattern sets in, whereby victims in one setting become instigators of violence in the other. Largely missing from Huntington's discussion, however, is a sustained attention to mobilization strategies, including the kinds of resources employed to mobilize support.

This is where Collier's paper offers some challenging insights. I refer specifically to his analysis of the role of diasporas and access to financial resources as crucial factors in explaining the risk of civil war. On the other hand, serious questions arise as to whether the financial viability of rebel factions, including refugee diasporas, is entirely reducible to the opportunities offered by commodity export economies. If this were the case, the whole of the continent would be tottering on the brink of insurrection. Not just any export commodity but gold and diamonds are the rebels' best friends.

Whether through gem trading or any other source of profits, financial viability matters. There is no denying the cardinal importance of the looting of gold and diamond resources in eastern Congo in the funding of the war effort by Kigali and Kampala and of the deadly rivalries over the loot in pitting Rwanda against Uganda in Kisangani. Nonetheless, "financial viability" only tells part of the story. Crucial as they are in explaining the failure or success of mobilized diasporas, contextual opportunities are not limited to financial viability; equally important is the political viability of rebel and refugee movements, most notably their ability to negotiate political and military support. This is true not only of the RCD factions today, but was certainly the case for the second generation Tutsi refugees in Uganda in the 1980s.

Where the Collier thesis seems most vulnerable is in the rejection of objective socioeconomic indicators as a source of civil violence: "Objective measures of social grievance, such as inequality, a lack of democracy, and ethnic and religious divisions, have no systematic effect on risk . . . because civil wars occur when rebel organizations are financially viable."[18] Quite aside from the fact that the argument simply doesn't hold up in the face of the overwhelming evidence to the contrary—a fact that Collier might conceivably explain away by relegating Rwanda, Burundi, and eastern Congo to deviant cases—one wonders why one set of independent variables (objective measures of social grievance) should exclude the other (financial viability).

Categorically dismissing rebellion as "protest motivated by genuine and extreme grievance," Collier offers a striking analogy: "For a few moments suspend disbelief," he writes, "and suppose that most rebel movements are pretty close to being large-scale variants of organized crime. The discourse would be exactly the same as if they were protest movements."[19] Nowhere, however, does he consider the alternative proposition that the state might qualify as the criminal and the rebels as victims of state crimes. This is, of course, the central argument set forth by Bayart, Ellis, and Hibou in their recent work on the criminalization of the state.[20] This is not meant to deny the propensity of rebel and refugees, and refugees turned rebels, to engage in criminal activities, yet it is important to note that the phrase covers a wide spectrum of illegal activities and that such criminal activities often pale in comparison with those carried out by the state. Rwanda under Habyalimana, Zaire under Mobutu, and the Burundi armed forces under Buyoya all exhibit, to some degree or another, at one point or another, what can only be described as a criminal behavior of the worst kind, including political assassination, theft, and corruption on a grand scale. It is difficult to avoid the conclusion that the result has been to promote huge social and economic inequalities, along with corresponding "genuine and extreme grievances," and thus pave the way for the exclusionary policies that lie at the heart of ethnic violence in the Great Lakes.

The Herbst thesis has the merit of looking at a range of variables seldom taken into account by political scientists: the combined effect on state failure of low population densities, weak and artificial boundaries, and the resultant inability of the state to control its hinterland; this, he adds, is in striking contrast with the historical record of European states, all of which have experienced "the brutality of interstate war" as a major ingredient of state consolidation.[21] On each of these counts, however, the recent history of the Great Lakes offers massive counter-factual evidence. The region claims the highest population density in the continent; the precolonial boundaries of the interlacustrine kingdoms of Rwanda and Burundi were fairly well delineated, at least by comparison with the rest of Africa; control of these states over the hinterland was relatively well established; and the "brutality of interstate war" was a major feature of their precolonial histories, though by no means comparable to the devastation caused by the internal and interstate wars currently ravaging the region. What Herbst leaves out of the picture is the impact of colonial and postcolonial history. He leaves out what Crawford Young has so ably brought into view—the enduring disabilities arising from the impact of the colonial state on African societies.[22] Predictably, Herbst makes no reference to the multifaceted crises of exclusion and social marginalization around which much of this discussion revolves and for which there are many parallels in the continent. Only by confusing optimism with fantasy and reality with illusion, can one take comfort in the view, implicit in the Herbst thesis, that the violent confrontations in former Belgian Africa will ultimately bring to the region the benefits of state consolidation along a bloodstained path similar to the one historically taken by European states.

Policy Implications

By postulating exclusion as a crucial dimension of the Great Lakes crisis, we do not mean to suggest that its conceptual opposite is the only solution to the region's woes. Inclusion is a theme that admits many variations. It can easily mask a policy of cooptation and serve as a substitute for a genuine sharing of power; carried to an extreme, with little or no attention paid to contextual realities, the result may be chronic instability, as happened in Burundi in 1995, following the so-called Convention of Government of 1994. The diffusion of ethnic violence across national boundaries, sustained by external forces, imposes severe limitations on the benefits of power sharing.

The case of Burundi is instructive in this respect. A key provision of the precarious peace deal worked out in Arusha (Tanzania) in July 2000, through Nelson Mandela's painstaking facilitating efforts, involves a broadly based three-year transitional government incorporating the representatives of fifteen parties, almost evenly distributed between predominantly Tutsi and Hutu parties. For the next eighteen months a Tutsi (Pierre Buyoya) will serve as president and a Hutu (Domitien Ndayizeye) as vice president; during the following eighteen-month period, the roles will be reversed. This power-sharing arrangement is bolstered by more fundamental concessions to the Hutu majority, such as a commitment to restructuring the all-Tutsi army on the basis of ethnic parity. Demands which until recently were non-negotiable have now been met, such as the presence of a 1,400-strong South African peace keeping force; others will be negotiated in months ahead, such as the restructuring of the army, the dismantling of regroupment camps, and the appointment of an international judicial commission to address issues of justice and impunity. Incentives to cooperate go beyond the allocation of portfolios to a wide array of coalition partners. To the extent that the Burundi state is becoming less hegemonic and more open to the demands of the Hutu majority, it has gone a long way towards promoting a climate of trust. Nor has the international community faltered in its efforts to reward cooperative behavior, as shown by the promise of a generous aid package from the European community ($440 million).

Despite efforts to widen the scope of Hutu-Tutsi cooperation, the Arusha framework faces an uncertain future. Inclusionary strategies so far have failed to convince the leaders of two extremist Hutu rebel groups, the FDD and the Palipehutu-FLN, to lay down their arms. That their obduracy is in part motivated by the financial and military support they have come to expect from external actors—whether from Zimbabwe or Congo-Kinshasa or from their ethnic kinsmen in the Congo or Tanzania—is reasonably clear. Equally plain is that Hutu extremism is bound to generate a response in kind from Tutsi hard-liners. Expectations of strategic assistance from external actors are not limited to any one group. They constitute major incentives for extremists at both ends of the ethnic spectrum not to cooperate in power-sharing arrangements.

If so, there are compelling reasons for encouraging the full implementation of the Lusaka accords (1998), especially as regards the withdrawal of foreign armed forces, the disarming of the so-called "negative forces" (the interahamwe militias and Mai-Mai factions), and the resumption of an inter-Congolese dialogue. The success of the Arusha accords is intimately linked to a global settlement in the Congo. Only if the rebel factions in Burundi are deprived of the support of secondary level participants (i.e., Zimbabwe or Congo-Kinshasa) will they join in the peace process or at least desist from violence. The same is true of the rebel RCD factions in the Congo, currently supported by Uganda and Rwanda.

Given the considerable economic stakes they have in the conflict, neither Rwanda nor Uganda are likely to envisage a withdrawal of their armies unless faced with vigorous pressure from the international community. Though providing convenient justification for their presence in eastern Congo, security concerns are of secondary importance for Presidents Kagame and Museveni; far more significant as a policy imperative are the enormous profits derived from the wholesale plunder of the Congo's mineral wealth. This is where a major reappraisal of strategic priorities is needed from donors, specifically from the World Bank, the United States, and Great Britain. By turning a blind eye to the "imperial" designs of Rwanda and Uganda in eastern Congo, while at the same time rewarding their economic performance, donors are in effect subsidizing their war effort. The time has come to recognize the fundamental contradiction involved in the pro forma support of the Lusaka accords and assistance policies designed to undermine their full implementation.

A more fundamental contradiction exists between the ethos of participatory politics and the exclusionary implications of the foreign-linked clientelism operating in much of the Great Lakes region. Reinforcing the neopatrimonial features of their domestic politics, Rwanda and Uganda have developed multiple linkages—economic, military, and political—with their respective client factions, but these linkages extend far beyond the boundaries of the Great Lakes. Corporate interests in the West and elsewhere in the world also have stakes in the rents generated through the illicit exploitation of the Congo's resources. The unpalatable truth is that the multiplicity of interests in support of the regional status quo far exceed the pressures of the United Nations for implementing the Lusaka accords. Nonetheless, no matter how daunting the obstacles ahead, Lusaka is the only roadmap for charting a new course towards peace. From all the evidence, this basic truth has yet to sink in among certain key members of the international community.

Part II
Rwanda and Burundi: The Genocidal Twins

Chapter 3
Ethnicity as Myth

Ethnicity is never what it seems. What some see as ancestral atavism, others see as a typically modern phenomenon, anchored in colonial rule. Where neo-Marxists detect class interests parading in traditional garb, mainstream scholars unveil imagined communities. And whereas many see ethnicity as the bane of the African continent, others think that it could provide the basis for a moral social contract and that it contains within itself the seeds of openness and accountability.

So overwhelming is the evidence that points to the demonic face of ethnicity that it is tempting to forget its more benign traits. Yet not everything about ethnicity translates into bloodshed and genocide or into frenzied ethnic cleansing. Ethnic communities also generate responsible, civic-minded leaders, anxious to speak on behalf of their constituents and willing to protect them against the abuses of the state. The sense of belonging to an ethnic community need not be synonymous with conflict and competition. John Lonsdale's argument about the significance of "moral ethnicity" readily comes to mind. Drawing a distinction between "political tribalism" and "moral ethnicity," he defines the former as "the use of ethnic identities in political competition with other groups" and the latter as "a positive force which creates communities from within through domestic controversy over civic virtue."[1] Moral ethnicity, he wrote, is an expression of "the common human instinct to create out of the daily habits of social intercourse and material labor a system of moral meaning and ethical reputation within a more or less imagined community."[2]

Ethnicity does not necessarily mean conflict, nor is conflict everywhere traceable to politicized ethnicity. Illustrating this point are the violent struggles in Somalia, one of the most conflict-ridden states anywhere in the continent, and the class-based intra-Zulu confrontations that have punctuated the recent history of Natal. Similarly, the recent war in the Democratic Republic of the Congo cannot be reduced to ethnic polarities. Even where mass murder is clearly aimed at a specific ethnic community, as in Rwanda during the 1994 genocide, it is not easy to pin the blame on ethnicity. What, indeed, does ethnicity mean when the groups in conflict share the same language, the same national territory, the same customs, and have for centuries lived more or less peacefully side by side?

Clearly then, ethnicity can be many things, both good and bad. The crucial question, therefore, for anyone attempting to understand its role in conflict is, What causes it to become a force for evil? What, in other words, accounts for the transformation of moral ethnicity into political tribalism, and tribalism into genocide? What are the mechanisms through which peaceful ethnic cohabitation gives way to death and destruction?

John Lonsdale gives us a clue: "Tribalism," he writes, "remains the reserve currency in our markets of power, ethnicity our most critical community of thought."[3] In the market place of electoral competition, tribalism is the bad currency that drives out the good currency, in a kind of Gresham's law of ethnic politics. Moral ethnicity is the first casualty of the inflationary spiral of ethnic claims and counterclaims. Nonetheless, to invoke political tribalism in an attempt to explain genocide leaves out a crucial dimension of ethnicity. Ethnicity has a capacity to be manipulated for the pursuit of preeminently immoral goals, to profoundly alter collective perceptions of the "other." It can be distorted using images whose purpose it is to draw rigid boundaries between good and evil, civic virtue and moral depravity, freedom and oppression, and foreigners and autochthons.

This chapter focuses on the effect of mythmaking on ethnic strife in the Great Lakes region of Africa. After an examination of the meaning of ethnicity, attention is given to the origin and development of myths in central Africa, especially to the traditional Rwandan myths of origins and the so-called Hamitic hypothesis, a myth started by the Europeans. The last part of the chapter is devoted to a consideration of how and why these myths were turned to genocidal purposes. It is my contention that the history—in whose name hundreds of thousands of innocent Tutsi men, women, and children were slaughtered—is, in large part, myth. So is the view of the past that lies behind Rwanda's claims to huge chunks of North and South Kivu. And so, also, is the reading of history implicit in the construction of new identities in eastern Congo, the so-called Banyamulenge. Mythmaking, in sum, is what transforms social conflict into irreconcilable moral standoffs.

Ethnicity: Invented, Imagined, or Mythologized?

In order for ethnic entrepreneurs to make capital out of tribalism, a tribe must exist. The term *tribe*, however, as has been emphasized time and again, is hardly appropriate to describe communities whose pedigree is traceable to the accidents of colonial rule. The tribal names that have passed down into modern usage are, in most instances, misnomers. The tribes were born of European ignorance, with their existence given formal recognition in statistical records or in the writings of early European administrators, explorers, and missionaries. Prior to these European records, they had no real existence.

ETHNICITY INVENTED

Should we speak then, not of tribes but of "invented" communities? Examples abound of ethnic entities whose birth certificate bears traces of an "invented tradition," to use Terence Ranger's phrase. The classic example is the case of the Bangala of northern Congo. First "discovered" by Henry Morton Stanley, who called them "unquestionably a very superior tribe," the Bangala, as Crawford Young reminds us, "were accorded official anthropological recognition when an entire volume was devoted to them in 1907 in the first ethnographic survey of the Zaire peoples."[4] The Dinka of the Sudan, likewise, derive their ethnonym and thus part of their collective identity from a similar misreading of the facts by a European explorer who took the name of a local chief to designate a collection of quite separate communities.[5] The Acholi of northern Uganda are another example. According to Atkinson, the term *Acholi* was invented by Arab traders (Kutoria) from the Sudan to refer to a variety of Luo-speaking lineages and chiefdoms.[6] Even as late as the 1930s, "the Acholi were referred to as 'Gangi' or 'Shuli' and they had no fixed territorial boundaries."[7] Each of these invented communities, along with many others, would not have been out of place in the volume edited by Ranger and Hobsbawm on *The Invention of Tradition*.[8]

ETHNICITY IMAGINED

Evocative though it is, the term *invention* does not do justice to the diversity of voices that contribute to the making of a community. To speak of an invented tradition does little to illuminate the ideological orientation or normative underpinnings of such a group. Nor does it bring out the different constructions placed upon it by different categories of social actors at different moments of history. Ranger himself came to recognize the limitations of the term *invention* and to prefer the notion of imagination. Drawing from the insights of Feierman and Lonsdale, he noted that the word *imagining* has the advantage of stressing ideas, images, and symbols, which are useful vehicles for understanding how traditions are formed.[9] The history of any modern tradition, Ranger emphasized, is immensely complex. It is not the product of one, but of many, conflicting imaginations. Over time, the meaning of the imagined is defined and redefined. In Africa, as Ranger explained, traditions imagined by whites were reimagined by blacks; traditions imagined by particular interest groups were reimagined by others.

We should therefore, perhaps, speak of imagined communities rather than invented ones. Ranger's understanding of the exegesis of tradition certainly seems to apply to the Great Lakes region of Africa. Here, Africans appropriated the Hamitic tradition imagined by Europeans. This same tradition was again reimagined by Hutu intellectuals to forge ideological weapons directed at the Tutsi minority. To describe Hutu and Tutsi as "invented communities" is hardly appropriate. Both existed long before the advent of colonial rule. To see them as imagined identities does point to the changing perceptions of one group by another, as well as to the processes involved in the emergence of a new "tribe" in eastern Congo, the Banyamulenge.

ETHNICITY MYTHOLOGIZED

Yet there is surely more than political imagination at work in the continuing carnage in the Great Lakes. What gives ethnic conflict in the region its peculiarly savage edge are the myths that have grown up around Hutu and Tutsi. Behind the twisted memories, distorted histories, and demonized ethnicities that have contributed to the bloodshed lie mythologies, which have thus been summoned to legitimize the butchery. Ironically, in Rwanda, it is the very thing that should have welded the people together that has served to do the most to tear them apart. The Rwandan myth of origins, at least in its original conception, conjures up a normative charter-holding society together in a unified trinity of Tutsi, Hutu, and Twa. And yet, in time, this very myth of origins became the quarry for destructive ideologies.

In the context of this discussion, *myth* is used in both its conventional and metaphorical senses. In its conventional sense, a myth is a legend. Mythmaking may thus simply refer to the creation of such a legend. In such an instance, the purposes of mythmaking are often benign. Myths of origins, for example, are not uncommonly designed to foster social cohesion. Mythmaking may, by contrast, carry far more negative connotations. In the metaphorical sense, mythmaking involves the deliberate denial or distortion of historical reality in a situation of crisis and conflict. The aim of mythmaking of this sort is to inspire division and to inflame ethnic passions.

The Origin and Transformation of Rwandan Myths

Ancient Rwanda had a rich collection of myths and ideologies long before the coming of Europeans. The traditional myths of origins, which provided a virtual charter of Tutsi supremacy, continue to play a central role to this day, though their meaning has radically changed over time. They are still the main frame of reference for conservative Tutsi elites, but since the early fifties, they have been given a quite different symbolic meaning by Western-educated Hutu elites.

These myths have been studied by Marcel d'Hertefelt,[10] who identified five essential themes: the celestial origins of the Tutsi; the fundamental and "natural" differences among Tutsi, Hutu, and Twa; the superior civilization that the Tutsi brought to Rwanda; the threat of divine sanctions against those brazen enough to revolt against the monarchy; and the notion of divine kingship.

The first of these themes finds expression in the story of Kigwe, the founding hero of the royal clan, who descended from heaven, accompanied by his bother Mututsi and his sister Nyamparu. The second is the subject of numerous folktales and dynastic poems. A typical story is that of the stratagem used by God to determine who should rule over whom. So as to test their dependability, God decided to entrust Gahutu, Gatutsi, and Gatwa each with a pot of milk to watch over during the night. When dawn came, gluttonous Gatwa had drunk the milk; Gahutu had gone to sleep and spilt his milk; only the watchful Gatutsi had stayed up through the night to keep guard over his milk. The third is the theme of Tutsi civilization as inherently superior. Nowhere is this theme more tersely summed up than in the opening statement of a folktale of central Rwanda: "Dead are the dogs and the rats, giving way to the cows and the drum." (The cows here allude to the Tutsi, who, according to legend, introduced pastoralism; the drum was a symbol of power.) Rwanda has no official history before the arrival of the Tutsi. Just as in the dark ages of pre-Islamic civilization (*jahiliya*), it is assumed that until the Tutsi arrived, there was little worth remembering, much less recording.[11]

Why did these early myths take this shape? "The function of myth," says M. I. Finley, "is to make the past intelligible and meaningful by selection, by focusing on a few bits of the past that thereby acquire permanence, relevance, and universal significance."[12] Rwanda's myths of origins did more than make the past intelligible. Their function was also to make the present legitimate in the eyes of both Hutu and Tutsi.

In time, legends became reality. The myths gained a life of their own and came to be not so much fictitious stories but rather "a statement of a bigger reality." Its precedents, laws, and morals were, as Bronislaw Malinowski put it, "partially alive,"[13] and provided powerful moral justification for the all-encompassing "premise of inequality."[14] Indeed, it was this very ability of these myths to validate oppression that eventually led Hutu politicians to recast them in a radically new light.

Nineteenth-Century European Mythmaking: The Hamitic Hypothesis

By then, however, another myth had taken hold, one imported from nineteenth-century Europe that placed yet another construction on the history of Tutsi hegemony. Like its precolonial counterparts, the Hamitic myth underwent fundamental changes of substance and meaning; it therefore came to be seen and interpreted in very different ways by Hutu and Tutsi. It is indeed an ironic commentary on the malleability of myths that the same "Hamitic hypothesis"[15] should have provided European administrators and missionaries with a powerful argument in support of Tutsi domination, and thus subsequent generations of Hutu politicians with the most devastating ideological ammunition against it.

For the early Christian missionaries, the Tutsi stood as the finest example of the Hamitic race, described by Seligman as "pastoral 'Europeans,' arriving wave after wave, better armed as well as quicker witted than the dark agricultural Negroes."[16] In the eyes of these Christians, the Tutsi clearly belonged to a higher order of humanity than the Hutu. For this reason, they were seen as ideally equipped to act as the privileged intermediaries between the European colonizer and the "dark agricultural" masses. Tutsi superiority was manifested in their tall, arresting physique, their extraordinary capacity for self-control, and their ability to exercise authority.

The "scientific" authority of Diedrich Westerman, among others, also was cited in support of the view that the Tutsi were an exceptionally gifted and attractive race: "The Hamites are light skinned, with a straight nose, thin lips, narrow face, soft, often wavy or even straight hair, without prognathism. . . . Owing to their racial superiority they have gained leading positions and have become the founders of many of the larger states in Africa."[17] What made the Tutsi even more attractive was the fact that they were presumed to be of Ethiopian origin. This ancestry meant that at some point in the distant past, they must have been exposed to biblical influences, which would also explain why they were disposed to embrace Christianity. As Ian Linden puts it, "It seemed to the missionaries that Hamitic history had involved the progressive dilution of some religious essence preordained to flower into the fullness of Christianity."[18] All of this history and speculation was entirely consistent with the prejudices and preconceptions of nineteenth-century European ethnology, but it was also perfectly compatible with the view that some Tutsi had of themselves. Hamitic theories showed an uncanny fit with the mythologies of traditional Rwanda; once incorporated into the work of historiographers, it became increasingly difficult to tell them apart.

Reimagining the Myth in the Early Twentieth Century

Through much of the 1920s and 1930s, Rwandan historiography was cross-fertilized by the confluence of two complementary streams of mythologies: one specific to Rwandan society, the other borrowed from nineteenth-century European race theories. Court traditions gave Christian missionaries a striking illustration of the Hamites as "born rulers, superior in every respect to the 'dark agricultural' masses." The Hamitic frame of reference gave scientific respectability to the work of Tutsi historiographers. In the meantime, the coincidence of views between European and Tutsi historians gave European administrators a rationale for the most extreme and extensive application of indirect rule.

This said, it would be highly misleading to view the "invention" of Rwandan traditions as a straightforward, linear transfer of the Hamitic myth to historiographers and ultimately to African ideologues. If one can speak of "invention by tradition," then it is important to consider the twists and turns that have accompanied the reinterpretation of traditions. The work of Alexis Kagame is a perfect example. Kagame was a Tutsi historian of considerable reputation, as well as a social actor with strong political commitments. In this latter capacity, his endorsement of the Hamitic frame of reference is not nearly as significant as his attempt to put a modern, Eurocentric construction on Rwandan traditions by casting them in a juridical mold. His *Code des institutions politiques du Rwanda pré-colonial*, published in 1952, is a case in point.[19] Precolonial Rwanda was not just a "royaume Hamite," to use the title of a celebrated work by Father Pagès.[20] It was a traditional state system regulated by codes of laws, juridical norms, and unwritten rules. Just as the rituals of kingship were described as the *"code ésotérique de la monarchie,"*[21] Rwanda's precolonial institutions were carefully regulated by customary laws, much in the same way that in prerevolutionary France, the "fundamental laws of the realm" imposed specific restrictions on the king's authority. What made traditional Rwanda eminently modern and susceptible to constitutional transformation was not the plasticity of its traditions, but the fact that they were so carefully codified.

Kagame's intellectual processes speak volumes for his political goals. Both are excellently analyzed by Claudine Vidal. "If there is only one word to describe Kagame's philosophy of history," she writes, "it is *'le juridisme.'*" Kagame systematically draws analogs between Rwandan and European institutions. Thus, for example, he assimilates personal power to administrative functions, relations of subordination to contracts, and royal decisions to fundamental laws. In so doing, Kagame identifies precolonial Rwanda with a European nation that has gone beyond the stage of feudalism. He creates an image of it as an absolute monarchy tempered by a military code and offering safeguards against social injustice.²² Kagame had no interest in exalting the merits of an arbitrary, omnipotent kingship. His overriding concern was to show that the institution of kingship, by virtue of its rich array of customary codes, was remarkably well equipped to evolve into a constitutional monarchy. Kagame's history, in short, was designed to get Europeans to see that Rwandan traditions were neither arbitrary nor decadent. To the contrary, they contained within their folds the promise of a democratic renewal. Kagame's painstaking reinterpretation of traditional Rwanda was consciously designed to influence the basic constitutional choices facing the Belgian trust authorities in the decade preceding independence.

As a politically committed intellectual, determined to save the monarchy from itself, Kagame showed unusual foresight and imagination. As an historian, however, he showed little inclination to depart from the basic tenets of the Hamitic tradition; pre-Tutsi traditions went virtually unnoticed. Not until 1962, with the publication of Jan Vansina's pathbreaking work, *L'évolution du royaume rwanda dès origines à 1900*, did the flaws in Kagame's writings, and much of the historical literature on Rwanda, come to the attention of Rwandan historians.²³ The history of Rwanda as the story of exceptional men performing exceptional feats just did not stand up to the historical record. What was left out was the rich history of preconquest Hutu states, some of which survived until the 1920s, and some of whose customs, rituals, and conceptions of authority were assimilated by Tutsi clans (and all this happened long before the term *Tutsi* gained currency in the area).²⁴ Rather than a superior civilization imposing its rule on an inferior one, the evidence revealed a far more complex story. Ironically, much of what made the Hamites so captivating in the Europeans' eyes turned out to be the result of selective cultural borrowing from the supposedly inferior agricultural societies.

Here, then, was a view of history that came as close as any to reflecting Ranke's ideal of "how things really were." More important, it could provide a meaningful rationale for cooperation and mutual respect between Hutu and Tutsi. This possibility was not to be realized, however. As independence loomed on the horizon, confronting Hutu and Tutsi (and Europeans) with basic tactical decisions, the Hamitic view of history reasserted itself with a vengeance, but not without undergoing some extraordinary changes in meaning and substance.

The Politics of Memory in the Historical Present

Commenting on the distinction between myth and ideology, Benjamin Halpern makes the argument that "the study of myth is a study of the origins of beliefs out of historic experience," whereas "the study of ideology is the study of moulding of beliefs by social situations."[25] Though analytically distinct, the two are intimately linked to each other.

It was in Rwanda during the social revolution of 1959 to 1962 that the efforts of both Tutsi and Hutu to remember their past entered into their political agendas with unusual bluntness and profoundly divisive consequences. For the conservative Tutsi associated with the court, history ruled out reconciliation: "Since our kings have conquered the land of the Hutu by killing their kinglets (*bahinza*) and turning them into serfs, how can they now pretend to be our brothers?"[26] For the Hutu, however, it was precisely this kind of outlook that made revolutionary change imperative.

In the remainder of this chapter, we shall turn our attention to four examples of mythmaking, where memory operates selectively and in so doing, creates not just "imagined" communities but communities of fear and hatred. The first example of divisive mythmaking can be seen in the resurrection of the Hamitic myth in the political discourse of Hutu elites in Rwanda and Burundi. The second is to be found in the denial of genocide by both Hutu and Tutsi (the first in Rwanda, the second in Burundi). A third example of mythmaking is to be found in what might be called the *Rwanda irredenta* phenomenon. By this, we mean the efforts of postgenocide Rwanda to legitimize its claims to eastern Congo by rewriting the precolonial history of the region. A fourth concerns the emergence of a new "tribe" in eastern Congo, the so-called Banyamulenge.

Myth #1: The Resurrection of the Hamitic Hypothesis

Of these four myths, the first is evidently the most critical to an understanding of the other three. More than any other, it is the Hamitic myth that has had the most devastating impact on the texture of Hutu-Tutsi relations through much of the Great Lakes region, in effect providing ideological ammunition for the elimination of "Hamites" by "Bantus." Viewed through the lens of mythical representations, historical memory thus creates its own universe of death and destruction. "Men do not find truth," wrote Paul Veyne, "they create it, as they create their history."[27]

Initially fashioned by colonial historiography, the Hamitic hypothesis provided a simple model for understanding perceived distinctions between lower and higher orders of humanity. Recast in the form of an ideological weapon to discredit allegations of Tutsi supremacy, it reemerged with extraordinary virulence during the 1994 genocide.

Filtered through the prism of antimonarchical ideology, the Hamitic phantasm eventually morphed into a militantly anti-Tutsi vision. Already in 1959, the Hutu elites seized upon the myth and profoundly altered its meaning. They invoked the same mythical themes once taken to prove Tutsi superiority, but now used them to prove Tutsi foreignness and depravity. The Hamitic race, believed by Europeans to embody all that was best in humanity, was now presented by Hutus as the embodiment of the worst. Hamites represented cruelty and cunning, conquest and oppression. Where missionaries had invoked Semitic origins to suggest racial superiority, Hutu ideologues invoked them to argue that "the Tutsi are all originally bad." Where anthropologists had detected contractual exchange between Hutus and Tutsi, Hutu saw only proof of compulsion. That the native Hutus had adopted customs from the Tutsi was seen as the result of social domination, enforced by ruse and coercion. Even physical attributes once seen as marks of worthiness were denounced: what some perceived as Tutsi feminine grace was now vilified as yet another ploy designed to subjugate the unsuspecting Hutu.

In retrospect, early references to the *féodalo-Hamites* by Hutu revolutionaries seem relatively mild compared to the murderous frenzy of anti-Tutsi propaganda and the blatantly racist iconography that was diffused by the Hutu-controlled media on the eve of the genocide.[28] The cartoon in Figure 1 is a chilling example of how recent events in Burundi were recast in the frame of historical traditions with a view to casting aspersions on Tutsi cruelty: the death of the Hutu President Melchior Ndadaye (assassinated by elements of the Tutsi army in October 1993), is represented as involving a typically Tutsi-inspired martyrdom (impalement); watching his agony are soldiers of the RPF severing Ndadaye's vital parts, for the purpose of attaching them to the royal drum (Kalinga), as used to be the custom in traditional Rwanda.

Anti-Tutsi propaganda must be seen in the context of the pervasive fear created among Hutu by the RPF invasion of northern Rwanda on October 1, 1990. Another major background factor was the legacy of the Burundi genocide of 1972 that resulted in the extermination of at least 200,000 Hutu civilians.[29] The impact of the Burundi bloodbath on subsequent developments in both Burundi and Rwanda cannot be overemphasized. It is not a matter of coincidence that the few Hutu elites who survived the Burundi carnage were the first to articulate a stridently anti-Tutsi ideology, explicitly grounded in a Hamitic frame of reference. Formalized by the founder of the Palipehutu, Rémi Gahutu, this ideology flourished among a small group of Hutu exiles in Rwanda in the years immediately following the Burundi slaughter. The main themes are depressingly familiar. We learn that Tutsi domination over the Hutu can only be explained by taking into account the moral depravity of the Hamites. We hear of their consummate skill in the use of cunning and

Ethnicity as Myth 59

Figure 1. Melchior Ndadaye's assassination reinterpreted through the phantasms of extremist anti-Tutsi propaganda, from *Le Médaille-Nyiramacibiri*, no. 17 (November 1993): 10. Reproduced from Jean-Pierre Chrétien, ed., *Rwanda: Les medias du génocide* (Paris: Karthala, 1995), p. 365.
The Kinyarwanda text reads as follows:
Supervisor: Finish up that stupid Hutu and make sure his genitals are attached to our drum.
Ndadaye: You can kill me, but you cannot wipe out the other Ndadayes in Burundi.
Kagame: Finish him off quickly. Remember what a good job we did in Ruhengeri and Byumba. We have torn the children from their mothers and torn eyes from the men.

deceit; using, for example, poisoned gifts (beautiful women and cows) to reduce the Bantu into bondage. The Hutu exiles also stressed the unspeakable cruelties perpetrated during the 1972 genocide. They presented them as irrefutable proof of Hamitic perversity.[30]

From the narratives collected by Liisa Malkki in refugee camps in Tanzania, one gets an idea of the extent to which these ideas took hold among the Hutu survivors:

> In the past our proper name was Bantu. We are Bantu. "Hutu" is no tribe, no nothing! The Kihamite is the national language of the Tutsi. Muhutu is a Kihamite word which means "servant." Having been given cows as gifts by the Tutsi, the Hutu were used as a slave. It is indeed here that the Hutu were born. . . . We are not Hutu we are Bantu.[31]

From 1990 to 1994, much the same themes would emerge in the pages of *Kangura,* one of the most stridently anti-Tutsi of the forty-odd newspapers published at this time in Rwanda. The following are a few random examples:

- "The Tutsi have created out of whole cloth a tribe which does not exist: the Banyarwanda. The Banyarwanda exists nowhere in Africa; it is only mentioned to create confusion."
- "Public opinion must know that the only language of the Hutu is Kihutu, just as the Nande speak Kinande, the Hunde Kihunde."
- "Try to rediscover your *ethnie,* for the Tutsi have taught you to ignore it."[32]

What made the ideological climate of pregenocide Rwanda pregnant with intimations of disaster was the sheer force and frequency of appeals to racism diffused through the media, the extensive use of a racist iconography, and the systematic elaboration of Hamitic mythologies into a coherent body of categorical imperatives. This is nowhere more chillingly evident than in the "Ten Commandments of the Hutu," first published by *Kangura*[33] in December 1990. This doctrine is a veritable catechism of racist principles. At the heart of this ideology are a series of axiomatic truths:

- *The Tutsi are the embodiment of malice and wickedness.* "You know the trick they employed when they came to Rwanda: they pretended to have descended from heaven; in fact they came from the north of Africa. In Rwanda they found the pastures they needed for their cows. They approached the Hutu kinglets (*bahinza*), and with their customary malice they offered them women and cattle, until they overthrew the Hutu, seized power and kept it until the 1959 revolution."[34]
- *The Tutsi never change*—a point put across in a *Kangura* article titled "A Cockroach (*inyenzi*) Cannot Give Birth to a Butterfly." Thus, "history shows that the Tutsi have remained identical to themselves, they haven't changed; their malice and wickedness is what we have

experienced throughout history." Typical of their deviousness is the fact that some "changed their identity in order to gain access to positions reserved to the Hutu," which is why they have gained a dominant position in "the administration, commerce and the health sectors."[35]

- *Their long-term strategy is the creation of a Hima empire in the heart of the continent.* The Tutsi master plan, we are told, is a diabolical scheme "to restore the dictatorship of the more extremists of the Tutsi minority through genocide and the extermination of the Hutu; to institute in the bantu region of the Great Lakes (Rwanda, Burundi, Zaire, Tanzania and Uganda) a vast Hima-Tutsi empire, under the guidance of an *ethnie* that considers itself superior, like the Aryan race, and whose symbol is Hitler's swastika."[36] The killing of President Melchior Ndadaye in Burundi at the hands of an all-Tutsi army is thus seen as unmistakable evidence of Hamitic imperial ambitions, along with the fact that the RPF fought its way into Rwanda with the help of "the Tutsi Museveni."
- *Given the mortal threat facing the Hutu majority, it is imperative to delineate tribe from nation and for the Hutu to rediscover their true identity as Bantu.* Again to quote from *Kangura*: "The nation is artificial, only ethnicity (*ethnie*) is natural."[37] "You (the Hutu) are an important *ethnie* within the Bantu group," yet numbers alone may not suffice; what you must realize is that "a conceited (*orgueilleuse*) and bloodthirsty minority is working to create divisions among you, the better to dominate you and kill you."[38]
- *In these conditions, vigilance is the key. Watch out for spies and be particularly wary of Tutsikazi (Tutsi females).* In the words of the first of the "Ten Commandments," "Every Hutu must know that any Tutsikazi, regardless of where she works, is in the pay of her Tutsi *ethnie*. Consequently, will be treated as a traitor any Hutu who marries a Tutsikazi, or makes her his concubine or his protégée." The second commandment stipulates that "every Hutu must know that our women (Hutukazi) are more dignified and more conscious of their roles as mothers and wives," and the third enjoins Hutu females "to remain vigilant and bring back (their) husbands, brothers and sons to reason."[39]

Tutsi women, indeed, play a disproportionate part in Hutu discourse (and iconography). As the foregoing shows, the first three of the Ten Commandments are concerned exclusively with the threats arising from the presence of Tutsikazi among the Hutu communities. Tutsi women, furthermore, were a favorite target of Hutu cartoonists in search of pornographic effect. Warning against the dangers of potential Mataharis among Tutsi females was evidently a major objective of the

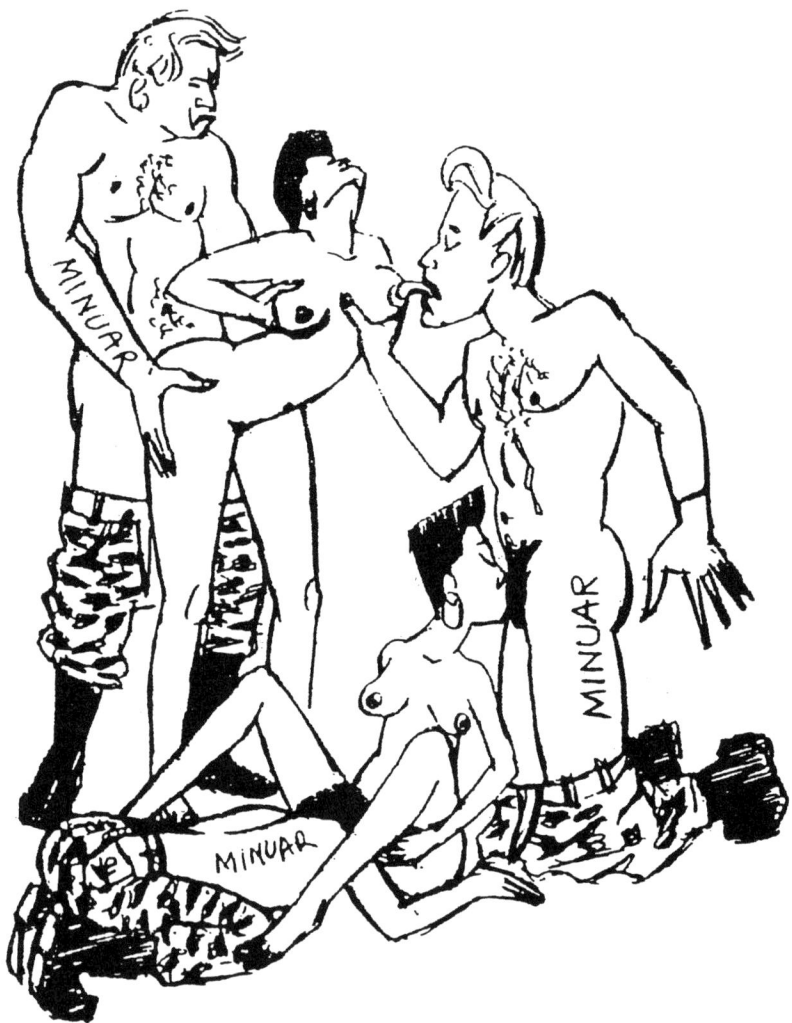

Figure 2. Extremist anti-Tutsi propaganda directed at Tutsi women and Belgian paratroopers in the MINUAR (the French acronym for the UN Mission in Rwanda). "The Force of Sex and the Belgian Paratroopers," from *Power*, no. 2 (December 1993): 12. Reproduced from Jean-Pierre Chrétien, ed., *Rwanda: Les medias du génocide* (Paris: Karthala, 1995), p. 366.

Hutu-controlled press. The more outrageous caricatures gleaned from the pages of *Power* and *Kangura-Magazine*[40] suggest, however, a deeper motivation. They reflect the seething anger and frustrations of many Hutu who saw in the greater attractiveness to Europeans of the typical Tutsikazi body a slur against their own "race." How the media exploited the legendary attractiveness of Tutsikazi to discredit both Tutsi women and the United Nations Mission in Rwanda is nowhere more shockingly illustrated than in the cartoon in Figure 2, published in *Power*, no. 2 (December 1993): 12.

What all this adds up to is a sustained and deliberate effort to recast the Hamitic frame of reference in such a way as to throw moral discredit on an entire ethnic community. By 1994, it was almost as if every Tutsi in sight was by definition an ally of the RPF and hence an enemy of the Hutu nation.

MYTH #2: THE DENIAL OF GENOCIDE

As an ideological construction designed to justify the annihilation of the Tutsi minority, the Hamitic myth must be seen as the central element behind the 1994 genocide. In the denial of genocide by some of its perpetrators lies another extraordinary form of mythmaking.

The term *genocide* has now become the most overused and arbitrary word in the political discourse of Hutu and Tutsi in Rwanda and Burundi. In both states, it is among the perpetrators that one encounters the most vigorous denial of involvement in ethnic massacres. Although many of the killers who are now in custody in Kigali or Arusha have admitted involvement in the Rwandan massacres, many more refuse to acknowledge their deeds. In flagrant contradiction of the facts, the argument one hears most often is that the killings were the result of a spontaneous outburst of collective anger, not the outcome of a planned annihilation.

Much the same sort of role reversal can be seen in Burundi, where the perpetrators are cast as victims. To this day, the 1972 genocide of Hutu by Tutsi has been virtually obliterated from the consciousness of most Tutsi. Radical Tutsi ideologues officially recognize only one genocide, the killing of thousands of innocent Tutsi civilians in October 1993, in the wake of President Melchior Ndadaye's assassination. They see this carnage as planned annihilation, even though it might better be described as an explosion of collective fear and anger, set off by a murder that conjured up haunting memories of the 1972 killings. They do not mention the subsequent repression of the Hutu by the Tutsi-controlled army that led to the death of thousands of Hutu and the exodus of some 300,000 of their kinsmen to Rwanda. Although, historically, the group that has suffered most from genocidal killings in Burundi are the Hutu, today it is the 1994 Rwanda genocide that impresses itself most forcefully on the mental retina of Tutsi politicians. The genocide brings into focus a simple equation: majority rule equals Hutu rule; Hutu rule equals the threat of Tutsi annihilation.

Both Hutu and Tutsi have been victims of genocide—most conspicuously and massively, the Hutu in Burundi and the Tutsi (and not a few Hutu) in Rwanda. Yet ironically, for many Tutsi, only they, as victims, have a proprietary right to genocide. A useful comparison might be made to the Serbs in former Yugoslavia, who see themselves as the perennial victims of historic massacres. "Deployed in this way," writes Roger Cohen, "genocide was no longer a horror but a form of immunity. It was a *passe-partout* allowing the eternal Serbian victim to butcher with impunity."[41] That there is more than a superficial parallel here with the situation in Rwanda has been made abundantly clear by the Kibeho massacre of Hutus in 1995 and the killings of tens of thousands of Hutu refugees in eastern Congo in 1996 and 1997.

MYTH #3: THE INVENTION OF GREATER RWANDA

Besides putting historical imagination in the service of genocide, perceptions of the past have played a crucially important role in "fixing" (in both senses of the word) geographical boundaries. This kind of mythmaking has had equally destructive political consequences. An apt example of this sort of distortion may be seen in the efforts of the Rwanda government to summon the precolonial past on behalf of its territorial claims to North and South Kivu.

Shortly after the search-and-destroy operation mounted by the RPA against the refugee camps in eastern Congo, President Pasteur Bizimungu held a press conference. Armed with maps of precolonial Rwanda, he informed his audience of the extent of the territorial conquest of Mwami Rwabugiri (1853–95) north and west of Rwanda's present borders. Stretching from Lakes Rweru and Cyohoha across the Virunga volcanoes all the way to Lake Albert and beyond, precolonial Rwanda, according to Bizimumgu, incorporated within its national boundaries much of eastern Congo.[42] The message, clearly intended to give legitimacy to the presence of RPF troops in North Kivu, could not have been clearer: much of the area included in eastern Congo was part and parcel of the precolonial kingdom.

By all accounts, however, Bizimungu's claims simply do not stand up to the historical record. This observation, however, is not to deny that raids were conducted by Rwabugiri in North Kivu, but it is patently at odds with the facts to claim that such raids were instrumental in cementing the political control of the monarchy. Even where tributary relationships were temporarily established with local authorities, the writ of the Rwanda monarchy was precarious at best.[43] Nor did the presence of Kinyarwanda speakers in eastern Congo, "Hutu and Tutsi," mean that they came under the effective control of the monarchy; in many instances, it meant precisely the opposite. The point is convincingly argued by David Newbury. The Kinyarwanda speakers, he argues, were "refugees, fleeing the expansion of the Nyiginya dynastic state at a time of intense competition among diverse political units in Rwanda. Thus, rather than being subjects of the royal court, these migrants were its opponents; their presence in Itombwe (South Kivu), in fact, represented the lack of state power in that region, not its presence."[44] Precolonial boundaries were anything but fixed. Even within Rwanda, relations between the Rwanda court and the Hutu communities in the north and the west were remarkably fluid. Many such communities remained virtually independent until brought into the fold of the monarchy by colonial troops. So far from restricting the scope of authority of the ruling dynasty, colonial rule had the opposite effect within Rwanda. As David Newbury points out, "The effect of European boundary agreements was to expand, not contract, the reach of the Rwanda state; in fact, with the help of European power, Nyiginya dynastic structures were extended to many areas that formerly had successfully resisted Rwandan expansion."[45] The historical evidence, in short, lends little credibility to Bizimungu's claims. They are entirely consistent, however, with the Rwanda government's definition of its security interests in eastern Congo. Though at odds with historical facts, the president's illusions had a clear political objective. Bizimungu was not satisfied with maintaining a military presence in eastern Congo to ward off the threats of crossborder raids. He felt that the military presence also had to be legitimized by history. Only by restoring the territorial integrity of precolonial Rwanda could the sovereignty of the new Rwanda be fully established.

MYTH #4: THE BANYAMULENGE: ETHNOGENESIS AS MYTHMAKING

The Banyamulenge are not pure invention. The term initially referred to "the people of Mulenge." These were a small group of predominantly Tutsi pastoralists whose traditional habitat was in Mulenge, a locality situated on the high-lying Itombwe plateau, south of Uvira (South Kivu).[46] The ancestors of the people of Mulenge were renegades from Rwanda. Having fallen foul of the ruling Niginya dynasty, they moved to the Itombwe area in the late nineteenth century. Others followed in search of greener pastures, some from Rwanda, others from Burundi.

Although they formed a culturally and linguistically distinct community, their name never appears in colonial records. Their political significance became apparent in the years following the independence of the Congo, when they found themselves embroiled in the so-called Muleliste rebellion of 1964 to 1965 in eastern Congo. Unlike many Tutsi who had fled Rwanda during the revolution of 1959, the Banyamulenge, upon realizing that their cattle was being slaughtered to feed the rebel army, refused to cast their lot with the Mulelistes. Instead, they joined the ranks of the National Congolese Army (NCA), a fact that further contributed to distinguish them as a separate community.

The "myth" of the Banyamulenge has two sides, both at odds with the historical record and both intended to serve a specific political objective. To begin with, there is what might be called the "foreigner in native clothes" version. For many "native" Congolese, the Banyamulenge are indeed Rwandan Tutsi in disguise. Their precolonial roots are vehemently denied, and so also are their claims to citizenship rights. They are seen as the Trojan horse of the Rwanda regime. Rwanda is where they belong.

The opposite version aims at reinforcing the claims of "indigeneity" of all Tutsi residing in North and South Kivu. From a small, highly localized Banyamulenge community, numbering no more than fifty thousand people, the term has come to designate perhaps as many as 130,000 ethnic Tutsi, irrespective of their place of residence or historical roots. Lumped together under the same ethnic rubric are those Tutsi who lived in North and South Kivu long before the advent of colonial rule, those who migrated to the area during the colonial period, and the tens of thousands of refugees who crossed into eastern Congo in the early 1960s during and immediately after the Rwanda revolution. There are no parallels in the continent for such an instant and extensive ethnogenesis.

Although this chapter is hardly the place for a detailed discussion of the singularly tragic history of the Banyamulenge, their tale is a notable one of hopes betrayed, alliances undone, and vicious factional struggles. Suffice it to say that their initially very close relationship with Kagame's Rwanda was predicated on the assumption that Rwanda would in time offer protection against the mounting threats to their security posed by self-styled "native" Congolese. Rwanda, in turn, quickly grasped the strategic advantage to be gained from this pool of potential allies. There is little question that the Banyamulenge played a significant auxiliary role during the destruction of the Hutu refugee camps in North and South Kivu in November 1996. This operation was conducted with extreme brutality by units of the RPA, assisted by hundreds if not thousands of ethnic Tutsi from eastern Congo, those very elements who today call themselves Banyamulenge. The high point in the convergence of interests between the Rwandans and the Banyamulenge came in 1998, with the creation in Kigali of the RCD. Despite or because of its subservience to Rwanda, many leading Banyamulenge joined the movement. The RCD, however, has been wracked by intramural disputes, the most serious being the dissidence of a large number of Banyamulenge troops in early 2002, led by a certain Musunzu. Only after a bloody repression by units of the Rwandan army was the rebellion finally quelled. But this has only reinforced the conviction of a growing number of Banyamulenge that they have been "instrumentalized"—their standard phrase—by Rwanda. As peace talks loom on the horizon, a growing number of Banyamulenge are trying to distance themselves from their former Rwandan patron, if only to evade the retribution that could be forthcoming if and when the Rwandan army withdraws from eastern Congo.

Partnerships dissolve, yet the myth persists. For most Banyamulenge, the label validates their claims to being authentically Congolese, and it refutes accusations that they might have acted as Rwanda's "fifth column" in the Congo. By the same token, the term settles once and for all the nationality question: an issue that during the Mobutu years lay at the heart of Tutsi grievances against Kinshasa. No longer is citizenship conditioned by length of residence. All Tutsi are now Banyamulenge and hence authentic Congolese citizens.

Is this a case of political tribalism, as John Lonsdale would put it, "flowing down from high-political intrigue"? Or is it an example of "moral ethnicity creating communities from within through domestic controversy over civic virtue"? It is possibly both. In North and South Kivu, as elsewhere in the region, history's myths are in violent conflict with history's realities. Adjusting one to the other is what much of the violence in the Great Lakes is all about.

Conclusion

Reflecting on the fortunes of the Hamitic hypothesis, Edith Sanders noted thirty years ago: "The word [Hamitic] still exists, endowed with a mystical meaning; it endures through time and history, and like a chameleon changes its color to reflect the changing light. As the word became flesh it engendered many problems of scholarship."[47] How one wishes the problems had remained restricted to the field of scholarship!

Amid all the bloodshed caused by the extension of civil war to the whole of the Congo, the myth has proven remarkably resilient. Bantu and Hamitic identities have now crystallized on a wider scale than ever before. The language used on all sides is clearly inspired by racist stereotypes. Hundreds, possibly thousands of ethnic Tutsi or Tutsi-looking Africans are reported to have been massacred in Kinshasa and other localities in the name of a threatened Bantu identity. The enemy can be easily identified by its physical markers, as warned by the national radio: "Watch the nose, it's thin and narrow, and the height: Tutsi are tall!" As one observer noted, "There was nothing subliminal about Kabila's messages. Like the infamous radio broadcasts that primed Rwanda's Hutu for the massacre of more than five hundred thousand Tutsi in 1994, the invitation was to kill."[48] Never before has the common imagination generated a more deadly potential for regional instability.

The final word must be left to Leszlek Kolakowski:

A myth may grow like a tumor; it may seek to replace positivistic knowledge and laws, it may attempt forcibly to take over all areas of culture, and may become encrusted in despotism, terror and mendacity. It may also threaten to relieve its participants of responsibility for their own situation, drain away the desire for freedom, and bring the value of freedom as such under suspicion.[49]

Such is the bitter lesson we have learned from the endless bloodshed in the Great Lakes, where the Hamitic myth is indeed growing like a tumor, with few signs of remission.

Chapter 4
Genocide in the Great Lakes: Which Genocide? Whose Genocide?

The title of this chapter is deliberately provocative. Can there be any doubt about the responsibility of the government of the late President Juvénal Habyarimana of Rwanda for what has been described as the biggest genocide of the end of the century? Can one seriously question the active involvement of high-ranking officials, the presidential guard, the local authorities, and the militias in the planning and execution of a carnage that took the lives of an estimated 800,000 people, three fourths of them Tutsi? Would anyone deny the critical role played by the Hutu-controlled media in providing incitements to genocide? The answer is clearly in the negative.

But there is another side to the story, inscribed in the very different perceptions that Hutu politicians and intellectuals have of what is and what is not genocide, who the real génocidaires are and who the victims are. Questions have also been raised by Western observers as to whether the Tutsi invaders, under the banner of the RPF, were not involved in the genocidal killing of innocent Hutu civilians. More recently, human rights groups, most notably Human Rights Watch,[1] have provided crushing evidence of massive human rights violations against Hutu refugees in eastern Congo by units of the all-Tutsi RPA, thus adding a third genocidal massacre to the record.

Regardless of whether it makes any sense, morally or intellectually, to hold a brief for the Hutu as a group, the issues it raises cannot be dismissed out of hand: Would the genocide have occurred if the RPF invasion had not taken place, threatening both the heritage of the 1959–62 Hutu revolution and the state born of the revolution? Why should the genocide of the Tutsi, and their presumptive allies among the Hutu population, mask the countless atrocities committed by the RPF in the course of their military operations in Rwanda? Can one turn a blind eye to the systematic killing of tens of thousands of Hutu refugees in eastern Congo by the RPA?

And what of Burundi? Can one seriously maintain, against every shred of evidence, that the only genuine genocide suffered by this God-forsaken land was the genocide of Tutsi by Hutu in October 1993? If, as Presidents Museveni and Kabila insist, historical depth is the essential condition for a fair investigation of the 1997 massacres of refugees, why not expand the mandate of the UN Commission of Inquiry back to the 1972 genocide of Hutu by Tutsi, to bring out the chain of causality between past and present atrocities?

These are not meant to be rhetorical questions. They go to the heart of the Hutu-Tutsi conflict and bring to light important dimensions of the continuing crisis in the Great Lakes. What makes these questions so highly controversial is not that there are no answers but that the answers given by Hutu and Tutsi point to radically different interpretations of the same ghastly events. The focus here is on the distortions inscribed in the cognitive maps of both victims and perpetrators—that is, memory—in response to the exigencies of the moment, in turn providing justification for further killings.

To move beyond the realm of conventional historical description is essential if we are to grasp properly the moral rupture involved in genocide. By the same token, failure to take this critical aspect into account—how the horrors of genocide profoundly alter the image that one has of the other—must be seen as a key factor behind the inability of "peacemakers" to come to terms with the psychological roots of ethnic conflict. The case of Burundi—the site of a fourth, yet seldom mentioned genocide—is a case in point.

A Forgotten Genocide

No other country on the continent has received more assiduous attention from so many conflict-resolution experts than Burundi over the last three years—and with so few results.[2] Since the assassination of its first elected Hutu president, Melchior Ndadaye, at the hands of the army on October 23, 1993, countless conferences, seminars, workshops, and peace missions have been organized by governmental and non-governmental organizations to prevent the country from sinking ever deeper into chaos. Whether the aim was to "structure the peace process," "initiate a dialogue to break the power of terror," "encourage the participation of citizens in peace-making," or "confidence-building," the hope was that sanity would ultimately prevail, that a compromise would be reached, and the killing would stop.

That so many well-intended peacemakers failed to come anywhere near achieving any of these objectives is not too surprising if one considers the depth of the antagonisms pitting Hutu against Tutsi. The anomaly lies in the failure of the peacemakers to see genocide as the central issue that underlies civil strife in both Burundi and Rwanda.

The 1972 genocide in Burundi, like the 1994 genocide in Rwanda, is indeed the cataclysmic event which lies at the root of the Hutu-Tutsi conflict. This is where the historical experience of Burundi (and Rwanda) differs markedly from that of most other war-torn societies in Africa. Dealing with "post-conflict" situations is one thing; healing the wounds of genocide is a very different matter.

Amazingly, the 1972 killings of Hutu by Tutsi—what Stephen Weissman calls "the first clear genocide since the Holocaust"—have sunk into near oblivion.[3] The most obvious explanation for this extraordinary case of historical amnesia is the conspiracy of silence, which to this day surrounds the circumstances of the killings, their scale, and their impact on subsequent developments.[4] Remarkably few observers seem to realize that the first genocide to be recorded in the annals of independent Africa occurred not in Rwanda but in Burundi, in the wake of an aborted Hutu-instigated uprising that caused the deaths of hundreds if not thousands of Tutsi civilians. Estimates of the number of Hutu killed during the ensuing repression range from 100,000 to 200,000. The killings lasted from April to November 1972, resulting in the death or flight into exile of almost every educated Hutu. Day after day truckloads of Hutu young men—primary and secondary school children, university students, teachers, agronomists, and civil servants—were sent to their graves.

Why dredge out of the shadows of history a carnage that took place twenty-five years ago? Because the 1972 genocide in Burundi provides the historical thread that enables us to make sense of subsequent developments. It explains the anti-Tutsi backlash in Rwanda that paved the way for the seizure of power by Juvénal Habyarimana in 1973 and the ascendency of northerners; it explains the rise of a radical political movement among those Hutu refugees who sought asylum in Tanzania (the Parti pour la Libération du Peuple Hutu, better known by its acronym, Palipehutu); and the very difficult problems posed by the resettlement of refugees in the days following President Melchior Ndadaye's election in 1993. Above all, it helps us understand why, after twenty-five years of unfettered control of the state, the army, the schools, and the nation's wealth, many Tutsi simply refused to contemplate a transfer of power to Hutu claimants, and why, ultimately, so few shrank from the use of violence to reverse the verdict of the polls.

Most importantly, memories of the 1972 genocide are the critical frame of reference for understanding the violent reaction of many Hutu against their Tutsi neighbors upon hearing of Ndadaye's assassination. Perhaps as many as 20,000 Tutsi men, women, and children were hacked to pieces or burned alive in October and November 1993 in an uncontrolled outburst of rage—a tragedy inseparable from the fact that for many Hutu on the hills, the death of Ndadaye was the harbinger of a replay of 1972. It is estimated that an equal number of Hutu were killed by the all-Tutsi army in the course of an equally blind and brutal repression, causing some 300,000 panic-stricken Hutu to seek refuge across the border into Rwanda. It is easy to see in such circumstances why these refugees needed little prodding to join Rwanda's militias, the *interhamwe*, when the genocide got under way. What emerges from all this is not just a peculiarly ignominious episode in the history of Burundi, but one whose repercussions on recent events in Rwanda and in Burundi has been profound.

In what must be seen as the epitome of "inversionary discourse" (to use David Apter's phrase), today the concept of genocide is widely used as a form of discourse by Tutsi extremists to discredit their Hutu opponents, the better to consolidate their grip on what is left of the state. The 1972 genocide of Hutu by Tutsi has been obliterated from their collective memory. If the term genocide has any relevance to the Burundi situation, it can only apply to the massacre of Tutsi in 1993. Thus, by projecting the 1994 Rwanda genocide into Burundi, a new version of the country's history emerges, in which one genocide is forgotten (1972), and another invented (1993). The political implications are clear: only the Hutu politicians qualify as "génocidaires," and none are more compromised in the killings of Tutsi than the top leadership of the Hutu-led Front Démocratique du Burundi (Frodebu). According to one version of what happened in 1993, since the Frodebu was all along involved in a gigantic plot to wipe out all the Tutsi, the army had no choice but to intervene and kill Ndadaye, the chief planner of the genocide, in order to prevent an even more devastating bloodbath: "what happened to our country is not accident, but a catastrophe engineered by the Frodebu."[5] In plain language, don't blame the army; the fault lies entirely with the Frodebu. Thus rewritten, the history of Burundi can be conveniently used to rule out all possibilities of compromise with Frodebu politicians.

Mythmaking: Through the Lens of Ethnicity

No group has a monopoly on mythmaking. As I have demonstrated elsewhere, the manipulation of the past in an effort to control the present was certainly very much in evidence in the writings of some Hutu ideologues associated with the Palipehutu, a stridently anti-Tutsi party born in 1980 in the refugee camps of Tanzania.[6] Genocide, we argued, leaves a profound imprint on the processes by which people write, or rewrite history, on what is being remembered, and what is being forgotten. What is being remembered by many Hutu is an apocalypse that has forever altered their perceptions of the Tutsi, now seen as the historic incarnation of evil; what many Tutsi have forgotten, or refuse to acknowledge, is that they, and not the Hutu, were the first to use genocide in order to consolidate their hold on the state.

Nor is Burundi the exception. Much the same sort of hiatus between perception and reality can be seen in Rwanda and eastern Congo. Consider the case of Rwanda: astounding as it may sound, to this day many Hutu will vehemently deny the reality of a genocide that killed an estimated 800,000 people (of whom approximately one fourth were Hutu from the south-central regions). Not that they would deny the existence of massacres; that they were systematically planned and executed is what they contest. The war, they say, was the principal cause of the massacres. Had the RPF not invaded the country on October 1, 1990, the massacres would not have taken place. The onus of guilt, therefore, lies entirely with the RPF.

Rejecting this extreme view (even though most would agree that there is reason to view the RPF invasion as the root cause of the genocide, just as the abortive Hutu uprising was also the triggering factor behind the 1972 genocide in Burundi), others among the Hutu community in exile claim that there was not one but two genocides, a genocide of Tutsi by Hutu and a "countergenocide" of Hutu by Tutsi.[7] The first received sustained attention in the media; the other went virtually unreported. The RPF troops, they claim, were wholly responsible for the wanton killing of thousands of Hutu civilians in the course of their military campaign, as they were for the killing of some 5,000 unarmed Hutu refugees at Kibeho in 1995, and more recently, for wiping out tens of thousands of refugees in eastern Congo. In short, the greatest disservice that the international community could render to the cause of peace, they say, would be to impute genocide only to the Hutu, as if the "good guy-bad guy" dichotomy were largely synonymous with the Hutu-Tutsi split.

Typically, and with utter disregard for the evidence, Tutsi officials generally advance the following counterargument: (a) although there were Hutu civilians among battlefield casualties, at no time have RPF troops engaged in cold-blooded executions of civilian populations; (b) the Kibeho killings involved at the most 300 persons, most of whom were former *interhamwe*, which is why they refused to return to their communes of origin; and (c) the search and destroy operations conducted in eastern Congo against Hutu refugees were targeted against *interhamwe* and ex-FAR and did not involve civilians.

Although the evidence collected by impartial observers casts serious doubts on each of these assertions, the more important point to stress is the tendency on the part of a growing number of Tutsi elites to substitute collective guilt for individual responsibility and to affix the label "genocidaire" to the Hutu community as a group. It is at this level that an ominous parallel emerges between the discourse of Tutsi extremists in Rwanda, within and outside the army, and their counterparts in Burundi: by attributing responsibility for genocide not to individuals but to a whole community—lumping together the perpetrators of genocide and innocent civilians, including those Hutu who risked their own lives to save those of their Tutsi neighbors—the result has been to create those very conditions that impel some Hutu to become rebels and ultimately "genocidaires."

What it all means from the standpoint of everyday relations between Hutu and Tutsi is nowhere more painfully conveyed than in the commentary of an American aid official to this writer after his visit to Bujumbura in September 1997:

> The more I deal with Burundi, the more I see and feel that the Hutu-Tutsi divide is not bridgeable in the foreseeable future, and may even have been deepened by events of recent years. A sort of caste system is definitely there, and those who have been accustomed to being on top are ready to do anything to maintain the social and political order as it is.... It is disturbing to me to see the very disdain even ordinary Tutsi have for Hutu, and how the ordinary Hutu meekly accept their status. I see how the ordinary Tutsi read the riot act to ordinary Hutu for even the most mundane infractions, or for nothing at all, when they would never do the same to another Tutsi. The poor Hutu just stand there and take it.... Another time I was in the Bwiza quarter with photocopies of photos appearing in your book. I was showing these to people, and they were commenting on them. The last photo was of President Ndadaye. When this photo appeared, all the small children surrounding us pounced quickly on it and began hitting it. I was really taken aback by this visceral, hateful reaction and greatly disturbed as these children tore the photo into dozens of pieces. How have even the small children learned such hate? What does this say about peace and reconciliation in our lifetime in Burundi? ... The people in the neighborhood still relish talking about how the pregnant Tutsi woman married to a Hutu man living in this compound was burnt to death. They recount in gory detail how the flesh burnt until the foetus was visible.[8]

Violence as Discourse

If the symptoms of Burundi's "sickness" are easy to detect, the causes of the malady are more difficult to identify. To invoke ethnic hatreds does not carry us very far. Asking ourselves what impels people to kill each other brings to mind Paul Richard's analysis of violence in Sierra Leone as a form of discourse which, in the absence of alternative outlets, seeks expression in bloodshed. To quote:[9]

> War itself is a type of text—a violent attempt to tell a story or to 'cut in on the conversation' of others from whose company the belligerents feel excluded. Understanding war as text and discourse is not an intellectual affectation but a vital necessity, because only when 'war talk' is fully comprehended is it possible for conciliators to outline more pacific options in softer tones.

David Apter makes a somewhat similar argument: "Violence," he writes, "is itself a mode of interpretation, with interpretation leading to violent events: protest, insurrection, terrorism."[10]

Looked at from this perspective, a certain logic begins to emerge in what otherwise could be dismissed as a case of tribal insanity. It is a logic that challenges some of the myths discussed earlier (e.g., the myth of Hutu as global genocidaires or the myth of Ndadaye's assassination as a preemptive strike made necessary to save the Tutsi from an impending genocide); by the same token, however, the violence through which this "text" expresses itself, in turn becomes the source of an "interpretation," which generates further violence.

Let us return for a moment to Burundi and take a closer look at the outburst of anti-Tutsi violence triggered by the news of Ndadaye's death in 1993: inscribed in the unspeakable atrocities[11] committed by Hutu against Tutsi was a very clear interpretation of Ndadaye's assassination as the harbinger of a replay of the 1972 carnage. In the words of one Hutu, shortly after the news of Ndadaye's death had reached his commune, "back in 1972 they got us, but this time they won't!" (*en 1972 ils nous ont eus; ils ne nous auront plus!*). Again: "since 1972 it is our blood that's being spilled! Now we hear that President Ndadaye has been killed. If they did that, that means we are next."[12] What all this adds up to is an unshakable conviction that the 1972 scenario was about to repeat itself.

From the vantage point of extremist elements within the Tutsi community, such an interpretation carries little or no conviction. The Tutsi "text" conveys a very different scenario, which might be summed up as follows: the wanton killing of innocent Tutsi families by their Hutu neighbors is traceable to a carefully planned attempt to annihilate the Tutsi community; the brains behind this dastardly plot are the Frodebu leaders; the most dangerous of the Frodebistes are those elements who joined Leonard Nyangoma's National Council for the Defense of Democracy (CNDD) and its armed wing, the FDD; only by physically eliminating the genocidaires within and outside the Frodebu can the Tutsi minority protect itself against genocide. Thus, with the Rwanda scenario held up as an omen of what the future holds in store, anticipation of genocide becomes justification for killing the potential génocidaires. There can be little question about the fear of the Tutsi minority that, if given the opportunity, the Hutu would not hesitate a moment to wipe them out, as happened in Rwanda. Meanwhile, as the number of Hutu officials killed increases, the threat of retaliation rises in proportion.[13]

By imputing genocidal motives to many key Frodebu leaders, by using scare tactics and assassination to exclude them from positions of responsibility in the National Assembly and the government, and by consistently denying them the status of legitimate interlocutors in the ongoing search for a negotiated solution; their accusers in effect gave them no other choice than to have recourse to violence and indeed genocide: a case in point is the horrendous killing of over 300 innocent Tutsi in Bugendana, on July 20, 1996, by bands of Hutu terrorists; such gratuitous carnage cannot be described otherwise than as a genocidal massacre.[14]

With the growing polarization of ethnic feelings, extremists at both ends of the spectrum are redoubling their efforts to make their voices heard, most of the time violently. On the Hutu side, Leonard Nyangoma's CNDD insists that peace and reconciliation are contingent upon a return to the status quo ante, that is to the pre-1993 coup situation, when the Frodebu held a majority of the seats in parliament, in government, and in the provincial administration. Any suggestion that power sharing is the quickest path to reconciliation is rejected out of hand as unacceptable. Not only is the 1993 coup seen as a flagrant breach of constitutional legality; so, also, are the subsequent power-sharing arrangements worked out by party representatives. Buyoya's coup of July 1996 merely prolongs the state of illegality created by the 1993 putsch. To paraphrase Richards, cutting in on the conversation of others (i.e., mainly Frodebistes and Upronistes) from whose company he feels excluded, Nyangoma's position can be reduced to the following propositions: (a) one does not negotiate with assassins; (b) the men responsible for Ndadaye's assassination must be brought to justice; and (c) nothing short of a return to the pre-coup legality can bring peace to the country.

Tutsi extremists, likewise, reject any thought of power sharing, but for different reasons. Nyangoma's mantra that one does not negotiate with criminals finds an echo in the Tutsi militia's insistence that one does not negotiate with génocidaires, a position also endorsed by the extremist wing of the predominantly Tutsi Union pour le Progrès National (Uprona). Because the label is now used to designate almost every Frodebu politician, as well as the CNDD/FDD leadership, it is difficult to see how a negotiated solution can be arrived at when virtually every Hutu of any standing is excluded from the negotiation by virtue of his participation in an alleged genocide.

The notion of collective guilt is the principal obstacle to national reconciliation. To hold all Tutsi collectively responsible for human rights violations is hardly more convincing than to assume that the hundreds of thousands of Hutu refugees in eastern Congo were all involved in the 1994 genocide. Nothing is more specious than the argument that after the destruction of the refugee camps in November 1996 and the return of perhaps as many as half a million refugees to Rwanda, the only Hutu left behind were the génocidaires and therefore, that it was entirely legitimate for the Rwandan army to kill them to prevent them from doing further harm. And yet this is precisely the subliminal "text" that underlies the "cleansing" operations of the Rwandan military in eastern Congo. In healing, dealing, and coming to terms with the crises in Burundi and Rwanda, two different strategies are being tested: one focuses on the concept of healing and draws its inspiration from South Africa's Truth and Reconciliation Commission (TRC), chaired by Archbishop Desmond Tutu; the other puts the emphasis on the pursuit of negotiations aimed at a power-sharing formula. Though by no means mutually exclusive, neither strategy has yet given proper attention to the different versions of the "truth" about genocide, which may be the reason why the results, so far, have been somewhat less than impressive.

The limitations of power sharing as a way of promoting overarching cooperation at the elite level are nowhere more cruelly evident than in the disastrous outcome of the so-called Government Convention of September 1994. After endless rounds of negotiations it was finally agreed that 55 percent of cabinet posts and civil service positions would go to the Hutu-dominated Forces du Changement Démocratique (FCD)—of which the Frodebu was the key component—and 45 percent to the Tutsi-controlled Coalition des Partis Politiques de l'Opposition (CPPO)—led by the Uprona—while vesting all decision-making powers in a National Security Council (NSC) made up of a majority of CPPO elements. That the convention turned out to be a less than ideal solution is not surprising if one considers that the net result was to rob the Frodebu of its electoral victory while reducing the constitution to a mere scrap of paper. As Filip Reyntjens correctly noted, "the Government Convention is the institutional translation of the October 1993 coup: the constitution has been shelved and the outcome of both the presidential and parliamentary elections swept aside as the president and parliament are placed under the tutelage of an unconstitutional body."[15] It is one thing to share power and quite another to surrender power under the pressure of extremist militias and urban mobs.

It is in Rwanda that healing strategies have been applied most consistently, if not always successfully, by church groups. At the heart of such strategies is the belief that unless people are willing to confess their crimes and ask forgiveness, there can be no basis for reconciliation. Negotiations, no matter how carefully orchestrated, are no substitute for healing. In the words of Frank Chikane, former Secretary-General of the South African Conference of Churches, "negotiations can result from political pressures or from a mutual decision by parties to avoid a war because the costs are too great. This does not necessarily mean that the parties have had a change of heart—they are simply relocating the battleground to the negotiation table."[16]

But how can a "change of heart" come about where there is neither truth nor justice or, better still, when justice is intended to reflect the victor's "truth"? In a fascinating discussion of the conditions for peace in Rwanda and South Africa, Mahmood Mamdani notes that in South Africa, the TRC "exemplifies the dilemma involved in the pursuit of reconciliation without justice," whereas Rwanda "exemplifies the opposite: the pursuit of justice without reconciliation."[17] One wonders, however, whether the parody of justice observable in Rwanda and in Burundi is not the main reason why the prospects for genuine reconciliation remain so bleak. This is not the place for a sustained inquest into their legal systems, only to note that there are reasons to doubt whether fair justice can be rendered where lawyers and magistrates are predominantly drawn from the Tutsi community, without recourse to a jury, and where the verdicts of the courts are overwhelmingly biased on the side of official "truths."

Could amnesty succeed where the justice system has failed? For Alex Boraine, the TRC's vice-chair, it is "morally defensible to argue that amnesty is the price that we had to pay for peace and stability."[18] Very few people in Rwanda or Burundi, Tutsi or Hutu, would agree, because there is no parallel in the recent history of South Africa for the scale of the genocidal killings experienced by Rwanda and Burundi. The point here is not that amnesty is not defensible or desirable, but only if it is applied selectively; for unless impunity is brought to an end, unless the organizers of the Rwanda genocide and the authors of the 1993 coup in Burundi, among others, are brought to justice, peace and stability will not be achieved.

Amnesty for the "rank and file" of the génocidaires, for the hundreds and thousands who may have killed because they had no other choice, would serve a salutary purpose if conducted along the lines of the TRC, with full disclosure of their deeds by the killers. This is where the mandate of South Africa's TRC holds important lessons. Again to quote from Boraine, "essentially the TRC is committed to the development of a human rights culture and a respect for the rule of law. . . . In attempting to do this, I believe that there is an irreducible minimum and that is a commitment to truth."[19] It is doubtful that the full truth will ever be known about the circumstances and scale of the atrocities committed in former Belgian Africa, but unless a concerted effort is made to get closer to the facts and move out of the fantasyland of official mythologies, the collective memory of Hutu and Tutsi will continue to enshrine the same myths, with little hope in sight that the killing may stop.

Chapter 5
The Rationality of Genocide

The image of Rwanda conveyed by the media is that of a society gone amok. How else to explain the collective insanity that led to the butchering of half a million civilians: men, women, and children? As much as the scale of the killings, the visual impact of the atrocities numbs the mind and makes the quest for rational motives singularly irrelevant. Tribal savagery suggests itself as the most plausible subtext for the scenes of apocalypse captured by television crews and photojournalists.

Ironically, just as tribalism is being reaffirmed by the media as the bane of the continent, Rwanda's descent into hell makes it a society not unlike others in Europe and Asia where genocide has been intrinsic to their recent historical experience. Seen in the broader context of twentieth-century genocides, the Rwanda tragedy underscores the universality—one might say the normality—of African phenomena. The logic that set in motion the infernal machine of the Rwanda killings is no less "rational" than that which presided over the extermination of millions of human beings in Hitler's Germany or Pol Pot's Cambodia. The implication, lucidly stated by Helen Fein in a recent publication of the Institute for the Study of Genocide, is worth bearing in mind: "Genocide is preventable because it is usually a rational act: that is, the perpetrators calculate the likelihood of success, given their values and objectives."[1]

The Rwanda genocide is neither reducible to a tribal meltdown rooted in atavistic hatreds nor to a spontaneous outburst of blind fury set off by the shooting down of the presidential plane on April 6, as officials of the Habyarimana regime have repeatedly claimed. However widespread, both views are travesties of reality. What they mask is the political manipulation that lies behind the systematic massacre of civilian populations. Planned annihilation, not the sudden eruption of long-simmering hatreds, is the key to the tragedy of Rwanda.

It is not my intention to dispose of one myth by promulgating another: the fantasy of a precolonial society where Hutu and Tutsi lived in an eternally blissful harmony. That Rwandan society was one of the most centralized and rigidly stratified anywhere in Africa cannot be denied, any more than the use of force in the conquest of peripheral Hutu kingdoms. But this does not mean that conflict was necessarily more intense

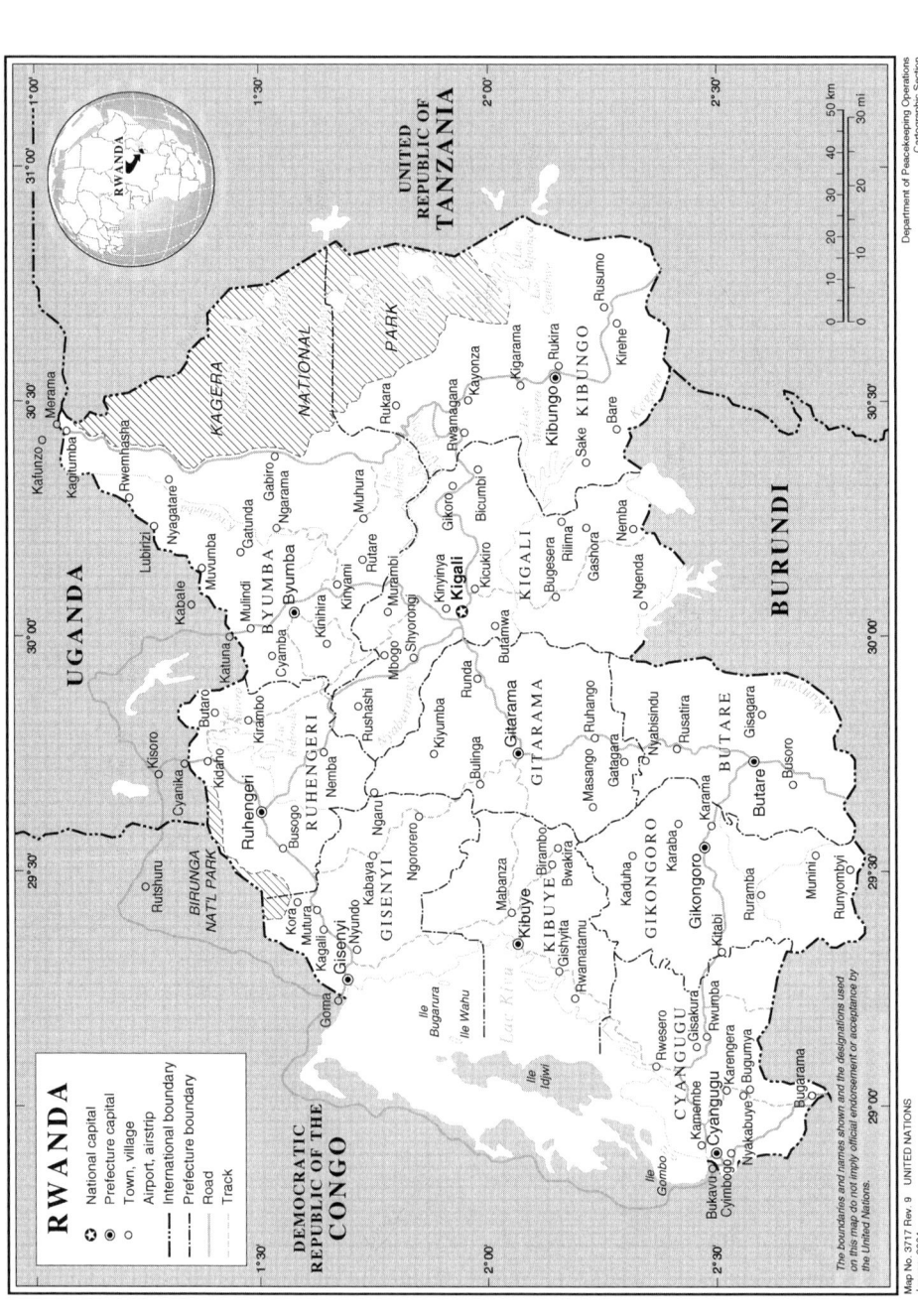

Map 3. Rwanda. Map no. 3717, rev 9, United Nations, January 2004. Reproduced by permission of the UN Department of Peacekeeping Operations, Cartographic Section.

or frequent between Hutu and Tutsi than between Tutsi and Tutsi. Much of the historical evidence suggests precisely the opposite.

The Legacy of Revolution

Although there is general agreement among Rwanda specialists that the roots of conflict lie in the transformation of ethnic identities that has accompanied the advent of colonial rule, the chain of events leading to the killings begins with the Hutu revolution of 1959–62—a revolution, I might add—that would have quickly fizzled had it not been for the sustained political, moral, and logistical assistance which the Catholic Church and the *tutelle* authorities provided the insurgents.[2] The result was a radical shift of power from Tutsi to Hutu and the exodus of thousands of Tutsi families to neighboring territories.

Few would have imagined that thirty years later, the sons of the refugee diaspora in Uganda would form the nucleus of a Tutsi-dominated politicomilitary organization, the RPF, that would successfully fight its way into the capital city and defeat an army three times its size.

Fewer still could have anticipated the price of their victory. On the eve of the October 1, 1990 invasion, no one within the RPF had the slightest idea of the scale of the cataclysm they were about to unleash. The assumption, fed through rumor and self-induced optimism, was that the Habyarimana regime was a pushover and would quickly collapse in the wake of the invasion. While grossly overestimating the strength of the internal opposition, the RPF did not anticipate the massive military support that President Juvénal Habyarimana was about to receive from the French. Nor did they foresee the catalytic effect of the invasion on Hutu solidarities and the growing determination of hard-liners within the government to manipulate ethnic hatreds for political advantage. The perceptions that the RPF leaders had of themselves—that of liberators, dedicated to the overthrow of a thoroughly corrupt and oppressive dictatorship—turned out to be sadly out of sync with the image that a great many Hutu had of their would-be liberators.

Counterrevolutionaries as Hamites

Different levels of meaning can be read into the invasion of Rwanda by the RPF, each corresponding to a distinctive set of actors. What the French saw as an intolerable Anglo-Saxon threat to their *chasse gardée*—"the Fashoda syndrome"—the hard-liners in the Habyarimana camp did not hesitate to denounce as a brazen attempt by externally supported counterrevolutionaries to turn the clock back to the prerevolutionary era, when Tutsi hegemony was the order of the day.

The Hamitic frame of reference added yet another ominous dimension to the counterrevolutionary image projected by the invaders. This is where the legacy of missionary historiography—evolving from speculation about cultural affinities between Hamites and Coptic Christianity, to politicized dogma about the Ethiopian origins of the Tutsi, now referred to as "féodo-Hamites"—contributed a distinctively racist edge to the discourse of Hutu politicians. Already the ideological stock-in-trade of Hutu revolutionaries in the fifties (who saw in "Hamitization" a Tutsi plot to exclude them from positions of responsibility), official references to the Hamitic peril gained renewed salience in the wake of the invasion. Thus Leon Mugesera, the Hutu "boss" from Gisenyi, who, in a much quoted statement, urged his followers to send the Tutsi back to their country of origins—Ethiopia—through the quickest route, via the Akanyaru river (known to have disgorged countless Tutsi corpses into Lake Victoria).

What emerges from the urgings of a Léon Mugesera and the incitements to violence distilled by Radio Libre des Mille Collines, the extremist outlet, is an image of the Tutsi as both alien and clever, not unlike the image of the Jew in Nazi propaganda. His alienness disqualifies him as a member of the national community; his cleverness turns him into a permanent threat to the unsuspecting Hutu. Nothing short of physical liquidation can properly deal with such danger.

The Regional Dimension of Hutu Rule: North versus South

Acceptance of the Hamitic myth by Hutu politicians was not limited to any particular region or locality, yet it was among the northern Hutu that it found its most receptive echo. The reason, in part, is historical. Unlike the Hutu of the southern and central regions, their northern kinsmen were incorporated rather late into the fold of the monarchy and with considerable assistance from the German Schutztruppe. To this day, the northerners, also known as Kiga, form a distinctive subculture. Their contacts with the Tutsi monarchy, and Tutsi culture in general, were few and far between; very few northerners married Tutsi women. For their awareness of a pre-Tutsi past, inhabited by kinglets (*abahinza*) and lineage heads (*kaburi b'imiryango*), landowners (*abakonde*) and clients (*abagererwa*), and sorcerers and prophetesses, there are few equivalents among southern Hutu. No wonder the thrust of their revolutionary efforts in the 1950s aimed at turning the clock back to the golden age of pre-Tutsi days.[3]

Nor is it too surprising if the army coup that brought Habyarimana to power in 1973 had its key political objective to take power away from the southern Hutu (led by the late president, Grégoire Kayibanda) and place it firmly into northern hands. And to make sure that power and privilege would remain a monopoly of the north, what was more natural, in Habyarimana's mind, than to order the massacre of anywhere from forty to fifty incarcerated Hutu politicians from the central and southern regions, thus eliminating at one fell swoop his regional enemies, the "révolutionnaires de la premiére heure"? (From this deed Habyarimana derived an additional benefit when some years later, he turned against Major Théoneste Lizinde, at the time his chief of security and now a key RPF personality, and accused him of having personally engineered the assassination of the southern politicians in Ruhengeri!)[4]

It was this critically important regional dimension in the distribution of power that inspired in the minds of the northerners a nightmarish vision of the RPF as a potential ally of Hutu politicians from the south. To the image of the Hamite as an essentially alien and predatory creature was added the frightening possibility that they might join hands with the Hutu opposition and undo everything that had been accomplished since the 1973 coup.

Since June 1991, when the legitimacy of multiparty democracy was finally recognized, the ruling Mouvement National pour la Révolution et le Développement (MNRD) had to reckon with several opposition groups, most notably the ethnically mixed Parti Libéral (PL), the Parti Social Démocrate (PSD), and the Mouvement Démocratique Républicain (MDR). All three parties could conceivably be viewed as potential allies of the RPF, but because of its substantial support among the Hutu masses of Butare and Gitarama, in the south, and because of its unique pedigree, traceable to the historic, southern-led Parmehutu, the MDR became the object of intense suspicion by northerners. This perhaps explains their determined and largely successful efforts to split it down the middle. The result was a growing rift between moderates and hardliners, the former led by Faustin Twagiramungu, the latter by Dismas Nsengiyaremye, Frodouald Karamira, and Donat Murego. That all three were once among Habyarimana's bitterest opponents, only to emerge as his staunchest supporters, is illustrative of how circumstances, as well as appropriate rewards, or thinly veiled threats, could bring about spectacular shifts of loyalty.

The Scuttling of Arusha

Whether as counterrevolutionary threat, vector of Hamitic hegemony, or potential ally of the Hutu opposition, the RPF, in the minds of the Habyarimana clique, had to be destroyed as a political force. This meant the rejection of any kind of political compromise with the RPF, including ad hoc alliances with its representatives during the transition to multiparty democracy.

Yet the concept of compromise was at the very heart of the Arusha accords, signed on August 4, 1993, after a year of off-and-on negotiations. In the power-sharing arrangement hammered out at Arusha, the RPF would have a total of five cabinet seats out of a total of twenty-one and eleven seats in the transitional national assembly out of a total of seventy, putting it on par with the ruling MNRD. Compromise, likewise, was the name of the game in the restructuring of the armed forces: 40 percent of the troops and 50 percent of the officer corps would consist of RPF elements. Agreement of sorts was also reached on the repatriation of refugees, the demobilization of troops, and most importantly, on multiparty elections twenty-two months after the signature of the accords.

By instigating ethnic violence on a substantial scale, the MNRD—assisted by its faithful ally, the crypto-fascist, rabidly anti-Tutsi CDR—knew that it could effectively derail the peace process. The killing of some 300 Tutsi in the Gisenyi prefecture in February 1993 was designed to do just that. It is surely not a matter of coincidence that the killings occurred shortly after the signature of one of the key power sharing agreements (technically known as "protocol of agreement with the RPF on the sharing of power within the context of a broadly based transitional government") on January 9, 1993.

The wanton killing of Tutsi civilians thus became the quickest and most "rational" way of eliminating all basis for compromise with the RPF: the reassertion of Hutu solidarities would soon transcend regional differences and make it virtually unthinkable for Hutu and Tutsi to agree on anything.

The pattern was set long before the Arusha talks got under way. In the weeks immediately following the October 1990 invasion, an estimated 300 Tutsi were massacred in cold blood in Kibilira. In retaliation for the RPF raid on Ruhengeri, in January 1991, came the physical elimination of at least a thousand Bagogwe cattle herders and their families, a Tutsi subgroup. In 1992, hundreds of Tutsi were killed in the Bugesera region when government sponsored rumors warned the Hutu that they were about to be massacred by the RPF and their civilian collaborators.[5]

The persistent indifference of the international community in the face of organized murder, coupled with France's rising levels of military assistance to the murderers, were powerful inducements for the regime to further strengthen its organizational capacities. By 1992, the institutional apparatus of genocide was already in place. It involved four distinctive levels of activity or sets of actors: (a) the akazu ("little house" in Kinyarwanda), that is the core group, consisting of Habyarimana's immediate entourage, namely, his wife (Agathe), his three brothers-in-law (Protée Zigiranyirazo, Seraphin Rwabukumba, and Elie Sagatwa), and a sprinkling of trusted advisers (most notably, Joseph Nzirorera, Laurent

Serubuga, and Ildephonse Gashumba); (b) the rural organizers, numbering anywhere from two to three hundred, drawn from the communal and prefectural cadres (préfets, sous-préfets, conseilleurs communaux, etc.); (c) the militias (interhamwe), estimated at 30,000, forming the ground-level operatives in charge of doing the actual killing; and (d) the presidential guard, recruited exclusively among northerners and trained with a view to providing auxiliary slaughterhouse support to civilian death squads. Thus came into being an organizational structure ideally suited to the task at hand.

Ndadaye's Assassination

With the assassination of President Melchior Ndadye of Burundi on October 21, 1993, genocide came to be seen increasingly by MNRD politicians as the only rational option; and compromise, along the lines of Arusha, as synonymous with political suicide. As the first Hutu president in the history of Burundi, Ndadaye's election brought to a close twenty-eight years of Tutsi hegemony.[6] His death at the hands of an all-Tutsi army six carried an immediate and powerful demonstration effect to the Hutu of Rwanda. As ethnic violence swept across the country, causing some 200,000 panic-stricken Hutu to seek refuge in Rwanda, the message conveyed by Ndadaye's assassination came through loud and clear: "Never trust the Tutsi!"

With Ndadaye's death vanished what few glimmers of hope remained that Arusha might provide a viable formula for a political compromise with the RPF. Though formally committed to implement the accords, Habyarmiana was fast losing his grip on the situation. Meanwhile, and as if to further bolster the posture of MNRD hard-liners, tens of thousands of Hutu refugees from Burundi, highly politicized by the events there, were now available for political mobilization precisely where they were most needed, in the south-central regions, seen by the akazu as the least "reliable."

Compounding the divisive effects of Ndadaye's assassination, the selection of candidates to the transitional organs of government unleashed a frenzy of competition for the spoils of office both within and among parties. Some opposition parties, such as the PL, or the PSD, found themselves overnight in the throes of bitter ethnic struggles; others seemed almost to disintegrate in factional squabbles between extremists and moderates. Political assassinations sometimes disposed of both, in tit-for-tat fashion.

Nonetheless, the prospect of a transition that would meet the expectations of "Hutu Power" (the phrase that came to designate the extremist fringe among opposition parties) and effectively reduce the influence of

RPF elements in government, seemed utterly illusory as long as Arusha provided the basic constitutional frame of reference for institutionalizing a compromise. Abeit for opposite reasons, RPF hardliners saw the implementation of Arusha with similar distaste.

The Shooting Down of the Presidential Plane: A Rational Plot?

The shooting down of Habyarimana's plane, on April 6, seemed consistent with the overall strategy of MNRD extremists. Despite the absence of as much as a shred of evidence in support of an akazu-sponsored plot, it is easy to see the logic that might have prompted such a move. Not only did Habyarimana's death remove once and for all the specter of Arusha (even at the cost of losing in the process a key member of the akazu, Elie Sagatwa), but by making it unmistakably clear that "it was the RPF that did it," the same extremists could now point to the "dastardly crime" as a moral justification for genocide. Who actually fired the missile that brought down Habyarimana's plane may never be known, any more than who ordered the missile to be fired. But if the implications of the Arusha compromise are any index, there is every reason to view the shooting of the plane as an eminently rational act from the standpoint of extremists, Hutu on Tutsi.

In Kigali the killing of opposition figures, Hutu and Tutsi, began moments after the crash, on the basis of pre-established lists. Two categories of potential allies of RPF were targeted: (a) moderate (as distinct from "Hutu Power") Hutu politicians from the south-central regions, most of them affiliated with the MDR and (b) opposition leaders (Hutu and Tutsi) identified with the PL or PSD. Therefore, far from being selected on the basis of ethnic criteria, the victims were generally seen as animated by a sense of compromise and conciliation toward the RPF, in short as potential traitors. Those two categories were disposed of in a matter of hours. Doing away with Tutsi civilians proved a more difficult undertaking, yet the scale and swiftness of the carnage leaves no doubt about the efficiency of the machete-wielding death squads.[7] If we are to believe the testimony of eye witnesses, there was a macabre rationality to the methods employed by the killers: as one survivor told this writer, "where large numbers of people had to be killed, as happened where dozens or hundreds had sought refuge in churches, the death squads went about it methodically: phase one involved breaking the ankles so as to prevent the victims from running away; once the victims were immobilized, they worked on the wrists and arms, to prevent them from fighting back; the killers could then turn to the last phase, using clubs, sticks, and machetes to break the skulls and necks." Horribly "rational" as well was the systematic slaughter of infants: after all, many of the RPF soldiers were toddlers when their parents fled their homeland during the 1959 revolution; why make the same mistake twice?

That a carnage of this magnitude could have been going on day after day, week after week, without interference from the international community speaks volumes for its lack of resolve in dealing with massive human rights violations. That they could literally get away with murder must have been a major consideration in the minds of the organizers of the killings. Given the extent of French backing—military, logistical, political, and economic—they correctly assumed that they could act with impunity. They knew that the Fashoda syndrome would work to their advantage; they knew that the French embassy would look the other way each time it was confronted with irrefutable evidence of massive human rights violations; and they knew, when the circumstances required, how to capitalize upon the close ties of friendship between President Mitterrand's son, Jean-Christophe, and his "buddy," Juvénal Habyarimana.

It is difficult to believe that the French were not aware of the potential for genocide created by the systematic manipulation of ethnic identities, by the mob killings of Tutsi over a period of years, and by the incitements to violence broadcast by Radio Mille Collines. If so, it defies Cartesian logic to comprehend how the self-styled "patrie des droits de l'homme" could shove under the rug such massive human rights violations in the name of the threats posed to its higher geopolitical interests by the Trojan horse of Anglo-Saxon imperialism. It took only a logic of calculated risks for the authors of the genocide to grasp the implications of this paradox. The lesson to be drawn is nowhere more clearly articulated than by Helen Fein: "Abusive powers will continue to abuse as long as it works: the movement to change the taken-for-granted assumption that sovereignty implies indifference to our neighbors' crimes (like respect for family implied by overlooking child abuse next door) is still to emerge from gestation in images of mass flight, chaos, blood and death."[8]

Chapter 6
Hate Crimes

The tale hardly bears retelling: in Rwanda an estimated one million people died in a frenzy of genocidal killings that was one of the most appalling bloodbaths of the twentieth century. Most of the victims were members of the country's Tutsi minority. Few were lucky enough to be shot; the majority were hacked to pieces, drowned, speared, or beaten to death with clubs, their bodies left unburied, at the mercy of stray dogs and vultures. Although the worst of the killings was the work of militias—the notorious *interahamwe*, "those who stand together"—the slaughter rapidly gained a momentum of its own, drawing participants from a wide cross section of the population that included government officials, town mayors and councilors, members of the clergy, teachers, and nurses.

This almost unthinkable crime is like a black hole, swallowing past, present, and future in its unfathomed enormity. It is a crime that demands justice, and there are now two autonomous jurisdictions prosecuting thousands of individuals accused of participating in the genocide—the Rwandan Public Prosecutor's Office and the International Criminal Tribunal for Rwanda in Arusha, Tanzania. In Rwanda the recent past is a crushing burden. But if the past is horrific, the question of the future still remains: the question of whether there can be reconciliation without justice or justice without truth. Rwanda is more profoundly divided now than at any other time in its history. Although the Tutsi-led government espouses non-racialism, dissension between Hutu and Tutsi has never been sharper. The Tutsi minority has no illusions about the threat posed to its security by Hutu-instigated raids across Rwanda's border with the Democratic Republic of the Congo. Meanwhile, Hutu fears of Tutsi vengeance acquire fresh urgency with each new report of violence in eastern Congo, much of it under Rwandan control.

Thinking critically about the genocide and its legacy is difficult, not least because the wounds are still so raw, the victims so many, the apportionment of guilt and responsibility so controversial. That the story of Rwanda is at all known in the United States today owes much to the work of Philip Gourevitch and Alison Des Forges. Gourevitch is a staff writer at the *New Yorker*. His reports from Rwanda are lively and informed; he has access to many of the principals, especially the leadership of the RPF. He is also an essayist in the tradition of Ryszard Kapuscinski and Robert D. Kaplan, and his book, *We Wish to Inform You That Tomorrow We Will Be Killed with Our Families,* is not just a masterwork of travel writing but a chilling account of the individual tragedies endured by genocide survivors. It has received numerous accolades—the 1998 National Book Critics Award—and sold surprisingly well for a book about Africa—and a book about genocide, at that.[1]

But as the author himself would admit, it is not a scholarly work. There are no footnotes, no indexes, and little documentation; much was left out or papered over in the crafting of this narrative. What is missing from Gourevitch's account is the how and why of the killings. It is one thing to describe the horror, another to explain the motivations that occasioned the carnage. Little is said of the impact of the colonial and precolonial past on Hutu-Tutsi relations, of the significance of regional differences in Rwanda's political culture, of the 1959–62 Hutu revolution, of the divisions among Hutu in the days immediately preceding the invasion of the country by the RPF—or the invasion itself for that matter. The absence of attention to the history and politics of the country creates a portrait of genocide that is insensitive to the complexity of its circumstances. In essence, Gourevitch's story reduces the butchery to a tale of bad guys and good guys, innocent victims and avatars of hate. His frame of reference is the Holocaust.

Very different is the story told by Alison Des Forges, an activist, writer, and consultant at Human Rights Watch, in her 750-page tome on the Rwandan tragedy, *Leave None to Tell the Story.* Trained as a historian and long recognized as a Rwanda expert, Des Forges has conducted a thorough and richly documented inquest into the roots and mechanics of the carnage. Aided by eight research assistants and informed by dozens of interviews, as well as a firm grasp of the country's tortured history, the author takes us into the belly of the beast. With exemplary meticulousness, Des Forges lays bare the workings of the propaganda machine, the organization of the killings, the strategies of slaughter, and the social structures that provided support (including the clergy); she brings out the regional dynamics at work and leaves no doubt as to the mix of obfuscation and indifference that marked the international community's response. Like Gourevitch, Des Forges believes that foreign intervention could have prevented the genocide—or at least ended it much earlier, when the body count was much lower.

Unlike Gourevitch, however, she also sees the other side of the genocidal coin—the human rights abuses, killings and other abuses committed by the RPF during and after the genocide, including the ruse of holding public meetings designed to round up and kill Hutu civilians.

(Hence the joke that *kwitaba imana*, "to die" in Kinyarwanda, was the same as *kwitaba inama*, "to attend a meeting.") Des Forges also discusses "murders committed by assailants who went from house to house, and the hunting down and murder of people in hiding."[2]

There is a temptation, in writing about the genocide, to tell a story of good and evil. This is understandable: the evil committed in the name of Hutu power numbs the mind. But there is more to the story than Tutsi victimhood and Hutu guilt. It is easy to see why this Manichaean temptation has come to inform the consciousness of some genocide survivors and perpetrators. But considered as a foundation for moral inquiry, or a guide to public policy, it carries the seeds of renewed confrontation.

To criticize this Manichaean thinking is not to endorse what Alain Finkelkraut has called the "dogma of equidistance"—the idea that all who have sinned are equally sinners. In the first place, it is simply to observe that not every Hutu has blood on his or her hands. If it's true that 10 percent of the Hutu population participated in the killings as organizers, executioners, or unwilling accomplices surrendering to threats, that leaves 90 percent of the population that did not—5.8 million Hutu whose hands are clean. Thousands of Tutsi were saved from the machete by Hutu neighbors who put themselves and their families at considerable risk.

Guilt and innocence do not run parallel to ethnic lines. But in Rwanda today, guilt and innocence are increasingly becoming ethnicized: because the Tutsi were so thoroughly victimized, they are now beyond reproach. Genocide exonerates its victim of all subsequent sins. This is true not only in Rwanda but also in Yugoslavia; it is happening today in Kosovo, where members of the Kosovo Liberation Army have engaged in the wanton murder of Serbian civilians. In *Hearts Grown Brutal: Sagas of Sarajevo*, Roger Cohen noted the tendency of Bosnian Serbs to invoke earlier "genocides" they suffered at the hands of Croats, Muslims, or Turks as a pretext for retaliating in kind. "Deployed in this way," Cohen writes, "'genocide' is no longer a horror but a form of immunity. It [is] a *passe-partout* allowing the eternal Serbian victim to butcher with impunity."[3]

"The experience of others," observes Nelson Mandela, "has taught us that nations that do not deal with the past are haunted by it for generations." But what, exactly, does the experience of others tell us? The record is ambiguous. At one extreme, there is Cambodia, where not a single Khmer Rouge soldier or officer has been prosecuted for the murder of more than a million people between 1975 and 1979. Twenty years later, a culture of impunity has taken root. At the other extreme, there is Germany, where the Nazi past is insistently scrutinized not just in the media but also, more important, in the schools. As Tina Rosenberg noted in the *New York Times*, "No nation has done more than Germany to deal with its past. No country has announced its guilt more loudly, paid more in reparation . . . or put more of its citizens on trial for war crimes."[4]

Much has been written about the parallels between the Nazi Holocaust and the Rwandan genocide. But Rwanda is not Germany. The point is not only that one happens to be a minute, underdeveloped, overpopulated, poverty-stricken state and the other, a highly developed industrial society. There are major differences between the genocides themselves. The most obvious, perhaps, is that unlike the Nazi Shoah, the Rwanda genocide can best be described as retributive. Although Germans may have fantasized about Jewish world domination, Jews did not invade Germany with the military backing of a neighboring state; in Rwanda, the Tutsi-dominated Rwandan Patriotic Army initiated a civil war four years before the genocide, with support from the government of Uganda. There are other salient differences: the technology of extermination in Rwanda bears little resemblance to the efficient, modern death camps of the Third Reich. (This also explains another crucial difference: where the Nazis kept detailed records of those they killed, the documentation on Rwanda is notoriously unreliable.) The circumstances of the Rwandan genocide are more complex, and the chain of events that led to the killings is much less clear. It took decades for Germany to face up to its past; in Rwanda, the wounds are still raw.

Where a significant parallel does emerge between Germany and Rwanda is in the proportion of Jews to non-Jews exterminated by the Nazis, as compared to the proportion of Tutsi to Hutu killed during and after the genocide. Of the eleven million who died in Nazi concentration camps, six million were Jews and five million non-Jews. Although the figures for Rwanda are far less reliable, research conducted by Filip Reyntjens suggests a similar ratio of Tutsi to Hutu. At least 600,000 Tutsi were slaughtered during the genocide, between April and July 1994; the number of Hutu killed by Hutu could be as high as 50,000. But if we consider the number of Hutu killed during and immediately after the RPF's advance on Kigali (between 5,000 and 10,000 each month from April through July and 5,000 for the month of August, according to figures cited by Alison Des Forges), then add the Hutu refugees killed by Rwandan troops in Zaire in 1996 and 1997 and those who died of disease and starvation there, we arrive at a figure of perhaps half a million deaths. If so, the proportion of Hutu to Tutsi casualties parallels that of non-Jews to Jews during the Holocaust. Significantly, in each case the identity of the victims enters our consciousness selectively: just as the Holocaust is overwhelmingly identified with the agony of European Jewry, the Rwandan genocide is generally seen as an attempt to exterminate the Tutsi. Non-Jews, like non-Tutsi, seldom figure in the accounting.

There are no quick fixes or simple recipes for Rwanda to come to terms with the past. But one thing is clear: there can be no reconciliation without justice, and there can be no justice without truth. This holds not just for Rwanda but also for Burundi and eastern Congo, where mutual hatred between Hutu and Tutsi still threatens to ignite a wider disaster. The quest for truth must transcend both ethnic and geographical boundaries. In none of these states, however, are we getting any closer to the facts. We know so little about so many questions. Exactly how many people died in 1994? How many of them were battlefield casualties; how many died of disease and malnutrition; how many died at the hands of the génocidaires? How many Hutu were killed by Hutu? How many Tutsi? Who shot down President Habyarimana's plane on April 6, 1994—thus setting the genocide in motion? How many refugees died in the course of the RPF's search-and-destroy operations in eastern Congo? How many refugees returned to Rwanda after the destruction of the camps? With so much still in dispute, there is ample room not just for speculation but for mythmaking as well.

The whole history of Rwanda is shrouded in myth. There are the myths of origins of the Tutsi kingdom and the legends that gave legitimacy to the "premise of inequality"[5] between Hutu and Tutsi; there is the Hamitic myth that Catholic missionaries imported from nineteenth-century Europe; and the stridently racist mythology that Radio Mille Collines used to exhort Hutus to genocide. The Hamitic idea, which presumed the innate cultural superiority of the Tutsi and claimed that Ethiopia was their original homeland, was pressed into service to legitimize Tutsi overrule under the Belgian colonizers. The inversion of this mythical discourse, emphasizing the foreignness, cunning, and perversity of Tutsi "feudal exploiters," played an equally decisive role in legitimizing Hutu ascendancy in the last years of colonial rule. It also lent ideological justification to the génocidaires. In a much-quoted statement, Léon Mugesera, a leading figure of the ruling party, told the Tutsi in November 1992, "Your home is in Ethiopia, and we are going to send you back there quickly, by the Nyabarongo," referring to earlier massacres, whose victims were dumped into that river.[6]

There are other myths with less storied pedigrees. For some analysts, traditional Rwanda was an ethnic nirvana; there was no trace of ethnic tension until the Belgians came to sow the seeds of division between Hutu and Tutsi. That myth, assiduously promoted by the ideologues of the RPF, contrasts with an enduring myth among Hutus that no genocide ever took place. What happened in Rwanda in 1994, on this view, was nothing more than a spontaneous uprising of normally peaceful people in the face of external aggression. Clearly, no single group has a monopoly on mythmaking.

What caused the carnage? A great deal hangs on this question. The history of the killings lends itself to very different explanations and understandings, each fraught with implicit ideologies.

There is a wide array of underlying causes to choose from or to gather into a meaningful account:

- the invasion of Rwanda by the RPF on October 1, 1990;
- the murderous ambitions of the small coterie of northern politicians surrounding President Juvénal Habyarimana, who set in motion a killing machine (the so-called *akazu*);
- the propaganda machine built around Radio Mille Collines;
- the political culture of submission to higher-ups inscribed in the norms and habits of Hutu society;
- the land problem and high population densities;
- the legacy of Belgian colonial rule and the "structural violence," to use Peter Uvin's phrase,[7] inherited from the shortsightedness of international development assistance;
- the psychological impact of specific events in neighboring territories (such as the assassination of Burundi's first Hutu president, Melchior Ndadaye, in October 1993);
- the unanticipated consequences of the introduction of multiparty democracy;
- the auxiliary role played by the French in training Habyarimana's army, combined with the appalling passivity of the international community in the face of an impending massacre;
- the concessions accorded to the RPF in the 1993 Arusha accords and the fear they inspired among Hutu extremists that a Tutsi military and political takeover was imminent;
- and last but not least, the mysterious shooting down of Habyarimana's plane on April 6, 1994, for which the RPF was immediately held responsible by Radio Mille Collines, even though there was no solid evidence that such was the case.

Clearly, all these considerations (and many more) must be taken into account if we are to understand the roots of the cataclysm. Yet the impulse in Rwanda—and elsewhere—has been to make the evidence fit one's own preconceptions. To this day, Hutu and Tutsi view the same historical reality through radically different lenses.

Regardless of whether they admit the reality of genocide, there is only one explanation for most Hutu ideologues: the RPF invasion in 1990. Everything else is secondary, except perhaps the destruction of

Habyarimana's plane. From this vantage point, the invading Tutsi army must bear full responsibility for a tragedy they brought onto themselves and their people. A similarly blinkered view of history can be seen in the argument made by Tutsi intellectuals that the immediate cause of the tragedy must be found in the sheer perversity of Habyarimana's genocidal clique, abetted by the dual complicity of the French in supporting his regime and the international community in failing to intervene.

In the lengthy catalog of sins each side brings against the other, there is seldom any mention of local politics. Although theories of ethnicity and the delayed impact of the colonial encounter are strenuously debated, the history of politics in the years leading up to the Rwandan genocide is typically neglected. But local electoral contests—alongside the changes that convulsed Rwandan politics and society in the 1990s—explain a fundamental aspect of the genocide: the killing of Hutu by Hutu.

Land hunger is one of the longest-standing issues in Rwanda—a poor, densely populated, exceptionally fertile country. For many landless peasants, the genocide was not an end in itself but a kind of do-it-yourself land reform: an opportunity to grab land from their neighbors, Tutsi and Hutu alike. Catherine André and Jean-Philippe Platteau have shown that in villages where the shortage of land was particularly acute—particularly in the northwest—land grabbing was a major motivation in the killing of Hutu by Hutu.

Inter-Hutu politics was characterized by violence even before the genocide in Rwanda. In a 1998 article in *Africa Today*, Michele Wagner, who spent time in a southern village (Nyakizu) as a Human Rights Watch participant-observer in 1995, pieced together a chilling account of a struggle for power among aspiring party leaders in the months preceding the genocide. Wagner shows the extreme brutality involved in the rise of a local administrator: the manipulation of patronage (including access to land) went hand in hand with political assassination, the destruction of property, the deployment of murderous youth gangs (usually after accusations of witchcraft), intimidation, and theft. All of this was portrayed as part of a process of *kubohoza* ("liberation"), converting members of the ruling party, Habyarimana's Mouvement Républicain National pour la Démocratie et le Développement (MRNDD) to the cause of the opposition MDR. Not coincidentally, the "moderate" Hutu killed during the genocide were largely members of the MDR. "From late 1990 until 1994," Wagner writes, "Rwandan citizens developed the techniques, practices and patterns of behavior that would enable genocide."[8]

Multiparty democracy was introduced in Rwanda in 1991, one year after the onset of the civil war between the government and the RPF. The genocide of 1994 was, among other things, a crescendo of the murderous calculus of political advantage that had been unleashed by electoral competition. Here, too, genocide was a means to an end: to bludgeon opposition parties into submission. The MRND had controlled Rwanda for the better part of two decades; if the MDR were to join forces with the RPF in the new political framework set up by the Arusha accords, Habyarimana and his entourage might lose power. Preventing that eventuality from coming to pass was among the first orders of business for the *interahamwe*.

If it is crucial to understand the diverse causes and consequences of the Rwandan genocide, it is increasingly difficult to do so. To speak of shared responsibility for the genocide, or of Tutsi violence against Hutu—indeed, to criticize the present-day government of Rwanda at all—is to risk the accusation of sympathizing with the killers. Respected academics who deviate from the party line have been denounced as Hutu apologists; human rights organizations that catalog abuses have been pilloried as partisan or out of touch. Roger P. Winter, the director of the U.S. Committee for Refugees, reveals the antinomies of this new form of political correctness in his blanket attack on groups like Amnesty International and Human Rights Watch. Such groups, Winter told the *Washington Post*, are rendering a profound disservice to the people they are trying to help. Unmindful of the sheer fragility of post-genocide polities, Winter argues, human rights activists forget that "there is a time to shout and a time to help"—and now the best way to help is to keep silent on human rights violations.[9]

Some of this may be attributable to the strange fascination of American foreign policy professionals—particularly in the Pentagon—with Paul Kagame, Rwanda's vice president and minister of defense. Kagame led the RPF to victory in Rwanda; his army is credited with ending the genocide. He is widely admired as the architect of the plot to shut down the Hutu refugee camps in eastern Zaire—an action that led to the overthrow of Mobutu Sese Seko, one of Africa's most hated tyrants. Kagame is the hero of Gourevitch's book; not coincidentally, he is among the best regarded of the "New African leaders" supported by American policy analysts, second only to Yoweri Museveni, Uganda's president (and Kagame's mentor). Kagame has the ear of many in the West, not least because he knows how to appeal to its shame for not acting to end the genocide itself. Very little is said about the 120,000 Hutu suspects still languishing in overcrowded prisons; about the Rwandan army's continuing activities in the eastern Congo (in violation of the Lusaka accords); or about brutal raids against Hutu communities suspected of harboring génocidaires in Rwanda itself.

This wall of silence applies to the past, as well. One merit of *Leave None to Tell the Tale* is its presentation of the history of the "Gersony

Report." Robert Gersony, an official at the UN High Commission for Refugees, was charged with finding ways to expedite the repatriation of Hutu from refugee camps in eastern Zaire, where some one million fled after the RPF takeover. Gersony, originally sympathetic to the RPF, discovered evidence of "clearly systematic murders and persecution of the Hutu population in certain parts of the country."[10] After intense lobbying by the Rwandan government and the U.S. State Department, however, the UN suppressed the information. Des Forges's repeated requests to obtain a copy were met with a uniform response from the United Nations: "The Gersony Report does not exist." The situation was similar in the summer of 1997, when Roberto Garreton, UN Special Rapporteur on Human Rights in the Democratic Republic of Congo, led a UN team to investigate allegations that the Rwandan-backed, Tutsi-led rebel movement that overthrew Mobutu had murdered thousands of fleeing Hutu refugees and buried them in mass graves. After months of stonewalling and harassment from Kabila's government, Garreton quit the Congo without visiting a single alleged grave site. There were no adverse consequences for Kabila and none for his patron, Kagame.

It is time to end the conspiracy of silence surrounding human rights violations committed by the RPF government. Rwanda today is a thinly veiled military ethnocracy. What is missing in the governing clique is the political will to affect a genuine political opening to the non-Tutsi majority. And yet it is important for the government to create the illusion that such a will exists: approximately two-thirds of the national budget comes from foreign assistance, which is predicated on the idea that aid will help end divisiveness. There are indeed Hutus in the current Rwandan government: the president, Pasteur Bizimungu, is a Hutu, as are half of its cabinet-level ministers.

What may be more important than who is in the government, though, is who is not. In August 1995, two Hutu members of the government, Seth Sendashonga and Faustin Twagiramungu (the minister of the interior and prime minister, respectively) were forced to resign after expressing their concern over human rights abuses committed by the army. In May 1998, Sendashonga—a brilliant mind, erstwhile member of the RPF, and early opponent of Habyarimana—was gunned down in Nairobi, allegedly by hit men recruited by the Rwandan embassy. A third Hutu cabinet member, Alphonse Marie Nkubito, minister of justice, died in mysterious circumstances shortly after resigning in 1995. Those Hutu who remain in the government do so by avoiding criticism of the army's activities.

The army is the central element in the Rwandan political equation. The political decisions with the gravest consequences for the nation (and for the Great Lakes region as a whole) are undertaken by the RPF's Tutsi leadership, not by the political establishment. The takeover of Kigali in 1994 and the toppling of Mobutu in 1997 were brilliantly executed, ending the genocide and removing the primary sponsor of the génocidaires. But the attempt to overthrow Mobutu's successor, Laurent-Désiré Kabila, has foundered amid regional anger at Rwandan imperialism. Rwanda's behavior in the eastern part of the Congo has become increasingly erratic: its surrogate, the RCD, keeps recruiting non-Tutsi Congolese to assume symbolic leadership posts, only to marginalize them if they seem too independent. (Only the intervention of Uganda, Rwanda's former ally, prevented the assassination of estranged RCD leader Ernest Wamba dia Wamba in August 1999.) The *interahamwe*, once on the defensive, now find employment as mercenaries in rebellions throughout the region: in Angola, fighting with UNITA; in Uganda, fighting with forces that hope to topple Museveni; and in the DRC, where they form the backbone of Kabila's counterinsurgency forces. Military solutions offer no solution to this conflict, though they have a logic of their own.

Today Kagame is caught in a bind: yielding to the security imperative only creates further insecurity. Rwanda's military presence in eastern Congo continues to generate enormous resentment; both Congolese and Rwandan Tutsi are perceived as bitter enemies by non-Tutsi Congolese. But as the situation in the Congo deteriorates, Rwanda's case for sending more troops gains strength. And each expansion of the conflict defers the hope of political liberalization yet again.

There is no epiphany in sight, only a sense of continuing crisis, rooted in the same political exclusion that prevailed before the genocide. There is more than a touch of Kafkaesque irony in this situation. The bizarre has been normalized. One form of ethnic supremacy has given way to another. Commenting on the "ultimate and horrible paradox" of post-genocide Rwanda, Gérard Prunier recently observed that although the génocidaires lost the battle, in a sense they have won the war. "The atrociousness of their ideology has tainted the victors," he wrote in *Le Monde Diplomatique*. "It has contaminated all social relations and perverted political calculations."[11]

Can Rwanda reinvent itself? Can it ever reach across the Hutu-Tutsi chasm and chart a new path toward national reconciliation? The first step is not to ethnicize guilt and innocence but to seek the truth, however uncomfortable. The génocidaires must be held responsible for genocide; but not every Hutu is a génocidaire, nor even a potential génocidaire. It is one thing for courts of law to seek out truth about who killed whom, where, when, and how; and quite another for all of us to deal with the more ambivalent truth of why the genocide happened in the first place. It is this latter truth that needs to be established if Rwanda is to move forward.

Not every Tutsi is a victim. And victimization is no excuse for future barbarism. As one reflects on the continuing crisis in the Great Lakes, it is well to bear in mind Tzvetan Todorov's warning, echoing Primo Levi: "Vengeance settles nothing; it adds new violence to old violence. But this addition does not stop the violence. On the contrary, it only prepares the way for new explosions. . . . What is important is not that justice be more or less severe, it is simply that justice exists."[12] Justice, like innocence, belongs to individuals, not groups. Until that lesson is learned, there is little hope for an end to Rwanda's continuing agony.

Chapter 7
The Politics of Memory

"Never again! Plus jamais!" The message—so often heard, so seldom heeded—was delivered loud and clear to those present in the Amahoro stadium in Kigali on April 7, 2004, on the tenth anniversary of one of the most monstrous bloodbaths of the last century. Relayed through public speeches, survivors' reminiscences, and multiple banderoles; even the name of the venue—"Peace"—gave symbolic significance to that defining moment.

This was a time to remember the enormity of the crimes committed a decade ago while the international community looked the other way. This was a time for all Rwandans to commune in remembrance of their common agony; a time for recognition.

Unlike on a similar occasion in 1995, when a posthumous homage was paid to Hutu and Tutsi victims, this time, as in previous years, Kagame's discourse, in turn mournful and accusatory, made no mention of ethnic identities. To do so would have been indecently superfluous and in any case, contrary to the public ban on all references to ethnicity. There are no Hutu or Tutsi in today's Rwanda, only Banyarwanda (Rwandans).

In justification of this drastic reconfiguration of collective identities, Rwandan officials are prompt to point out that the aim of the state at this critical juncture is to build a nation, and the first step toward this daunting task is to do away with ethnic labels once and for all. The logic of the argument is straightforward: "if awareness of ethnic differences can be learned, so too can the idea that ethnicity does not exist."[1] The rationale is equally clear: "divisionism"—ethnic, regional, and political—has been the bane of Rwanda and indeed the root cause of the genocide; the time has come to lay the foundation for a national community free of the stigma of ethnicity. This is why the crime of divisionism has been added to the penal code: besides providing the government with a convenient weapon to ban almost any type of organized opposition, it offers the new nation builders a unique opportunity to legislate ethnic identities out of existence.

Although there are obvious and compelling reasons to remember the atrocities of 1994, the question is whether the exclusion of ethnic memories for the sake of a spuriously unifying official memory can bring the people of Rwanda—Hutu, Tutsi, and Twa—any closer to building the mutual trust necessary for a peaceful coexistence. Reconciliation, assuming it can ever be achieved, requires that the past be confronted, not obliterated. Recognition that guilt and victimization transcend ethnic boundaries is not enough. No less crucial is how ethnic and individual memories alter perceptions of the past, and by implication, the writing of history. The following is an attempt to explore the politics of memory in post-genocide Rwanda in the light of categories proposed by Paul Ricoeur: thwarted memory, manipulated memory, and enforced memory.[2]

The Ambivalence of Ethnic Memory

Memory—official or ethnic, collective or individual—is a preeminently subjective phenomenon. It blurs the boundaries between fact and fiction, between factual truth and interpretive truth. Blind spots, ethnic amnesia, and denials of historical evidence operate to mask unpalatable truths and magnify others out of proportion. "Memory," writes Stanley Cohen, "is a social product, reflecting the agenda and social location of those who invoke it."[3] This is true not only of the official memory invoked by the Kagame government, but of the ethnic and individual memories summoned by perpetrators and victims alike. In these conditions, the distinction between good faith and bad faith is not always easy to pin down. The reason for this is nowhere more convincingly articulated than by Primo Levi in his penetrating commentary on "the memory of the offense":[4]

> There are those who lie consciously, coldly falsifying reality itself, but more numerous are those who weigh anchor, move off, momentarily or forever, from genuine memories, and fabricate for themselves a convenient reality. The past is a burden to them; they feel repugnance for things done or suffered and tend to replace them with others. The substitution may begin in full awareness, with an invented scenario, mendacious, restored, but less painful than the real one; they repeat the description to others but also to themselves, and the distinction between true and false progressively loses its contours, and man ends by fully believing the story he has told so many times and continues to tell, polishing and retouching here and there the details which are least credible or incongruous or incompatible with the acquired picture of historically accepted events: initial bad faith has become good faith.

Anyone familiar with the discourse of the more radically inclined members of the Hutu and Tutsi communities on the roots of the genocide cannot fail to note the pertinence of Levi's comments: the "memory of the offense," whether falsified or fabricated, is always selective and thus acts as a key mechanism in the construction of a "convenient reality."

The clash of ethnic memories is an essential component of the process by which the legacy of genocide—the "memory of the offense"—is being perceived or fabricated by one community or the other: once filtered through the prism of ethnicity, entirely different constructions are imposed on the same ghastly reality—from which emerge strikingly divergent interpretations of why a genocide happened. Not only is the past seen through a different ethnic lens, but there are also major differences *among* Hutu and Tutsi in the way in which it is remembered or forgotten.

There are those fortunate ones, overwhelmingly Tutsi, who survived the carnage and witnessed at close range the horrors of genocide, who saw friends and neighbors and members of their own families shot, speared, clubbed to death, or hacked to pieces by mobs of enraged Hutu youth. And there are the *inkontanyi*, Kagame's refugee "warriors," who killed tens of thousands of Hutu civilians in "liberated" zones, and according to credible testimonies from RPA defectors, did not shrink from inflicting horrendous tortures on their suspected enemies.[5]

There are the blood-soaked Hutu génocidaires, and there are the "heroes" who risked or lost their lives in order to save their Tutsi neighbors. And there are those countless, anonymous Hutu who were witness to the cold-blooded killings perpetrated by Kagame's troops in Rwanda and eastern Zaire (now the DRC).[6] All, to some extent, experience the same dysfunctions of memory and emotional traumas so tellingly explored by Liisa Malkki among survivors of the 1972 genocide of Hutu in Burundi.[7]

Finally, there are the ideologues who manipulate the historical record for political purposes. They are found on both sides of the ethnic divide and beyond. Even in the absence of ulterior political motives, the deliberate travesty of the facts is not uncommon among foreign observers. A case in point is Helmut Strizek who, in a conference at the Sorbonne, on April 6, 2004, denied that the killings were planned, thereby implicitly denying the existence of a genocide. Christian Davenport, a professor of political science at the University of Maryland, also contests the appropriateness of the term *genocide*, arguing that what occurred was a "totalitarian purge, a politicide rather than ethnic cleansing or genocide." Moreover, the majority of the victims, according to Davenport, were Hutu, not Tutsi: "Our research strongly suggests that a majority of the victims were Hutu—there weren't enough Tutsi in Rwanda at the time to account for all reported deaths. . . . Either the scale of the killing was much less than is widely believed, or, more likely, a huge number of Hutu were caught up in the violence as inadvertent victims. The evidence suggests the killers didn't try to figure out who everybody was. They erred on the side of comprehensiveness."[8] Such assertions are enthusiastically received by some Hutu deniers, all too eager to bolster their claims by quoting from European "authorities." One example among others of Hutu *négationisme* can be found in the statement released on March 21 by the Association des Rescapés du Génocide des Réfugiés Rwandais en République Démocratique du Congo, which states: "Since there is no proof that the genocide was planned . . . how can one say that a genocide has been directed against the Tutsi of Rwanda in 1994?" Recent leaks to the press of the report by the French investigating magistrate, Jean-Louis Bruguière[9]—in which strong circumstantial evidence points to the implication of Kagame in the shooting down of Habyarimana's plane, on April 6, 1994—have given a new slant to the argument advanced by Hutu deniers: the mass murder of Tutsi was the direct outcome of the dastardly plot concocted by the RPF, and thus has nothing to do with the planning imputed to extremist Hutu elements. If one can speak of a genocide, the argument goes, the responsibility lies squarely with Kagame. A closer look at the evidence reveals a more complex reality. Nonetheless, critical questions remain about the role of Kagame in paving the ground for the carnage, including those raised by Bruguière in his as yet unpublished report.

Thwarted Memory

There are many ways in which memory departs from reality. In his magisterial work *Memory, History and Oblivion*, Paul Ricoeur refers to "thwarted memory, manipulated memory, and enforced memory" ("*mémoire empêchée, mémoire manipulée, mémoire abusivement commandée*").[10] Our fixation on "*le devoir de mémoire*" (the duty to remember), he argues, makes us lose sight of a more urgent task, which he calls "*le travail de mémoire*" (the labor of memory), which involves a more sustained effort to probe the relationship between history and memory and between memory and recognition. This is also Eva Hoffman's point when she writes, "the injunctions to remember, if reiterated too often, can become formulaic—an injunction precisely not to think or grapple with the past."[11] Thinking or grappling with the past is what is conspicuously missing from Rwanda's official memory—in other words, a sustained effort to recognize the profound ambivalence of the notion of guilt. What persists to this day, in Cohen's words, is "collective memory pressed into shape by being repressed."[12]

Ricoeur's notion of thwarted memory gives a clue to an understanding of the many blind spots in Rwanda's official memory. What is being thwarted through the ban on ethnic identities is the memory of atrocities endured by Hutu and Tutsi, where ethnicity, though singularly unhelpful for discriminating between victims and perpetrators, is crucially important for addressing the roots of the injuries suffered by each community.

What is being thwarted is the memory of those generally referred to as Hutu "moderates," a "ubiquitous, undefined phrase," as Nigel Eltringham correctly shows that "fails to communicate the proactive resistance these actors demonstrated."[13] Among them were Prime Minister Agathe Uwilingiyimana, three government ministers, the president of the Constitutional Court, the entire leadership of the PSD, forty-nine journalists killed because they aired criticisms of the genocidal crusade, and scores of human rights activists; along with tens of thousands of Hutu killed by other Hutu for no other reasons than they happened to belong to an opposition party or because they happened to look like Tutsi or because their spouses were Tutsi. What is being thwarted is the memory of those Hutu who steadfastly refused to surrender their Tutsi friends and neighbors to the militias and who gave them shelter and protection at considerable risk to themselves and their families. Exemplary is the story of Damas Mutezintare, a Hutu who saved nearly 400 Tutsi lives, 300 children and 80 adults, in his orphanage at Nyamirambo. "I haven't done anything special," he told the correspondent of *La Libre Belgique*, Marie-France Cros. "I just said to myself I've got to do something, but I wasn't sure what the results would be. . . . I've been lucky."[14] Not all such "heroes" were lucky enough to live to tell their story.

Summoning a de-ethnicized, victim-centered memory is not enough; what has yet to be given proper recognition is that Hutu and Tutsi were victims of a calamity for which responsibility is shared by elements of both communities. This sharing of responsibility is what Rwanda's official ideologues refuse to acknowledge. Instead, every effort is made to manipulate memory so as to exonerate the ruling elites of all responsibility in the circumstances that led to the abyss. Complex though they are, a key element in the chain of events leading to the butchery is the outbreak of the bitter civil war instigated by the RPF.

Manipulated Memory

"Tous les autres sont coupables, sauf moi" (all others are guilty except me). Céline's phrase[15] provides a subtext to Kagame's commemorative discourse on April 7, 2004. There are excellent reasons for lambasting the ignominious attitude of the French government throughout the crisis, as Kagame did on that occasion, as well as the culpable indifference of the international community and the disastrous consequences of Belgian colonial policies. Predictably, however, nothing was said of the responsibility borne by Kagame himself in unleashing the civil war that led to the genocide. This is not to deny the very obvious culpability of the Hutu génocidaires and their leaders in planning, organizing and carrying out the murder of approximately 800,000 people; only to underscore that the climate of fear and paranoia created by the civil war did at least as much as Radio des Mille Collines to heighten the receptivity of Hutu extremists to a "final solution." Again, it is not insignificant that among the one million Hutu internally displaced persons (IDPs) forced out of their homelands by incoming RPF troops[16]—most of them living in utterly inhumane conditions in makeshift refugee camps—many enthusiastically joined the killing spree. The key point here is that there would have been no genocide had Kagame not decided to unleash his refugee warriors on October 1, 1990, in violation of the most elementary principle of international law. If he deserves full credit for stopping the killings, an equally convincing case can be made for the view that he bears much of the onus of responsibility for provoking them.

Tempting as it is to see in the government of President Kagame the embodiment of moral virtue for bringing the genocide to an end, the mourning of Tutsi lives must not be allowed to obscure the crimes against humanity committed by Kagame's army. If, as claimed by the UN-commissioned Gersony Report, between 25,000 and 45,000 Hutu were massacred by the RPA in only three communes of Rwanda between the months of April and August 1994,[17] how many were similarly killed in the whole of Rwanda during the same period?

Again, the systematic extermination by Rwandan troops in eastern DRC of tens of thousands of Hutu refugees—conveniently lumped together as "génocidaires"—has been virtually "airbrushed out of history," to use Milan Kundera's phrase. Stephen Smith, in his absorbing sketches of Congolese history, estimates at 200,000 the number of Hutu killed in the course of search-and-destroy operations conducted by the RPA in 1996 and 1997, of whom "800 were machine-gunned in broad daylight in the port city of Mbandaka on May 16, 1997, the day Laurent-Désiré Kabila captured the capital."[18] Are we to assume that these victims of Kagame's "security imperative" are to be left out of the macabre accounting of 1994?

Admittedly, whether the killings in eastern DRC can be seen as genocide is open to debate. The terms *war crimes* and *crimes against humanity*, rather than *genocide*, are generally used to describe the systematic elimination of refugee populations after the destruction of their camps in 1996. Nonetheless, the June 1998 UN report on violations of human rights in the DRC does not shrink from evoking the "G-word" but adds a cautionary note: "The killings perpetrated by the AFDL constitute crimes against humanity, just as the denial of humanitarian assistance to Hutu refugees. The members of the team feel that certain types of murder could constitute acts of genocide, depending on the intention of the perpetrators, and request that such crimes and their motives become the object of further investigation."[19] Arguably, even in the absence of wholesale massacres comparable to those perpetrated against Tutsi in 1994, the thoroughly inhumane treatment visited upon Hutu refugees would fit Helen Fein's definition of "genocide by attrition" that occurs "after a group is singled out for political and civil discrimination. It is separated from the larger society, and its right to life is threatened through concentration and forced displacement, together with systematic deprivation of food, water, and sanitary and medical facilities."[20]

Enforced Memory

If there is ample evidence that the regime is manipulating the historical record for the sake of an official memory, in what sense can one speak of an enforced memory?

At the outset, in a legal sense, the decree on ethnicity rules out public expressions of ethnic memory. Intimations that Tutsi have killed Hutu or that Hutu have killed Tutsi are subject to the same legal sanctions, regardless of the commonly accepted truth that Tutsi is synonymous with victim and Hutu with perpetrator. The writing of history, like the summoning of memories, thus takes on the quality of a fairy tale, where ethnic identifications rarely come to the surface.

No less important examples of enforced memory are the rituals of the annual genocide commemoration, which again unfold as a tribute to victims whose ethnic identity hardly needs to be mentioned. As Claudine Vidal points out, "at every commemoration those in power have instrumentalised the representation of the genocide in the context of the political conflict at the time." Vidal continues, "The commemorations explicitly deny the status of victims to those Hutu who, even though they did not kill, were massacred so as to create a climate of terror. How can one speak of reconciliation when the exposure of skeletons has as its only purpose to remind the Tutsi that their own people were killed by Hutu? This is tantamount to keeping the latter in a permanent position of culpability."[21] This is a telling commentary on how the selectivity of public memory helps nurture ethnic enmities. As Vidal explicitly suggests, in essence the official history inscribed in the commemoration ceremonies was meant to give ideological legitimacy to the consolidation of Tutsi power. The elimination of public references to ethnic identity conveniently erases from the record the memory of Hutu victims or those "righteous" Hutu who died protecting Tutsi friends and neighbors. The only category left are the génocidaires.

The instrumentalization of genocide—of which the commemoration rituals are but one example—has been the subject of scathing criticisms by three well-known experts: Vidal, Rony Brauman, and Stephen Smith. They convincingly argue that public sympathy for the victims of the genocide, and more importantly, for the successor government that stopped the genocide, has been instrumentalized in ways that allow the Kagame government to commit further crimes with impunity. "The global criminalisation of the Hutu community," they write, "poses a major threat to civil peace. . . . Every Hutu is suspect since his community bears the onus of guilt for the genocide. . . . The official history of genocide makes no reference to Hutu victims or Hutu survivors, or those Hutu who saved Tutsi lives at their own peril."[22] What Filip Reyntjens calls "the genocide credit,"[23] enjoyed by Kagame, has helped deflect attention from the crimes committed by the RPF and instead win the current Rwandan government the sympathies of an international community all too eager to atone for its shameful behavior during the genocide. To a considerable extent, the skill with which the Rwandan authorities have capitalized on this genocide credit, goes far in explaining the reluctance of most outside observers to criticize Kagame's human rights record, including his suppression of ethnic identities by decree (as if one could change society by decree!). Enforced ethnic amnesia is the most formidable obstacle to reconciliation, because it rules out the process of reckoning by which each community must confront its past and come to terms with its share of responsibility for the horrors of 1994.

The Work of Memory: Recognition and Reconciliation

What, then, is the relationship between the politics of memory and the prospects for national reconciliation in Rwanda? The short answer is that this relationship is highly problematic. To speak of national reconciliation as a realistic short-term goal is to make exceedingly short shrift of the gaping wounds each community has inflicted on the other. The wounds will take generations to heal. The scars will remain forever etched into the collective consciousness of Hutu and Tutsi. But if forgiveness is not to be expected any time soon, can one find a redemptive element in what Eva Hoffman calls "recognition," that is, a "reckoning with the past," where "recognition of what actually happened—of the victims' experience and the perpetrators' responsibility, and ultimately the broader structures of cause and effect—can allow some healing to take place?"[24]

What makes the "duty to remember" so problematic as a path to reconciliation is that the phrase leaves out the crucial questions: What is to be remembered? How? By whom? And for what purpose?

No one was more dutifully conscious of the obligation to remember than President Kagame on April 7, 2004, but what was being remembered, in effect, was the collective agony of the Tutsi, not also the sufferings and losses of the Hutu. The exclusion of Hutu victims from

Rwanda's official memory can only strengthen the conviction of the majority of the population that the genocide has been shamefully instrumentalized for the benefit of the regime. "Memory is blind to all but the group it binds," writes Pierre Nora, "which is to say . . . that there are as many memories as there are groups, that memory is by nature multiple and yet specific, collective, plural and yet individual."[25] There is Kagame's official memory, "blind to all but the group it binds," and there is a Hutu memory. There is a Tutsi memory (which is not necessarily synonymous with official memory), and there a plurality of memories among Hutu and Tutsi. Each must find its place in the annual mourning ceremonies of April 7; oblivion is not an option if the promise of "never again!" is to be fulfilled.

What could be seen as the obvious alternative—giving free rein to ethnic memories—is no less problematic. These can be just as selective in their choice of victims, just as biased in their apportioning of blame, and just as blind to the larger historical picture as official memories. This is made cruelly clear in some of the statements and *prises de position* issued by the more militant Hutu refugee organizations in exile.

A more fruitful approach is the one explored by Hoffman in her wonderfully sensitive essay, "The Balm of Recognition." Commenting on "the current rhetoric," she writes, "memory always stands for victimological memory, embraced by particular groups, and foregrounding the darkest episodes of various pasts. . . . And yet there is something that troubles me about the current discourse of memory. For one thing, the injunctions to remember, if reiterated too often, can become formulaic—an injunction precisely not to think or grapple with the past. Moreover, the uses of collective memory to bolster a groups' identity, or a fixed identification with parental victimhood, seem sometimes to verge on a kind of appropriation or bad faith. . . . What we see is the marshalling of victimological, defensive memory for the purposes of aggression."[26] Instead she invites us "to look beyond the fixed moment of trauma to those longer historical patterns, to supplement partisan memory with a more complex and encompassing view of history—a view that might examine the common history of the antagonistic groups and that might, among other things, enable us to question and criticize dubious and propagandistic uses of collective memory."[27]

Recognition in this sense means more than mere remembrance; it means coming to terms with the unspeakable atrocities inflicted on Hutu and Tutsi, by Hutu and Tutsi; it means "to name wrongs as wrongs and to bring some of those responsible to account" irrespective of ethnic identities;[28] it means addressing the traumas experienced by the tens of thousands of survivors (and indeed many of the perpetrators); and it means placing the horrors of genocide in the perspective of the broader historical forces that have led to violence. All of this and more are included in what Ricoeur has in mind when he urges upon us the exigencies of a "travail de mémoire."[29]

The phrase, Ricoeur tells us, harks back to Freud's concept of *Durcharbeiten* (which he translates as "translaboration"), which Freud used to call attention to the obstacles to the psychoanalytic cure raised by the obsessive, repetitive memory of traumatizing moments. In Ricoeur's discourse, it brings into focus the need for a "critical use of memory." Rather than a one-sided compulsive urge to rehash the sufferings endured by one group at the hands of the other or allowing them to slip into oblivion, working through memory is first and foremost an exercise in narrative history. It aims at "narrating differently the stories of the past, telling them from the point of view of the other—the other, my friend or my enemy." As alternative perceptions are brought into view, past events take on a different meaning: "Past events cannot be erased: one cannot undo what has been done, nor prevent what has happened. On the other hand, the meaning of what happened, whether inflicted by us unto others, or by them upon us, is not fixed once and for all. . . . Thus, what is changed about the past is its moral freight (*sa charge morale*), the weight of the debt it carries. . . . This is how the working of memory opens the way to forgiveness to the extent that it settles a debt by changing the very meaning of the past."[30] Both Ricoeur and Hoffman are skeptical of injunctions to remember; both reject the notion of oblivion as a vector of forgiveness; and both are aware of the need to give a central place to the claims of a "critical memory," immune to appropriation and manipulation.

Under any circumstances the search for a critical memory in postgenocide Rwanda would be difficult enough, given the radically different narratives through which the past is interpreted. With the ban on ethnicity decreed by Kagame, the prospects are even bleaker. Enforced memory in today's Rwanda does more than suppress ethnic identities, it rules out "recognition" and makes the search for a "critical memory" an exercise likely to be denounced as a source of "divisionism" and therefore, liable to legal sanctions. Ironically, while aimed at eliminating the "divisions of the past," the decree on ethnicity makes them all the more pregnant with mutual enmities. The imposition of an official memory, purged of ethnic references, is not just a convenient ploy to mask the brutal realities of ethnic discrimination; it institutionalizes a mode of thought control profoundly antithetical to any kind of interethnic dialogue aimed at a rethinking of the atrocities of mass murder. This is hardly the way to bring Hutu and Tutsi closer together in a common understanding of their tragic past.

Chapter 8
Rwanda and the Holocaust Reconsidered

> *The only way to clarify the applicability of definitions and generalizations is with comparisons. The question of whether the Holocaust had elements that have not existed with any other form of genocide . . . is extremely important if we want to find out more about social pathology in general. When one discusses unprecedented elements in a social phenomenon, the immediate question is, Unprecedented in comparison with what?*
> —Yehuda Bauer, Rethinking Genocide *(2001), p. 39*
>
> *Because the Holocaust is often regarded as the apotheosis of genocide and is the best known genocide in the western world, it is the paradigmatic genocide for political manipulation and revising the past. . . . Comparisons based on either the Holocaust or the Gulag Archipelago as a single archetype which assume that there is one mechanically recurring script are bound to be misleading.*
> —Helen Fein, Genocide: A Sociological Perspective *(1990), pp. 55–56*

The Holocaust and the Rwanda genocide are two of the most terrifying and complex catastrophes of the twentieth century. Whether measured by the scale of the atrocities committed against Jews and Tutsi, the distinctiveness of their collective identities, or the deliberate, purposeful manner of their annihilation, there are compelling reasons for seeing in the Rwanda carnage a tropical version of the Shoah. Little wonder that time and again the better known of the two has been used as the paradigmatic frame for analyzing the other.

The aim of this discussion is to challenge—or at least problematize—this analogy by placing the concept of genocide in comparative discourse. The sense of revulsion inspired by mass murder on such an appalling scale is no reason to gloss over the singularity of each catastrophe. For if the points of convergence between them are undeniable, to treat Rwanda as the carbon copy of the Holocaust is likely to obscure its historical specificity and regional context and ultimately lead to a misunderstanding of the motivations behind the killings. Not only does it make short shrift of the very different logics at work in each case, one ideological, the other retributive; it also renders the prospects of national reconciliation in Rwanda even more remote. History, as someone said, never repeats itself, but it sometimes rhymes.

Before going any further, a few notes of caution. Although the title of this essay is meant as a rejoinder to Mark Levene's effort to identify the "common threads" linking Rwanda to the Holocaust, it is by no means intended to settle scores with the author.[1] There is much in his discussion that I find illuminating and pertinent. In pointing to its shortcomings—his neglect of the regional and historical contexts—my aim is to raise problems of analysis which are of immediate concern to historians of the Holocaust yet seldom appear to cross the minds of Rwanda specialists, namely, the relative importance of context and circumstance as distinct from intention or ideology. This where the ongoing debate among historians of the Holocaust—notably the controversies surrounding the intentionalist and functionalist schools—offers a particularly useful vantage point from which to look at the etiology of the Rwanda genocide.[2]

Contrary to the impression conveyed by most journalistic accounts, the history of Rwanda does not begin in 1994, or even in 1990, when a group of Tutsi "refugee warriors" invaded the country, setting in motion an extremely bloody civil war.[3] We need to remind ourselves of the pivotal role of the Hutu revolution of 1959–62, culminating in the overthrow of the Tutsi monarchy and the rise to power of politicians claiming to represent the voice of the Hutu majority. If, as Robert Melson has conclusively demonstrated, revolution and civil war were central elements in the background of the Holocaust and Armenian genocide, his thesis also finds a perfect illustration in the case of Rwanda.[4] Not the least of the merits of his model is that it offers a framework for understanding not just similarities but differences between the cases at hand. There are indeed significant differences between the Nazi revolution and the Hutu revolution, and Hitler's disastrous invasion of the Soviet Union (code named Barbarossa) in 1941 has little in common with the 1990 invasion of Rwanda by the RPF. In one case the perpetrator is the one invading his neighbor; in the other it is the perpetrator who is faced with an invasion from a neighboring state.

The distinction drawn by Helen Fein between *ideological* and *retributive* genocide is crucial to the argument set forth here.[5] Whereas the Holocaust is the classic example of an ideological genocide, rooted in the most stridently racist ideology, the Rwanda genocide is better seen as the by-product of the mortal threats posed to the revolutionary Hutu-dominated state by the RPF. Like all ideal types, these categories are analytic tools and thus do not take into account the full complexity of real life situations. This is not to suggest therefore that racist propaganda did not play a major role in inciting Hutu mobs to kill innocent Tutsi civilians; only to emphasize the extent to which threat perceptions enhanced the receptivity of the killers to the poisonous ideology distilled on the airwaves of the infamous Radio Mille Collines. Nor is this meant to ignore the anxieties inspired by Nazi allegations of a Judeo-Bolshevik plot; only that such fears belonged to the realm of pure fantasy, whereas in Rwanda they were part and parcel of the everyday reality of a vicious civil war.

To put it baldly: Jews did not invade Germany with the massive military and logistical support of a neighboring state; nor did they once rule Germany as the political instrument of an absolute monarchy; nor were they identified with a ruling ethnocracy; nor did Jewish elements commit a partial genocide of non-Jews in a neighboring state twenty-two years before the Holocaust. Again, Jews did not stand accused of murdering the head of state of a neighboring state (as happened in Burundi with the assassination of Melchior Ndadaye in October 1993). And although Jews were insistently accused by the Nazi propaganda mill of working hand in hand with Bolshevism to subvert the state, at no time did their actions, within or outside Germany, lend the slightest credibility to these accusations. Immensely more threatening was the military posture of the RPF on the eve of the Rwanda genocide.

Bill Berkeley, one of the few observers to call into question the parallel between the Tutsi's experience of genocide and that of the Jews, sums it up in a nutshell: "The Jews of Europe were never armed. There was no Jewish conspiracy to dominate Europe, nor had there ever been one. There had been no Jewish tyranny in Germany, as there were Tutsi tyrannies in Rwanda and Burundi, and there had been no Jewish-perpetrated genocides in, say, Austria, as there were Tutsi-perpetrated genocides against Hutus no fewer than three times in a generation in Burundi, just an hour's drive down the road."[6]

The Case for Parallelism

Once this is said, there is a sense in which the analogy remains unambiguously compelling: Tutsi and Jews share a sense of victimhood for which here are few other parallels in recent or past history; both have been the target of a "total domestic genocide," to use Melson's phrase.[7] It is not a matter of coincidence if the Rwanda genocide makes immediate claims on the collective memories of Jews everywhere, if Jewish commentators are instinctively drawn to identify with the agonies of the Tutsi, and if an exceptionally close relationship has since developed between the state of Israel and post-genocide Rwanda. Referring to the "murderous trauma which they have respectively endured," William Miles notes that "it is in this vein that contacts between the RPF and the

State of Israel have been close; that cash-strapped Kigali maintains an embassy in Jerusalem; and the Israeli branches of the Simon Wiesenthal Center and Amcha have actively assisted in survivor treatment and national healing programs in Rwanda, as well as advising Rwandan prosecutors on conducting war crime trials. In this sense post-1994 Tutsi are post-Shoah Jews."[8]

The analogy applies at another level as well, albeit a more complex one. In a fascinating discussion of the problems involved in " 'Judaizing' the Rwanda genocide", Miles draws attention to their collective self-awareness as "chosen peoples," not to mention the "positive affinities" supposedly inscribed in their biblical "sibling relationship": "Tutsi are also Jews in the more problematic sense of being—albeit in the African context—a 'chosen people,' one whose historically privileged status stemmed from colonial favoritism. (According to some Hamitic interpretations, divine patronage also played a part in Tutsi superiority)."[9] But as the author would readily concede, it is one thing to be "chosen" by a colonial administration imbued of the racially inspired notions of nineteenth-century European ethnography, and quite another to be a divinely chosen people (*am nivchar*) in the biblical sense. Of this crucial distinction Miles is fully aware. Nor is he oblivious of the ideological convergence between Hamitic and Aryan mythologies. For there is indeed a sense in which Tutsi claims to superiority—whether induced by early European colonizers and missionaries or stemming from a culturally ingrained disposition to see themselves as belonging to a higher order of humanity—remind one of nothing so much as of the way in which pseudo-scientific theories were turned into racist myths at the hands of Nazi ideologues.[10]

"Who, then, in the moral universe of Holocaust parallelism, are the Tutsi? Are they 'the Jews,' victims of intended extermination? Or are they 'the Nazis,' putative embodiment of a superior race?" The question Miles raises is one that defies simple answers. His position is unambiguous: "To posit that they are, in some sense, both Aryans and Jews is unacceptable."[11] I am inclined to think otherwise: seen through the prism of history, one might conceivably argue that they are *both* Aryans and Jews, albeit at different moments of their destiny. Their "Aryanness" is inscribed in the explicitly racist connotations of the Hamitic hypothesis—in part also in some of the myths of origins associated with the birth of the Nyginya monarchy—and their Jewishness in their tragic destinies, their shared victimization at the hands of a racist state.

This is only one of the many ambivalent issues raised by "Judaizing" the Rwandan genocide. Another has to do with the parallel relationship between the Nazi and Hutu revolutions, on the one hand, and genocide on the other.

The Historical Nexus: Revolution and War

Seldom is history determined by accident or contingency. Hitler alone does not explain the Holocaust, any more than Habyalima or his entourage, the so-called *akazu*, are the causes of the Rwandan tragedy. Like any major event in history, genocide must be contextualized. No one has done it more effectively than Robert Melson in his remarkable inquest into the roots of the Armenian and Nazi genocides. Rather than looking at any single individual or culture or *mentalité* for an explanation, he shows how in each case the combination of revolution and war provided the structural opportunities for the systematic extermination of Jews and Armenians.

Although providing the condition for the coming to power of "ideological vanguards," revolutions redefine "the identity of the political community as the 'people,' the 'nation,' the 'class,' the 'race'"; the occurrence of war heightens the sense of vulnerability of the new community and creates strong ties between domestic and external foes. As Robert Melson convincingly argues, "those that earlier have been labeled as 'the enemies of the revolution' are part of an insidious plot with the regime's international foes to undo revolution or even to destroy the state and the political community itself." Neither "expulsion, assimilation, or segregation" are viable options in dealing with such threats; systematic extermination is the only solution.[12] More often than not, genocide is the deliberate, calculated response of the self-appointed custodians of the revolution to the menace posed by counterrevolutionaries at home and abroad.

The Melson thesis brings to light a crucial parallel between the Holocaust and Rwanda. In both instances, the roots of genocide are traceable to the same lethal mix of revolutionary fervor and wartime conditions. Closer scrutiny of the evidence, however, shows that there are fundamental differences in the types of revolutionary upheavals experienced by each state and the character of the war that followed in their wake.

All revolutions involve the drastic and violent restructuring of the social order, but not all revolutions stem from the same ideological roots. The Nazi revolution was nothing if not stridently anti-Semitic, aiming at the regeneration of state and society in the name of Aryan "purity." Under the leadership of the Fuhrer, the master race would emerge as the only source of salvation in the face of a world Jewish conspiracy. The Rwanda revolution was an entirely different phenomenon. The aim was not to enthrone a master race but to end the hegemony of the Tutsi minority, the nearest equivalent of a master race during much of the colonial period, and in so doing free the Hutu masses of the shackles of the Tutsi-dominated monarchy.

The ethnic underpinnings of the Rwanda revolution (1959–62) cannot be denied any more than the anti-Tutsi violence that has accompanied the rise to power of the Hutu counterelites. As many as 20,000 Tutsi may have lost their lives (out of a total of some 350,000); tens of thousands fled the country, most of them to Uganda and Burundi, others to the Congo and Tanzania. Although some Tutsi do not hesitate to view the revolution as the first of the several genocides they have suffered at the hands of the Hutu, neither the scale nor the circumstances of the human losses have anything in common with the 1994 carnage.

Paradoxically, the exclusionary implications of the revolution were the flip side of its populist, egalitarian aspirations. The "emancipation" of the Hutu masses meant recognition of the claims of the humble and downtrodden—"le menu peuple," to use the self-description most frequently used by Hutu politicians—against the age-old domination of a "feudo-hamitic" monarchy. Though utterly oblivious of the rights of the minority, this revolutionary agenda attracted considerable sympathy and support from Brussels. It is noteworthy that the revolution got underway three years before the advent of independence in 1962; a successful transfer of power to Hutu politicians would have been unthinkable in the absence of the wholehearted support they received from the trusteeship authorities and the church. The tone of the revolution was populist and anti-feudal. Unlike most other varieties of African nationalism, its rhetoric was anything but anti-Western; its target was not the trusteeship authorities but the Tutsi-dominated Union Nationale Rwandaise (Unar), seen by Belgium as a dangerous radical movement, close to Lumumba's Mouvement National Congolais (MNC) and strategically allied to Communist China. In sum, to see in the Hutu revolution a tropical replica of Nazi revolutionary anti-Semitism makes little sense.

What does make sense is the perversion of the Hutu revolution into an increasingly anti-Tutsi crusade, culminating in the years following the RPF invasion with an outpouring of rabidly racist propaganda. It is tempting—but quite misleading—to explain the Rwanda genocide by projecting the events of 1994 into the past and infer therefrom an undiluted commitment to racism on the part of the Habyalimana regime and its predecessor under the presidency of Grégoire Kayibanda. To cite but one example, Peter Uvin refers to "the longstanding and deeply ingrained racism of Rwanda society," noting that "for decades Rwandan society has been profoundly racist. The image of the Tutsi as inherently evil and exploitative was, and still is, deeply rooted in the psyche of most Rwandans; this image was a founding pillar of the genocide to come."[13] This naively ahistorical view of the roots of the genocide makes short shrift of the fact that ethnic discrimination was indeed the hallmark of the traditional Tutsi monarchy long before it was appropriated by Hutu ideologues[14]—and suggests an obvious parallel with the Goldhagen argument: just as the Holocaust is historically linked to a long tradition of "eliminationist anti-Semitism,"[15] the Rwanda genocide is likewise anchored in a long-standing legacy of anti-Tutsi racism. This amounts to a gross oversimplification of a far more complex reality. Overt, officially sanctioned racism, as distinct from "anti-feudal" or "anti-monarchical" propaganda, was largely absent from the political discourse of Hutu revolutionaries in the 1950s. There was no *Mein Kampf* to provide ideological direction to the revolution, no Fuhrer to instill hatred in the minds of the masses, no *lebensraum* to justify conquest, and no Final Solution to deal with Tutsi threats—at least not until 1993, when the assassination of Melchior Ndadaye in Burundi set in motion a trend toward "cumulative radicalization," best illustrated by the rise of Hutu Power.

Anti-Tutsi sentiment has never been a constant in Rwanda history. It waxed and waned depending on the historical moment. The key variable was the salience of threat perceptions, a phenomenon closely linked to the political events in the region. Anti-Tutsi violence reached ominous proportions in 1963–64, in the wake of repeated attempts by Tutsi commandos—the so-called *inyenzi*, or "cockroaches" in Kinyarwanda—to fight their way back into the country.[16] The most disastrous of such raids occurred in December 1963, when a group of armed Tutsi refugees from Burundi nearly captured the capital city; in response, an estimated 5,000 Tutsi civilians were murdered by Hutu mobs in the Gikongoro prefecture. Ineffective though they were in bringing down the republic, the impact of these incursions on the radicalization of the Kayibanda regime has been profound. Several new elements, all of them harbingers of a future apocalypse, came into focus: (a) the growing identification of the enemies of the revolution with foreign enemies; (b) the conflation into the same subversive frame of exile and resident Tutsi elements, the latter supposedly acting as spies (*ibiyetso*) for the former; and (c) the radicalization of the domestic arena through the elimination of moderates.

The following years saw a distinct lowering of ethnic tension. As cross-border raids came to an end, so did anti-Tutsi violence—only to resurface immediately after the 1973 genocidal slaughter of Hutu by Tutsi in neighboring Burundi. Scores of Tutsi students were killed by their Hutu schoolmates in secondary schools and on the campus of the National University of Rwanda in Butare, causing another major exodus of Tutsi civilians to neighboring states. The 1973 pogroms played a major role in the army coup that brought Habyarimana to the presidency of the Second Republic and in vesting power in the hands of Hutu elites from the north. Possibly to enlist their support against its domestic opponents, the new regime at first showed unmistakable signs of sympathy towards the Tutsi minority. Few today seem to recall that in the years following his accession to power in 1973, President Habyarimana went to great lengths to integrate Tutsi elements into society and publicly stress the need for national reconciliation. In a 1976 document titled *Protocole de la Réconcilation Nationale entre les Rwandais*, written at the request of Habyalimana by a well-known Hutu politician, Joseph Gitera, a recurrent theme was the need to bring Tutsi, Hutu, and Twa in a common unifying ideological framework; a goal in keeping with the stated objective of the manifesto of the ruling party, the Mouvement National Révolutionnaire pour le Développement (MNRD).[17]

By the early 1990s, the government was faced with unprecedented challenges both from within and without. The plummeting of coffee prices sent the economy into a tailspin; the exigencies of structural adjustment placed further strains on the state; and famine conditions were reported in several southern prefectures, in turn intensifying the long-standing tensions between north and south. It was at this critical juncture, in a climate of rising tensions, that some 6,000 RPF troops, with considerable logistical and military support from Uganda, marched into northern Rwanda on October 1, 1990. Far from being viewed as a force dedicated to the overthrow of a dictatorship as they had hoped, the invaders were immediately perceived as Ugandan-supported counterrevolutionaries in league with a Tutsi fifth column inside Rwanda. Predictably, in a matter of weeks anti-Tutsi racism emerged full-blown. The ethnic cleansing of hundreds of Tutsi civilians in 1991 and 1992 were the premonitory signs of the 1994 apocalypse. The huge bloodletting—precipitated by the shooting down of the presidential plane carrying President Habyarimana and his Burundi counterpart, Cyprien Ntaramyira, on April 6, 1994—did not come to an end until a hundred days later, when the RPF finally seized power in Kigali. It is with reason that a retrospective homage is sometimes paid to the RPF for stopping the killings, but this does not detract from the fact that it bears much of the onus of responsibility for the carnage, for without the RPF invasion, there would have been no genocide.

The contrast with the wartime conditions ushered in by the Nazi invasion of Poland and the Soviet Union could not be clearer. Barbarossa was a war of conquest launched by the perpetrator state in the name of a racist ideology.[18] The invasion of Rwanda, on the other hand, immediately metamorphosed into a civil war in which the victims were, for the most part, ethnically identified with the invaders, not the perpetrators. The conflict was between Tutsi invaders anxious to overthrow a dictatorship (and return to their homeland) against Hutu defenders who saw in the invasion the fearsome prospect of a return to servitude.

Tempting though it may be in the light of these considerations to argue that in Rwanda genocide was brought onto themselves by the victims, this is far too simplistic as an explanation; in part because the Tutsi invaders were a very different group of people in terms of their history, social backgrounds, and generational ties from the victim group, namely, the resident Tutsi community of Rwanda; and because it ignores the crucial role played by Hutu extremists in the scuttling of the Arusha accords. Thus, in response to the argument that there would have been no genocide if the RPF had not invaded the country, one might argue with equal plausibility that there would have been no genocide had Hutu extremists not chosen the path of violence. Once this is said, the case of Rwanda comes as close as any other, and probably closer, to giving qualified validation to the provocation thesis.[19] For a more critical assessment of the provocation thesis, something must be said of the regional parameters of the Rwanda tragedy.

Intentionalist versus Functionalist Explanations

How much weight should one place on the intention to kill as against the chain of circumstances leading to the killings? This, in a nutshell, is the central question at the heart of the debates among German historians grappling with the roots of the Holocaust.

For the intentionalists, the role of Hitler in orchestrating mass murder is the irreducible, overriding element behind the annihilation of six million Jews; for the functionalists, "circumstance" is the key. Whereas some emphasize the significance of "cumulative radicalization" that stemmed from the incoherence of the Nazi state, or what Christopher Browning describes as "the chaotic decision-making process of a polycratic regime," others point to the disastrous consequences of Barbarossa.[20] As Arno Mayer puts it, "the radicalization of the war against the Jews correlated with the radicalization of the war against the Soviet Union."[21] An extreme and highly debatable interpretation is set forth by the most controversial of German historians, Ernst Nolte, in his book on Germany and the Cold War. For Nolte, the rise of anti-Semitism in its most murderous form is inseparable from the criminal record of Bolshevism during and after the Soviet revolution; anti-Semitism and fascism, according to this reasoning, were simply the means through which the German people were effectively mobilized against the external threat of communism. In Edouard Husson's words, for Nolte, "Hitler was, almost exclusively, an anti-Lenin."[22]

Such contrasting interpretations are directly relevant to Rwanda as they bring into focus two critical dimensions of analysis, one focusing on the role of the genocidal state, its ideologues, militias, and racist propaganda; the other drawing attention to the domestic and regional contexts in which the killings occurred. Although I am in general agreement with Christopher Browning and others who point out that the intentionalist and functionalist arguments are in some ways complementary rather than mutually exclusive, I would give considerably more merit to the former in explaining the Holocaust.

The intentionalist dimension of the Holocaust is nowhere more pithily captured than in the following quote from Ian Kershaw's magisterial history of the Third Reich:[23]

Never in history has such ruination—physical and moral—been associated with the name of one man. . . . Hitler's name justifiably stands for all time as that of the chief instigator of the most profound collapse of civilization in modern times. The extreme form of personal rule which an ill-educated beer hall demagogue and racist bigot, a narcissistic, megalomaniac, self-styled national savior was allowed to acquire and exercise in a modern, economically advanced, and cultured land known for its philosophers and poets was absolutely decisive in the terrible unfolding of events in those fateful twelve years. . . . Hitler was the chief inspirator of a genocide the like of which the world had never known, rightly to be viewed in coming times as a defining episode of the twentieth century.

Replacing the name of Hitler by that of Habyarimana and the Nazi regime by the Hutu regime can only convey a totally misleading view of the roots of the Rwanda bloodbath.

To emphasize Hitler's pivotal role in the extermination of Jews in no way diminishes the centrality of ideology; they are two sides of the same anti-Semitic coin. Yehuda Bauer's major difference between the Holocaust and other forms of genocide is that "pragmatic considerations were central with all other genocides, abstract ideological motivations less so."[24] This is where the Rwanda genocide deviates radically from the Holocaust: if by "pragmatic considerations" is meant a conscious attempt to counter the clear and present danger of a Tutsi take-over, these loomed considerably larger than ideological ones. It is not without reason, therefore, that Bauer views Rwanda as "a pragmatically motivated genocide."[25]

It is easy to see why some would find incongruous, if not downright offensive, the use of the term *pragmatic* to describe the monstrous crimes committed against innocent Tutsi civilians. All the more so when one considers the murderous role played by the Hutu-controlled media in fanning the flames of genocidal murder. Several observers have chronicled the outpouring of scurrilous accusations leveled against the Tutsi community through the airwaves of Radio Mille Collines and in the pages of Kangura.[26] Racist propaganda is not enough, however, to explain the spiral to murder. To leave out of the picture Hutu perceptions of the multiple threats to their security posed by Tutsi elements within and outside Rwanda is to miss the key factor that made Hutu extremists—and others—so receptive to rabidly racist propaganda.

Fear and hatred—both contributing, in Helen Fein's words, to place prospective victims "outside the universe of obligation"[27]—were crucial motives behind the Rwanda bloodbath. Behind the paranoid fears raised by the RPF invasion lay the widespread suspicion that Tutsi everywhere in the region were in league with the invaders. This is where the regional context played a major role in magnifying the threat posed by the RPF. Nowhere was the image of the Tutsi as the embodiment of a mortal danger more hauntingly evident than in Burundi, where Tutsi hegemony was achieved at considerable cost in human lives. From the assassination of Burundi's first Hutu prime minister (Pierre Ngendadumwe), in 1965, by a Tutsi refugee from Rwanda to the assassination of its first Hutu president (Melchior Ndadaye) in 1993, the history of the country is written in blood, mostly Hutu blood.[28]

The 1972 carnage marks a turning point in the escalation of ethnic violence in Burundi. In response to a local Hutu-sponsored insurgency, as many as 200,000 educated Hutu males, including university students and secondary school children, may have died at the hands of the all-Tutsi army. Surprisingly, little attention has been paid to this watershed event in the long chain of circumstances leading to the Rwanda tragedy. Whether referred to as partial genocide or selective genocide, the 1972 killings have been a pervasive presence in the historical memory of a great many Hutu through the entire region.[29] Nothing has had a more profound effect in crystallizing anti-Tutsi sentiment than the presence of those tens of thousands of Hutu refugees who sought asylum in Rwanda. This is even more true of the some 350,000 Hutu who fled Burundi into Rwanda after the assassination of Melchior Ndadaye in 1993. It is no coincidence if these were among the most dedicated murderers of Tutsi during the 1994 bloodbath.

Ethnic memories transcend boundaries. Just as the flow of Tutsi refugees into Burundi during the Rwanda revolution contributed in no small way to polarize Burundi society, the genocide of Hutu in Burundi served as a powerful magnifier of the danger posed by the RPF. What needs to be underscored is the consistency with which history has influenced the receptivity of the Hutu masses to anti-Tutsi propaganda: from the assassination of Ngendadumwe in 1965 to the assassination of Ndadaye in 1993, from the systematic elimination of scores of Hutu politicians in 1965 and 1969 to the 1972 genocide, and from the confiscation of the electoral victory of Hutu candidates in 1965 to the 1993 coup, the image of the Tutsi projected by the recent history of Burundi has been consistently threatening, whether as murderers of elected Hutu officials or genocidaires. The incredible fantasies conveyed by the Hutu-controlled media on the eve of the genocide are inseparable from their collective memory of past catastrophes.

To argue with Mark Levene that "there was at least a kernel of truth in the Hutu fear of the Tutsi" is, to say the least, an understatement.[30] Even more surprising is Yves Ternon's contention that "there has never been in Rwanda the threat of a seizure of power by the Tutsi, who only represent in 1994 10 percent of the population and have been persecuted for the last thirty years."[31] If anything, the deadly cross-border raids of the early 1960s, not to mention the invasion of October 1, 1990, suggest precisely the opposite. The fact is that by 1993, fear was omnipresent in many sectors of Rwanda society.

The introduction of multiparty elections in 1991 was the signal for a violent competition among rival Hutu parties; and as the Arusha talks conferred upon the RPF the status of a legitimate opposition party, another source of anxiety arose among MRND extremists: the ominous possibility that the Hutu opposition would work out a deal with the RPF to take over the state. All of this gives considerable plausibility to Jacques Semelin's proposition that "fear, exploited by propaganda, has played a fundamental role in the construction of a criminal project, a project subsequently implemented with method and organization."[32] The situation of collective psychosis arising from a political environment saturated with tension and chronic violence is a key element in the background of the 1994 catastrophe.

The comparison with the regional context of the Holocaust is instructive. For if there are ample grounds on which to disagree with Nolte that Nazism was in essence a response to the "class genocide" of the Bolsheviks, and the Holocaust a preemptive strike against the communist threat from the east, in Rwanda the perceived threats arising from both the domestic and regional environments were infinitely more substantial. One can only agree with Mark Levene that "the Nazi projection of threat (by contrast with the situation in Rwanda) remained entirely in the realms of fantasy."[33] By the same token, there are excellent reasons to question Alain Destexhe's dismissal of "background circumstances" as irrelevant to an understanding of the Rwanda genocide. "In Rwanda," writes Destexhe, "some commentators were very quick to explain that the killings were due to background 'circumstances': the war, the death of the Hutu president, the 'excesses of crowds gripped by fear and ancient hatred,' the 'justifiable anger of the people,' the 'provocations by the Tutsi' and their 'historical domination of the country,' etc. A consequence of this kind of reasoning is that 'collective guilt leaves us with no one to blame. . . . Therefore, so the argument continues, genocides and systematic massacres fall in the same category as volcanic eruptions or earthquakes.'"[34] Not only does attention to "circumstance" not rule out the apportionment of blame, it provides important clues to an understanding of the element of rationality underlying the motivation to kill.

The Rationality of Mass Murder

There is evidently more to genocide than a sudden outburst of murderous irrationality rooted in fear and prejudice. As Jacques Semelin reminds us, human beings are capable of committing the most heinous crimes to promote specific political objectives, for ideological reasons, to save their own lives, or because they feel they can act with impunity. These are some of the most disturbing facts brought out by students of genocide.[35] But what kind of rationality can conceivably explain the systematic extermination of six million Jews? Where is the logic behind the killing of hapless Tutsi civilians, men, women, and children, and the cold-blooded murder of one's nearest kin and neighbors?

The works of Hannah Arendt, Raul Hilberg, and Christopher Browning point to the vulnerability of "ordinary men" to the conditioning impact of racist propaganda, the polarizing effects of "race war," and the crushing weight of an all-embracing bureaucratic machinery.[36] Is there any reason to believe that the same forces that conspired to the extermination of Jews did not also operate in Rwanda? The answer must necessarily remain speculative. Nothing comparable to the sustained, empirically grounded research conducted by Hilberg and Brown is as yet available for Rwanda. Nonetheless, enough is known of the circumstances of the killings in Rwanda to suggest significant variations in the logic at work in each case.

Perhaps the most obvious refers to the greater salience of ideological motives in the planning and orchestration of the Holocaust. Without trying to minimize the impact of anti-Tutsi propaganda in the years following the RPF invasion, the impetus to kill all Tutsi cannot be traced to a long-standing ideological commitment. "What I view as singular about the Holocaust," Helen Fein writes, "is the length of warning time, its transnational scope and Hitler's announcement of his intention to eliminate the Jews two decades before their extermination."[37] None of these singularities applies to the case of Rwanda.

What, then, is the rationality that impelled tens of thousands of Hutu extremists to engage in mass murder? Taking a leaf from Yehuda Bauer, one might invoke "pragmatic" reasons, but the phrase is too vague to capture the different sets of actors involved at different junctures of the crisis and the diversity of their motives.

From the October 1990 invasion to April 1994, the overriding objective was to prevent the RPF from seizing power but throughout this period, recourse to violence served different intermediate goals.

The Instrumental Uses of Violence

It is useful to distinguish three phases in the sequence of violence leading to the ultimate carnage, each corresponding to separate but convergent motivations. During the first phase, stretching from October 1990 to the opening of the Arusha talks in August 1992, hundreds if not thousands of Tutsi civilians in the north and west of the country were massacred by youth groups (the infamous "réseau zero") acting under the supervision of communal authorities. The aim was essentially to physically eliminate those Tutsi elements who might join hands with the aggressors, while at the same time accelerate the polarization of as yet immobilized peasant communities. Contrary to an all-too-frequent opinion, the murder of Tutsi civilians was not a spontaneous mass phenomenon. It required the dismantling of interethnic social mechanisms for controlling the use of force, along with the manipulation of ethnic identities against a common enemy. The pattern revealed by the Kilibira, Bugogwe, and Bugesera massacres in 1991 is one in which trained activists were spurred on by state officials to engage in random acts of anti-Tutsi violence.

Next came the crucial period of the Arusha negotiations, from August 1992 to August 1993. The worst killings during that time occurred in the Gisenyi and Ruhengeri prefectures in February 1993, taking the lives of an estimated 300 Tutsi. The RPF responded by launching a massive and largely successful attack against government positions in the north, thus causing a temporary suspension of the peace talks. By then multiparty democracy had been formally endorsed by the Habyarimana government, and the civil war had given way to a long drawn-out negotiation among five different parties. The key players, the RPF and the MRND, were now joined by three opposition groups, the multiethnic PL, the MDR, with its roots in the south-central region, and the PSD. Significantly, the most rabidly anti-Tutsi party, the CDR, had been left out of the talks at the request of the RPF and was thus disqualified from participating in the so-called broadly based transitional government (BBTG) agreed upon in Arusha. The exclusion of the CDR, together with the rejection by its leadership and other extremist fringe groups of certain key provisions of the Arusha accords, were the decisive factors leading to the killing of Tutsi civilians in 1993. The aim, in short, was the scuttling of Arusha. The point has been conclusively demonstrated by Bruce Jones: referring to CDR extremists and hard-liners within the MRND, he notes that "these extremists reacted bitterly to the provisions of the Arusha accords which called for power-sharing and, especially, the integration of the armed forces.... The genocide was, in the first instance, an attempt by these extremists to maintain their power by destroying the Arusha accords and its supporters, including the moderates within the government parties who were among its first victims."[38]

Before the onset of mass murder, extremists had another practical purpose in mind: the use of force as a means of seizing power from their immediate Hutu competitors within and outside their respective political formations. *Ukubohoza*—liberation—the Kinyarwanda term to designate the campaign of violence directed by members of the opposition against the ruling MRND speaks volumes for the kind of rationality underlying the use of force.[39] *Intimidation* is a better word to describe the criminal activities orchestrated by the MDR in the south to wrest control, first from the local MRND cadres, then against the PSD, and ultimately against the Tutsi. The process is excellently analyzed by Alison Des Forges in her discussion of how the burgomaster of Nyakizu, Ladislas Ntaganza, managed to use every resource at his disposal, including force, to break the power of the MRND; then to turn against his former ally, the PSD; and ultimately to manipulate ethnic solidarity to enlist the support of Burundi refugees against the Tutsi: "Asked how to define the basis of Ntaganzwa's power, people said repeatedly and simply: fear."[40]

Much the same strategy was used by radical politicians to rid themselves of their moderate rivals within their own parties. As the date for the installation of the BBTG neared, intraparty competition for access to the transitional government became increasingly fierce, putting anti-Tutsi demagoguery at a premium. Nothing seemed to pay higher dividends than to accuse one's rival of being soft on the FPR. As anti-Tutsi rhetoric picked up momentum, so did violence. Before long, every opposition party (except the PSD) was split right down the middle between radicals and moderates. The result, in the words of Vincent Ntezimana, a leading MDR personality, was "l'éclatement de l'opposition pacifique."[41]

The phenomenon is directly linked to the emergence of Hutu Power (locally referred to as Hutu Pawa), a label that came to designate extremists across a wide spectrum—not just CDR or MRND fanatics but anti-Tutsi zealots within the PL and the MDR. The precipitating factor leading to the birth of Hutu Power was the assassination of President Ndadaye in Burundi. As Alison Des Forges puts it, "The movement known as Hutu Power, the coalition that would make the genocide possible, was built on Ndadaye's corpse."[42] News of Ndadaye's death had an immediate and devastating impact on Hutu attitudes. Almost overnight, many moderates turned into radicals and radicals, into Hutu power extremists; and those who did not were as likely as not to be faced with accusations of disloyalty (*ibisiyo*). Ndadaye's death made a chimera of the implementation of the Arusha accords and with the flood of Hutu refugees from Burundi fleeing into southern Rwanda, anti-Tutsi sentiment gathered fresh momentum, driving home what many already suspected: "You simply cannot trust the Tutsi."

The Security Dilemma

The crash of the presidential plane, on April 6, 1994, took the lives of two Hutu presidents, Habyarimana of Rwanda and Cyprien Ntaramyira of Burundi, bringing to three the total of Hutu presidents killed in six months. Although responsibility for the shooting down of Habyalimana's plane remains a mystery, few Hutu doubted that the RPF was directly implicated. In an atmosphere already saturated with fear and uncertainty it is easy to see why Hutu extremists quickly yielded to their long-standing plan of using force preemptively. By shooting down Habyalimana's plane, the RPF made dramatically clear that it was about to strike first; rather than wait for Kagame to preempt; for Hutu extremists in the government and the army, the exigencies of security—indeed survival—called for an immediate response. The decision to apply the full force of genocidal violence against all Tutsi, as well as every Hutu suspected of Tutsi sympathies, stemmed from a straightforward, rational choice proposition: either we kill them first, or else we'll be killed. Thus framed, the logic of the "security dilemma" left no alternative but to annihilate the enemies of the nation.

The argument that crisis situations generate irrational fears that are rationally exploited by perpetrators of mass violence is nowhere more dramatically illustrated than by the renewed outpouring of racist propaganda, diffused through Kigali's hate-radio, in the days following the crash. In drawing attention to the critical nexus between irrational fears and the rational manipulation of such fears, Rothchild and Groth give us a clue to an understanding of how the shooting down of Habyarimana's plane played into extremist hands: "Ethnic psychosis may create rational opportunities . . . this kind of atmosphere, quintessentially irrational, is paradoxically compatible with a perfectly rational exploitation of mass psychosis by communal brokers and entrepreneurs."[43] The entrepreneurs of death saw their opportunity and proceeded to exploit it to the full: the global targeting of all Tutsi as the common enemy went hand in hand with the setting in motion of the institutional machinery of murder, of which the key elements were the prefectoral and communal cadres and militias.

The Grassroots Killers

Tempting though it is to portray all "grassroots killers"[44] as zombies mechanically responding to orders from above, reality on the ground tells a more complex story. Admittedly, much more research is needed before we get a coherent picture of the full range of motives that led the lower-echelon genocidaires to kill friends and neighbors, as well as relatives; there is as yet too little of the kind of fine-grained, local-level investigation conducted by Alison Des Forges in the prefectures of Gikongoro and Butare. Relatively little is known of the dynamics at work in regional arenas.

What is reasonably clear, however, is that we are here dealing with very different kinds of phenomena from those so carefully analyzed by Christopher Browning in his groundbreaking work, *Ordinary Men*. For if the men of Reserve Police Battalion 101 killed for reasons that had little to do with the threat of sanctions, and more to do with peer pressure, careerism, and self-serving ambition, the same is not true of the grassroots killers in Rwanda. Many Hutu were driven to kill their Tutsi neighbors because they knew they had no other option; refusal to comply meant that they themselves would be killed the next day.

Again, while there is reason to agree with Browning that the psychological constraints of binding orders were little more than a convenient alibi for the men of Battalion 101 and notwithstanding Stanley Milgram's assertions to the contrary,[45] in the case of Rwanda, the culture of obedience cannot be dismissed out of hand. Several commentators have correctly emphasized the extent to which conformity is a dominant trait of Rwandan political culture. People, whether Hutu or Tutsi, rarely challenge authority. Compliance with orders from above is part and parcel of what Filip Reyntjens describes as "social conformism": "many Rwandans tend to do what their neighbours do or what a person of authority tells them to do."[46] Not every Hutu fits the pattern of Milgramite robots, however; indeed, many took great risks to save the lives of their Tutsi neighbors. As reported by Des Forges, "some Hutu tried to protect their Tutsi neighbours, particularly those to whom they were bound by the ties of marriage, clientage, or long-standing friendships. Other Hutu opposed the killings on the grounds of principle."[47] Sometimes, the killing of one Tutsi, unknown to the killer, did not prevent the same individual from going to great lengths to save the life of a Tutsi friend. Clearly, the "culture of conformity" argument cannot be accepted without strong qualifications, but the fact remains that it has a far greater explanatory force in Rwanda than in Nazi Germany.

Given the extreme poverty of the country, among the poorest of the poor, it goes without saying that economic motivations loomed infinitely larger in Rwanda than in Nazi Germany. That some Hutu killed for no other reason than to pillage and loot Tutsi property is well established. "The killers pillaged the goods of their victims," writes Alison Des Forges, "whether Tutsi in flight or local residents. One witness recounts seeing 'people returning from Nkakwa with bags of beans, clothing, mats.... One man came by with cushions for a couch. He had six of them. He wanted to sell them to buy beer.... People were returning with things which they had found free. There was no punishment. It was like a festival.'"[48] Nor were wealthy Hutu necessarily safe. In those northern communes where land hunger was especially acute, scores of landowning Hutu were killed by their landless kinsmen. In many instances, the dynamics of grassroots murder were closely related to intraethnic class differences and with land ownership; rather than ethnicity being the key determinant of the victim's identity. Nonetheless, as reported by Maurice Niwese, cases occurred where putting a Tutsi label on a wealthy Hutu served to legitimize the theft of his/her property.[49]

Finally, and most importantly, many Hutu became killers because of an enduring sense of ethnic hatred born of the sufferings and hardships they experienced at the hands of the RPF. I refer to the hundreds of thousands of internally displaced persons from the north, who were driven from their homes by the advancing RPF army. After the RPF offensive of February 1993, an estimated one million were forced out of their homelands and regrouped into some forty IDP camps. As James Gasana noted, the IDPs were "explicitly targeted by the RPF rebellion, expelled from their homes and continuously shot at in the camps to force them to move farther into the government-controlled zone"; the result was entirely predictable: "families were separated and scattered ... health centers were overwhelmed, mortality increased; suspension of schooling and lack of occupation for the young led to increased delinquency and crime." Speaking of the "social, environmental and political problems caused by the huge displacement of civilian populations between 1990 and 1994," the same observer draws attention to "the singular contribution" of the IDP phenomenon to the "combustion of ethnicity."[50] Even more decisive was the contribution of the young IDPs to the ranks of the MRND militia, the *interahamwe*. It is hardly a matter of coincidence if among the scores of young thugs manning the checkpoints of the capital, the vast majority were recruited among the IDPs of Nyacinga camp, near Kigali. Seething hatred of every Tutsi in sight, rather than greed or binding orders, is what lay behind the scenes of mayhem in Kigali, Butare, and Gikongoro.

What all this adds upto is a picture of considerable complexity. The killings cannot be reduced to any single motive. The circumstances that caused Hutu to become killers differed from prefecture to prefecture, sometimes from commune to commune, and although anti-Tutsi propaganda played an important role in driving the genocidaires to murder, its impact varied widely from one sector of Hutu society to another. Rather than being the result of a genocidal Leviathan orchestrating the killings from above, the carnage is better seen as the work of key "patrons" or big men, within the army and the government, each trying to make the most of their privileged access to the militias, prefects, and burgomasters to mobilize the masses behind the killing machine.[51]

Impunity: A Common Denominator

Reflecting on the lessons of Bosnia and Rwanda, Helen Fein brings to light yet another rational dimension behind the horrors of mass murder. "Genocide is preventable," she writes, "because it is usually a rational act: that is, the perpetrators calculate the likelihood of success, given their values and objectives."[52] Certainly, no one familiar with the extent of French complicity during the Rwanda bloodbath, or indeed with the extraordinary indifference of the international community in both Rwanda and Bosnia, can avoid the conclusion that the organizers of the killings entertained few doubts that they could literally get away with murder. The French patron was seen as offering a diplomatic guarantee of impunity as well as the military and financial means with which to prosecute the carnage.

France's patron role in Rwanda finds a parallel of sorts in the supportive part played by Germany during the Armenian genocide. In his discussion of "German complicity" in the Armenian genocide of 1915–16, Manus Midlarsky writes that "the Berlin-Baghdad railway, the symbol and reality of Germany's extension of influence into the Middle East, of course depended on continued Ottoman cooperation, made easier, in the German view, by complicity in the genocide of the Armenians."[53] In the same vein, Norman Naimark points out that "The Germans themselves had played a central role in the Young Turk administration, and a number of Wehrmacht generals had earlier served as advisors to the Ottoman forces during the war. Some German officers may even have played a role in the Armenian genocide itself."[54]

But even in the absence of an external patron to assist the genocidaires, the sheer passivity or indifference of the international community can be interpreted as a tacit approval of their plans. Rwanda and Bosnia are cases in point, but so is Germany in the thirties; although signs of Hitler's genocidal designs could be detected as early as the 1920s and 1930s, France and Great Britain found in their appeasement policies the justification they needed to refrain from intervening.

If impunity is indeed the rational foundation for genocidaires to become recidivists, public indifference goes a long way to explain impunity. One of the lessons of history that has yet to sink in is that unpunished crimes can provide a precedent for later crimes. In 1939, addressing a group of Nazi leaders and Wehrmacht generals, Hitler is reported to have said, "Who, after all, speaks today about the annihilation of the Armenians?"[55] Could some Hutu in Rwanda have referred to the 1972 bloodbath in Burundi in similar terms?

The first step to prevent the recurrence of genocide is to see to it that the perpetrators are brought to justice and meted out a punishment proportional to their crimes. But as Leo Kuper reminded us many years ago, the sanction of immunity afforded by the concept of national sovereignty is not the least of the obstacles in the way of sanctions. Helen Fein puts it even more graphically: "Abusive powers will continue to abuse as long as it works: the movement to change the taken-for-granted assumption that sovereignty implies indifference to out neighbors' crimes . . . is still to emerge from gestation in images of mass flight, chaos, blood, and death."[56]

One final note: to bring an end to impunity is one thing, just how to calibrate the scale and severity of the punishment is another matter. This is where the Holocaust holds a lesson for the rulers of Rwanda. The men most directly responsible for planning and implementing the Holocaust—some thirty people altogether—were identified, tried, and sentenced to die. Although some have argued that the punishment decreed at Nurenberg was disgracefully benign in view of the magnitude of the crime, and that those elements who escaped punishment hardly became pillars of democracy, there is another side to the coin that must be looked at. Can one imagine what the effect would have been on the German people and the future of democracy in Germany had every German involved in the Holocaust, at one level or another, or in one capacity or another, been brought to justice and condemned? Had tens of thousands been sent to the gallows, as some had wished, one wonders whether Germany would have become a flourishing democracy, or would have experienced much success in coming to terms with its past. In Rwanda today, very few of the "brains" behind the genocide have been identified, and none of those currently in detention in Arusha have been dealt a death sentence; meanwhile, scores of mid-level killers have been tried in Kigali and inflicted the death sentence, while some 130,000 Hutu suspected of participating in the killings are still languishing in jail, seven years later. The least that can be said is that the prospects for national reconciliation in such circumstances seem very remote. This is yet another difference from the Holocaust, and perhaps not the least consequential.

Chapter 9
Burundi 1972: A Forgotten Genocide

> *Through the spring and summer of 1972, in the obscure Central African state of Burundi, there took place the systematic killing of as many as a quarter million people. Even among the awesome calamities of the last decade, the tragedy in Burundi was extraordinary in impact and intensity. Though exact numbers can never be known, most eyewitnesses agree that over a four-month period, men, women and children were savagely murdered at the rate of more than a thousand a day. It was, wrote United Nations observers, a staggering disaster.*
> —Passing By: The United States and Genocide in Burundi, 1972 *(Carnegie Endowment for International Peace, 1973), p. 1.*

Thirty-five years ago Burundi was the scene of a horrific bloodletting when from late April to September 1972 anywhere from 200,000 to 300,000 Hutu were massacred by a Tutsi-dominated army. When the slaughter stopped, most of the educated adult Hutu males were either dead or in exile. From this appalling surgery emerged a state entirely dominated by Tutsi elements from the south, the so-called Tutsi-Hima. For the next seventeen years, Tutsi hegemony remained unchallenged.[1]

Outside a small circle of Africanists and genocide scholars, who in the West remembers this tragedy? To speak of a forgotten genocide is hardly an exaggeration. Compared to the sustained media hype attracted by the Rwanda bloodbath, the 1972 killings in Burundi received precious little press coverage and even less scholarly attention.[2]

This is all the more surprising considering the highly emotional reaction of the White House at the time. Indeed, one person who remembered the Burundi tragedy long after its occurrence was Richard Nixon. After receiving a rather bland, non-committal memo from Henry Kissinger, briefly stating the scale of the killings, and noting that neither the USSR nor the People's Republic of China (PRC) was involved, thus posing no threat to U.S. interests, Nixon flew into a rage. His handwritten reaction, scribbled on the memo, conveys something of his anger:

This is one of the most cynical, callous reactions of a great government to a terrible human tragedy I have seen. When the Paks try to put down a rebellion in

Map 4. Burundi. Map no. 3753, rev. 6, United Nations, September 2004. Reproduced by permission of the UN Department of Peacekeeping Operations, Cartographic Section.

East Pakistan, the world screams. When Indians kill a few thousand Paks, no one cares. Biafra stirs us because of Catholics; the Israeli Olympics because of Jews; the North Vietnam bombings because of Communist leanings in our establishment. But when 100,000 (one third of the people of a black country) are murdered, we say and do nothing, because we must not make blacks look bad (except, of course, when Catholic blacks are killed). I do not buy this double standard. Tell the weak sisters in the African Bureau of State to give a recommendation as to how we can at least show moral outrage. And let's begin by calling our Ambassador immediately for consultation. Under no circumstances will I appoint a new Ambassador to present credentials to these butchers.[3]

Whatever else can be said of Nixon's outburst, it provides a jarring note to the seeming indifference of the American public at the time. Today, even among those who claim awareness of what happened, the term "massacre" is the preferred label, as if the use of the G-word in this context might suggest an equivalence with the vastly more destructive Rwandan bloodbath. Adding to the opaqueness of the phenomenon, until recently every effort was made by the Burundi authorities to erase from public memory all references to 1972, whether as genocide or as massacre.

Seen in comparative perspective, the events of 1972 raise important questions: In what sense could they be described as genocide? To what extent is reluctance to use the G-word the result of deliberate obfuscation or semantic manipulation? How does comparison with Rwanda help comprehend the dynamics of mass murder in Burundi, and vice versa? And what does it tell us about the nature of the post-genocidal state?

Manufacturing the Truth

Given the lack of a common consensus among scholars as to what really constitutes genocide, there is no precise answer to the first question—only tentative approximations of whether the criteria one chooses are met in any given case. In what must be seen as a landmark in the field of genocide studies, Jacques Sémelin has gone further than most in discriminating between mass murders, massacres, and ethnic cleansing, on the one hand, and genocide on the other.[4] Rather than take the scale of the killings as a key variable, he argues, the dynamics of violence offers a more reliable guide for differentiating between ethnic cleansing and genocide. Unlike ethnic cleansing, which seeks to purify and expel, genocide involves the planned annihilation of a group as ethnically, culturally, or religiously distinct, and for no other reason than it is perceived as a vector of social contamination. The targeted group takes on the quality of the unacceptable other—*l'autre en trop*. The aim is to eradicate in order to purify (p. 413). It allows for no exit. In contrast with the mass murders committed in the USSR under Stalin, he argues, where violence was targeted against all suspected enemies in order to enforce submission, in the case of genocidal murders committed in Armenia, Nazi Germany, or Rwanda, the aim is excision. In one case, the mere fact of incarceration is deemed sufficient proof of guilt; in the other culpability is rooted in identity.

In Burundi, global eradication of an entire ethnic community was not on the killers' agenda. The principal target were civil servants, educated males, including the near totality of the secondary school population, and university students. On the other hand, there can be no doubt about the intent of the Burundi authorities to annihilate a major segment of the Hutu population, solely because of their "Hutuness," irrespective of whether they posed a threat to society or the government. That a genocide happens to be selective does not make it less of a genocide. To borrow Robert Melson's distinction,[5] whereas Rwanda offers the clearest example of a total genocide, Burundi can best be described as a partial genocide. To invoke this distinction to deny the genocidal quality of the Burundi killings strikes me as singularly disingenuous—and when the deniers happen to be of Jewish origins, as surprisingly incongruous.

It is one thing to eschew the use of the G-word on definitional grounds, and quite another to do so for political or ideological reasons. This is where some disturbing parallels emerge between Rwanda and Burundi. In both instances, perpetrators have insistently denied the reality of planned murder. For many Hutu extremists in Rwanda, including officials directly involved in the process of extermination, the carnage was a spontaneous outburst of collective anger against the Tutsi invaders, entirely beyond the control of government authorities. In Burundi the standard argument heard in official Tutsi circles was that the only génocidaires were the Hutu insurgents and that in taking immediate steps to stop the bloodshed, the government saved the country from the horrors of what surely would have been a genocide of Tutsi.

Again, in the months following the assassination of the first popularly elected Hutu president, Melchior Ndadaye, on October 23, 1993, a recurrent theme in the official propaganda was that the only genuine genocide recorded in the country's history was the planned extermination of Tutsi civilians in the wake of Ndadaye's murder.[6] Imputing genocidal intentions to the victims has been a constant leitmotiv of Tutsi politicians and at least one well-known European historian, Jean-Pierre Chrétien.

Much the same tendency to shift responsibility away from themselves can be seen among Hutu extremists in Rwanda when they refer to Kagame as a genocidaire, or when they claim that a double genocide was committed, one against the Hutu another against the Tutsi. At issue here is not so much the crimes imputed to Kagame, for these are well established, but whether these can be described as genocide.

Unlike what happened in Rwanda, in Burundi the perpetrators won the day. In such circumstances, contesting the official version of the killings entails risks. No effort was made at the time by the international community to call for an investigation of the killings. No international tribunal ever materialized. Until the publication in 2007 of the thorough inquest by Jean-Pierre Chrétien and Jean-Francois Dupaquier,[7] the principal source information about the circumstances of the killings were the stories told by Hutu exiles and missionaries, not the ideal outlet for piecing together a coherent picture of what actually happened. Small wonder if the corpus of reliable data for Burundi does not come anywhere near the massive outpour of literature on Rwanda.

The manufacturing of an official truth by the winning party is a characteristic shared both by the Rwanda government under Kagame and its counterpart in post-genocide Burundi, under President Michel Micombero. Just as in Rwanda the winner's truth has served as a screen for concealing the crimes committed by Kagame's RPF, so also with the abominations perpetrated by President Micombero's army twenty-two years earlier. Nonetheless, there is no equivalent in Burundi for the extent of disinformation displayed by the Kagame regime since coming to power in July 1994. Only recently has the responsibility of the RPF in triggering the carnage been reasonably well established, thanks to the remarkably detailed accounts authored by dissident elements of the RPF, notably Lt. Abdul Joshua Ruzibiza.[8] From the crushing body of evidence gathered in his narrative, Ruzibiza conclusively demonstrates the participation of RPF units in the killing of hundreds of thousands of Hutu civilians in Rwanda and eastern Congo, as well as Kagame's personal responsibility in the shooting down of Habyalimana's plane.[9] There is nothing comparable to Ruzibiza's chilling exposé when it comes to Burundi.

Rwanda and Burundi: Comparative Perspectives

For all the distortions and lacunae surrounding the Burundi tragedy, certain facts are beyond controversy.[10] The following are worth noting:

- Whereas the victims belonged overwhelmingly to the Hutu majority, the perpetrators were drawn from a specific segment of the Tutsi minority, the Tutsi-Hima, the real holders of power at the time; they are heavily concentrated in the south, in the province of Bururi, and are culturally distinct from the northern-based and socially "higher-up" Tutsi-Banyaruguru.

- The killings occurred in response to a localized, Hutu-led insurgency, presumably involving the participation of Congolese elements (often mistakenly referred to as "Mulelistes"); hundreds or perhaps thousands of Tutsi civilians were massacred by the insurgents.
- The repression of the insurgency—and the subsequent massive elimination of Hutu civilians—was largely conducted by government troops, assisted by the youth wing of the ruling party, Uprona, and by an unknown number of Tutsi refugees from Rwanda.
- In the wake of the slaughter, hundreds of thousands of Hutu men, women, and children fled the country, seeking asylum in neighboring states, most of them in Tanzania and Rwanda. The most militantly anti-Tutsi party, the Palipehutu was born in 1980 in a refugee camp (Mishamo) in Tanzania. What might be called the "Palipehutist" streak in Burundi politics is still visible today in the radical, violently anti-Tutsi ideology of the FNL.

This brief summary is enough to suggest a number of significant points of convergence with Rwanda.

For one thing, both genocides can best be described, in Helen Fein's terminology, as *retributive genocides,* coming about in response to perceived threats to the state: in Rwanda, the menace stemmed from an invasion of armed Tutsi refugees under the banner of RPF on October 1, 1990, whereas in Burundi, the outbreak of a Hutu-led insurgency on April 29, 1972 in the regions of Nyanza Lac and Rumonge was immediately seen as a clear and present danger by the Bujumbura authorities. Retribution rather than ideology must be seen as the primary motivation behind the killings.

In both instances, exclusion was the underlying factor behind the threats posed to the state: in one case suppression of all meaningful opportunities for Hutu politicians to participate in their own government; in the other, denial of the Tutsi community in exile to return home and become full citizens of Rwanda and continued imposition of a second-rate citizenship status for the resident Tutsi community. The exclusionary implications of what Leo Kuper calls "plural societies" are a central element in the background of genocide in each state.

In each case, episodic massacres served as the harbingers of a more deadly crisis. Scores of Hutu intellectuals and politicians were killed in Burundi in October 1965 in the wake of a bungled Hutu-led coup against the royal palace, the latter motivated by the refusal of the monarchy to acknowledge the victory of Hutu candidates in the legislative elections of May 1965. Again, in September 1969, allegations of an impending coup led to the arrest and execution of scores of influential Hutu personalities in the army and the government. In Rwanda, an aborted raid by Tutsi refugees from Burundi in December 1963 led to an exceptionally brutal reaction, resulting in the deaths of an estimated 10,000 Tutsi civilians. The history of violence in each state thus confirms the proposition that genocide is the culmination of preexisting outbursts targeted against specific communities.

In each state, the key participants in the killings were army units and youth groups affiliated with the ruling party, the Jeunesses Révolutionnaires Rwagasore (JRR) in Burundi and the *interahamwe* in Rwanda; identified respectively with the Uprona and the MNRD. Furthermore, a number of refugees also joined the killing spree. Just as in Rwanda scores of Hutu refugees from Burundi turned against Tutsi civilians, so also in Burundi, where Tutsi refugees from the 1959–62 revolution in Rwanda, lent a helping hand to the killers. Just how many were involved is impossible to tell, though there are reasons to believe that the refugee presence in the ranks of the génocidaires loomed far larger in Rwanda. The point to be stressed is that the multiplicity of actors in each state also points to a variety of motives, ranging from vengeance to blind obedience, from fear to greed, and from ethnic hatred to ideological militancy.

In some major respects, however, the Rwanda context stands conspicuously apart from that of Burundi. Only in Rwanda do we find a textbook illustration of the thesis advanced by Robert Melson that a revolutionary heritage, coupled with a civil war, are the quintessential factors associated with genocide. Rwanda is one of the very few states on the continent to have experienced a genuine revolution (as distinct from a mere turnover of personnel in office). Only if we remember the magnitude of the stakes involved in this unique event, and what a return of Tutsi rule really meant—in symbolic, as well as economic and political terms—can we grasp the sheer brutality of the violence unleashed against the Tutsi minority. Again, the horrors committed by both sides during the three-year civil war must be seen as a key contributory factor to the genocide.

Not only was Burundi spared a civil war—the overthrow of the monarchy on November 26, 1966, by Captain Micombero, was little more than a palace revolution—but the essential goal of every Tutsi-dominated government since independence was to prevent a Rwanda-type revolution from happening. Burundi was the archetype of the counterrevolutionary state. And while the country did indeed sink into a long bitter civil strife after Ndadaye's assassination, at no time before the 1972 carnage did Burundi experience violence on scale comparable to Rwanda. That Melson's conditions failed to materialize in Burundi does not mean that the genocide label does not apply; all it means is that we are dealing with a case that departs significantly from that of Rwanda.

There is yet another way in which Burundi stands apart from Rwanda: in the chain of events leading to the crisis there is nothing remotely comparable to the critical part played by the shooting down of President Juvenal Habyalimana's plane on April 6, 1994 in triggering the bloodbath. What Sémelin calls "le passage à l'acte"—the transition from the will to kill to the act of killing—stemmed from a radically different set of circumstances.

Le passage à l'acte

The outbreak of the Hutu insurrection on April 29 was the precipitant that led to the killings. In a matter of hours, terror was unleashed by roving bands of Hutu against Tutsi civilians. Countless atrocities were reported by eyewitnesses. In Bururi all military and civilian authorities were killed. After seizing control of the armories in Rumonge and Nyanza-Lac, the insurgents proceeded to kill every Tutsi in sight, along with a number of Hutu who refused to join the rebellion. A plausible estimate would put the number of Tutsi civilians killed at anywhere from 1,000 to 2,000. At this point, in an attempt to build a political base, the insurgents retreated to the locality of Vyanda, near the provincial capital of Bururi, and proclaimed a mysterious *République de Martyazo*. A week later government troops brought the experiment to an end. Meanwhile, on May 30, after proclaiming martial law, President Micombero requested immediate military assistance from President Mobutu. With Congolese paratroopers holding the airport, the Burundi army moved in force into the countryside. What followed was not so much a repression as a hideous slaughter of Hutu civilians. The carnage went on unabated through the month of August. By then virtually every educated Hutu element, down to secondary school students, was either dead or in flight.

The following excerpts from the cables sent by the deputy chief of mission (DCM) at U.S. embassy in Bujumbura, Michael Hoyt, give us a sense of the pervasive fear that gripped the country in the weeks following the insurgency: May 25, "a missionary from the interior fears Hutu may be reaching the breaking point . . . increasing number of educated Hutu in eastern Burundi have fled toward Tanzania;" May 26, "no respite, no letup. What apparently is a genocide continues. Arrests going on around the clock. Charge d'affaires' laundry boy fled JRR band last night, says they are killing most Hutu on the spot." July 11, "Tutsi reprisals unabated in the interior but have slackened somewhat in Bujumbura . . . in the north the Hutu take cover upon arrival of any vehicle, reflective pervasive fear. Tutsi continue to be haunted by fear for their own survival no matter how casually they may saunter around"; July 21, "in two days following July 14 three new ditches filled with Hutu bodies near Bujumbura airport. Arrests have continued throughout the week in Bujumbura, in the hills around town, in Ngozi region and in central Burundi.

Military units sent north of Bubanza to carry out widespread organized reprisals."[11] Furthermore, adds a cable of July 25, "Repression against Hutu is not simply one of killing. It is also an attempt to remove them from access to employment, property, education and the general chance to improve themselves."[12]

It is not a matter of coincidence if the outbreak of the insurrection occurred when a crisis of unprecedented proportions pitted one group of Tutsi elites (the southern-based Hima) against another (the Banyaruguru). In the months preceding the slaughter, the country seemed to be tottering on the brink of anarchy, with the long-simmering struggle between them threatening to get out of hand. Already in July 1971, charges of conspiracy were brought against a group of leading Banyaruguru and on January 14, 1972, a military tribunal issued nine death sentences (four officers and nine civilians) and seven life sentences against them. On the eve of the insurrection, the country was awash with rumors of plots and counterplots. The ruling Hima clique, headed by Micombero, saw its legitimacy plummet. Nothing could have done more to solidify Tutsi solidarities than the looming threat of a violent Hutu uprising.

In addition to the two-fold threat of a Hutu rebellion and a Banyaruguru-instigated coup, the return to Burundi of the deposed king (*mwami*), Charles Ndizeye, appeared to pose yet another challenge to the regime. His tragic fate bears testimony to the fear he inspired: seen as a potential rallying point for the Hutu masses (and a strong candidate to defend the cause of the Banyuruguru), the deposed king was assassinated in Gitega at the very outset of the rebellion.[13]

It was in this context of crisis and fear that the decision was made to set in motion a process of extermination that would effectively remove the Hutu threat for the next fifteen years, along with the monarchical threat, and pave the way for a restoration of Tutsi unity in the face of a common danger.

In his captivating discussion of what he terms "le dispositif de bascule dans le meurtre de masse," Sémelin shows how potential killers become génocidaires in response to the self-reinforcing pressures of vertical and horizontal nets, how once they are caught in this infernal machine—*l'engrenage*—the act of killing becomes thinkable, realizable, eventually an almost routine activity. Though little is known of the organizational underpinnings of the killings that went on in the countryside, the evidence available from the U.S. embassy cables and other sources shows that the military provided the essential command structure, whereas the JRR served as the horizontal network through which individuals of the same ethnic background, age group, and ideological persuasion forged new bonds of solidarity in their common involvement in the act of killing. Writing in 1967, this is how a Belgian journalist described the JRR: "These young men, generally without weapons, set up roadblocks, stop traffic, sometimes for days, molest, insult, kidnap their political rivals, without eliciting much of a reaction from the government authorities, who seem to fear them. Escaping all means of control . . . they constitute a readily available social net (masse de maneuvre) which could easily turn against their leaders, but meanwhile accept to perform on their behalf all kinds of criminal acts."[14] By 1972, the JRR had effectively morphed into gangs of killers.

The principal architect of the killings, however, was not an army man but a high-ranking civil servant, Arthémon Simbananiye, Minister of Justice in the Micombero government, and since then retooled into a "born again Christian." It was the same Simbananiye who reportedly admitted at the height of the massacres, "at least we'll have peace for the next thirty years." Apocryphal or not, the statement clearly conveys the fear shared by many Tutsi that their survival was at stake. Central to the rationalization that presided over the killings lay the conviction that the physical elimination of Hutu was the only practical course of action for ensuring the survival of the Tutsi minority.

Are we then dealing with a concerted attempt to enforce submission or should it be described as a case of eradication, to use Sémelin's distinction? Probably both. Only through the eradication of tens of thousands of their kinsmen would future generations of Hutu learn to accept submission as the lesser of two evils. Exactly where submission ends and eradication begins, as key features in the dynamics of violence, is a moot point.

Although the killings were intended first and foremost to crush the insurrection, there was a great deal more at stake. The underlying objectives of the government in orchestrating the huge bloodletting were (a) to ensure long-term stability of the state through the wholesale elimination of all educated Hutu elites and potential elites, (b) to transform the instruments of force—army, police, and gendarmerie—into a Tutsi monopoly, (c) to rule out the possibility of a return to the monarchy (hence the killing of King Ntare in Gitega on May 1), and (d) to create a new basis of legitimacy for the Hima-dominated state by projecting the image of the state as the protector of all Burundians against their domestic and external foes. On each count Micombero's policy of prophylactic elimination met with considerable success. For the next sixteen years, Burundi experienced unprecedented peace. The country was by now virtually bereft of educated Hutu elites. The ever-present threat of another bloodbath discouraged all forms of protest. From a fragile edifice threatened from within and without, the state had now become the all-powerful, unchallenged instrument of Tutsi hegemony.

The Regional Fall-Out

A retrospective look at the regional context brings into focus the wider implications of the crisis. It calls attention to a central feature of the historic relationships between Rwanda and Burundi, that is, the back-and-forth dialectic by which ethnic conflict in one state impacts upon the other, a phenomenon already discernible in the "self-fulfilling prophecy" unfolding in the years immediately following their independence.[15] As has been noted time and again, the Rwanda revolution had a profound effect on the hardening of the ethnic fault line in Burundi, as it provided the nascent Hutu elites in Bujumbura with a republican model to emulate, and the Tutsi with a nightmare scenario to be avoided at all costs, by force if need be. This nightmarish vision of the Hutu insurrection as the first step toward the proclamation of a Hutu-dominated republic certainly loomed large in the spectrum of motives that led to the carnage. And it also figured prominently behind the extensive purges of 1965 and 1969.

In Rwanda the backlash of the 1972 killings took the form of violent anti-Tutsi pogroms in secondary schools and at the University of Rwanda, resulting in scores of victims. The growing unrest and incitements to violence by Hutu politicians were the pretexts for the seizure of power by a group of officers from the north, under the leadership of Juvenal Habyalimana. The events of 1972 in Burundi thus played an important, though indirect, part in bringing about the birth of the Second Republic and by the same token, in helping bring about a shift of power away from the south-central region (Nduga) to the north (Kiga). One can only speculate as to what would have been the fate of Rwanda if the northerners had not seized power. Even though the culturally distinct Kiga are in general notoriously more distrustful of Tutsi than the southern Hutu, this is hardly sufficient evidence for arguing a direct causal relationship between 1972 and 1994.

Once this is said, there can be little doubt that memories of the Burundi carnage must have contributed to the radicalization of anti-Tutsi sentiment in Rwanda. Relayed by the tens of thousands of Hutu refugees who found asylum in Rwanda, stories of atrocities committed by the Tutsi army found a receptive audience on the hills and in the bars of the capital. The fresh outflow of refugees caused by the "incidents" of Ntega and Marangara in 1988, when thousands were killed by Tutsi soldiers, underscored once again the brutality of the military and gave added weight to the tales of horror told by their predecessors.

The 1972 crisis in Burundi marked the birth of a state entirely dominated by Tutsi elements. It is easy to see in such circumstances why in 1993 some Tutsi extremists within the army and the government found it intolerable to surrender power to a Hutu president. But perhaps the most dramatic blow-back effect of 1972 found expression in the orgy of violence triggered by the news of Ndadaye's assassination, when thousands of innocent Tutsi civilians fell under the blows of enraged Hutu youth. As one Hutu clergyman reported, "When we told them (*les excités*) not to spill blood, they said, 'Look, since 1972 it is our blood that's being spilled! Now we hear that President Ndadaye has been killed. If they did that it means we are next!'"[16] Memories of 1972 suddenly surfaced with an emotional charge made more potent by intimations of yet another massacre of Hutu populations.

All genocides are alike in the horror they evoke. Yet they each stand as singular events, rooted in the particularities of specific historical situations. Although the parallels with Rwanda are undeniable, the Burundi genocide cannot be seen as a carbon copy of the far more devastating bloodbath of 1994. Each state bears traces of its tragic heritage. How to come to terms with the past in order to reinvent their destinies is the daunting task facing both states as a fragile peace looms on the horizon.

Chapter 10
Burundi at the Crossroads

Burundi has many claims to fame, none to be envied. Despite widespread assumptions to the contrary, it has the sad distinction of having experienced the first genocide recorded in Central Africa. Although overshadowed in public attention by the far more extensive carnage in Rwanda, to this day the killing of an estimated quarter of a million Hutu at the hands of a Tutsi-dominated army remains deeply etched in the collective memory of the Hutu people. If trust is in such dramatically short supply in Burundi society, this is largely the legacy of a mass crime that has never been officially recognized for what it is.

Burundi also has the highest rate in Africa of heads of state and of government officials to be sent to their graves by an assassin's bullet. The list includes Prince Rwagasore in 1961, Pierre Ngendandumwe and Joseph Bamina in 1965, ex-king Ntare in 1972, and Melchior Ndadaye in 1993—not to mention the death of President Ntaryamira in the crash that took the life of President Habyarimana in April 1994. But if the actuarial risks of holding office are nowhere higher than in Burundi, measured by the rage and anger it provoked among Hutu masses, Ndadaye's murder was unlike any other. It unleashed one of the most vicious and intractable civil wars on the continent, resulting in an estimated 300,000 casualties. This is as close as Burundi came to a meltdown. If for no other reason, it must be seen as a turning point in the country's violent history.

No other strife-torn country on the continent has received more sustained remedial attention from as many international actors as Burundi since 1994. In addition to countless formal diplomatic initiatives from the United Nations, the European Union, the African Union, South Africa, and Tanzania, not to mention the cohorts of special envoys, no fewer than seventeen international NGOs have desperately been searching for a solution to the conflict, but with minimal results. In retrospect, the sheer number of actors involved in crafting conflict prevention and resolution strategies must be seen as the principal factor behind their limited achievements. From their different definitions of the nature of the conflict stemmed different agendas and strategies, sometimes working at cross-purposes with each other, while presenting the parties to the conflict with ample opportunities for manipulation.

Dimensions of the Burundi Crisis

Each of the foregoing brings into view key elements in the background of the present crisis. The first relates to the critical importance of the 1972 genocide in shaping the collective memory of the more radical Hutu factions, notably Agathon Rwasa's FNL. Its radical, populist, anti-Tutsi streak is rooted in an enduring awareness of the horrors suffered by the Hutu at the hands of the Tutsi army. To this day, official denials that anything like a genocide of Hutu even happened only reinforces the FNL's uncompromising stance on the Hutu-Tutsi conflict. The genocidal quality of the 1972 tragedy has never been explicitly acknowledged by the 1995 UN-appointed commission of inquiry into the circumstances of Ndadaye's death—which on the other hand gave prominent emphasis to "acts of genocide" committed by Hutu against Tutsi in the wake of Ndadaye's assassination—or for that matter by any of the international actors involved since the visit of the UN Commission, a fact which did not go unnoticed by Hutu politicians.[1]

Ndadaye's death did more than give Hutu radicalism a new lease on life. It has set the stage for the involvement of a large number of international actors and created new sources of division among Hutu and Tutsi. The two phenomena are interlinked. Beginning with the appointment of the UN secretary general's special envoy Ahmedou Ould-Abdallah in 1994, international actors—most notably Ould-Abdallah but also former Tanzania president Julius Nyerere in his capacity as facilitator of the Arusha talks—played a key role in legitimizing the fractiousness of the Burundi political arena in the name of "inclusiveness," while doing next to nothing to tame the forces of Hutu and Tutsi radicalism.

As the predominantly Hutu Frodebu split between moderates and radicals, an endless process of fragmentation began to set in, eventually reaching unprecedented proportions during the Arusha conference (1998–2000). At first the principal line of cleavage was between those who insisted on going back to the status quo ante (meaning a predominantly Frodebu government and a Hutu president, as well as a return to the 1992 constitution) and those who, albeit reluctantly, were willing to work out a power-sharing agreement giving equal representation to Hutu and Tutsi. A host of other divisive issues arose—constitutional (over the election of Ndadaye's successor), judicial (whether or not to prosecute Ndadaye's assassins), strategic (whether to use force or to seek political accommodation)—that helped further fragment the political arena. Radicalism by then had ceased to be the monopoly of the Hutu. With Hutu and Tutsi split into a large number of parties, and parties into factions, the state found the key to its survival in its seemingly limitless capacity to absorb its potential enemies.

Though much has been said of ethnicity as a point of entry into the analysis of Burundi politics, today's dilemma goes beyond the Hutu-Tutsi question. Not that ethnicity will ever go away. But there is little doubt that in recent times its salience has tended to recede, bringing into view a far more complex picture. A more relevant point of reference, besides regional loyalties, is the split between extremists and moderates on both sides of the ethnic fault line, as well as various shades of extremism in each camp. Whether a viable state system can be reconstructed through a power-sharing formula, incorporating some twenty different factions, is the central question facing the Burundi authorities today. How to stitch together a reasonably stable coalition government in a context of growing political fragmentation, increasing rural poverty, severe land hunger, chronic violence, persistent discords about the legitimacy of Arusha, and continuing vulnerability to the intrusion of regional forces—such are the dimensions of the dilemma facing domestic and international actors in today's Burundi.

Before going any further, and to properly grasp the continuing hold of the past on the present, a brief excursus into the country's history is in order.

The Past as Present

This is not the place for a detailed account of Burundi's tortured history since independence in 1962;[2] suffice it to note the lasting significance of three critical junctures. The first concerns the impact of the Rwanda revolution on the hardening of ethnic enmities in the years immediately following the advent of self-government; the second has to do with the legacy of the 1972 genocide; and a third relates to the momentous consequences of Ndadaye's assassination.

THE SELF-FULFILLING PROPHECY

There is no need to explore the precolonial record of armed confrontations between Rwanda and Burundi to appreciate the importance of the regional context in shaping the course of Burundi politics. The regional dimension comes into clear focus in the wake of the Rwanda revolution (1959–61), when tens of thousands of Tutsi refugees fled to Burundi, each with tales of horror on their lips. The result was to drastically alter the texture of Hutu-Tutsi relations. From a society where ethnic tensions were largely eclipsed by a far more significant tug-of-war between princely factions (Bezi vs. Batare), each drawing support from both Hutu and Tutsi, Burundi began to look more and more like its neighbor to the north. At the root of this phenomenon lies what we referred to elsewhere as a self-fulfilling prophecy: along with Hutu efforts to emulate the Rwandan republican model, Tutsi perceptions of Hutu politicians as potential enemies would make their originally false imputations true.[3] Thus, although traditional Burundi differed from Rwanda in many significant ways, the Hutu revolution in Rwanda set in motion a process of ethnic polarization that reached unprecedented intensity during the 1972 genocide. By then, however, power was firmly in the hands of the predominantly Tutsi army.

There are obvious differences between the 1972 carnage in Burundi and its 1994 counterpart in Rwanda in terms of scale (in Burundi estimates range from 150,000 to 300,000 killed, as against 600,000 to 800,000 in Rwanda) and target group. Yet they both qualify as retributive genocides in that they came about in response to a perceived threat from the victim group: in Rwanda the threat came from the October 1, 1990 invasion of the RPF; and in Burundi, from a violent, though highly localized, Hutu-led insurgency that led to the killing of hundreds, if not thousands, of Tutsi civilians. In both instances, the killings were conducted by army units and *jeunesse* groups, with substantial auxiliary support provided by refugee communities (Hutu from Burundi in Rwanda, and Tutsi from Rwanda in Burundi). And in both countries, the ultimate outcome was the emergence of a state system with all the qualities of a military ethnocracy. Unlike what happened in Rwanda, however, in Burundi the genocidaires came out on top.

THE LEGACY OF 1972

The planned, systematic extermination of Hutu elites and potential elites (including university students and school children), as well as many who would hardly qualify as either, was meant to achieve several long-term objectives: (a) to insure the stability of the state by the wholesale destruction of its presumptive opponents; (b) to transform the instruments of force—the army, the police, and the gendarmerie—into a Tutsi monopoly; (c) to rule out the possibility of a restoration of the monarchy (hence the killing of ex-king Ntare in Gitega, on May 1); and (d) to create a new basis of legitimacy for the ruling elites—most of them recruited among the Bururi-based, Tutsi-Hima subgroup—by projecting an image of the state as the benevolent protector of all Burundians against their domestic and foreign foes.

On each count, the government of President Michel Micombero met with considerable success. For the next sixteen years, Burundi experienced a period of unprecedented peace under Tutsi hegemony. Those Hutu most likely to resist such hegemony were either killed or in exile. But as subsequent events were to demonstrate, this surface impression of a country at peace with itself was profoundly misleading.

THE RISE OF HUTU RADICALISM

The most threatening of all the problems inherited from the 1972 bloodbath is the enduring vitality of Hutu radicalism. It is worth recalling that the Palipehutu, the principal vehicle of anti-Tutsi radicalism, was born in 1973 in the refugee camp of Mishamo in Tanzania.[4] Today the most vehemently anti-Tutsi of the half-dozen political parties identified with Hutu interests is the armed wing of the Palipehutu, the so called Palipehutu-FNL, led by Agathon Rwasa. Its closest rival on the scale of radicalism is the CNDD-FDD, an offshoot of the Frodebu, currently headed by Pierre Nkurunziza. It is significantly less exclusionary in terms of membership, however (its leadership includes a substantial number of Tutsi elements), which helps explain why, after years of foot dragging and fruitless negotiations, it has finally agreed to the terms of the cease-fire negotiated in Pretoria in October 2003 and joined the government. As I write these lines (January 2004), the FNL has yet to follow suit. Yet both are heirs to the Palipehutist ideology in their uncompromising rejection of Tutsi hegemony. The roots of this ideology are part and parcel of the 1972 legacy. It is not a coincidence that the most uncompromising advocates of the Hutu cause, including Agathon Rwasa of the FNL, and Pierre Nkurunziza and Jean-Bosco Ndayikengurukiye of the CNDD-FDD, have all lost many of their relatives in the 1972 bloodbath.

If the rise of Hutu radicalism is indeed inseparable from the refugee problem, the latter has more wide-ranging ramifications. It brings into focus the land problem and the bitter contestations that have arisen since 1972 and 1993 over the ownership of the plots left behind by fleeing refugees. Many were taken over by Tutsi claimants who insist on hanging on to their ill-gotten gains. To add complexity to the issue, some Tutsi have since sold or leased the refugee's properties to Hutu elements who now press their claims as rightful owners. The seriousness of the issue of the restitution of the refugee's land was dramatically brought to light after Ndadaye's election to the presidency, when violent confrontations erupted between scores of Hutu returnees and the Tutsi claimants, which in turn contributed in no small way to his demise. To this day, the land issue remains unresolved. It may still prove a major obstacle in the way of a lasting solution to the Hutu-Tutsi conflict.[5]

NDADAYE'S MURDER: THE DESCENT INTO HELL

Unlike previous cases of political assassination (Prince Rwagasore in 1961, Ngendadumwe in 1965), Ndadaye's murder, on October 21, 1993, caused a tectonic shift in the country's political landscape. It marks

Burundi's descent into a hellish cycle of ethnic violence and counterviolence from which it has yet to fully recover.

In trying to make sense of the motives behind this cataclysmic event, we are once again reminded of the legacy of 1972. Having reaped the economic and political benefits of Tutsi hegemony for decades, extremists within and outside the army were quick to grasp the implications of a transfer of power to the leading representative of the Hutu majority. And none were more eager to challenge the verdict of the polls than those Tutsi who had taken over the refugees' land, cattle, and houses. The risks of eliminating Ndadaye seemed slight given that the army was, and still is, to a considerable extent, the monopoly of the Tutsi minority. Missing from this harebrained calculus, however, was the possibility of a massive and violent outburst of Hutu anger, fed by memories of 1972. The sudden eruption of anti-Tutsi violence only hours following the news of Ndadaye's death, resulting in countless atrocities and random killings of Tutsi civilians, was the triggering factor behind an equally devastating display of anti-Hutu violence by the army. How many lives were lost is anybody's guess—estimates vary between 30,000 to 100,000; what most observers agree on is that as many Tutsi were killed by enraged mobs of Hutu as Hutu by the army's blind repression. From then on, Hutu radicalism only served to encourage Tutsi extremism and vice versa.

Once again hundreds of thousands of Hutu refugees fled to neighboring states. Some 350,000 sought refuge in Rwanda and at least as many to Tanzania and the Congo. In the wake of this mass exodus, a new set of actors emerged on Burundi's doorstep. To this day, the regional dimension is inseparable from the convoluted course of Burundi's domestic politics.

The Regional Nexus of the Burundi Crisis

How Burundi politics has affected the wider regional crisis, and vice-versa, draws attention to three watershed events, each linked to the other through a complex ethnic dialectic: Ndadaye's assassination, the Rwanda genocide, and the outbreak of the Congo's second civil war in August 1998.

The first gave a powerful stimulus to the crystallization of Hutu Power in Rwanda and thus contributed significantly to the radicalization of Hutu politics on the eve of the carnage. Among the Burundi refugees living in Rwanda, many took an active part in the killings of Tutsi in 1994. Furthermore, the seizure of power by Paul Kagame's RPF in July 1994 led to the mass exodus of some two million Hutu refugees from Rwanda into the Congo, Tanzania, and Burundi: in each of these external "sanctuaries," informal alliances emerged between them and their kinsmen from Burundi, thus injecting a new source of tension between Hutu and Tutsi, both within and outside their countries of origin, while at the same time posing major security threats to the newly established Tutsi regime in Kigali and what was left of the state in Burundi after Ndadaye's demise. By 1995, a convergence of ethnic interests led to a mutually supportive relationship between Leonard Nyangoma's CNDD-FDD and groups of *interahamwe* and ex-FAR in eastern Congo, yet at no time did anything like a coherent cross-national alliance materialize between them.

Today the persistence of intra-ethnic divisions is nowhere more evident—and politically consequential—than in multiplicity of political parties represented in the government: the post-Arusha coalition includes no fewer than seven Hutu parties (the so-called G-7) and ten Tutsi parties (G-10). Behind this extreme fragmentation of the social landscape lies a variety of factors: some having to do with sub-ethnic or regional loyalties, others with personality differences, and others still, with genuine disagreements over questions of tactics and strategy. Seen from a broader perspective, however, the phenomenon brings into focus two critical elements: one refers to the drastic transformation of the geopolitical map of the Great Lakes in the wake of the 1998 civil war in the Congo; and another has to do with the impact of the Arusha peace talks on the process of political fragmentation.

The 1998 Civil War in the Congo

With the outbreak of the second civil war in the Congo, new patterns of alliances came into being that made ethnic and national divisions largely irrelevant. Opportunism was the rule; the quest for tactical advantage the guiding principle. The result has been an endless series of intramural tiffs and discords among presumptive Hutu leaders.

The straightforward split between moderates (Frodebu) and radicals (CNDD-FDD), brought to light in the days following Ndadaye's death, proved extremely short-lived. Forced into exile into eastern Congo by the relentless pressure of the Burundi army, the CNDD-FDD, then led by Leonard Nyangoma, suffered huge losses in the wake of the destruction of the refugee camps by the RPA in and around Uvira in late 1996, only to be faced with further onslaughts by Tutsi troops as they crossed into Burundi to seek asylum in Tanzania. Bitter internecine quarrels erupted over what some described as a bungled operation.

By 1998, with the outbreak of the second civil war in the Congo, disagreements over whether to fight their way back into the country from Tanzania or to join hands with Kabila's army and its Mai-Mai auxiliaries drove a deep wedge between the two leading FDD personalities, Leonard

Nyangoma and Jean-Bosco Ndayikengurukiye. After deciding to cast his lot with Kabila, Jean-Bosco surfaced as his most faithful ally in eastern Congo. But his meteoric rise as Kabila's man in Katanga—at one point serving as his all-powerful emissary in Lubumbashi—did little to boost his popularity among those FDD troops who had stayed in Burundi and fought tooth and nail against the Burundi army. Predictably, another split emerged between the "internal" and "external" wings of the FDD, with Nkurunziza eventually stealing much of Jean-Bosco's thunder. After the routing of the FDD and their Congolese allies by the RPA at the battle of Pweto in 2000, Jean-Bosco found himself increasingly isolated, a fact that goes a long way toward explaining his decision to negotiate a peace accord with the government.

The internal rifts suffered by the FNL-Palipehutu tell a similar story of one leader replacing another against a background of bitter quarrels over tactics and strategy, over the misappropriation of funds collected from refugees, and with even deeper disagreements between the "external" and "internal" wings.

As the infiltration of Hutu rebels from the Congo and Tanzania picked up momentum, they were joined by a growing number of Hutu civilians, by force or by persuasion. The army's response was to order hundreds of thousands of Hutu peasants out of their homes into "regroupment camps," so as to minimize the risks of "contagion" from the rebellion. The move proved utterly counterproductive. By 1997, an estimated 600,000 Hutu had been forced into what critics of this policy called "concentration camps."[6] Most of these were located miles away from the nearest road, making it almost impossible for humanitarian workers to provide assistance. The few outside observers who were able to reach them described the conditions in the camps as totally inhumane. Lacking the barest necessities of life, without infrastructures, running water, or electricity, thousands died of sickness, malnutrition, and hunger. Many who refused to leave their homes were killed by the army. Only after insistent protests from the international community were most of the camps dismantled. The important point to note, from the standpoint of this discussion, is that the majority of the camps were located in the rural province of Bujumbura. That the province also happens to be the stronghold of the FNL is not a matter of coincidence.

The hellish conditions created by the government's regroupment policies (so ominously reminiscent of French policies during the Algerian war) go far in explaining the FNL's remarkable staying power in Bujumbura Rural province, the appeal of its populist ideology, its capacity to recruit thousands of child soldiers, and for that matter, the strong element of biblical mysticism that enters into Agathon Rwasa's exhortations. The sufferings endured by the Hutu populations at the hands of the army within and outside the camps seemed entirely consistent with the 1972 genocidal killings of Hutu by Tutsi.

What happened in 1972 is still fresh in the memory of some FNL leaders. As one of its spokesmen, Pasteur Habimana, recently told this writer, "I have been holed up in the forest since 1973; I am fifty years old. The truth must be told about the many Hutu killed by Tutsi. We need to tell the truth. *Le problème du Burundi c'est le mensonge!* The members of parliament represent no one. . . . How can we agree on a fifty-fifty sharing of power with the Tutsi when they represent 15 percent of the population? . . . In 1972 I saw my brothers being killed. I was twenty years old. I remember everything."[7] The streak of fanaticism in the FNL's ideological stance is unmistakable. It helps explain why it rarely shrinks from the use of violence to force young Hutu, many of them teenage boys, to join its ranks. The closest parallel that comes to mind is not so much the FDD as the Lord's Resistance Army (LRA) in Uganda.

Arusha: The Rush to the Trough

Although the exclusion of both the CNDD-FDD and the FNL from the Arusha peace talks—largely at the request of the Tutsi parties—has contributed to their growing radicalization in the years following the Buyoya coup in July 1996, the more important point to note is the phenomenal proliferation of parties unleashed by the Arusha peace process.

The reason for the rapid increase in the number of participants is not hard to find: participation in the conference was the safest guarantee any politician could get that he might be included in a future government in one capacity or another. The significance of the "rush to the trough" phenomenon to an understanding of the post-Arusha dilemmas cannot be overestimated. For one thing, it has given birth to a flurry of parties (Hutu and Tutsi) that are nothing more than the convenient vehicles of small coteries of aspiring urban politicians. Their popular legitimacy is nil. Furthermore, the sheer number of parties represented in the government—with more knocking at the door—has led to an institutional monstrosity: a top-heavy political machinery whose sole purpose is to provide as many jobs as are needed to meet the requirements of political stability. The government is not meant to govern; its purpose is to offer an attractive alternative to the rebellion. What it fails to offer is a package of social and economic policies that could meet the demands of the peasant masses, and thus offer a meaningful alternative to the rebellion.

With the benefit of hindsight, one might argue that the inability or unwillingness of the facilitators to admit to the negotiating table some of the key players, the CNDD-FDD and Palipehutu, is where the role of external actors appears to have been singularly counterproductive.

The Role of International Actors

It is impossible in the context of this discussion to do justice to the enormous complexity of the subject. Those readers who are undeterred by the Kafkaesque complications of the twists and turns of the Arusha peace process will read with profit the masterful account of these tortuous negotiations by a key participant, Howard Wolpe, who served as the United States special envoy to the Great Lakes during the Clinton years.[8] Our main concern here is to highlight some key issues.

Reflecting on "the profusion of players" in Burundi, "each with its own agenda and favored solution," Fabienne Hara argues that the result has been to "undermine the coherence of the international community's response, and lead to competition among various Burundian factions for recognition and support."[9] Though primarily concerned with the adverse effects of the "parallel diplomacy" conducted by NGOs, there are reasons to believe that her judgment could apply just as well to the involvement of regional and intergovernmental organizations. Indeed, she suggests that much in her comments on the "sheer number of special envoys (which) reflects the diversity of their agendas and motivations, and tends to jeopardize the official claim that the international community wants peace, or at the least the same peace, for the region. . . . In the end it appears that every political tendency in Burundi has found a temporary ally among the international negotiators, who, in turn, become part of the problem."[10]

Given the intractable nature of the Burundi crisis, it is all too easy, with the benefit of hindsight, to emphasize the shortcomings of the international community as it tried to grapple with the challenge of conflict resolution in a political arena suffused with ethnic hatreds, factional strife, and revenge killings. Nonetheless, granting that the blame cannot be shared evenly, there are ample grounds on which to question the wisdom of some of its peace initiatives.

The first point to be reiterated is not so much a lack of foresight or wisdom on the part of any single actor as it is a commentary on the plurality of actors involved. As Fabienne Hara conclusively demonstrates, much of the problem about the role of international actors is reducible to their different agendas and definitions of the Burundi crisis. It is a well-known fact, for example, that Museveni and Nyerere held radically different perceptions of the roots of the crisis, and the same could be said of the very different approaches followed by the Community Sant'-Egidio and the Arusha facilitators. Countless other examples could be cited.

A straightforward assessment of the role played by regional actors is rendered extremely difficult by the ambivalence of their performance and the controversy surrounding the consequences of their interventions. A case in point is the boycott strategy pursued by the Central and East African states in 1996 and 1997, following Buyoya's coup in July 1996. This initiative, forcefully supported by Nyerere, came in for the strongest criticisms from a number of NGOs, including the International Crisis Group (ICG), as well as virtually all of the special envoys. Aside from creating confusion about the role and efficacy of the international community, critics of the boycott argued that it penalized mostly the rural masses, did little to prevent continuing transactions with neighboring states, and in the end encouraged radical Hutu factions to make political capital out of the boycott. Yet, seen from another perspective, it is entirely conceivable that Buyoya may not have agreed to a significant political overture (notably the reopening of the National Assembly and the readmission of opposition parties in the political arena) in the absence of such sanctions.

The next point is equally subject to debate: it refers to the less than constructive role played by the UN Special Envoy, Ahmedou Ould-Abdallah, in legitimizing power sharing as a conflict resolution strategy. Anyone familiar with his highly controversial *apologia pro vita sua*, *Burundi on the Brink: 1993–1995*, cannot fail to note his pro-Tutsi sympathies, a fact perhaps not unrelated to his aristocratic origins as a representative of the Mauretanian *bidan* ("white") community. Consider, for example, the rationale invoked by the author to explain the fifty-fifty sharing of governmental and administrative positions inscribed in the 1994 Convention of Government: the seizure of power by the RPF in Kigali is presented to the reader as one of the justifications for giving the Burundi Tutsi an equal share of power with the Hutu![11] To quote: "It was impossible to ignore this completely new political context, especially with two million Hutu refugees in Zaire and Tanzania, many of them under the effective control of the army of the former Rwandan regime."[12] Nor can one ignore some of the more debatable statements and patent inaccuracies offered by the author (including the notion that ex-president Bagaza financed the political campaign of the Frodebu!). Not only did the Convention of Government turn out to be a dismal failure, but its architect also deserves considerable credit for legitimizing a power-sharing formula that would exclude the more radical elements in the spectrum of Hutu parties—possibly as a concession to what he refers to as "the spiritual dimension" of his mission.[13]

Just as Boutros-Ghali's Special Envoy may have been swayed by his ethnic origins, one is also reminded of the criticisms addressed to Mandela for projecting his experience of apartheid into the Burundi context: it has been said that by coming down so harshly on the Tutsi minority during the Arusha talks, Mandela tended to equate the plight of the Hutu community with that of the African majority and the Tutsi claims, with those of the white minority. This is a fair criticism, but the Mandela stance on the Hutu-Tutsi question may have nudged the Tutsi hard-liners into a more pliant attitude than would have been the case otherwise. Whatever the case may be, we are again confronted with the problem of how best to accommodate divergent agendas into a coherent framework for conflict resolution.

By 2003, South Africa had emerged as the decisive actor in the peace process. It played a central role in the long drawn out negotiations that led to the Global Cease-fire Agreement of November 16 with Nkurunziza's CNDD-FDD, justly described as a milestone on the road to peace. For this remarkable achievement, much of the credit goes to Deputy President Zuma and President Mbeki. Both took an active part in the two day-and-night-long meetings that finally broke the deadlock over the restructuring of Burundi's security forces. As much as their strong personal commitment to the peace process, the fact that South Africa was able to assert itself as the uncontested leader in the negotiations—in no small part because of Mandela's earlier commitment—goes a long way toward explaining their successful outcome.

Prospects for Peace

For all their shortcomings, compared to the situation of near anarchy prevailing through the late 1990s, the Arusha Accords stand as a major breakthrough. The successful transition to multiparty democracy has come about because of the long and painful negotiations undertaken first in Arusha, then in Pretoria and Bujumbura. Following the start of the disarmament, demobilization, and reintegration (DDR) in 2004, Burundi adopted a new constitution by referendum in March 2005, and a new electoral code was approved by the transitional parliament. After a six-month extension of the transitional period, communal elections were held in early June 2005, giving Nkurunziza's CNDD-FDD 55 percent of the seats in communal councils. Despite reported cases of extremists trying to disrupt the vote by throwing grenades near the polling stations, large crowds showed up to cast their ballots. Similarly, when legislative elections were held in July 2005, scores of people were injured and polling stations disrupted when grenades were thrown near queues of people waiting to vote. UN peacekeepers protecting international observers were also fired on. But despite more shelling around the capital, large numbers defiantly voted. With a majority of the legislative seats, Nkurunziza was elected president in August 2005. Given the power-sharing formula inscribed in the constitution and the obligation for parties to include Hutu and Tutsi in their list of candidates, a reenactment of the 1993 scenario seems unlikely.

The election of Nkurunziza fulfills two of the core objectives established by the multitude of external interveners in Burundi: the need to transfer power from the Tutsi minority to the Hutu majority and from military control to civilian control. But it is too early to make predictions about whether the experiment will hold. The potential dangers stem from the continued threat posed by the FNL and from the difficulties involved in the DDR. Despite Rwasa's repeated overtures, the FNL has yet to mutate from an armed faction into a political party. In September 2005, the FNL rejected a government offer of peace talks. Although most observers agree that it is not in a position to derail the transition, it still has a significant nuisance potential. The slow pace of the DDR process, combined with the appalling conditions prevailing in some regroupment camps, is another source of concern as it raises the possibility that many of the candidates for demobilization could retool themselves into armed bandits. Formerly under the National Commission for Demobilization, Reinsertion, and Reintegration (NCDRR), the program is intended to run over a four-year period, at the end of which some 26,000 ex-rebels are expected to be either demobilized or reintegrated into the Burundi armed forces. As of May 31, 2005, however, only 9,300 had been demobilized, along with 2,939 child soldiers and 515 female soldiers. Little wonder if a growing number of ex-rebels appear determined to engage in banditry as the next best thing to languishing in cantonment sites.

Furthermore, a number of critically important issues—impunity, justice, national reconciliation, the reinsertion of Hutu refugees, and the restructuring of the army—have yet to be resolved.[14] Of these, the most potentially explosive concerns the fate of the refugee and internally displaced populations. Taking into account the 1972 and 1993 exodus, there were roughly 800,000 refugees in Tanzania and 300,000 internall displaced persons at the time Arusha got under way. Since then, tens of thousands have returned to their homeland. Many live in dire circumstances. The worst off among the refugees are those who are returning on their own (*rapatriés spontanés*) rather than through the United Nations High Commission for Refugees (UNHCR) as they face countless exactions by armed bandits, militias, and camp custodians. All are living in fear and with few prospects for a better future inside Burundi.

Protocol IV of the Arusha Accord provided for the reinsertion of the refugees through a politically independent commission, the Commission Nationale de Réhabilitation des Sinistrés (CNRS). Although presently under the control of the Frodebu, the commission has been placed under the jurisdiction (*tutelle*) of the Ministry for the Reinsertion and Reinstallation of Displaced and Repatriated Persons (MRRDR), itself headed by one of the Tutsi parties of the G-10 coalition. At stake here is a competitive struggle for the control of the refugees. Given that the overwhelming majority are CNDD-FDD sympathizers, it is easy to see why the Frodebu would want to reap the political benefits of their reinsertion, and why the MRRDR would insist on exercising control over hundreds of thousands of potential opponents. To this political infighting must be added another dimension: the competition for the control of the financial resources given by international donors to meet the costs of reinsertion. Meanwhile, the five-stage action plan elaborated by the CNRS has remained a dead letter. So, also, have the provisions of the Arusha accords concerning the restitution of their landed property to the refugees. The implication of this mess is tersely stated in the report of a local NGO: "It is imperatively urgent that the CNRS plan a coherent and global strategy in order to avoid another civil war, that one linked to property rights."[15]

Conclusion

There are no simple recipes for ensuring a durable peace, only some tentative steps toward trust and mutual tolerance. The following come to mind:

- External regional pressure in support of the peace process must continue, via the Great Lakes Initiative, and the lead role must be assumed by South Africa. No other African state can match its expertise and degree of commitment or claim a more impressive track record. Furthermore, the continuous close contacts it has established with the protagonists, together with its well-deserved reputation as an honest broker, make South Africa the single most qualified partner in helping the Burundi government resolve the many issues left pending since the signature of the Arusha Accords.
- The regional dimensions of the peace process cannot be left out of the political equation. Nowhere in the Great Lakes region is peace divisible. The conflicts that affect Burundi are bound to affect its neighbors and vice versa. Unless this seemingly banal truth is recognized and acted upon, the prospects for peace in the region are bound to remain elusive. It is imperative, therefore, that the forthcoming UN-sponsored conference on the Great Lakes establish a set of policy priorities for regional actors; these should be designed to address the interconnectedness of conflict-generating issues: ranging from the plundering and illicit diversion of natural resources by

domestic warlords and foreign interlopers to the continuing flow of small arms into the region; from the plight of refugee populations to the recruitment of child soldiers by armed factions; and from conflict-promoting economic activities by foreign corporations and the absence of minimum standards of conduct and effective regulatory mechanisms.
- Military means alone may not suffice to break the hold of the FNL in the countryside: only by offering the rural masses on the hills a meaningful alternative to violence, through the implementation of social and economic policies designed to meet their immediate needs, can they be persuaded to desist from supporting the rebellion; hence, the need to strengthen the institutional capacity of the government. One example among others of how to proceed are the highly promising workshops recently organized in specific localities under the guidance of Howard Wolpe of the Woodrow Wilson Center (WWC), and with funding from the World Bank, to develop the requisite "skills, knowledge and models for more effective economic recovery, policy development and implementation." The lessons learned from the WWC experiment could provide a model for donors, as well as the framework for testing similar initiatives in other parts of the country.[16]
- Among Burundi's civil society organizations (CSOs) the Observatory for Governmental Action (Observatoire pour l'Action Gouvernementale [OAG]) and Ligue Iteka have established for themselves an impressive record as watchdogs of government action: both have repeatedly drawn attention to human rights violations committed by Hutu and Tutsi and made specific recommendations to bring such violations to an end. They deserve the full support of the international community in their efforts to denounce restrictions of press freedoms and human rights abuses, including arbitrary arrests, extra-judicial murders, and inhumane prison conditions. No other two CSOs have done more to promote mutual trust between Hutu and Tutsi.
- The time has come for the international community to recognize the potential for renewed ethnic strife inherent in the problems faced by refugees and displaced persons: the international community, through the African Union, should bring maximum pressure to bear on the CNRS and MRRDR to work jointly towards a viable action plan; additional funding from the United Nations is urgently needed to cope with the logistics of the problem. And unless a more proactive role is played by the Commission de suivi des accords d'Arusha to monitor and assist the implementation of the action plan, the refugee problem could easily spin out of control and reignite ethnic strife.

- The top-heavy governmental machinery born of the Arusha Accords is unlikely to succeed in resolving the country's economic problems as long as its primary purpose is to serve as a political machine for rewarding political allegiance. A sustained effort should be made by donors to promote the development of the private sector as a source of employment. As long as the state remains the only source of rewards, its legitimacy and efficiency will decline in proportion to its size. Useful though it may have been in the short run as an integrating apparatus, its long-term viability is very much open to question. It simply cannot serve as a substitute for private enterprise.
- Private enterprise is not an unmitigated blessing. It can easily play into the hands of the more enterprising elements in society, namely, Tutsi elements, and thus create the basis for persistent social inequalities. The phenomenon is already apparent in some sectors of the economy (my guess is that 90 percent of the taxis operating in Bujumbura are owned by Tutsi elements). Along with the encouragement of private enterprise, it should be the responsibility of the government to see to it (possibly through an affirmative action type of guideline) that entry into the private sector, and therefore access to credit facilities, not be the privilege of any particular group, whether by design or by circumstances.
- None of the above can become reality unless minimal conditions of security exist in the urban and rural areas. This is why the international community must make an additional effort to fund the expansion and professionalization of the African Union-sponsored African Mission in Burundi (AMIB). Currently, limited to some 3,000 men from South Africa, Mozambique, and Ethiopia, the AMIB should expand to twice its present size if it is to provide adequate protection to opposition leaders and at the same time, provide effective security in and around the cantonments.
- Last but not least, the reality of the 1972 genocide can no longer be ignored while the killings of Tutsi, in the wake of Ndadaye's murder, qualify as the only example of "genocide" officially acknowledged. It is not by blocking out the past that Burundi will build its future. The time has come to set the record straight. Neither community has been spared the horrors of genocidal killings or the burden of responsibility for such killings. Public recognition of this irreducible fact would go a long way toward promoting a sense of trust between Hutu and Tutsi and help them come to terms with their tragic past.

The foregoing should disabuse us of the notion that free and fair elections are all that is needed to ensure a safe passage to multiparty democracy. As Fareed Zakaria reminds us, free and fair elections are no guarantee that those elected will heed the rule of law and protect basic individual rights, including minority rights.[17] The threat of "illiberal democracy" is particularly ominous in a country like Burundi, where today, as in the past, the tyranny of the Hutu majority remains the perennial concern of the Tutsi minority. Whether this threat is likely to materialize is anybody's guess. What seems reasonably clear is that much remains to be done before a consensus of sorts emerges among Burundians on how they want to be governed, by whom, and for what purpose.

Chapter 11
Burundi's Endangered Transition

> *When Nkurunziza and his men fought in the bush, their fight was legitimate, their promises reassuring. Today we've lost our illusions. We thought they were serious when they attacked corruption, human rights violations, bad governance, ethnicism and tribalism, clientelism and nepotism as a mode of government. We've been duped. We really believed that they wanted to change things and bring order to the exercise of power* (la gestion du pouvoir). *What a disappointment! Since they've come to power they never stopped doing the opposite of what they preached. They are even worse than their predecessors.*
> —A Hutu resident of Bujumbura, personal communication, September 14, 2006

Few other states in the continent can claim to have emerged from a ten-year civil war under more promising circumstances than Burundi. The transition process, however long and painful, has been exemplary. Beginning with the Arusha agreement of 2000, a constitutional formula was finally worked out whereby the rights of the Tutsi minority could be reconciled with the demands of the Hutu majority.[1] The 2005 legislative and presidential elections went remarkably smoothly, giving birth to a consociational government[2] headed by a Hutu president, Pierre Nkurunziza, where Hutu and Tutsi held respectively 60 and 40 percent of the ministerial portfolios. A similar proportion obtained in the National Assembly; and in the Senate, Hutu and Tutsi held a parity of seats. This is no small feat when one considers the sheer intensity and destructiveness of the Hutu-Tutsi conflict in the years preceding the transition.

The hopes raised by such auspicious beginnings may soon prove illusory, however. A year later the country finds itself in the throes of a major governmental crisis. In late July, rumors of a plot aimed at the overthrow of the government led to the arrest of several leading politicians, Hutu and Tutsi. Human rights organizations have accused the government of major abuses, ranging from extra-judicial executions to arbitrary arrest and torture. Adding to an already tense climate, on September 5 came the announcement that Burundi's second vice-president, Alice Nzomukunda, had handed in her resignation in protest against the unwarranted meddling of the ruling party's chairman, Hussein Radjabu, in the political life of the country.[3] The European Union (EU) representative in Burundi, meanwhile, disclosed a major corruption scandal related to the EU-funded Rehabilitation Program, involving an estimated five million euros. Whatever the outcome of the crisis, there can be little doubt that it has seriously dented the government's legitimacy.

It is difficult in such circumstances not to recall the widespread optimism that greeted the election of Melchior Ndadaye, the first Hutu candidate to the presidency, in July 1993, only to be followed a few months later by his assassination by elements of the all-Tutsi army—the triggering factor behind the ensuing civil war. To predict such tragic denouement is clearly premature, and today's fault-lines are not nearly as polarized as in 1993. But there is no denying the sense of anxiety and frustration felt by many Barundians who, in voting for Nkurunziza, had pinned their hopes on the banner of a pluralist democracy. The present crisis portends the eventual unraveling of the carefully calibrated power-sharing formula inscribed in the 2005 constitution.

If history never repeats itself, in Burundi as elsewhere, it provides important clues to an understanding of the present.[4] Some people suffer from inherited diseases; Burundi suffers from its inherited history. In order to grasp the roots of the current crisis, something must be said of the historical legacy bequeathed by previous regimes.

Historical Perspectives

There are many ways to read this troubled situation, and they all point to specific episodes in the country's convoluted history. There is, to begin with, the irreducible fact that in the forty-five years since independence, at no time has Burundi experienced as much as a glimmer of democratic rule. Although elections were held in 1965 and 1993, they each led to military dictatorships, accompanied by widespread violence. From the coming to power of Michel Micombero (1966–76), to his overthrow by Jean-Baptiste Bagaza (1976–87), and the latter in turn by Pierre Buyoya (1987–93), Burundi has been governed by a mixed assemblage of civilians and army men, with the army acting as the ultimate arbiter of conflict within and outside government. Beginning with the drastic purges of the military in 1965 and 1969, the trend has been increasingly in the direction of Tutsi dominance, reaching its most extreme form in the aftermath of the 1972 genocide.

Besides having been subject to decades of military rule, Burundi has the sad distinction of being the first state in the Great Lakes region to have experienced genocidal violence, a fact largely obscured by the far more devastating bloodletting in Rwanda. Unlike what happened in Rwanda in 1994—a total genocide—the 1972 killings, involving a wholesale massacre of Hutu elites, has been described as a "selective" genocide, with the victims numbering anywhere from 200,000 to 300,000.[5] Nonetheless, the points of convergence with Rwanda are unmistakable. In both instances, the killings occurred in response to what was perceived by the state as a major threat to its survival. In Rwanda, the menace came from the armed invasion of the Tutsi-dominated RPF on October 1, 1990; in Burundi it took the form of an externally supported Hutu uprising, in late April 1972, which took of the lives of thousands of innocent Tutsi civilians. In both cases, the roots of disaster must be found in the policies of exclusion long practiced by the ruling elites, which made it almost impossible for the Tutsi in Rwanda and the Hutu in Burundi effectively to exercise their political rights. And just as in Rwanda the outcome of genocidal violence has been the rise of a thinly veiled military ethnocracy, so also in Burundi where the state, like the army, became the monopoly of Tutsi elements. From 1973 to 1993, Burundi was in essence a Tutsi state. Furthermore, in each case, genocide has generated massive flows of refugees and IDPs, many of whom became actively involved in externally based insurgencies.

This brings into focus two critical challenges faced by the Nkurunziza government as it tried to make good on its promise to restore security to the country: the persistence of Hutu radicalism as an enduring element of the social landscape and the refugee problem. To these we shall return in a moment. Suffice it to note that although both are traceable to the 1972 bloodbath, the challenges they posed to the state were made even more daunting by the massive eruption of violence triggered by the 1993 crisis. The long civil war that followed in the wake of Ndadaye's assassination accelerated the flow of refugees to neighboring states and further intensified ethnic hatreds.

The disastrous consequences of the failed 1993 democratic transition must be seen as a key reference point for an understanding of the current crisis. As will be recalled, the pro-Hutu opposition party Frodebu scored a major victory at the polls against the former ruling pro-Tutsi Uprona in the presidential and legislative elections in June and July 1993. "One of the most remarkable transitions to democracy yet seen in Africa," is how one Western embassy described the elections—a judgment which subsequent events showed to be sadly premature.[6] Hutu elation over the election of the Frodebu's leader, Melchior Ndadaye, proved just as short-lived: Ndadaye was last seen on October 21, 1993, when the Tutsi-dominated army moved against the presidential palace, a prelude to the arrest and massacre of key Frodebu personalities. With the news of Ndadaye's death reaching the countryside, ethnic violence suddenly rose to a frightening pitch of intensity, with groups of enraged Frodebu militants turning against Tutsi civilians. Perhaps as many as 15,000 to 20,000 Tutsi were massacred. Probably as many Hutu were killed by the army in the course of the ensuing repression.

The coup rapidly collapsed, however, in the face of the international outcry caused by the army's brazen attempt to reverse the verdict of the polls. Although a compromise of sorts was reached over an interim government, consisting of notoriously undistinguished personalities—Hutu and Tutsi—every effort was made by hard-core Tutsi politicians and army men to recapture power. In Filip Reyntjens's terms, "a creeping coup followed, which aimed at destroying the legitimacy, and indeed the very existence of Frodebu and at imposing a de facto constitutional order that in effect consolidated the achievements of the October 1993 coup. This strategy increasingly radicalized political life and handicapped the search for a peaceful solution."[7]

Ethnic radicalism found expression in the growing strength of hardcore Hutu holdouts, traceable to the creation in 1983 of the Palipehutu in a refugee camp in Tanzania (Mishamo) and the emergence of a breakaway faction led by Agathon Rwasa, the FNL. Although largely confined to Bujumbura Rural province, near the capital, the FNL has confronted the new government with major security threats and forced the army into military engagements that led to countless human rights violations. Whether the cease-fire agreement recently negotiated in Dar es Salaam will hold is anybody's guess.

The radical strand in the post-coup dispensation took another and equally ominous form with the split between radicals and moderates within the Frodebu. Whereas the latter opted for collaboration, others chose to enter into armed rebellion. It was in June 1994 that a well-known Hutu politician, Leonard Nyangoma, until then Minister of the Interior, decided to launch a new political movement, the CNDD, whose armed wing, the FDD, in time became hard to distinguish from its parent organization. Although the movement spawned several dissident factions, under Nkurunziza's leadership the CNDD-FDD developed into a powerful politicomilitary organization. Its carefully calculated decision to join the transitional government headed by Damien Ndayizeye in 2003 signaled its mutation from a rebel organization to a legitimate political party.

The process of fragmentation reached its peak during the Arusha negotiations, beginning in July 1998 and ending with the formal signing of the so-called Arusha Peace and Reconciliation Agreement on August 28, 2000. From four main parties in 1996, no fewer than seventeen had come into being in 2000, of which ten were pro-Tutsi (G-10) and seven, pro-Hutu (G-7). Most of these newcomers had no constituencies to speak of beyond a handful of relatives and friends, their main concern being to position themselves for government jobs.

In the sheer proliferation of parties lies a major difference between the 1993 and 2005 transitions. Whereas in 1993 electoral competition took place in a highly polarized field, in 2005 it unfolded in a far more pluralistic environment, with several Tutsi and Hutu parties vying for the vote of their respective ethnic constituencies; and the predominantly Hutu CNDD-FDD claiming the support of not a few Tutsi. As we shall see, the 2004 constitution formalized a power-sharing arrangement that not only legitimized the rights of the Tutsi minority but made possible the representation of smaller parties, Hutu and Tutsi, in the institutions of government.

This brief excursus into the country's recent history shows the persistence of ethnic conflict as an irreducible fact of Burundi politics, combined with a trend in the direction of a more politically fragmented environment, where opportunities for cross-ethnic alliances greatly minimize the risks of a bipolar confrontation. In this more flexible context lies a major difference between the 2005 transition and that of 1993. The downside of the equation is no less important to bear in mind: if the present government suffers from a conspicuous lack of competent civil servants, this is traceable to the circumstances of a prolonged insurgency that made it impossible for the CNDD-FDD recruits to acquire the kinds of professional skills needed after the guns fell silent. To this must be added the devastating economic costs of a ten-year civil war, which in addition to causing the loss of an estimated 300,000 human lives, has driven the economy into a poverty trap from which it is unlikely to extricate itself in the foreseeable future.

The Costs of Civil War

Where the wounds of civil war have yet to heal and the memory of ethnic domination is still present in many people's minds, institutionalizing multiparty democracy is a very long shot. Even more so where the constraints of unsustainable population growth are added to the burden of extreme poverty. Burundi ranks 162 on the Human Development Indicator list. It claims one of the highest population densities on the continent. In a quarter of a century, its population doubled, from 3.5 million in 1972 to seven million in 1998. The implications require little elaboration: where exploding birth rates outstrip the rate of economic growth and where land hunger drives an ever larger number of peasant families to the edge of starvation, the prospects for democratic governance are dim, irrespective of the leaders' intentions. This is a large part of the dilemma facing the Nkurunziza government.

Even before the advent of civil war Burundi ranked among the poorest of the poor. Its gross national production (GNP) dropped from US$223 in 1989 to an average of US$116 from 1998 to 2001. Already in 1985 it was estimated that 55 percent of the urban population and 85 percent of the rural population lived below absolute poverty levels. Since 1993, the economy has been contracting even further. Whereas levels of economic and social development remained fairly constant between 1973 and 1993, the post-1993 period registers a dramatic decline in a number of indicators. Consider the following statistics:[8]

- Malnutrition among children under five increased from 6 to 20 percent since 1993; some 24,000 persons are treated monthly for malnutrition; only 55 percent of the population has access to water sources within less than fifteen minutes' walking distance.
- Cases of major endemic diseases have increased over 200 percent since 1993, with HIV cases rising to 20 percent in urban areas and 6 percent in rural sectors; today less than 20 percent of the population has access to a health center.
- Primary school enrollment dropped from 70 percent in 1993 to 44 percent; at the regional level, four provinces claimed a school enrollment of less than 30 percent of the school-age population, reaching 9 percent in the most violence-stricken areas.
- Food production per capital index (average 1989–91 = 100) dropped from 107 in 1980 to 77 and 81, respectively, in 2000 and 2002.

Poverty has been made worse by the collapse of basic public services through much of the country and the shrinkage of government revenue, from 20 percent to 12 percent of GDP since 1992. It is estimated that about 30 percent of the state's revenue went to the military in 2001, representing almost 10 percent of the GDP, as against 3.3 percent in 1992. In short, from 1993 onward, social and economic indicators plummeted, and rural poverty doubled.

How economic scarcity connects with conflict is perhaps best illustrated by the disastrous "regroupment" policy implemented by the Buyoya government shortly after coming to power in 1996. In order to "protect" peasant communities from rebel exactions, hundreds of thousands were forced into a dozen or so regroupment camps, most of them located in Bujumbura Rural province. Prevented from tilling their land and largely dependent on international assistance for their sustenance, some 300,000 peasants were forcefully removed from their traditional homelands. The conditions in the camps were described by journalists as thoroughly inhumane. Many did not survive the ordeal. "The camps are an unquestionable human disaster," one journalist reported in 1999.

"Crowded in huts made of mud, metal sheeting and palm leaves, several dozen people have died of cholera and dysentery. There are reports of a fire in one camp that spread to 50 huts. A drunken soldier reportedly opened fire on a crowd last month killing five civilians. . . . People complain about shortages of food, water, medicine, and said both the rebels and the army are stealing their crops and pieces of the homes they left behind. . . . It would be hard to name any other place where forced relocation of a third of a million people would not touch off major international protest."[9] Although officially described as a highly successful counterinsurgency strategy, a more realistic assessment would point to the enormous resentment generated by this initiative.[10] The dismantling of the camps under pressure from local and international NGOs, in 2000, ultimately played into rebel hands. For those Hutu peasants who experienced firsthand the indignities of regroupment, joining the rebellion was the only sensible choice.

Whereas persistent violence between rebel groups and the army sharply increased levels of poverty, the net result of increasing rural poverty has been to greatly intensify the potential for continued conflict. Despite the absence of reliable statistical data to substantiate the correlation between rising levels of poverty and the growing receptivity of the rural masses to the appeals of the FNL, this is a point on which many observers would agree. Many would suggest that since many of the FNL-controlled areas were off-limits to NGOs, the result has been to magnify the sense of despair and economic precariousness of the peasant population. Turning to the FNL for succor made sense in view of its proclaimed ideology, in part grounded in the promise of divine salvation for those willing to sacrifice themselves for the cause.

How to bring rebel groups into the fold of the Arusha process turned out to be a major impediment to the transition process; and for the relative success met in bringing them on board, much of the credit goes to the South African facilitator, Jacob Zuma. Whereas most of them, including the CNDD-FDD and its splinter organizations, eventually agreed to join the transitional government, the obstinately uncooperative attitude of the FNL is among the many obstacles faced by the Nkurunziza government.[11]

Institutionalizing the Transition

The 2005 elections are best seen as the culmination of long and difficult negotiations that began in Arusha (Tanzania) in 1998 under the auspices of the ex-Tanzanian president, Nyerere, who with the strong support of the Carter Center, assumed the thankless task of facilitator. The end result was the Arusha Peace and Reconciliation Agreement signed on

August 28, 2000, in the presence of Bill Clinton and Nelson Mandela—the pivotal reform package designed to chart a new course towards national reconciliation and democracy. A three-year interim period followed during which a transitional government came into being. In accordance with the interim constitution, during the first eighteen months the transition government would be headed by a Tutsi (Pierre Buyoya), with a Hutu serving as vice-president; during the next phase it would be the turn of a Hutu to serve as president (Domitien Ndayizeye) with a Tutsi as vice-president. At the end of the transition period, a new constitution would be adopted by referendum and elections held leading to the investiture of a new government.

It is to the credit of the participants in the conference that they were able to lay the foundation for a remarkably smooth transition, based on a constitutional dispensation that came to reflect the power-sharing formula agreed upon in Pretoria on October 20, 1994. Nonetheless, there are several features of the Arusha process that need to be underscored if we are to comprehend some of the difficulties faced by Nkurunziza in the wake of his landslide victory at the polls.

To begin with, the Arusha Accords, as Reyntjens correctly notes, "was in effect a non-accord . . . (since) some Tutsi parties among the 19 signatories agreed reluctantly and expressed reservations on essential provisions. They signed the accord but did not subscribe to it."[12] Such being the case, there is reason to question the extent to which the Tutsi participants were really committed to the transition process. Their recalcitrance was made clear when, after the death of Nyerere in 1999, Nelson Mandela took over as facilitator and immediately came under fire from certain Uproniste quarters for what some described as a pro-Hutu bias. Again to quote from Reyntjens, "Nelson Mandela needed all his charisma and skills, as well as the support of the region, to avoid total breakdown."[13]

The core provisions of the accord are found in five protocols drafted by the five committees appointed to deal with specific sets of issues: the nature of the conflict, democracy and good governance, peace and security, reconstruction and development, and guarantees for the implementation of the agreement. Much of the agenda inscribed in the protocols did not go beyond the stage of pious intentions. Except for the protocol dealing with democracy and good governance, which deals with the transitional institutions; and the protocol on peace and security, setting forth the principle ethnic parity in a restructuring of the security forces; the others have remained a dead letter or were only partially implemented. Thus, the commission in charge of rewriting the country's history (in accordance with the wishes of the committee on the nature of the conflict) has yet to give birth to anything more substantial than a "work in progress"; the long awaited Truth and Reconciliation Commission has yet to materialize and that applies as well to the International Judicial Commission supposed to investigate "acts of genocide, war crimes and crimes against humanity." In line with the recommendations of the committee on guarantees for the implementation of the agreement, a UN-chaired International Monitoring Commission (IMC) did come into being, responsible for "following, controlling, supervising and coordinating the implementation of all the stipulations of the accord." Its track record, however, has been less than scintillating. It is widely recognized in Bujumbura that its first chairman, Bernahu Dinka, an Ethiopian and close friend of Kofi Annan, turned out to be a total disaster. Great hopes were raised by the appointment of a National Commission for Refugee Rehabilitation, as recommended by the committee on reconstruction and development, only to be quickly dashed by bitter internal political wrangling and accusations of corrupt practices.[14] In short, many of the auxiliary institutions expected to assist the transition either remained in limbo or proved too weak to properly discharge the functions thrust upon them.

Many of the important decisions reached in Arusha were made under considerable external prodding. It is no exaggeration to say that there would have been no accord signed, or else a very different one, without the combined pressures of Tanzania, South Africa, and the United States. Much credit goes to the members of the regional initiative on Burundi, notably Uganda, Tanzania, and South Africa for persuading the Tutsi parties to accept the presence of a South African military presence—which in the past had been strenuously resisted by President Buyoya and the Tutsi hard-liners—along with a reform of the Burundi armed forces aimed at widening its bases of recruitment. Again, Nyerere played a crucial role in facilitating the admission of representatives of rebel factions to the transitional government. Even so, bringing on board the full range of rebel forces proved extremely arduous and time consuming.

Their official label notwithstanding, it is sadly ironic that at the time of the Arusha Accords neither peace nor reconciliation were yet in sight. More than three years would elapse before a cease-fire was reached with the principal rebel movement, Nkurunziza's CNDD-FDD, in November 2003 and two years before the minority wing of the same rebel movement, led by Jean-Bosco Ndayikengurukiye, agreed to lay down their arms. Thus many of the key members of the new government never had the opportunity to take part in the negotiations that went on between 1998 and 2000. Nor did they participate in the first phase of the transition. As minister of state in the Ndayizeye government, Nkurunziza exercised the responsibilities of his office for barely a year. For much of the period following Ndadaye's assassination, he fought alongside rebel troops against a Tutsi army while jockeying for power among insurgent leaders. The same is true of Hussein Radjabu, the all-powerful president of the CNDD-FDD. However impressive their track records as rebel leaders, their peacetime performance bears traces of their very limited experience in the art of governance.

The Politics of Power-Sharing

No other constitution on the continent enshrines the complexities of power-sharing with greater attention to minority rights and women's rights than the Burundi constitution of 2004. Drafted with the assistance of South African advisers, it comes closer than any other African constitution, past or present, to putting into practice Lijphart's model of consociationalism.

The logic of the model is predicated on the assumption that majority rule is a recipe for failure where society is deeply divided by religious, racial, or ethnic fault lines. In such an environment, the existence of group identities needs to be recognized and accommodated through inclusion rather than exclusion. The challenge, therefore, is to work out a formula whereby minority rights can be reconciled with the claims of the majority. The best way to achieve this, according to Lijphart, is to encourage elite cooperation through a grand coalition cabinet. At least three other conditions are required: (a) group autonomy, meaning that for issues of common interest, decisions should be made by all members of the grand coalition; on all other issues, autonomy is the rule; (b) proportionality, here seen as "the basic standard of political representation, public service appointments and allocation of public funds"; as such, it serves "as a guarantee for the fair representation of ethnic minorities"; and (c) the minority veto, described as "the ultimate weapon that minorities need to protect their vital interests," and which "works best when it is not used too often and only with regard to issues of fundamental importance."[15]

Not all plural societies are equally well prepared to handle the complexities of the model. As Lijphart has argued, power-sharing works best where ethnic segments are of roughly comparable size, and where more than two protagonists face each other across the ethnic fault line. This is where the Burundi case appears to be a distinctly poor candidate for a successful implementation of consociational rule. Furthermore, the requirement of group autonomy is particularly difficult to implement where ethnic communities intermingle at the grassroots, as is clearly the case in Burundi.

Previous experiments in power-sharing would seem to confirm this assessment. The 1994 Convention de gouvernement (CG), aimed at creating the basis of a compromise between the pro-Hutu Frodebu, winner of the 1993 elections, and its long-time rival, the Uprona, never came anywhere near its stated objectives. Engineered by the UN Special Representative in Burundi, Ahmedou Ould-Abdallah, the CG carried the principle of parity to an extreme (where even the embassies' personnel was evenly divided between Frodebistes and Upronistes). The singular flaw in the CG is that it blissfully ignored the fundamental fact that the Frodebu had won the elections. Rather than creating cohesion, the result was to foster paralysis at every level of government.

The Arusha process, likewise, tried to give equal recognition to the claims of Hutu and Tutsi in the appointment of a transitional government. But this did little to promote harmony. As noted earlier, sharp disagreements arose between the G-10 and the G-7 on certain fundamental issues. Furthermore, whereas the sheer proliferation of Hutu and Tutsi parties was instrumental in injecting a measure of flexibility in the negotiating process, incorporating so many claimants into the government seriously complicated consensus-building. In the words of one well-informed observer, "the Arusha negotiations were characterized by constant strategic repositioning, fragmentation of political parties and back-tracking."[16] Many of the parties represented in the transitional government were denounced by their opponents as self-serving opportunists (*ventriotes*). Their presence did not go unnoticed by those rebel organizations that claimed a substantial following but were consistently denied recognition (at least until 2003). The *ventriotes*, one might add, did not fare well in the elections; only a very small percentage of the G-10 and G-7 parties ended up with seats in the government after the 2005 election. Their exclusion remains a source of lingering tension, which could eventually find an outlet in the emergence of new opposition movements.

The new dispensation is in many ways a major improvement over previous arrangements. To remedy the disparity in size between Hutu and Tutsi, the framers of the 2004 constitution have made allowances for a system of representation that more than doubles the demographic weight of the Tutsi minority. With 40 percent of the seats in the government and the National Assembly—as against 60 percent for the Hutu majority—the Tutsi are thus entitled to a significant share of power in the institutions of government. Even more generous is their representation in the Senate, with 50 percent of the seats. Again, when the presidency is in Hutu hands, the vice-president is a Tutsi. At least 30 percent of the seats in parliament must be occupied by women, and three Twa will be co-opted to serve as parliamentarians. As for the local institutions of government, not more than 67 percent of the mayorships are to be held by any ethnic group. Although the mayors are elected by the municipal councilors, they in turn form the provincial electoral colleges in charge of electing two senators each. Their political reach, therefore, goes beyond the local level.

Although the principle of minority overrepresentation met with broad agreement among Hutu and Tutsi, the critical issue during the constitutional debates hinged upon the political affiliation of Tutsi representatives. Could any Tutsi candidate qualify, irrespective of party affiliations, or only those Tutsi who belonged to all-Tutsi parties, that is the G-10 parties? After much wrangling, it was agreed that Tutsi members of predominantly Hutu parties (such as the Frodebu or the CNDD-FDD) could indeed qualify as representatives of the Tutsi community, contrary to what Tutsi hard-liners advocated. This is in ironic contrast to the standard position of most Tutsi politicians in the wake of the 1993 elections, when the Frodebu scored a landslide victory: "'true democracy,' they argued, involves 'political' rather than 'demographic' majorities," thus calling into question the validity of an electoral victory delivered by an overwhelmingly ethnic vote. By 2004, however, the shoe was on the other foot, with ethnic and political loyalties expected to coalesce, a strategy designed to discourage Tutsi candidates from switching to the "enemy."[17]

Institutionalizing ethnic parity within the army is perhaps the most remarkable achievement of the Arusha conference. The result has been to bring about a sea change in the composition of what used to be an all-Tutsi military. The central question today is whether the fifty-fifty ratio among the troops also will apply to the officer corps. We touch here upon a highly sensitive issue, that became a major bone of contention in the recent peace talks between the FNL and the government (of which more later). The question it raises, from a broader perspective, is whether a restructuring of the officer corps would not be seen by hard-core Tutsi elements as a threat to their minority veto and thus pave the way for yet another army takeover. In a brilliant piece of analysis, Daniel Sullivan suggests that a key factor behind the 1993 assassination of Ndadaye was the widely shared assumption among Tutsi officers that he had every intention of breaking the Tutsi monopoly on the armed forces. Thus, the army seized power to neutralize the threat to its minority veto.[18] Sullivan's argument goes far in explaining why today many high-ranking officers are resisting attempts to apply ethnic parity to the higher ranks: what is at stake here is their minority veto. Whether such a move would automatically lead to an army coup is doubtful, however, given the enormous human costs such a move would entail, not to mention the presence on the ground of a 7,000-strong multinational force, the United Nations Operation in Burundi (ONUB).

The 2005 Elections

No fewer than four rounds of elections were held in 2005—actually five if one takes into account the constitutional referendum of February 28,

TABLE 1. NATIONAL ASSEMBLY: PARTY STRENGTHS AND ETHNIC PROFILE (2005)

Party	Seats	Hutu	Tutsi	Twa
CNDD-FDD	64	43	21	
Frodebu	30	23	7	
Uprona	15		15	
CNDD	4	3	1	
MRC	2		2	
Twa	3			3

Source: Filip Reyntjens, "Briefing: Burundi: A Peaceful Transition After a Decade of Civil War," *African Affairs* 105 (2006): 128.

2005: municipal elections on June 3, elections to the National Assembly on July 4, indirect elections for the Senate on July 29, and finally, on August 19, the indirect election of the president in a joint session of the National Assembly and the Senate.

Nkurunziza's CNDD-FDD emerged from all four races as the clear winner. In the communal elections, it received 62.6 percent of the vote, compared to 20.9 percent for its nearest competitor, the Frodebu. The CNDD-FDD kept its lead in the legislative elections, with 58.23 percent of the votes compared to 22.33 percent for the Frodebu, thus winning 59 seats in the National Assembly compare to forty-one for its rival. The Tutsi parties, represented by the Uprona and the Mouvement de Réhabilitation du Citoyen (MRC), ended up with, respectively, fifteen and two seats in the National Assembly. As Reyntjens observes, "the CNDD-FDD, generally presented as a Hutu party, came out as the most interethnic party, as 30 percent of its elected MPs were Tutsi."[19] By contrast neither the Uprona nor the MRC were able to send a single Hutu to the National Assembly. Let us note, finally, that since fewer of the constitutionally prescribed number of Tutsi deputies won seats in the National Assembly (thirty-five Tutsi and sixty-five Hutu), article 164 of the constitution immediately kicked in, in effect authorizing the Electoral Commission to co-opt eighteen deputies (four Hutu, eleven Tutsi, and three Twa).[20]

As the Table 1 shows, out of a total of 118 deputies, sixty-nine are Hutu and forty-six Tutsi; of these, however, more than half are affiliated with the CNDD-FDD (twenty-one) or the Frodebu (seven).

Although the electoral process was by no means free of violence, the consensus of international observers is that it was generally "free and fair." The CNDD-FDD's triumphant march to victory came as no surprise, given the solid support it received from the Hutu electorate, and the fact that it was able to attract the candidacies of not a few Tutsi who, on the eve of the elections, thought it wise to jump on the most promising bandwagon.

What did strike many observers as an unexpected turn of events was Nkurunziza's swift loss of popular legitimacy in the months immediately following his meteoric rise to the presidency.

Consociationalism Unhinged

Few African heads of state have come to power with a more impressive fund of good will and popular sympathy than Pierre Nkurunziza. In the eyes of many of his followers, he stood as the man to spoke truth to power, who fought tooth and nail to wrest power from the Tutsi oligarchs, and who did not shy from wrestling his internal enemies to the ground. A self-proclaimed born-again Christian, who sees himself as God's messenger, and former physical education instructor at the University of Bujumbura, he seemed well equipped for the job. His motives for joining the CNDD-FDD were both political and personal: of his six brothers, two lost their lives in killings that followed Ndadaye's assassination, and three subsequently died as rebels fighting the Burundi army.

His early public policy pronouncements augured well. His key priority, he said, was to make it possible for all children to attend primary school free of charge, along with free health care for children under five. Especially well received was his insistence on transcending ethnic and regional divisions. No sooner was he installed in the presidential chair than he declared, "with our new political orientation, everything is possible," including reconciliation with Rwanda, despite Kigali's radically different approach to building a new society. In a recent visit to Rwanda, he threw his arms around Kagame, in traditional fashion and said: "Our problem is not ethnicity; it was a scapegoat our predecessors used to cover up for their leadership failures and greed."[21] Many would have agreed with Paul Kaiser's optimistic assessment of Nkurunziza's rising political fortunes, penned in January 2006: "He has successfully reinvented himself as a novice statesman willing to admit his mistakes of the past, and symbolically lead the way in challenging the Burundian people to support his 'genuine cause' of ethnic reconciliation, political stability, and improving the quality of life for the Burundian people."[22]

Less than a year later, however, much of the early popular enthusiasm for Burundi's new leader has all but vanished. The government is facing a major crisis of confidence within and outside his own party, in parliament, and in the society at large. Not all of the underlying factors are as yet clearly identifiable, though many are. What seems reasonably clear is that the crisis is not reducible to one single event or set of motives. It has come about as a result of the accumulation of interrelated challenges to the government. First came the flurry of criticisms of the government's human rights record from various domestic and international NGOs;

then, like a bolt out of the blue, came the decision of the Frodebu to withdraw its support from the government, resulting in a major internal crisis within the party; the seemingly endless and (until recently) inconclusive cease-fire negotiations with the FLN was yet another source of disillusion about Nkurunziza's performance; a fourth stemmed from the accusations of corruption directed at the government, corroborated by disclosures by the media of large-scale misappropriations of EU financial assistance. On top of all this, as if he had not already suffered enough discredit, Nkurunziza invoked the convenient pretext of a plot against the security of the state to arrest scores of prominent personalities, all of whom, until proven innocent, are presumed guilty.

Human Rights Violations

Though most of the provinces remained at peace in the months following the elections, FNL attacks never stopped in rural Bujumbura, Cibitoke, and Bubanza. Nor did the army desist from its brutal retaliatory actions. The vast majority of human rights violations registered in late 2005 and early 2006 involved the deliberate killing of civilians by both the FNL and the armed forces (the latter now known as the Forces de Défense Nationale [FDN]). The most extensive reporting of such abuses is found in a February 2006 Human Rights Watch (HRW) report: much of it reads like a catalog of atrocities, ranging from revenge killings against "uncooperative" civilians to summary executions, abductions, mutilations, and torture. The abuses committed by the FNL are richly documented, as are the war crimes, arbitrary arrests, and collective punishment attributed to government security forces. "In December 2005 and January and February 2006, agents of the Documentation Nationale (DN) and army soldiers resorted to large-scale arbitrary arrests and detention of persons denounced as FNL collaborators by former FNL combatants. . . . Some of the victims told HRW that they were tortured in a small windowless room called 'the morgue' located in a small building run by the DN near the offices of the general prosecutor and the courts. . . . On January 25 government forces awakened residents of Muyira zone in Kanyosha commune (Bujumbura rural) just before dawn and ordered them to assemble at a nearby field. There, twelve captured FNL combatants picked out fifty-two persons as FNL collaborators and they were detained. The next day authorities detained others, including women and children."[23] This is only a small sample of the "incidents" recorded by HRW. Such abuses are of course part of a long established pattern of violence, but the fact that they occurred so soon after the elections, under Nkurunziza's watch, meant in effect that very little had changed since the advent of the new government. This is where popular disillusion began to set in. Especially revealing of the brutal incompetence of the government is that many of the atrocities denounced by NGOs were not isolated incidents but were for the most part orchestrated at the top, by the state intelligence agency, the DN, and the Interior Security Police (PSI).

In these conditions it is easy to see why the human rights issues were soon at the forefront of the attacks directed at the government by opposition parties.

Cracks in the Grand Coalition

In March 2006, Frodebu chairman Léonce Ngendakumana announced that his party was pulling out of the government. In addition to citing the failure of the ruling CNDD-FDD to consult with other parties in the government on certain key policy decisions, he also accused Nkurunziza of showing little regard for human rights. What could have led to a major crisis was quickly defused when the three Frodebu cabinet ministers—Barnabé Mbonimpa (health), Elie Buzoya (agriculture), and Odette Kayitesi (environment)—refused to comply. Although the outcome seemed to strengthen the government's position, this did little to solve the bitter internal quarrels within the ruling coalition.

Particularly embarrassing for Nkurunziza was the public display of mutual recriminations and accusations between his campaign manager and CNDD-FDD deputy, Mathias Basabose, a Tutsi, and the party chairman, Hussein Radjabu. In a press conference on April 11, Radjabu unleashed a violent attack against his former friend and companion in arms, accusing him, among other misdeeds, of having pocketed large sums of money in connection with a procurement contract concerning the rehabilitation of the road link Rumonge-Bujumbura. Basabose's response came in the form of a public statement claiming his innocence, and in turn lambasting Radjabu for his own corrupt behavior, reminding him of the huge kickbacks he allegedly received in connection with the sale of the Falcon presidential plane. The Basabose-Radjabu quarrel was given wide coverage in the local media before it was seized upon by opposition parties. The Frodebu, in particular, had a field day denouncing the "corrupt practices, kickbacks and influence peddling institutionalized by the party in power" and admitted its "sense of consternation in the face of the grave disclosures made by the party chairman El Hajj Hussein Radjabu and his right arm man, deputy Mathias Basabose."[24]

Adding to the fragility of the coalition, on September 5 came the announcement that Alice Nzomukunda, the country's second president, and second-highest-ranking official in the CNDD-FDD, had resigned in protest at the interference of the party chairman. "The reason for my decision," she said, "are the countless political difficulties we are facing, having to do with issues of security, contempt for the law, the justice system, the management of the finances of the state," all of which, she added, are traceable to "the total incompetence of the CNDD-FDD president, Hussein Radjabu."[25] She was later quoted as saying that "Radjabu was not respecting the country's institutions and was obstructing efforts to create a functional peacetime government"—to which the spokesman for the CNDD-FDD, Evariste Nsabiyumva, flatly replied, "what Nzomukunda says about the party chairman are big lies."[26] Although the vacancy was promptly filled by Marine Barampama, ex-secretary general of the Women's League of the ruling party, the procedure adopted by the government immediately came under fire from opposition deputies. Not only was the quorum of two-thirds of the membership of the National Assembly not met, the formalities of a secret ballot were deemed superfluous. It was by acclamation that the new vice-president was formally installed to replace her predecessor. Adding to the confusion, a private radio station, Radio publique africaine, informed its listeners that the newly appointed candidate was of foreign origins, the offspring of a Congolese mother (Kitenge Makangila) and a Tanzanian father (Shabani Meri), and that she had changed her name from Mwamini Shabani to Marine Barampama.

Between the Basabose-Radjabu confrontation and the brouhaha over Nzomukunda's resignation and replacement five months later, the credibility of the government came in for further questioning, this time from the EU.

Government Corruption

Compounding the discredit arising from allegations of financial wrongdoing by the two CNDD-FDD heavyweights, the scandal surrounding the European-funded Burundi Rehabilitation Program (BRP) caused further embarrassment to the government. Set up in 2001 for the specific purpose of rehabilitating the country's infrastructures, the BRP has become synonymous with claims of corruption and forgery involving millions of euros. On the basis of the investigation by the EU's Office de lutte anti-fraude (OLAF), the EU representative in Burundi, Georges Marc André, disclosed in June that widespread irregularities had occurred in the disbursement of funds. Some of the entrepreneurs working for the BRP, he said, were "forced to give bribes to get tenders." European funds, he added, "were allocated to Burundians to improve their living conditions, but instead of serving the interests of the Burundian community it has been used to enrich some individuals. That is unacceptable."[27] Although he declined to name names, it is widely believed that the top ranking officials in the BRP were on the receiving end of the line. Again, although André declined to say how much was involved, the total amount is estimated at five million euros (6.3 million dollars). In response, the prosecutor-general, Jean-Bosco Ndikumana, announced that legal proceedings would soon get under way but added that such cases of embezzlement would normally fall under the jurisdiction of the anti-corruption court, which is "not yet operational." If so, the same obstacle would presumably stand in the way of an investigation of the Radjebu and Basabose cases in the near future.

Among other shady deals, Radjabu is reported to have misappropriated a considerable sum over the sale of the presidential plane, a Falcon 50, soon to be replaced by a later model. He is said to have turned down an offer of $500 million and settled instead for a $300 million sale to another bidder, thus raising questions about who pocketed the difference. Some critics of the government claim that he has a major stake in the purchase of vehicles for parliamentarians and has the last word in selecting companies putting out tenders for the marketing of sugar. In lieu of the previous competitive procedure, the rumor in Bujumbura is that the government, notably the Minister of Commerce, engaged in a rather opaque bidding procedure giving control of the sugar market to seven traders, of whom four are members of parliament (MPs) affiliated with the CNDD-FDD. As for Basabose, the least that can be said is that his probity is very much in doubt. Despite his vehement denial that he benefited from under-the-table payments from a Rwandan contractor in connection with the rehabilitation of the Bujumbura-Rumonge road link, it is an open secret in Bujumbura that some 120 million Burundi Francs were paid by the same bidder to the CNDD-FDD treasury. Exactly who raked off the largest amount from the deal, Basabose, Radjabu, or other party hacks, is impossible to say.

Although many questions are yet to be answered, there is little doubt about the sense of disillusion shared by many Burundians in the face of mounting evidence of government corruption. Such a display of dishonesty by politicians and civil servants would be objectionable under any circumstances; in a country as poor as Burundi, where two-thirds of the population lives below poverty levels, such practices are unlikely to go unnoticed by the opposition, least of all by those poverty-stricken rural voters who placed their faith in the new leaders.

The Crackdown on Alleged Plotters

As if to cut short the litany of criticisms directed at his government, in late July Nkurunziza used the pretext of a plot against the security of the state to arrest a number of leading personalities suspected of involvement in this criminal conspiracy. The list of the persons rounded up reads like a who's who of the previous transitional government: among others, Domitien Ndayizeye, a key Frodebu personality and former transitional president;[28] Alphonse-Marie Kadege, ex-vice president under Ndayizeye and member of the Uprona; Déo Niyonzima, secretary general of the Parti pour la Réconciliation des Peuples (PRP);[29] and Alain Mugabarabona, head of the FNL-Icanzo, a dissident wing of the FNL. With the arrest of Colonel Damien Ndarisigaraniye, on August 2, the list of those arrested rose to nine, but government spokesman Ramadan Karenga said all those under arrest were on a list of fifteen "wanted for preparing the overthrow of elected institutions."[30]

Whether the crackdown came about in response to a genuine plot or is better seen as a machination orchestrated by the government to neutralize its opponents remains unclear. Until the government makes public the evidence at its disposal, the latter seems the more plausible interpretation, a view shared by the two major opposition parties, the Uprona and the Frodebu. The Uprona chairman, Aloys Rubuka, made clear the party position on the real significance of the arrests, which he described as a calculated cover-up: "The government wants to cover up the economic and political crisis whereby some senior country officials are involved in offences notably including the theft of sugar (from a state run firm), the illegal sale of an aircraft of President Pierre Nkurunziza, fraudulent tendering for government contracts, in addition to a crisis in the National Assembly on its internal regulations."[31] The Frodebu, for its part, "called on the international community, particularly the United Nations, the African Union, the European Union, and members of the Great Lakes initiative on Burundi to closely follow the situation in Burundi in order to prevent any social and political havoc."[32] A more subdued message came from the chairman of the Centre national d'alerte et de prévention des conflits, Charles Ndayiziga: in addition to complicating the ongoing negotiations with the FNL, "the scant information on the arrests is also worrying. We do not know much on that issue," adding that "we need to know the identity of the 'hidden forces' that may be working with the arrested people."[33] Their identity has yet to be revealed.

There is no indication of an ethnic motive behind the arrest of suspected plotters and the fact that both Kadege, a leading Tutsi figure, and Ndayizeye, the Hutu ex-president of the transitional government—known for their radically divergent political sensibilities—should be inculpated in the same conspiracy, makes the accusations against them all the more implausible. Despite the mystery surrounding the crackdown, what seems beyond doubt is that the person directly responsible for the arrests is none other than the CNDD-FDD chairman, Hussein Radjabu.

The Radjabu Enigma

Relatively little is known of the man who is increasingly seen as the real power behind the scenes. Lionized by some,[34] excoriated by others, he remains something of an enigma. A Hutu from Muyinga in the north, Hussein Radjabu belongs to the Muslim minority. His early career path as an agricultural assistant (*vulgarisateur agricole*) enabled him to develop close ties with the rural communities he came in contact with. Like many who lost relatives at the hands of Tutsi extremists—his father was killed in 1972, and in 1995, his wife was mortally wounded in Bujumbura by Tutsi militias, the infamous Sans Défaite et Sans Echec—he first joined the Paliphehutu, which he helped organize in the provinces of Bubanza and Cibitoke. He then switched to the Frodebu when Ndadaye emerged as the most credible candidate to the presidency in 1992. They became close friends and together were instrumental in converting local Palipehutu branches to the cause of the Frodebu. He was among the first to join the CNDD after Ndadaye's assassination. His talent as a grassroots organizer quickly caught the attention of Leonard Nyagoma, who appointed him as commissioner in charge of mobilization and propaganda. By all accounts, he played an important role in facilitating the rise of Nkurunziza to the leadership of the party and consistently sided with him when challenged by his rivals on matters of tactics and strategy. He would soon make excellent use of the manipulative skills he so successfully displayed in the course of the early intraparty struggles.

After Nkurunziza's victory at the polls, Radjabu shrewdly took advantage of his wartime experience and contacts to solidify his grip on the party, to the point where he now wields more influence than any other CNDD-FDD official within or outside the government. There are no holds barred in the methods he uses to rid himself of his potential enemies. Nor does he entertain any scruples in taking his cut on procurement contracts or the sale of public property; or in riding roughshod on the constitution. His use of symbolic gestures, one might add, are sometimes bizarre.[35] All of which has created a powerful backlash against the government.

Illustrative of this growing disenchantment are these comments from a well-informed Hutu observer: "It is he (Radjabu) who is responsible for the large-scale corruption going on in the government, for it is he who is in charge of giving procurement contracts. . . . What the Tutsi raked off in years, Radjabu and his cronies want to do in a few months time. . . . It is he who is responsible for human rights violations. He deeply distrusts the press, the civil society, and anything that smacks of an opposition. And who do you think is behind the manufacturing of imaginary coups and the arrest of alleged plotters against state institutions, and many other dirty tricks? Hussein Radjabu of course!"[36]

Although many would agree with such strictures, nagging questions remain about the scope of his influence. One concerns the extent to which something resembling a Muslim network has been put in place. Although there are reasons to doubt the existence of such ties, just how significant is the weight of Islam in shaping the government's foreign policy is hard to tell. Beyond dispute is that he is a devoted Muslim, having recently gone to Mecca on pilgrimage, and there is strong evidence that he is casting about for stronger diplomatic and commercial ties with the Sudan and Libya. Although rumor has it that he has sent a number of young men to Khartoum for military training,[37] the principal motive for this diplomatic overture lies in the prospects of economic and financial assistance from his newly found allies, should the European Union fail to deliver.

At the domestic level, many wonder as to whether his distrust of the media—recently shown by his personal attacks on Emmanuel Nsabimana, a journalist working for Radio ONUB, a station operated by the local UN mission—may not eventually lead to a more systematic repression of press freedom. The international NGO Reporters Without Borders recently admitted being "appalled by ruling party chief Hussein Radjabu's threatening comments towards the press on September 3," and urged Nkurunziza "to reestablish a relationship of trust with the independent media, which have had a rough ride in recent weeks."[38] So far there is little indication that any such relationship is about to materialize.

Finally, there is the question of his relationship with the security forces. The integration of former CNDD-FDD rebels into the police, the FDN, and the security apparatus, has produced a symbiosis of sorts between the party and the instruments of force. But the process has yet to be completed. Tutsi elements are still dominant in the upper ranks of the army. As we shall see, this has been a major stumbling block in the negotiations with the FNL. The problem has yet to be resolved. The key question is whether the incorporation of former CNDD-FDD troops into the army can be carried to the point where parity is achieved without provoking resistance from the Tutsi-dominated officer corps. Although Radjabu has proved himself adept at pushing his pawns on the political chessboard, whether he can press for further drastic changes in the structure of the armed forces and still rely on their continued loyalty is moot.

The Challenges Ahead

The biggest challenge is the institutionalization of a functioning democratic state, but to meet this challenge other issues must be resolved, ranging from the residual threats posed by the FNL and the future of the DDR program to refugee problems and governance.

The Persistence of Hutu Radicalism

Hutu radicalism has deep roots in the history of Burundi. In its most recent incarnation—Agathon Rwasa's FNL—it embodies a legacy of accumulated sufferings, anger, and frustration traceable to the 1972 bloodbath. The mass killings of Hutu by the Tutsi-dominated army created the context and motivation for the creation of the Parti pour la libération du peuple Hutu, (Palipehutu), born in 1980 in a refugee camp in Tanzania (Mishamo) at the initiative of the late Rémy Gahutu.[39] It is not for nothing that the formal designation of the FNL is Palipehutu-FNL: its stridently anti-Tutsi ideology, its mystical overtones and stern commitment to the cause of the Hutu people (in opposition to the Hutu "collaborators") bear the stamp of its early parent organization. Today the FNL makes no bones of the fact that "both the CNDD-FDD and the Frodebu have betrayed Burundi's mostly Hutu population by seeking political posts instead of improving living conditions for the majority."[40]

The inherited radical streak in the FNL ideology is graphically conveyed by the words of Pasteur Habimana, the FNL spokesman, to this writer in 2003: "Burundi's problem is that we are told lies! [*Le problème du Burundi c'est le mensonge!*] The members of parliament represent no one.... How can one agree on a fifty-fifty sharing of power with the Tutsi when they represent 15 percent of the population? In 1972 I saw my brothers being killed. I was twenty years old. I remember everything!"[41] There is indeed an irreducible core of fanaticism in the FNL's ideology, which finds expression in a blind recourse to violence, often perpetrated by teenage boys, going into battle chanting religious hymns. Such was the case during the devastating assault on Bujumbura, which lasted five days in July 2003 and caused scores of civilian casualties as well as the death of 310 rebels, mostly children, at the hand of the Burundi army.[42] That the FNL strongholds should be located in Bujumbura Rural, and therefore within striking distance of the capital, is not surprising when one recalls that the province claimed the largest concentration of regroupment camps. Nor is it a matter of coincidence, therefore, if the bulk of its combatants were child soldiers: as recent research convincingly shows, access to IDP and refugee camps correlates strongly with the recruitment of children as insurgents.[43]

Given the nature of the FNL's ideological appeal, its long history of resistance to Tutsi hegemony, and its capacity to mobilize popular support, it is not surprising that the signing in Dar es Salaam on September 7, of a "comprehensive cease-fire agreement" between the FNL and the government should have been received with cautious optimism by the international community.[44] Adding to such doubts is that the cease-fire was finally signed after considerable pressure from members of the Regional Initiative for Peace in Burundi (RIPB), notably presidents Yoweri Museveni of Uganda and Thabo Mbeki of South Africa. Furthermore, the crucial issue of the restructuring the Forces de Défense Nationale (FDN) high command appears to have been shoved under the rug. No where in the text of the agreement is there as much as a passing reference to this long-standing demand of the FNL. Further complicating the situation is the apparent unwillingness of a small FNL breakaway faction, led by Jean-Bosco Sindayigaya, to abide by the terms of the agreement.

Whether the cease-fire will hold long enough to allow the demobilization of FNL combatants, and ultimately pave the way for the restoration of peace in Bujumbura Rural, is anybody's guess. How to follow through the stipulations of the accords concerning the work of the Joint Verification and Monitoring Mechanism (JVMM), the movement of combatants to assembly areas, and their reinsertion into civilian life is a key problem facing the new government.

The Demobilization and Reinsertion of Ex-combatants

The demobilization of former CNDD-FDD fighters, as well as elements of the FDN has made notable progress under the supervision of the National Commission on Demobilization, Reinsertion, and Reintegration. Over the last year, according to figures released by the ONUB, 16,724 adult combatants and 3,015 child soldiers were demobilized, to which must be added 7,332 FDN troops. According to the most recent figures available (June 2006), a total of 20,294 ex-combatants have been demobilized. This brings within reach the target of a down-sized FDN of 30,000.

To this must be added the dismantling of militias, consisting essentially of the Tutsi-dominated Gardiens de la paix. By June of 2006, it was estimated that a total of 28,125 militia members had been demobilized, including 18,616 Gardiens de la paix.

However impressive its short-term achievements, the reinsertion program has yet to meet the long-term needs of the majority of demobilized combatants. Many are still waiting for their demobilization stipends or transitional subsistence allowance (TSA), the latter amounting to $515 per head for private soldiers. The Gardiens de la paix, on the other hand, are eligible for a single reinsertion payment of $91. By March 2006, an estimated 16,681 ex-combatants had received demobilization assistance. Although long-term reintegration programs are under way (involving 2,677 ex-combatants), whether sufficient external resources can be mobilized to sustain such programs over the long run is highly problematic.

Much the same problem is facing those FNL combatants currently being assembled for demobilization. How to accommodate their demands for reinsertion is only one aspect of the problem. Another is that some local FNL leaders "are recruiting civilians into its ranks as potential beneficiaries of demobilization fees," while others "have been collecting taxes, ranging from $0.50 to $1.50 per cow."[45] It is with no little apprehension that civilians watch the ex-rebels emerge from their rural hideouts in military fatigues, in search of food. Recently the governor of Bubanza province urged the government "to provide food for the combatants to prevent them from stealing from civilians," adding that "a team was needed to monitor the enforcement of the cease-fire accord between Rwasa's FNL and the government."[46] In these conditions it is doubtful that the timetable set for the disarmament, demobilization, and reintegration process—thirty days after the signing of the accord—will be met.

Seen from a broader perspective, the security sector reform undertaken by the government raises problems of *political* integration. As noted earlier, implementing the sixty-forty ethnic apportionment within the army high command remains a highly sensitive issue. Of the fifteen generals currently on active duty in the army, fourteen are Tutsi, of whom five are from Bururi. The Minister of Defense, Chief of Staff, and camp commanders are, likewise, Tutsi holdovers from the former Forces Armées du Burundi (FAB). Forcing them into early retirement is not an option. The new Burundi national police (BNP), on the other hand, has emerged as a notably heterogeneous force, consisting of elements recruited from different sectors, namely, from the previously Tutsi-dominated Police de Sécurité Publique (PSP), the Police Judiciaire (PJ), the Police Pénitentiaire (PP), the ex-FAB (about 10,600), as well as half a dozen former Hutu-dominated rebel movements. A total of 16,000 ex-combatants have been integrated into the BNP. Given such an extraordinary mix of ethnic and regional origins, professional backgrounds, and political horizons, doubts are bound to arise about the stability and reliability of the BNP as a constabulary force.

Overall it is difficult to disagree with the assessment offered by two well-informed observers: "One of the biggest challenges for the future will be the reintegration of the ex-combatants into civilian life. This process is only just beginning. Demobilized ex-combatants were given payments to support them for 18 months, calculated on salary scales in the armed forces, which allowed the former fighters some time for socio-economic integration. *The long-term goal, however, is for them to acquire a sustainable social and economic role in a peaceful society.*"[47] The issue is rendered all the more problematic by conditions of extreme economic scarcity, in part a reflection of a severe land hunger. Access to land ties in directly with another burning issue: how to reintegrate hundreds of thousands of refugees and internally displaced persons.

THE PROBLEM OF REFUGEES AND IDPs

It is estimated that during 2004 and 2005, approximately 170,000 refugees returned from Tanzania, and 1,500 returned in the first months of 2006. Out of a total of 411,000 refugees registered in Tanzania in early 2004 (a conservative estimate), some 342,000 remain outside the country, awaiting repatriation. These figures are based on the 1993 caseload; they do not include the refugees who fled the 1972 carnage. More than a million people were forced out of their homes during the killings, of whom as many as 300,000 sought refuge in Tanzania and other neighboring states, notably Rwanda. Referred to as "long-term refugees," 68,000 are said to have returned home since 2000. Furthermore, omitted from these statistics are tens of thousands who either did not register, moved to Dar es Salaam, or are currently living in Tanzanian village communities outside the camps.

There are, in addition, some 100,000 IDPs distributed among 160 camps in Burundi, down from 140,000 living in 182 camps in April 2004. Both the IDPs and the returnees live in the direst of circumstances. The worst off are those returning on their own, the so called *rapatriés spontanés*, as they are faced with frequent exactions from bandits (*wajambazi*), militias (*banamugambo*), and camp custodians (*basungusungu*). More importantly, they do not qualify for food aid from the United Nations High Commission for Refugees (UNHCR) and other humanitarian agencies. As one of them lamented, "when food is distributed we never know who gets it. Since I came back I have never received one single soya bean."[48] Unlike the *rapatriés spontanés*, those who return under UNHCR auspices can expect a three-month aid package consisting of food rations, household goods, tents, and other implements. Although the aid package will help them keep their heads above water for a few months, what happens to them in the longer term is anyone's guess.

The crux of the problem is the extreme scarcity of land. A survey conducted in 1999 indicated that 28.6 percent of the refugee respondents identified the land problem as a "crucial" obstacle to their return.[49] Today this percentage is likely to be much higher. The salience of the land issue is due in part to the enormous population pressure on the land, leading to an endless fragmentation of landholdings.[50] Another reason is that the land that once belonged to the refugees has in the meantime become somebody else's property. Germain Ntibarufata's story is not atypical: currently awaiting resettlement in Rukaramu, along with eighty-nine other families, the land he once owned at Kajaga, in Mutimbuzi commune, has been seized by the government and allocated to private developers while he and his family were in exile. "Nice homes and hotels have been built on our land," he said; "they told us we would get other land, but we have been waiting for four years now."[51] Summing up the dilemma faced by humanitarian agencies, one UNHCR official candidly admitted that "as long as the land issue is not settled, the UNHCR will only bring them emergency aid."[52]

One of the few bright spots on the horizon is the decision of the government to set up a commission on land and other properties, within the Ministry of National Solidarity, Human Rights and Gender, a move intended "to ease resettlements and solve disputes arising from the repatriation of long-term refugees." According to the commission's chairman, Abbot Aster Kana, "the team would neither operate as a conciliation body nor as a court: the commission would review complaints and help restore property to their owners."[53] It is worth noting, however, that the mandate of the commission extends far beyond the refugee's plight. In Kana's words, "it would work for all landless people such as the Batwa, the indigenous hunter-gatherer, forest-dwelling communities who are often neglected in society."[54] Providing land for the returnees is already an enormously complicated and politically sensitive issue; extending the commission's mandate to "all landless people" may not be the best way to attend to the urgency of the refugee demands.[55]

If the past record of administrative efficiency in meeting the demands of refugees is any index, there are reasons to doubt the capacity of the present government to live up to their expectations. In conformity with the Arusha Accords, a CNRS was created to handle the refugee problem. Its work, however, was immediately stymied by a conflict of jurisdiction, with strong political overtones. Although the CNRS was under the control of the Frodebu, it was financially and administratively accountable to the MRRDR, headed by one of the G-10 (Tutsi) parties. The result was administrative paralysis. The five-stage action plan elaborated by the CNRS remained a dead letter. So also, the provisions of the Arusha Accords concerning the restitution of their landed property to the refugees. Although this sort of political infighting is unlikely under the present dispensation, there is no denying the magnitude of the administrative challenge involved in the resettlement of hundreds of thousands of refugees eager to recover their lost property.

What makes the refugee problem so politically sensitive is that the occupants of refugee lands are unlikely to let go of their property for the benefit of the previous owners. It is common knowledge among refugees that "expropriated land (has been) allocated to influential political and military figures without adequate compensation to those from whom it has been taken."[56] Again, "commissions appointed to look into the land availability for the resettlement of refugees have at times appropriated the land for themselves or their wives."[57] Many recipients of these ill-gotten gains are either Tutsi, or Hutu to whom the land has been sold by previous Tutsi occupants. Coming to grips with illegal seizures of property going back to 1972, 1988, and 1993 is a daunting task. It is easy to see, in such circumstances, why so little has been done to meet the claims of the returnees.

Compounding these difficulties is the rampant corruption surrounding the allocation of humanitarian aid for refugee resettlement. A well-informed analyst detects a "predatory logic"—"des logiques prédatrices et de captation des fonds humanitaires"—in the dysfunctions that once crippled the MRRDR,[58] eventually resulting in the arrest of the minister and his cronies. Similar malpractices have been reported at the local and provincial levels. "The land reserve," some observers noted in 2004, "intended for allocation to the landless is manipulated, resulting in some people waiting for years, while others, who are not actually landless, receive plots rapidly due to favoritism and bribery."[59] In view of the recent scandal over the misappropriation of EU funds earmarked for the Burundi rehabilitation program, it would be surprising if such practices were to come to an end in the foreseeable future.

A Governance Deficit

There is no little irony in the fact that while Nkurunziza served for nearly two years as Minister of Governance in the transitional government under president Ndayizeye, today the lack of transparency, administrative efficiency, and respect for constitutional norms are among the most damning criticisms addressed to the government. In a report to the Netherlands Institute of International Relations, Willy Nindorera makes a strong case for "reinforcing the democratic culture of the CNDD-FDD," noting that the government is "in large part the product of an old rebellion which has not totally achieved its metamorphosis." There is, he adds, a carry-over of the *pratiques du maquis* into the context of the newly emergent state institutions. Among such practices he mentions clientelism, obsession with secrecy, and a highly personalized line of command, with the party "intervening in the affairs of the state to the point where it substitutes itself for the ministers and civil servants."[60] He might have added the tendency to revisit the past to settle scores with former rivals.

Such strictures are of course anathema to most CNDD-FDD incumbents. They point to the presence in the government of highly competent ministers and civil servants and do not hesitate to dismiss such accusations as unfounded. That some officeholders are indeed well qualified is undeniable. A case in point is the Minister of Foreign Affairs, Antoinette Batumubwira, whose track record cannot be faulted.[61] Others could be mentioned. The fact remains, however, that there is considerable room for improvement in the realm of governance.

While there may be exceptions to the rule, by and large the *pratiques du maquis* observed by Nindorera translate into a highly dysfunctional state, where the ruling party—not to mention key personalities within the party—seeks to assert itself as the only legitimate decision maker. There is no evidence that the process of consultation and cooperation so crucial to the successful implementation of consociational rule is being heeded. Laws are rammed through parliament without any real debate. The state and the party are two faces of the same coin. The grand coalition principle—identified by Lijphart as the key to effective power-sharing—has morphed into a wobbly coalition of party blowhards, threatened to dissolve at any moment into internecine struggles and settling of accounts. Hovering over these tiffs and intramural enmities is a strong whiff of machine politics. The spoils of office are distributed to the faithful, irrespective of their qualifications. Contracts and favors (access to free housing, vehicles, award of export-import licenses, appointments to parastatal institutions, and so forth) are awarded on the basis of loyalty to the party bosses at the central or regional levels, who are then in a position to build their own clienteles. Little wonder if the provincial governors, all of them nominated by the party, have emerged as powerful chiefs, strangely reminiscent of their precolonial counterparts. The most artful manipulator of resources is, of course, Radjabu, who has powerful allies in the government (notably the Ministers of Communication and Justice), as well as in the provinces and probably in the police and armed forces. His most faithful crony is none other than the all-powerful Adolphe Nshimirimana, the head of the National Intelligence Agency, the much feared Service National de Renseignement (SNR). Structurally, it seems that little has changed since the days of Tutsi hegemony in the 1970s and 1980s, except that ethnic and regional identities as a criterion for power and privilege are not nearly as significant as they used to be, at least for the time being.

Compounding the handicaps of a *maquis*-inspired approach to day-to-day administrative problems is the dearth of qualified civil servants, especially among Hutu. This is how a confidential source describes the situation: "As a result of the war, many civil servants have been either physically eliminated, or displaced and turned refugee [*sic*], fleeing to other countries. Burundi is left with a civil service that is ill-equipped, underpaid, and consisting of many elderly civil servants who are not tuned in to the requirements of modern organizations (no computer skills; no information infrastructure)." Sometimes administrative records are disposed of in the most erratic and arbitrary fashion, as in Gitega, where according to the same source, "all files on deaths and births as well as land titles were simply burned as those in charge did not know what to do with them." Although a *Statut de la fonction publique* has recently been elaborated, one wonders how long it will take before the new rules and code of conduct are internalized and acted upon by the new generation of civil servants.

One of the most worrisome aspects of this rising CNDD-FDD hegemony has been the increasingly tense climate between the ruling party and the civil society. The convening of the party congress in Bururi, in June, was the occasion for the organizers to make clear their distaste for whatever criticisms might come from civil society organizations. Of these, the media are seen as the most nefarious and have consequently paid the heaviest price. Not only are they perceived as a threat to the government but the fact that for historical reasons, most are headed by Tutsi elements makes this menace particularly ominous. One observer volunteered the opinion that "the hostility of certain figures or groups in civil society and the CNDD-FDD reaction to them could potentially stoke the embers of a greater clash."[62] Further complicating the situation, he adds, is "the tendency of opposition parties and civil society to act as if the system of governance was much better and cleaner before and was not previously riven by corruption, impunity, lack of accountability, and clientelism."[63] At stake here is not only the capacity of the civil society to fulfill its role as a potential source of opposition and a vitally important channel of communication between the populations at large and the decision makers, but also, and more significantly, the future of Hutu-Tutsi relations.

Governance issues, then, arise at several levels and in different contexts, but they all come into focus through the prism of state legitimacy. Electoral legitimacy is one thing; trust in the government is something else. It stems from the capacity of the state to meet the moral and political expectations of the electorate, or in Lockean terms, from the trust of the people in their rulers. That good governance fosters trust and legitimacy is an axiom that has yet to be fully realized by Burundi's new rulers.

Conclusion

The foregoing is not meant as a call for disengagement by donors, but rather the opposite. Although many of the problems faced by the new authorities will not be resolved by more foreign aid (*pace* Jeffrey Sachs)—indeed the result may be precisely the opposite—development assistance may indeed make a significant difference if it is properly targeted and prioritized.[64]

If the aid package is to be made more effective, a serious attempt must be made to engage the Burundi authorities in a more constructive dialogue. A close observer recently emphasized "the difficulties in the interface between the top of government and donors." After lamenting the fact that "very few donors have contact with Radjabu," he goes on to explain that their success in "engaging with sectoral planning (e.g., education and possibly health)" has had little impact on the political climate, "even if aid is a huge percentage of the country's GDP."[65] If so, a convincing case can be made for a more concerted approach in dealing with the principal decision makers, including Radjabu. A key objective of such a dialogue should be to define the terms on which conditionality could be applied, including the withholding of further assistance to specific sectors (e.g., rehabilitation, health, education) unless the present conditions of transparency and accountability are significantly improved. For the sake of giving greater resonance to their views, donors should reach out to the members of the Burundi regional initiative (BRI), and in concert with them, explore the ways in which the present climate can be improved. International pressure, in short, should not be limited to European donors alone.

Restoring the economy is of course one of the most urgent tasks facing the international community, but this can only be accomplished if the country enjoys sustained peace and stability. Peace has been reestablished through much of the country; consolidating the peace is where the challenge lies. Security sector reform (SSR) should be a key priority, especially with regard to the DDR and police training. In view of the size of the BNP (20,000), and its lack of internal cohesion and training, immediate attention should be given to a comprehensive police training program. This involves a broad range of interventions, from skills (crowd control) to technical competence and operational capacities. How this form of assistance could be combined with the current ongoing DDR program is one of the many issues donors should concern themselves with. Given that a very substantial number of BNP recruits are former rebels, their integration into a reconstituted police force, comprising a fair number of Tutsi elements from the former police and gendarmerie corps, raises obvious questions. How to facilitate the integration of such disparate elements should figure prominently on the DDR agenda.

With regard to economic recovery, the World Bank deserves much credit for coming to grips with the macroeconomic dimensions of poverty. Its poverty reduction strategy program bears testimony to a sustained effort in the direction of pulling the country out of the poverty trap. Nonetheless, the microeconomic, grassroots dimensions of rural poverty, especially in provinces most directly affected by civil conflict, are generally neglected. This is where a major effort is required from donors.

Consider the following description of the conditions prevailing in the rural sectors: "The majority of the people have only tiny amounts of cash moving through their hands each year. Coffee payments have dropped significantly and although there is an improved security situation, market access is still a problem. Transport is almost non-existent on the roads (except for beer and Coke trucks), and most people do not even have access to a basket or barrow to use to carry produce as they walk to the market. Activities that could possibly change this are ones that are unappealingly time-consuming and labor-intensive for donors.... As for bigger businesses, these are more likely to benefit from donors' preferences to support economies of scale and export revenue-generation.... As an economic development strategy, it reinforces the divide between 'haves' and have nots.'"[66] How to meet the needs of the rural poor in a country devastated by civil war—not to mention the recent torrential rains that have destroyed homes and crops and the spread of bacterial diseases attacking banana and cassava, Burundi's main staple—and where infrastructures are thoroughly inadequate, is indeed a daunting challenge.

CSOs should figure prominently on donors' agendas. As Western analysts never tire of reminding us, a healthy and "vibrant" civil society is an essential ingredient of democracy. Not all such organizations, however, are equally in sync with the ethos of democracy. Burundi is no exception. Furthermore, there is always the risk that by strengthening CSOs, donors unwittingly end up creating the conditions of a backlash against the recipients. This seems to be particularly relevant in the case of Burundi, where criticisms of government policies by the media are often seen as evidence of disloyalty to the state. Thus, although donors should make every effort to strengthen the civil society, they should exercise caution in their choice of partners, and remain fully aware of the possible costs.

In the context of present day Burundi, where state institutions are fragile and where the newly elected leaders are desperately trying to adjust to a civilian form of government and are confronted almost daily with new and formidable challenges, it is the responsibility of donors to take the full measure of the obstacles ahead.

Part III
The Democratic Republic of the Congo: From Failed State to Fragile Transition

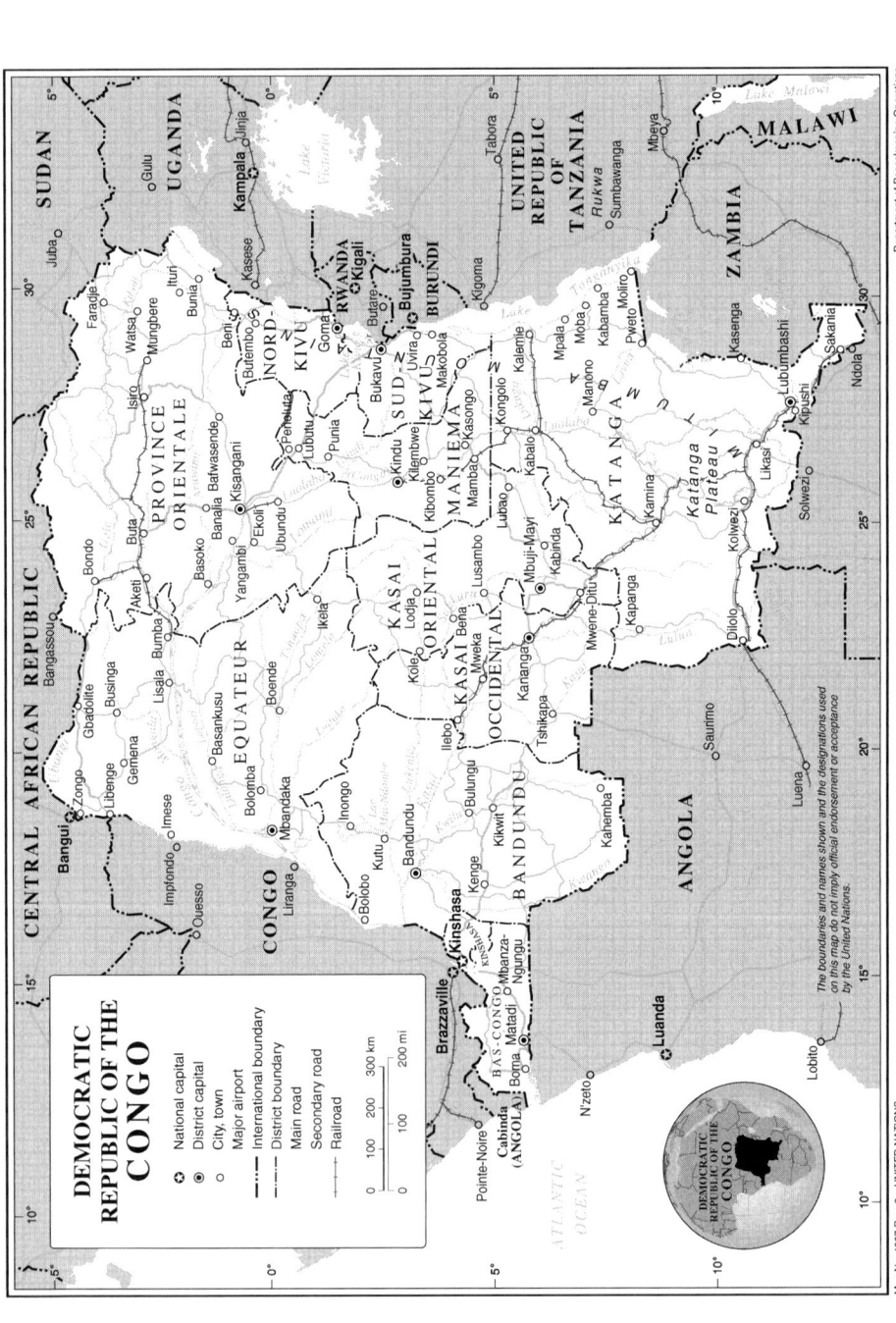

Map 5. Democratic Republic of the Congo (DRC). Map no. 4007, rev. 8, United Nations, January 2004. Reproduced by permission of the UN Department of Peacekeeping Operations, Cartographic Section.

Chapter 12
A Blocked Transition: Zaire in 1993

Zaire is the only country in the world to claim two prime ministers, two governments, two parliaments, two constitutions, and two transitional constitutional acts. The phenomenon—euphemistically referred to in Zaire as *dédoublement*—bears testimony to the total impasse currently facing the country.

At the root of the continuing deadlock lies a fundamental disagreement over the pace and manner of the transition. Against the claims of the opposition—a loosely knit coalition of parties known as the Union Sacrée (US)—that it has full authority to define the rules of the transition, Mobutu and his allies—the so-called Mouvance Présidentielle (MP)—insist that the only source of legitimacy lies in the 1990 revised constitution of the Second Republic, tailored to his autocratic stature. This means to say that he alone has the right to determine the basic outlines of a transitional framework and to set the timetable for presidential and legislative elections.

On each count, the disaccords between the US and the MP are virtually unbridgeable. Yoked together in a mire of contradictions and disagreements, they can neither live with each other nor without each other. For if there can be no question that the Conférence Nationale Souveraine (CNS), and now its successor institution, the Haut Conseil de la République (HCR), embodies an alternative source of legitimacy to that of the Mobutist state, once all is said and done, power—that is, access to guns and money—lies with the presidency.

The state in Zaire has virtually ceased to perform its intended functions, but the HCR is utterly impotent to act as a surrogate. While the security forces are a permanent threat to the civilian population, private militias are emerging in parts of North Kivu, protection rackets proliferate in Lumbubashi and Kinshasa, and mutinies are reported in Kolwezi. Meanwhile, the extreme fluidity of political alignments and ceaseless combinations among members of the political class make it impossible to predict what the next round might be like.

Toward a "Global Political Compromise"

The critical issue now facing the political class is whether the July 1992 compromise—the so-called Compromis Politique Global (CPG)—hammered out between the MP and the US can provide the basis for a democratic transition.

What many at the time saw as a major breakthrough came about after a protracted trial of strength between Prime Minister Nguz Karl I Bond (Mobutu's candidate) and the CNS. Tensions came to a head on February 16, 1992 when in response to Nguz's decision to suspend the CNS, thousands went on a protest march in the streets of Kinshasa—only to be savagely repressed by units of the Civil Guard.

Not until July was a "global compromise" finally reached that among other things (a) recognized the right of the CNS to elect a Prime Minister, (b) acknowledged the prerogatives of the President as the Head of State and Supreme Commander of the Armed forces during the transition, (c) called for a neutral transitional government "free of partisan militancy and exclusivism," and (d) suggested a pre-electoral timeframe of eighteen to twenty-four months. An important stipulation of the compromise—promptly violated by Mobutu—was that "the present National Assembly will not stand as a transitional institution," because "no institution can impose its will on the people or on any other institution"—a provision that contained within itself the seeds of endless conflict.

As if to give them greater legitimacy, the terms of the compromise were subsequently enshrined in a basic constitutional document—officially known as "*Acte portant dispositions constitutionnelles relatives à la période de transition*," in short, "*Acte de la Transition*" (hereafter referred to as the Transitional Constitutional Act). Adopted by an overwhelming majority of the CNS on August 4, this document incorporates and elaborates upon the key provisions of the Global Compromise, with the added provision that the country would again be known as the Congo.

As subsequent events showed, the election by the CNS of the US leader Etienne Tshisekedi as the prime minister, on August 15, marked the limits of Mobutu's tolerance in recognizing the terms of the Global Compromise and the Transitional Constitutional Act.

President versus Prime Minister

Arguing that the CNS had violated the terms of the compromise by changing the name of the country; that Tshisekedi had failed to put together a government of "national union" of neutral complexion, as had been agreed upon by the parties to the compromise; and that he went far beyond his prerogatives as Prime Minister in sacking the Governor of the

Central Bank, Nyembo Shabani, on October 1; Mobutu proceeded to use every means at his disposal, including force, to reassert his control.

On October 1, armored units of the Forces Armées Zairoises (FAZ) were ordered to the Central Bank to reinstate Governor Shabani; a few days later the National Assembly met at the Palais de la Nation at the request of Mobutu, a move clearly intended to challenge the legitimacy of the CNS; and on October 27, a carefully selected group of CNS members, mostly identified with the MP, met with Mobutu and publicly came out in support of a neutral and more broadly representative transitional government. On December 1, a presidential ordinance dismissed Tshisekedi from office and appointed him as *formateur* in hopes that he would heed the presidential warnings and reshuffle his cabinet. Tshisekedi remained obdurate. Resisting pressure from the newly elected HCR—that, after the dissolution of the CNS in December, emerged as a kind of surrogate parliament—Tshisekedi decided to maintain his cabinet, with seven ministries out of a total of twenty-two (including Interior, Justice, and National Defense) under the control of his own party, the Union Démocratique Populaire et Sociale (UDPS). Mobutu responded with a presidential ordinance vesting full authority with senior civil servants (*secrétaires généraux*) to run the day-to-day tasks of the administration. To induce compliance with Mobutu's directives, each received an additional month's salary as a bonus.

The crunch came in January 1993, after Mobutu decided to issue a new five-million-zaire banknote in an attempt to reduce the printing costs of his sharply devalued currency. The move was immediately declared illegal by Tshisekedi. His call was largely heeded by traders and shopkeepers. Upon discovering that they would not accept the new banknote, scores of infuriated soldiers went on a looting spree; spreading violence, arson, and chaos through the capital city and other localities. This was not the first time that disgruntled soldiers had gone on rampage, but there was no precedent for the scale of the devastation. An estimated 1,000 human lives were lost at the hands of the Division Spéciale Présidentielle (DSP); hundreds of millions of dollars worth of property went up in flames; and not a few of the looting operations conducted by FAZ commandos were specifically targeted against enemies of the regime, including Union des Démocrates Indépendents (UDI) turncoats.

Mobutu Seizes the Initiative

In the atmosphere of fear and consternation that enveloped Kinshasa, Mobutu moved swiftly to exploit the situation to his advantage—first by blaming Tshisekedi for the rioting; then by appointing General Eluki, known for his total loyalty to Mobutu, as his chief of staff, replacing

General Mahele, suspected of being too "liberal"; and finally by making it unambiguously clear that Tshisekedi was no longer qualified to serve as prime minister. By then there was a growing sentiment among some members of the US that Tshisekedi had outlived his usefulness. Capitalizing on this sense of frustration and disaffection, Mobutu quickly proceeded to restore his power base through an appropriate mixture of intimidation and reward.

In a move clearly intended to intimidate the HCR and cast discredit upon it, on February 24, 1993, units of the Civil Guard were instructed to surround the Palais du Peuple and make sure that none of the *conseillers* attending the session would be allowed to leave the building. Not until three days later would they be allowed to go home.

As if to add to the debilities of the HCR, and in clear violation of the terms of the Global Compromise and the Transitional Constitutional Act, on March 9 Mobutu resurrected the National Assembly (elected in 1987), with the firm intention of using it as a counterweight to the HCR.

Having dissipated all doubts as to where power lay, Mobutu now turned to the task of splitting the opposition by dangling the prospects of a nomination to the post of Prime Minister before a pool of receptive candidates. This was the main purpose of the conclave summoned by Mobutu, March 9–18. Among the key members of the US attending the conclave were Albert Ndele, Thomas Kanza, Cléophas Kamitatu, and Faustin Birindwa. By appointing Birindwa as prime minister, Mobutu exposed the venality of at least some members of the opposition while at the same time driving a deep wedge between hardliners and moderates. All four "ministrables" were immediately expelled from the US.

With a new parliament and a new prime minister, Mobutu could finally turn to the last and most important step: the construction of a new constitutional formula for the transition. Approved by an overwhelming majority of the National Assembly on March 26, the so-called Acte Constitutionnel Harmonisé provides for a constitutional formula radically different from the one embodied in the constitutional document of August 1992 adopted by the HCR: the president remains the central figure during the transition, with the prime minister, the National Assembly, the HCR, and the courts and tribunals all reduced to an ill-defined limbo.

The central obstacle in the way of a democratic transition lies in the historical legacy of the Mobutist state: although presidential and legislative elections were held in 1970, 1975, 1977, 1982, and 1987, at no time did they threaten Mobutu's autocracy; even when several candidates were allowed to compete under the banner of the Mouvement Populaire de la Révolution (MPR), as happened in 1977, 1982, and 1987, electoral processes were little more than plebiscitary rituals. For the overwhelming majority of the Zairians, the concept of democracy has no meaningful resonance.

Prolonged obeisance to the politics of patronage has insured the emergence of a political class utterly lacking in vision and maturity, primarily concerned with jockeying for power, ever ready to switch sides as long as the price is right, and with few notable exceptions, blissfully indifferent to the fate of the rural masses.

More specific handicaps include (a) sharp disagreements among political parties about the timetable and manner of the transition, (b) an extremely weak and fragmented civil society, with few crossethnic ties, and (c) a security situation characterized by countless human rights abuses, in some areas (Shaba and North Kivu) reaching the proportions of a near genocide.

Electoral Formats and Political Discords

As noted earlier, disagreements among political parties center on (a) the timeframe for electoral processes, (b) whether these should start at the local level first, then the legislative and presidential levels, or the other way around, (c) the distribution of power in the new constitutional dispensation.

Reaching agreement on these issues is made all the more complicated by the sheer number of contestants and the fluidity of political alignments. Switching sides—referred to in local parlance as "*vagabondages politiques*"—is a common practice among Zairian politicians. Coalition partners may share a common stand on one issue and not on others; and party leaders in the capital city may approach legal and constitutional issues from one perspective and regional and local leaders from another. All of which also raises serious questions about the durability of a consensus, should one emerge.

The number of registered parties increased from 3 in April 1990 (following Mobutu's speech of April 24, when he first recognized the legitimacy of a multiparty system) to 255 when the CNS met for the first time, to over 500 at the time of this writing. These are for the most part regrouped into a smaller number of platforms, each gravitating around the US and the MP.

Included in the former—recently renamed—Union Sacrée de l'Opposition Radicale (USOR) are the following constituent groups, each consisting of a constellation of satellite parties: Front Uni de l'Opposition (FUO), Collectif Progressiste (CP), Alliance des Forces Indépendentes pour le Changement Intégral (AFICI), Cartel des 18, and Indépendents.

The MP, on the other hand, includes Cartel des 40, Consensus, Alliance des Démocrates pour des Elections Libres (ADELI), and Union des Forces Nationalistes et Lumumbistes (UFONAL). The ADELI is made up of three separate parties: the MPR, which served as the pivot of the Mobutist state for a quarter of a century; Karl I. Bond's Union Fédérale des Républicains Indépendants (UFERI), with its political base in Shaba; and the Bula Mandugu wing of the Front Commun des Nationalistes (FCN). As of September 1993, the other wing, headed by Gérard Kamenda, was said to have joined the USOR.

The key players in the spectrum of political parties are the UDPS, the Parti Démocratique Social Chrétien (PDSC), and the Union Fédérale des Républicains Indépendents (UFERI). The first two are key partners in the USOR, and the third is one of the pillars of the MP, along with the MPR. Its staunchly federalist stance did not prevent the UFERI from entering into an alliance of convenience with the normally "unitarist" Mobutist forces, a situation that helps explain why the unitary versus federal issue appears to be the least contentious. On other issues, however, the prospects of a compromise between the USOR and the MP are not nearly as promising.

The position of the Mouvance Présidentielle on the timing of the elections is clear—the sooner the better. This means a constitutional referendum in October, presidential elections in December, and local and parliamentary elections sometime in the spring of 1994.

The USOR, on the other hand, insists on a longer time frame; so as to insure that Mobutu will not interfere in the electoral process and to give the opposition parties enough time to organize their campaigns. Broadly speaking, the USOR position is set forth in the Transitional Constitutional Act: a period of eighteen to twenty-four months should precede the elections, and these should start at the local level first and proceed from the ground up.

Unlike the MP, which argues that there is no need for a census or an electoral register, both are generally seen by the USOR as an important condition for free and fair elections, along with international monitors. Tshisekedi (UPDS) and André Boboliko (PDSC), among others interviewed, made it clear to me that they viewed a census as the first step towards putting together an electoral register. The last census was taken in 1984 and is said to be less than reliable. (The Zairian human rights activists that I interviewed unanimously endorsed the USOR position on a pre-electoral timeframe of eighteen to twenty-four months, though some would prefer an even longer period of time, ranging from three to four years. Most would agree that immediate priority should be given to setting up an electoral register and that close ties should be established with NGOs for monitoring purposes.)

More substantial are the differences between the MP and the USOR on constitutional issues. Where the MP insists on a strong executive and

TABLE 2. PARTIES' STANDS ON KEY ISSUES

Issues	USOR	MP
Strong president	Against	For
"Délai butoir"	For	Against
PM responsible to National Assembly	For	Against
Federal system of government	For	Against
Presidential "reserved domain"	Against	For

a weak parliament, the USOR argues precisely the reverse. Specifically, a weak executive for the USOR means (a) a figurehead president and a prime minister accountable to the National Assembly, (b) a *délai butoir* clause, meaning that after fifteen days of its passage by the National Assembly, a bill becomes law regardless of whether or not it is promulgated by the President, (c) a federal system of government allowing substantial autonomy to the regions, and (d) rejection of a presidential "reserved domain" that would enable the president to control such key portfolios as Foreign Affairs, Interior, and Defense. On each count, the position of the MP is diametrically opposed to that of the USOR (except for a compromise of sorts over the unitary vs. federal issue). Furthermore, unlike the MP, which insists on recognizing the 1967 parliament as a "key organ of the transition," the USOR takes the view that only the HCR can claim the role of a surrogate parliament before elections. In the words of the *Compromis Politique Global,* "the HCR has the power to pass laws in order to meet the needs of the transition."

The principal constitutional divergences between the USOR and the MP are summed up in Table 2. A protracted deadlock on these issues may not prevent Mobutu from going ahead with the presidential poll in December, but if so it will provide the opposition with further ammunition to boycott the elections. Even if agreement is reached before the elections, the sheer number of parties, along with their overwhelmingly ethnoregional underpinnings, is reason enough to expect considerable ethnic violence during the campaign and question the likelihood of a viable consensus in the post-electoral phase of institutional consolidation.

The Missing Middle: A Weak and Fragmented Civil Society

Democracy requires a great deal more than parties and elections. It requires participatory structures through which social demands can be formulated and acted upon. Such demands—the raw materials out of which parties normally build their platforms—are nowhere more weakly articulated than in Zaire.

Set against a quarter of a century of patrimonial rule, the organizational weakness of Zairian society must be seen as the logical consequence of the Mobutist state. Patrimonial rule sets sharp limits on the organization of independent power centers; state-society relations are mediated through personalized linkages, of a patron-client variety; and social demands are funneled upwards from clients to patrons, rather than through crossethnic associations capable of mobilizing widespread support from their constituents. In such circumstances, the organization of social life has little to do with professional associations, trade unions, or cooperatives. The civil society is largely reducible to a congeries of kin groups and ethnic associations.

The situation I observed in Goma (North Kivu) is not atypical: whereas the local branch of the Union Nationale des Travailleurs Zairois (UNTZ) seemed in a state of suspended animation, with a skeletal membership and average monthly dues amounting to the equivalent of $50; ethnic associations (or *mutualités*), on the other hand, were flourishing. Here is a sample of the most active:

Association Culturelle Bahunde
Bushenge (Mutuelle des Bahunde)
Kyahanda (Mutuelle Nande)
Bunakima (Mutuelle des Banyanga)
Mogo (Mutuelle des Originaires de Goma)
Banyamunigi (Association des Hunde de Goma)
Umoja (Mutuelle Bayarwanda)
Magrivi (Mutuelle des Agriculteurs et Eleveurs des Virunga)

Asked why parties and trade unions had such shallow roots in Goma and its vicinity, the answer I received from local notables was everywhere the same: "Political parties mean nothing to us. The same goes for the UNTZ. We'd rather be with people of our own kind. At least we know they can provide us with help and protection when we need it." Reports from other regions point to much the same sense of frustration over the inability of parties to respond to local concerns. Although interviews with local party officials convey an image of strong public support for their respective organizations, the weight of the evidence suggests otherwise. In the absence of strong party organizations, ethnic associations will become the most serviceable frameworks for setting up vote banks. Thus to the extent that much of the social space has been preempted by ethnic associations—which seems to be the case almost everywhere—it is easy to see why electoral processes might intensify interethnic competition and lead to further violence.

Except for the UDPS, the UFERI, and the PDSC, all of which have substantial roots in the countryside—the first primarily in Kasai Oriental, the second in Shaba, and the third in Bas-Zaire—few parties are likely to emerge as a dominant force at the regional or national level. Furthermore, since all three tend to be identified with specific ethno-regional aggregates—the PDSC with the Kongo, the UFERI with the Luba/Shaba and the UDPS with Luba/Kasai—there is every reason to expect electoral competition to translate into ethnic confrontations, with Shaba emerging as the most likely candidate for another round of ethnic unrest.

Not only does this situation pose major threats to the electoral process—and possibly induce Mobutu to have recourse to force to bring it to an end—but it also casts grave doubts about the next phase: in the absence of strong civic and professional associations to counterbalance the power of the government, a successful consolidation of democratic institutions seems most unlikely.

Insecurity: The Omnipresent Threat

The dominant trend in the security situation has been from repressive actions directed against regime opponents to something approximating organized anarchy.

Specifically, there are strong indications that Mobutu is no longer able to exercise effective control over the FAZ, as shown by their propensity to engage in recurrent looting sprees. Furthermore, there has been a major increase in the scale of human rights abuses committed by non-state agents, most notably in Shaba and North Kivu. Even if such were his intentions, Mobutu is in no position to guarantee minimum security conditions during the elections. To the extent that he still has a measure of control over certain units, as well as over the DSP, the intimidation and harassment of opposition candidates is not to be excluded.

Estimates of the size of the Zairian armed forces vary between 120,000 and 175,000. The core units are the DSP and the Garde Civile (GC). Officially described as consisting of "unités de la force terrestre chargées d'assurer la sécurité du Président," the DSP is Mobutu's praetorian guard. Headed by his brother-in-law (General Nzimbi) and much more generously treated than other units in terms of salaries and privileges, its 12,000 troops are essentially recruited among Mobutu's own ethnic group, the Ngbandi. Its loyalty to Mobutu seems assured.

The same applies to the 14,000 strong GC, headed by General Baramoto, also of Ngbandi origins. His meteoric rise through the ranks—illustrated by his instant promotion from the rank of sergeant to ur-star general—owes much to his unquestioned loyalty to According to Baramoto, Bas-Zaire (a predominantly Kongo tributes the largest number of troops to the GC; next comes , and third Equateur, with an almost even proportion of Ngbandi, Ngwaka, and Ngombe. Like the DSP, its pay scales are substantially above those of the regular FAZ units. Its reputation as an instrument of political repression is well established. On a number of occasions—beginning with the attacks against students on the Lubumbashi university campus in May 1990, against UDPS members in Mbuji-Mayi in April 1991 and in Kinshasa in September 1991, and followed by countless other "interventions" of a similar kind—the GC has been called upon by Mobutu to intimidate, beat, or kill his political opponents.

In dealing with the rise of anti-regime forces, Mobutu uses every means at his disposal, including force. After the killing of some forty DPS supporters in Mbuji-Mayi by the security forces in April 1991 came the shooting of some sixty peaceful demonstrators on February 16, 1992, and the targeted killings—locally known as *actions ponctuelles*—of various opposition figures and the destruction of their property—all of which come under the rubric of what Msgr. Monsengwo described to me as "state terrorism."

Another form of political violence is associated with non-state agents. A case in point is the "ethnic cleansing" undertaken by the Jeunesses wing of the UFERI—the so-called JUFERI—against Kasaian elements in several localities of Southern Shaba (Likasi, Fungurume, Lwena, Kanzenze, Musokantanda, and Kolwezi): under the leadership of a certain Jeannot Tshiyuka, the UFERI youth groups have morphed into gangs of terrorists high on drugs and alcohol. Although there can be little doubt that responsibility for the anti-Kasaian pogroms came from above, when interviewed by this writer, Governor Kyungu (Shaba) insisted that the Jeunesses evolved into a totally uncontrolled, self-recruiting group: "les membres se recrutent eux-mêmes." Responding to Kyungu's call, "Debout Katanga!" ("Up on your feet Katanga!"), they sprang into action shortly after Tshisekedi was appointed for the second time to the post of prime minister in August 1992. Since then, an estimated 150,000 Kasaians have been forced out of Shaba, leaving much of their property—houses, cars, bicycles, cattle, and land—in the hands of the Jeunesses.

North Kivu is another case in point: in March 1993, an estimated 3,000 Banyarwanda were massacred at the hands of Bahunde, Banyanga, and Banande elements in Walikale and Masis. Despite evidence of involvement on the part of the regional authorities, the killings were the work of rural elements, many of them landless, infuriated by the provocations of Kinyarwanda-speaking activists, many affiliated with the Magrivi. Tensions between Banyarwanda migrants (Hutu and Tutsi) and "natives" had been building up for years. That many of the large landowners in Masisi happened to be Banyarwanda of Tutsi origins contributed in no small way to focus popular resentment against all Banyarwanda. Like the Kasaians in Shaba, the majority of the Banyarwanda (numbering approximately half a million) were born in North Kivu. Although the sudden influx of thousands of Tutsi elements from Rwanda after the 1959–62 Hutu-led revolution put additional strains on land resources, the key issue revolves around the rights of Banyarwanda as a group: following the decision of the CNS to withhold recognition of their rights as Zairian citizens, Magrivi activists proceeded to make clear their discontent by staging a civil disobedience campaign in Walikale, much of it targeted against local authorities. In the climate of intergroup tension that existed at the time, this was the signal for a violent retribution. Violence spread quickly from Masisi to Bwito, where Tutsi elements took advantage of the situation to kill hundreds of Hutu. Yet a few miles south, in Bwisha, Hutu and Tutsi joined hands to kill every Hunde in sight. In addition to the loss of thousands of human lives on both sides of the ethnic fault line, an estimated 120,000 homeless people have found refuge in mission stations.

Just as a distinction must be made between state and non-state agents as vectors of human rights violations, it is important to distinguish between violence that is explicitly political in character and acts of arson and looting by troops, angered by long delays in the payment of their salaries, followed by the refusal of local traders to accept their freshly printed five-million Zaire notes. In practice, however, the distinction is not nearly as clear. As reported recently by Amnesty International, the January 1993 looting involved more than just the destruction of property. The pillages were an opportunity to settle scores with personal or political enemies, and in the process a fair number of anti-Mobutist elements were eliminated. According to reliable sources, in Kinshasa alone 113 persons were killed in January 1993, including twenty seven identified as "militaires"; 156 were seriously wounded by bullets. One informant told this writer, however, that at least 1,000 FAZ troops involved in looting were shot dead by the DSP. Meanwhile, millions of dollars worth of property were destroyed by FAZ elements.

Although the January 1993 and September 1991 pillages have received a fair amount of publicity, much less has been heard of other looting sprees—in Lubumbashi on October 23, 1991; in Mbanza-Ngungu on January 28 and 29, 1992; in Goma in December 1992; in Mbandaka in September 1992; in Kisangani, Goma, and Rutushuru in January 1993; and in Lisala in August 1993.

With the prospects of Mobutu running out of cash, further destruction and bloodshed seems likely. Zaire has reached the stage where the army is increasingly spinning out of control. Furthermore, the issue of

TABLE 3. DISTRIBUTION OF ETHNOREGIONAL
IDENTITIES AMONG FAZ GENERALS

Provinces	Generals
1. Equateur	31
Ngbandi	10
Mbuja	10
Libinza	4
Mongo	4
Ngombe	3
2. Haut Zaire	7
3. Bandundu	6
4. Maniema	5
5. Bas-Zaire	5
6. Kasai Occidental	3
7. Kasai Oriental	2
8. Sud Kivu	2
9. Shaba (Katanga)	1
Total	62

Source: *La Tempête des Tropiques*, no. 109 (August 21–24, 1993): 7.

ethnicity intrudes into this situation with equally ominous implications: the anti-Kasaian pogroms in Shaba have triggered serious mutinies among predominantly Kasaian FAZ units in Kolwezi; and the killing of an estimated 1,000 FAZ looters by DSP troops in Kinshasa in January 1993 must have left in its wake a rich potential for further conflict within the military.

Table 3 shows the ethnoregional origins of FAZ generals as of August 1993.

Although half of the FAZ generals come from Mobutu's region (Equateur), and one third of these are of Mobutu's own ethnic group (Ngbandi), the more important point is that Ngbandi elements are overwhelmingly concentrated in the DSP and the GC. In both, recruitment into higher ranks can best be seen as a patronage operation designed to reinforce the loyalty of the officer corps to the supreme patron. Merit is of secondary importance to personal devotion to Mobutu. In such circumstances one can readily appreciate the difficulty of persuading Mobutu to reorganize his armed forces. All efforts to achieve a more equitable ethnic balance among the upper ranks and to professionalize the army will be strenuously resisted by Mobutu and his cronies.

Nonetheless, to the extent that the situation threatens to get totally out of hand and result in the disintegration of what little is left of the security apparatus, both the Organization of African Unity (OAU) and the United Nations should be alerted to the extreme gravity of the situation and encouraged to bring maximum pressure on Mobutu to allow a reorganization of the FAZ.

The Economy in Shambles

The crisis which currently assails the economy holds equally somber implications for free and fair elections: as the economic pie shrinks, the competition for scarce resources becomes all the more intense, thus giving a fresh impetus to ethnic tensions (as happened in Shaba and North Kivu); and where eruptions of violence have led to a substantial flight of capital and expertise, the result has been to drive the economy even further into the ground. This is what happened in Shaba after hundreds of highly qualified Kasaians—Gécamines technicians, teachers, nurses, doctors, and entrepreneurs—were driven out of the region at gunpoint by JUFERI gangs; this is also what happened in Kinshasa and Lubumbashi in the wake of the pillages, when scores of well-to-do Zairian and non-Zairian businessmen suddenly decided to pull up stakes and to take their savings to South Africa.

The catastrophic effects of the looting on the economy go far beyond the flight of capital and expertise. Infrastructures, plants, and equipment have been destroyed; employment has declined, and the purchasing power of the urban masses has plummeted. Many had no alternative but to return to their villages. The rural sectors are in no better shape, however. The contribution of industrial crops—tea, coffee, and cotton—to the economy is but a fraction of what it used to be. Almost everywhere people are going back to a subsistence economy. Speaking of the "almost forgotten countryside," one recent visitor to Bas-Zaire noted: "people scratch out a living any way they can ... [on roadsides] charcoal, manioc, tomatoes, and bananas are offered to the declining number of passers-by." Again, to quote from the same source: "the modern economy is in full retreat, with a handful of businessmen hanging on as the economy plunges to less than half its former levels, and infrastructures crumble." Although the foregoing was inspired by a visit to Matadi—where port facilities, we are told, operate at just 30 or 40 percent of their capacity—it applies equally well to just about every other part of the country.

The industrial sectors are virtually paralyzed. From a total copper production of 130,000 tons in 1991 (approximately one fourth of its 1985 level), Gécamines is expected to produce less than 50,000 tons in 1993. Not only copper but every other mineral product (cadmium, zinc, silver, cobalt) registers a sharp decline in output. Diamonds remain the regime's best friend, but here again the output is declining (a large volume of diamond exports avoid official channels, however, which also could explain the registered drop in official exports).

Given the heavy reliance of the Zairian economy on industrial exports for foreign exchange, it is easy to see why annual inflation runs into four figures. The zaire's value against other foreign currency keeps tumbling day after day; it dropped from 4.5 million zaires to the dollar at the beginning of my trip to six million three weeks later.

A successful transition to democracy is the indispensable first step to deal effectively with the economic crisis, yet the profoundly destabilizing effects of the crisis on Zairian society pose a mortal threat to the transition. Not only do resource scarcities have a multiplier effect on ethnic tensions; they also generate a heightened awareness of the shocking social disparities between rich and poor, between those members of the political class whose foreign bank accounts allow them to engage in conspicuous consumption, and the urban poor who cannot meet even minimal food requirements.

Given the fact that few parties have anything resembling a "*projet de société*," let alone a coherent economic program, one can see why, for many Zairois, the game of politics is seen as utterly irrelevant to their immediate concerns, and why their attitude is marked by a growing sense of alienation and disaffection towards politics and politicians. These are far from propitious omens for the holding of democratic elections.

Chapter 13
Ethnic Violence, Public Policies, and Social Capital in North Kivu

Few works of political science have received a more universal acclaim than Robert Putnam's trailblazing inquest into the roots of democracy in contemporary Italy, appropriately titled *Making Democracy Work: Civic Traditions in Modern Italy*. Judging from the theme of this conference, the impact of his contribution is not limited to the American academic community. Although one may not agree with all of his ideas, their boldness is undeniable: more than an elegantly crafted case study of modern-day Italy, *Making Democracy Work* holds profoundly important implications for anyone trying to elucidate the conditions of successful democracy.

Incongruous though it may seem to use Putnam's concept of social capital in the context of Kivu politics—where the prospects for civic-mindedness are even more remote than in the most tradition-bound areas of the Mezzogiorno—the exercise is not entirely without merit. Besides pointing to some vulnerabilities in Putnam's thesis, it provides a convenient point of entry into the roots of violence in eastern Congo.

This is not meant to be an exhaustive discussion of either the Putnam thesis or Kivu politics. The aim, rather, is to offer an exemplification of how to think about the significance of social capital in the context of North Kivu, a notoriously violent and complex political arena.

The Putnam Thesis in a Nutshell

Although the crux of Putnam's argument is Tocquevillian in inspiration, the empirical evidence bears testimony to his skill in combining quantitative data with meticulous tracking of historical specificities. His debt to de Tocqueville lies in his contention that democracy can only flourish in a soil nurtured by strong associational ties. Just as involvement in secondary associations generates social capital, social capital in turn makes for trust and cooperation. In brief, only where communities have inherited a substantial stock of social capital will their members develop the habits of trust, along with the norms and networks of civic engagement, that are the essential conditions of successful democracy.

Putnam is not the first to have coined the expression "social capital." As he himself admits, credit goes to Glen Loury for introducing the concept, and to James S. Coleman for further elaborating upon it.[1] Where Putnam breaks new ground is in his effort to trace the origins of social capital to specific historical conditions. In so doing, he offers new insights into the prospects for democracy in Third World politics. His verdict, as one might expect, is not exactly encouraging for the latter-day Stakhanovites of democracy employed by USAID and other well-intended agencies:

The fate of the Mezzogiorno is an object lesson for the Third World today and the former Communist lands of Eurasia to-morrow, moving uncertainly toward self-government. The "always defect" social equilibrium may represent the future of much of the world where social capital is limited or nonexistent. . . . Without norms of reciprocity and networks of civic engagement, the Hobbesian outcome of the Mezzogiorno—amoral familism, clientelism, lawlessness, ineffective government and economic stagnation—seems likelier than successful democratization and economic development. Palermo may represent the future of Moscow.[2]

The central lesson to be drawn from his analysis is that institutional reform is no substitute for social capital. Not that reform cannot change political practice; rather, the point is that changes in behavior do not occur overnight: "Most institutional history moves slowly. Where institution building (and not mere constitution writing) is concerned, time is measured in decades."[3]

How does all this relate to an understanding of the crisis in the Great Lakes? Or, better still, how does the crisis in North Kivu relate to an understanding of Putnam?

Some Neglected Aspects of Social Capital Formation

Instead of invoking the absence of social capital to explain the horrors of ethnic cleansing, genocidal violence, and regional insurrections in eastern Congo, a more fruitful approach is to ask ourselves why social capital failed to materialize in the first place, or, alternatively, what caused initial stocks of social capital to evaporate?

Putnam would predictably argue that the roots of chaos lie in the weakness of associational ties among the societies of North and South Kivu and the corresponding fragility of networks of civic engagement: thus if one is to grasp the texture of Kivu society, one must look at Palermo and its corrupt, personalized, mafioso-cum-clientelistic style of politics.

This is somewhat misleading, however; for, along with corruption and patron-client nets, until recently the social landscape in Kivu was dotted with scores of secondary associations, or *mutuelles*, mostly identified with specific ethnic communities. Until the early 1990s, in no other part of the Congo did the civil society look more promising as a potential *countre-pouvoir* to the Mobutist state.

As anyone even remotely familiar with Kivu politics must admit, the key to violence must be found in factors and circumstances that transcend the realm of associational life. To the growing scarcity of land resources caused by successive waves of immigration from Rwanda, must be added the multiplier effect of the nationality issue on ethnic conflict. More than the absence of social capital, land hunger and insecurities of land rights arising from the withdrawal of citizenship from Banyarwanda immigrants is what transformed North Kivu into a tinder box.[4]

Critics of Putnam, most notably Margaret Levi,[5] have noted at least two areas where his argument falls short: (a) one is that he makes exceedingly short shrift of the role of the state as a variable in processes of social capital accumulation; and (b) another is his failure to properly identify the different levels at which trust operates. Furthermore, questions also could be raised about the propriety of looking at civic-mindedness as a determinant of economic growth, rather than the other way around.

The evidence from eastern Congo makes these criticisms all the more persuasive. To leave out of the accounting the role of the state—the colonial, as well as the postcolonial state—in creating the conditions of social conflict is to shove under the rug the most critical factor in the background of the crisis. Again, if we are to grasp the dynamics of conflict, we must factor in the different levels at which trust may obtain. And we must recognize that trust within a specific community may increase in proportion to the degree of distrust directed at another.

Ethnic Fidelities and Societal Enmities

Social capital cuts both ways: it can reinforce trust and cooperation within a given community, or it can mobilize collective energies against neighboring communities. The flip side of trust among kindred souls is the distrust of outsiders. Trust operates at different levels—at the interpersonal level, within the context of secondary associations, and toward government officials. To repeat: failure to take these distinctions into account must be seen as a major weakness in the Putnam thesis; another is his neglect of government policies in transforming ethnic fidelities into interethnic enmities.

Looking back to the post-independence history of the Kivu, one cannot fail to notice the extraordinary efflorescence of associational networks built around ethnic communities.[6] As of 1992, a partial listing would include Acuba (Association Culturelle Bahunde), Kyahanda, Bushenge,

Bunakima, Mogo (Mutuelle des Originaires de Goma), Magrivi, and Acogenoki (Association Coopérative des Groupements d'Eleveurs du Nord Kivu). Most were identified with specific ethnic communities: Bushenge and Acuba with the Hunde, Kyahanda with the Nande, Bunakima with the Nyanga, Magrivi with the Hutu, and Acogenoki essentially with the Tutsi. As elsewhere in Africa, these associations served to reinforce the cultural awareness and social solidarities of their members. In promoting the interests of their members, they became actively involved in Kivu politics. To the extent that they operated as functional alternatives to political parties, they became a major instrument of ethnic mobilization in the hands of ambitious politicians.

In time, the Hunde and Nande mutuelles emerged as powerful vehicles of distrust towards all immigrants from Rwanda—Hutu and Tutsi. Regardless of the date of their arrival, all Banyarwanda came to be seen as collectively responsible for their economic distress. Thus, a key member of the Bushenge Association, identified with Hunde interests, freely admitted to this writer in 1993 that the Banyarwanda mutuelle Umoja was the object of "intense detestation," and the same could be said of the predominantly Hutu Magrivi.[7] Thus, if social capital is meant to refer to "features of social organization such as trust, norms and networks that can improve the efficiency of society by coordinating actions,"[8] by 1993 the social capital of the mutuelles was principally used to coordinate action against Banyarwanda immigrants.

Immigration and Land Hunger

The roots of the Kivu crisis are directly traceable to the rise of a settler-sponsored, agricultural capitalism nurtured and encouraged by the colonial state.

Beginning in the 1930s, yielding to the pressures of the *colonat*, the Belgian authorities embarked on a cast resettlement scheme designed to encourage the immigration of Banyarwanda elements from neighboring Rwanda. The aim was two-fold: provide Belgian planters with a cheap labor force and offer an outlet for the growing population pressure in Rwanda. In the memorable words of District Commissioner R. Spitaels, later appointed head of the Mission Immigration Banyarwanda (MIB): "To encourage the flow of immigration into the Kivu is not just a wise administrative measure but also, and above all, an act of humanity and a duty (*devoir de tutelle*) that will allow the development (*mise en valeur*) of certain uninhabited regions of Kivu."[9] The MIB was the necessary tool for implementing the white settlement scheme already under way under the auspices of the Comité National du Kivu (CNK), a chartered company set up in 1928 to convert "vacant lands" into protected park lands and plantations.[10] By 1935 over 200,000 hectares had been in effect expropriated and turned into state domain.

With the influx of tens of thousands of Banyarwanda in the 1930s, land hunger among the indigenous "tribes" became increasingly widespread as each migrant family was given five hectares of cultivable land to provide for their sustenance. Adding insult to injury, in the 1930s the colonial authorities proceeded to carve out autonomous *chefferies* in areas normally under Hunde jurisdiction. In Masisi, for example, the Gishari was handed over to a transplanted Tutsi chief (Wilfried Bucyanayandi), and in Rutshuru, the Hunde chief of Bwito (Kamoli) was dismissed and sent into exile to Bukavu, and his *chefferie* was incorporated into Bwisha, a solidly Hutu area, under the command of a Munyarwanda chief.

The 1940s and 1950s saw no let up in the flow of Banyarwanda. By November 1959, according to official statistics established by the agent territorial, R. Deman, 184,089 Hutu (referred to as *bantous hamitisés*) were reported to be permanently settled; to these must be added 53,233 Tutsi (*"hamites"*). The Banyarwanda stood as the third largest group in the province after the Banande (390,704) and the Bashi (382,572). It is important to note that the vast bulk of the immigrant population was concentrated in the territories of Masisi (75,136 Hutu and 37,567 Tutsi) and Rutshuru (91,489 Hutu and 8,073 Tutsi); later to become the flashpoints of ethnic violence between immigrants and Hunde. In Rutshuru, Hutu and Tutsi were ten times as numerous as the indigenous Hunde population (10,193); in Masisi, almost two-thirds of the population were immigrants from Rwanda.[11]

The date of these statistics is worth bearing in mind: 1959 marks the outbreak of the Hutu revolution in Rwanda, and with the arrival of some 60,000 Tutsi refugees from Rwanda in the early 1960s and 1970s, yet another complicating factor was introduced into an already tense situation.

Before going any further, it is important to note that the expression "Banyarwanda" hardly does justice to the variety of identities and statuses subsumed under this all-encompassing label. We already mentioned the presence of both Hutu and Tutsi among Banyarwanda immigrants. The next point to be emphasized is that many so-called Banyarwanda were permanently settled in the region long before the inception of colonial rule. For centuries Masisi and Rutshuru had been the traditional homelands of independent Hutu communities. Whereas some local chiefs (*bahinza*) were conquered and temporarily brought under the control of the Rwanda monarchy, others successfully resisted encroachments from the Mwami's armies. In any event, such Hutu states as existed at the time of the armed expeditions organized under Ruganzu Ndori in the eighteenth century and Kigeli Rwabugiri in the latter half of the nineteenth century,[12] were never fully integrated into the fold of the Rwanda kingdom.

Nor were the Tutsi without precolonial roots in the area. Their presence in the eastern part of Rutshuru can be traced back to the nineteenth century if not before. The same is true of the so-called Banyamulenge in South Kivu, on the high plateau area east of Uvira, known as Mulenge.[13] If so, to treat all Banyarwanda as migrants and use their migrant status as a pretext for denying them citizenship rights is both historically inaccurate and politically unacceptable.

But if many Banyarwanda could legitimately claim North Kivu as their home, having lived in the area for decades if not centuries before colonial rule, tens of thousands of others moved into the region after independence, in the early 1960s and 1970s. These were no ordinary migrants; all were political refugees from the Hutu revolution, fleeing threats to their lives. The vast majority were Tutsi (though some Hutu accompanied their patrons into exile) and were significantly better off in terms of material wealth and education than their predecessors. Furthermore, they shared a political consciousness that inevitably impelled them to become actively involved in the politics of the province. Many joined hands with Congolese insurgents during the 1964–65 rebellion in hopes of securing a safe sanctuary for the overthrow of the Hutu regime in Rwanda.[14] Although the rebellion ultimately failed, this did not prevent them from making the most of their resources to acquire large tracts of land in Masisi and to distinguish themselves as an influential business community in Goma and Bukavu.

Patron-Client Nets: The Chiefs, the State, and the Land Problem

Where the Kivu situation brings to mind a striking parallel with Italy's Mezzogiorno is in the extent to which patron-client ties, personalized connections, and extortion were the prime mechanisms for the sale of land to rural entrepreneurs. Through much of the 1970s and 1980s, chiefly authorities were the privileged intermediaries through which huge tracts of land were sold to Tutsi and Hunde farmers, resulting in the expulsion of hundreds of Hutu and Hunde peasant families.

The networks ran from the *chefs de groupements* and *sous-groupements* at the grassroots level, to the *chefferie* and *territoire*, and extended to the core agencies of the Mobutist state through the good offices of a leading Tutsi émigré, Rwema Bisengimana, who by 1970 wielded enormous power in his capacity as Mobutu's *directeur de cabinet*.

The critical links were the paramount chiefs, or *grands chefs*, like Ndeze in Rutshuru and Kalinda in Masisi. To the extent that they were able to combine their chiefly status with important positions in the administration and the party hierarchy, they could claim authority on both traditional and political grounds and make the most of this situation to secure compliance with their decisions.[15] It is not a matter of coincidence that the most powerful of such chiefs, Andre Kalinda, combined the functions of chief of the Bahunde with those of *administrateur de territoire* for Masisi. Kalinda, however, also had close personal connections with Bisengimana and with the Acogenoki, the Tutsi-dominated cattle herders' cooperative. Just as the Acogenoki played a crucial role in getting a large-scale cattle ranching project under way in the early 1970s, Kalinda was no less instrumental in supervising the land sales required for the implementation of the project.

The beneficiaries of the project in Masisi were both Tutsi and Hunde, but one of the more privileged recipients was none other than Bisengimana himself. As Bucyalimwe Mararo notes, "the biggest ranch of Osso and most of the neighboring Kalonge passed into the hands of the Tutsi; the beneficiary of the Osso concession (the ranch that had the largest number of white settlers' cattle in Masisi . . .) was Bisengimana Rwema, who was at that time Mobutu's chief of staff."[16] The extent of the holdings handed over to other recipients speaks for itself: Kasugu (Tutsi) and Ndakola (Hunde) each received 10,000 hectares, Ngizayo (Tutsi) 2,000, Muhima (Hunde) 700, and so forth.[17]

Such massive land sales could not but adversely affect a large number of peasant families, including Hutu families whose land rights, they felt, had been fully individualized under the auspices of the MIB. What Bucyalimwe refers to as "the collaboration between Hunde customary authorities and cattle keepers in land expropriation" resulted in the eviction of hundreds of peasants from their holdings. This is how Bucyalimwe reports the eviction of peasants at Mushwa Hill: "The cattle keeper and Acogenoki branch president, Rumiya Ntamvutsa (Tutsi), used his relationship with Tito Muhabura, the *chef de groupement*, to dispossess several Hutu families of their lands at Mushwa Hill. Taking advantage of his influence and using his money, he succeeded in getting an ownership certificate from the Provincial Land Service in 1977 to expel these families from their lands where they had lived since 1955–56. In an ad hoc report, Tito Muhabura suggested seventy families had been evicted from their lands, Whereas the populations concerned put the number at 234 families."[18] There is reason to believe that what happened on Mushwa Hill was not an isolated case.

Neither the Hunde chiefs nor the Tutsi cattle ranchers could have succeeded in their enterprise without an "enabling" legislation. From this standpoint, 1971, 1972, and 1973 were very good years for both. In 1971, an *ordonnance loi* stipulating that all Banyarwanda and Burundians living in the Congo on June 30, 1960 could claim citizenship rights was adopted, thus making it legally possible for them to own land. Although the January 5, 1972 law[19] pushed back the required date of residence for citizenship to January 1, 1950, it appears that in many cases citizenship papers were freely granted to Tutsi refugees irrespective of their date of arrival. Thus, when the law on Zairianization came into effect in 1973, a number of Tutsi refugees claiming the rights of Zairian citizens became the legal recipients of plantations and ranches previously owned by Belgian settlers. The Osso ranch, handed over to Bisengimana, is a case in point. Meanwhile, the July 1973 general property law, virtually abolished customary land rights (hence reaffirming the principle set forth by the Bakajika Law of 1966) and declared all public land the domain of the state. The result has been to render null and void the claims of long established peasant families and indigenous groups, many of whom invoked the hallowed sanctity of customary rights to hang on to their land, while giving a blank check to the chiefs-turned-politicians to engage in sales of real estate in violation of customary land rights.

In short, the years following independence saw a continuation of the historical process of land alienation inaugurated by the colonial state to serve the interests of rural capitalists. It is easy to comprehend the anxieties of those peasant families who saw themselves pushed out of their holdings by the incessant demands of planters and cane farmers. The violent outbreaks of 1993 were inscribed in the land grabs of the 1970s and 1980s.

The Nationality Question and the 1993 Outbreaks

The land problem and the nationality question are but two sides of the same ethnic coin. Access to land presupposes access to citizenship; withdrawal of citizenship rights from the Banyarwanda meant the end of their security in land rights.

This is where the June 29, 1981 nationality law marks a turning point in the relations between "immigrant" and "indigenous" communities. By a stroke of the pen, the Legislative Council repealed the 1972 law and instead limited citizenship rights to those persons who could show that one of their ancestors "was member of a tribe, or part of a tribe, established in the Congo prior to October 18, 1908," when the Congo formally became a Belgian colony (which in effect meant the rehabilitation of Article 6 of the 1964 Luluabourg Constitution).[20]

Behind the palpable absurdity of this stipulation lies a clear intention collectively to deprive all Banyarwanda of citizenship rights. The dismissal of Bisengimana in 1977, following his alleged involvement in kickbacks from a textile plant in Kisangani, cleared the way for Hunde and Nande politicians to bring pressure to bear on Mobutu to contest the stipulations of the 1972 legislation. In yielding to their demands, the Mobutist state tried to play one group off against another. The immediate effect, however, was to create further confusion and insecurities among the Banyarwanda.

Some Banyarwanda hoped that the nationality issue would be resolved to their satisfaction at the National Conference in 1991, but this was not to be the case. The party delegations representing the interests of "foreigners" were refused admission to the conference. The civil society delegates did not fare much better. In his capacity as president of the civil society section, Kaseso, a Nande, was able to win enough support to counter the claims of the Magrivi president, Nyabirungu;[21] proponents of a return to the 1964 Luluabourg Constitution won the day. To make things even worse, the "geopolitique" argument—whereby positions of authority in the provincial administration should be reserved for those originating from that province—appears to have received widespread support among the participants.

The long-simmering tensions generated by the debate over the nationality question came to a boil in 1993 when violence suddenly erupted in and around Masisi, causing an estimated 10,000 deaths and the displacement of some 250,000 people. What touched off the waves of violence that swept across the region from March to July was the killing of a number of Banyarwanda, essentially Hutu, at the Ntoto market in Walikale. "Like the fire in a dry forest," writes Bucyalimwe Mararo, "the violence spread all over the north and west of Masisi and the Bwito area in the Rutshuru zone (all areas of heavy settlement by Rwanda immigrants) as the Hutu raised arms for self-defense or counter-offensive. The face of the war changed quickly, shifting from one-sided massacres of Hutu to armed confrontation."[22] How many of the victims, among Banyarwanda, were Hutu and how many were Tutsi is unknown. It is clear that (a) violence was directed against all Banyarwanda irrespective of their ethnic identities; (b) it was instigated by indigenous "tribes" (Hunde, Nande, and Nyanga), assisted by Mai-Mai and Bangilima warriors; and (c) the killings occurred in response to a widespread campaign of civil disobedience organized by the Magrivi, in large part directed against traditional authorities.[23]

As a result of this tragic turn of events, the so-called *mutuelles tribales*—for example, Kayanda for the Nande, Bushenge for the Hunde, Umoja for Hutu and Tutsi, Acuba for the Hunde-Nyanga-Tembo, and so forth—became even more tribalistic. Nor were NGOs immune from the contagion of mobilized ethnicity. As Willame notes, "the Adventist and Catholic Churches were described as pro-Tutsi, the Neo-Apostolic Church was believed to be dominated by Hunde and Nyanga, the Groupe d'Etudes et d'Action pour le Développement (Gead) was seen as pro-Tutsi, etc."[24] On the other hand, Hutu and Tutsi responded to this surge of xenophobic violence by developing closer ties. Bucyalimwe Mararo speaks of a "Hutu-Tutsi coalition." Whatever the case may be, the Hutu-Tutsi alliance proved extremely short-lived. With the capture of power in Rwanda by the Tutsi-dominated Rwanda Patriotic Front (RPF) in July 1994, followed by the massive outpouring of Hutu refugees across the border into Goma, the stage was set for a major reshuffling of ethnic alliances. From then on, the split between Hutu and Tutsi emerged as the critical frame of reference in Kivu politics; only to be supplanted, after the destruction of the refugee camps by the RPF in November 1996, by the growing polarization between Tutsi (now calling themselves Banyamulenge) and "native" elements.

The massive exodus of Hutu refugees from Rwanda opens up a new and even more tragic chapter in the history of the region. To do justice to these developments would require more space and time than we can afford.[25] Let us, in conclusion, return to Putnam.

Concluding Thoughts

The foregoing is not intended to dismiss the relevance of social capital as a key ingredient of civic-mindedness, indeed, as the germ from which democracy may flourish. The point of this discussion is to underscore how extraordinarily difficult is the production of such capital in a multiethnic environment as suffused with social inequalities, economic scarcity, and contested citizenship rights as eastern Congo. Clearly, to take Putnam to task for not dealing with these issues would be unfair. Italy, after all, is not the locus classicus of ethnic conflict. And although there are parallels between the clientelistic structuring of politics in the Mezzogiorno and the situation in North Kivu prior to 1994, the manipulation of patron-client nets for purposes of ethnic mobilization lends an entirely different texture to Kivu society.

Nonetheless, the evidence from eastern Congo does raise some nagging questions about Putnam's attempt to establish a direct causal connection between social capital and democratic performance. To leave public policies, or the role of the state, out of the global picture is to rule out a critically important dimension in the dynamics of social capital accumulation—or destruction. As the case at hand shows, if the colonial state emerges as the historic villain in preparing the ground for ethnic conflict, the successor state does not fare much better. Behind the surge of xenophobic violence lies not only the perverse short-sightedness of colonial immigration policies, but the contradictions and confusion created by the Mobutist state over the nationality question.

Equally questionable is Putnam's contention that "civics helps explain economics, rather than the other way around."²⁶ Here again, the history of the Kivu shows that the causal link between civic-mindedness and economic growth is far more complex than Putnam would have us believe. There is indeed enough evidence to show that the greatest threat to social capital stemmed from the growing conditions of economic scarcity engendered by colonial immigration policies. The nationality question was, of course, a key element behind interethnic violence in the early 1990s, but the issue also had a direct bearing on access to land because citizenship rights were seen as governing rights in land. This is not to deny the importance of political participation as a major stake in the nationality question; only to suggest that for many Banyarwanda, access to power and access to land were inseparable.

Where the relevance of Putnam to the eastern Congo comes clearly into view is in his contention that "social context and history profoundly condition the effectiveness of institutions."²⁷ Few would deny that the volatility of Kivu's social context is inscribed in the perverse effects of colonial and postcolonial history. What must be underscored here is not just the impact of history, but the recasting of precolonial history as a means of legitimizing Rwanda's territorial claims to large parts of eastern Congo. Unsurprisingly, since the outbreak of the Rwanda-sponsored, anti-Kabila rebellion in August 1998, it is the story of Mwami Rwabugiri's precolonial incursions that provides the legitimizing myth for Rwanda's military presence in North and South Kivu. The crucial question today is not whether colonial history has had a destructive impact on political institutions, but whether the rewriting of precolonial history by Rwandan ideologues is at all compatible with the exigencies of peace and stability in the Great Lakes region.

Chapter 14
The DRC: From Failure to Potential Reconstruction

The African continent is littered with the wreckage of imploded polities. From Guinea Bissau to Burundi, from Congo-Brazzaville to Congo-Kinshasa, and from Sierra Leone to Guinea and Côte d'Ivoire, failed or failing states confront us with an all too familiar litany of scourges—civil societies shot to bits by ethnoregional violence, massive flows of hapless refugees across national boundaries, widespread environmental disasters, rising rates of criminality, and the utter bankruptcy of national economies.

In its most recent avatar—the DRC—the former Belgian colony is widely seen as the epitome of the failed state, whose descent into hell has set loose a congeries of rival factions fighting proxy wars on behalf of half a dozen African states. *Statelessness* conveys a more realistic picture of the rampant anarchy in many parts of the country. Carved into four semi-autonomous territorial enclaves, three of which are under the sway of rebel movements, it is the most fragmented and violent battleground on the continent. The scale of human losses is staggering. According to the International Rescue Committee, the death toll since 1998 could be as high as three million. In comparative terms this is roughly the equivalent of the human losses of 9/11 on a daily basis over a three-year period. Meanwhile, disease, starvation, and homelessness are said to have affected sixteen million out of a total population of approximately fifty million.[1] The economy is in ruins, with approximately half of the country's mineral wealth mortgaged to President Joseph Kabila's allies; the other half, looted by invaders.

There is no precedent for the multiplicity of external forces involved in the destruction of the state and the plundering of the country's human, economic, and environmental resources. In 2001, at least six states were militarily involved, officially or unofficially: Rwanda, Uganda, and Burundi on the side of the rebellion; and Angola, Zimbabwe, and Namibia on the side of the Kabila government in Kinshasa. Putting the pieces back together is all the more problematic because of the extent to which intervenors are using the chaos to serve their own interests. Even though their objectives may differ, they each have a stake in perpetuating the breakup of the state.

The two key players, Rwanda and Uganda, once united in a common crusade against President Mobutu Sese Seko's dictatorship, are now at daggers drawn over the loot in eastern Congo; in the process dragging their respective client factions into violent turf battles. Born in a suburb of Kigali (Kabuga) in August 1998, with the blessings of Rwandan President Paul Kagame, the Congolese Rally for Democracy (RCD) is presently split into two rival factions, one based in Goma, in North Kivu (the pro-Rwanda RCD-Goma, led by Adolphe Onusumba Yemba), and the other in Bunia, in the Kibali-Ituri province (the pro-Uganda RCD-Bunia, recently led by Ernest Wamba dia Wamba, and now by Mbusa Nyamisi). Both wings have been torn by violent struggles for leadership, confronting their external patrons with difficult choices. Also supported by Uganda, a third rebel movement led by Jean-Pierre Bemba, the MLC— renamed Front de Libération du Congo (FLC), following its merger with the RCD-Bunia in January 2001—fought pitched battles against Laurent Kabila's ragtag army in the Equateur province, in the north, and now claims—implausibly—to control some 900,000 square kilometers "from Zongo on the Ubangi river all the way to Kanyabayonga in North-Kivu."[2] Approximately half of the DRC is under the fragile control of rebel movements kept alive by substantial infusions of direct military assistance from their respective sponsors. When not fighting each other, the strategic positions, including the key localities in the border area between Rwanda and Uganda, are held by units of the RPA and Uganda People's Defense Forces (UPDF). The DRC is the only country in Africa with approximately half of its national territory under foreign military occupation.

As if to further complicate the task of reconstruction, foreign-linked factionalism goes far beyond the three rebel movements currently tied to Rwanda and Uganda. A plethora of loosely knit factions have emerged in the interstices of the three-cornered struggle going on between Kinshasa, Kampala, and Kigali. One group, the Mai-Mai, tactically linked to Kabila, brings together a loose assemblage of local warlords, all vehemently opposed to the RCD-Goma and its Rwandan patron. Another consists of Hutu armed groups from Rwanda and Burundi, the former generally identified with the remnants of Rwanda's militias, the *interahamwe*, the latter with the Burundi-based FDD. A third (and more ambivalent) faction, the FRF, led by Muller Ruhimbika, draws its support from a small segment of the Tutsi community indigenous to South Kivu (the so-called Banyamulenge); although openly critical of the presence of the Rwandan army in the DRC, it can hardly be described as pro-Kabila. In this extraordinarily fluid, deeply fragmented environment, the only glue holding together this disparate group of counterinsurgents is common hatred of the Rwandan occupying forces and their local

Laurent Kabila's assassination, on January 16, 2001, followed by an impromptu transfer of presidential authority to his twenty-nine-year-old son, Joseph, raised further questions. What hidden hand, if any, lay behind the bodyguard's bullet? Kabila *père* had made enough enemies at home and abroad to be at risk of an attempt on his life. Whether Kabila *fils* can avoid his father's egregious mistakes—his utter insensitivity to the demands of the civil society, his sheer ruthlessness in dealing with his suspected opponents within and outside the army, his stubborn refusal to implement the Lusaka accords and cavalier dismissal of the UN-appointed facilitator, Sir Katumile Masire (derisively called the "complicator")—and in time chart a new course toward peace and reconstruction remains to be seen.

What accounts for the failure of the state in the DRC? Plausible though it is to detect historical continuities between the horrors of the Léopoldian system and Mobutu's brutally exploitative dictatorship, or between the sheer oppressiveness of Belgian rule and the excesses of the successor state, in the last analysis, Mobutu himself must be seen as the determining agent behind this vertiginous descent into the abyss.[3] What set Mobutu apart from other neopatrimonial rulers was his unparalleled capacity to institutionalize kleptocracy at every level of the social pyramid and his unrivaled talent for transforming personal rule into a cult, and political clientelism into cronyism.[4] Stealing was not so much a perversion of the ethos of public service as it was its raison d'etre. The failure of the Zairian state was thus inscribed in the logic of a system in which money was the only political tool for rewarding loyalty, a system that set its own limitations on the capacity of the state to provide public goods, institutionalize civil service norms, and effectively mediate ethno-regional conflicts.

Only through the concerted efforts of the Western troika, the United States, Belgium, and France (and after the United States and Belgium had secretly orchestrated the assassination of Patrice Lumumba), could Mobutu come to power and rule the Congo for thirty-two years with such an appalling combination of brutality, cunning, and manipulative perversity.[5] Although the massive infusions of financial assistance from the International Monetary Fund (IMF) and the World Bank contributed in no small way to satisfying Mobutu's incessant demands for cash, once confronted with their reluctance to oblige, it took all the pressure the United States could bring to bear on both institutions to ensure that the aid money would keep flowing into Mobutu's private pockets.[6] For decades, maintenance of the state system overruled reason.

Seen through the prism of the crises of the 1990s, the end of the Cold War emerged as a watershed in the unraveling of the Mobutist state. In

1990, after accumulating arrears of $70 million, the IMF, no longer facing a U.S. veto, suspended its loans to the country, while other donors cut off their assistance. Mobutu responded to the advent of multiparty democracy by buying off opposition parties. The urgent need for cash was met by printing tons of paper money. Spiraling inflation inevitably followed, driving the economy further into the ground.

From then on, the cancer rapidly spread, paralyzing one sector after another. As the delivery of political rewards beyond Kinshasa became increasingly uncertain, the control of the state shrank correspondingly. And when the salaries of the military could no longer be paid, the more disaffected troops took to the streets and went on looting sprees through the capital city, killing hundreds. If internal security was nonexistent, so was the capacity of the state to meet external threats. As the Rwandan army crossed into eastern Congo in October 1996, preparing the ground for Kabila's triumphant march to Kinshasa, the state had already ceased to exist.

On May 17, 1997, eight months after its creation, the victorious AFDL marched into Kinshasa. Its spectacular success in carrying the banner of "liberation" to the gates of Kinshasa is a commentary on the extent of disaffection generated by the Mobutist dictatorship; more to the point, it speaks volumes for the degree of institutional paralysis afflicting the apparatus of the state.

Anatomy of Disaster: Failure, Collapse, and Fragmentation

As the history of the Congo shows, the failure of one set of institutions is not enough to explain systemic collapse. The unraveling of the armed forces in 1964–65, after the Muleliste insurrection, did not bring about the disintegration of the state. External military assistance, coupled with substantial infusions of financial aid from the United States, made it possible for the state to recover, if only momentarily, from what could have been an insurmountable challenge. By the early 1990s, however, the Congo had lost its strategic significance to the West, and the costs of an external rescue operation seemed greatly to outweigh the benefits. At a time when multiparty democracy was in vogue, bolstering Mobutu's dictatorship had ceased to be a realistic option. Moreover, the multiplicity of opposition forces released by the National Sovereign Conference, and the continuing tug of war between the transitional institutions and the Mobutist state, forced donors (primarily France, Belgium, and the United States) to question how best to assist the transition, or indeed whether any assistance, short of military intervention, could make a difference.

Donors' inaction meant a continuing deadlock over the pace and manner of the transition. The resulting paralysis of decision-making mechanisms ushered in one crisis after another. None of the seven prime ministers appointed in 1991 and 1992 proved equal to the task of restoring governmental authority. The economy went into a tailspin when the rate of inflation jumped from 261 percent in 1990 to 6,800 percent in 1994.[7] Mobutu's insistence on printing new paper money against the advice of Prime Minister Etienne Tshisekedi led to the latter's resignation in December 1992. When local traders refused to accept the newly minted five-million-zaire banknotes, several units of the armed forces responded by going on looting sprees through Kinshasa and elsewhere. The most violent and extensive of a series of pillages by the army occurred in January 1993, when devastation spread to several areas in the Lower Congo and the Kivu provinces. Faced with major ethnoregional conflicts in North Kivu and Shaba (now renamed Katanga) by 1993, the Mobutist state had lost all capacity to mediate the crises effectively. Rather than serving as an instrument for the state, the army had become a loose cannon, and at times an active participant in local insurrections. From 1991 to 1993, failure metastatized from one institutional sector to another, reducing the Zairian state to utter impotence.

It is difficult to pinpoint precisely when the Mobutist state failed. In 1992, a senior U.S. diplomat noted that Zaire had all the earmarks of a hollowed-out state.[8] But if failure was already patent in 1992, it did not become conclusive until late 1996, with the destruction of the Hutu refugee camps of eastern Zaire by the RPA and the emergence of Laurent-Désiré Kabila as the self-proclaimed leader of the AFDL. That it took only six months for the poorly equipped and poorly led anti-Mobutist coalition to reach the gates of Kinshasa demonstrated the weakness of the Zairian Armed Forces (ZAF), rather than the strength of the AFDL.

Mobutu's appalling performance from one crisis to the next suggests the strongest reservations about structural explanations in any attempt to account for the demise of the Zairian state. More than the carryover of the Bula Matari syndrome into the postindependence years—evocative of underlying historical continuities between the ruthlessness of the Léopoldian regime and the autocratic features of the Mobutist state—Mobutu must be seen as the chief architect of disaster.[9]

Mobutu's unrelenting efforts to thwart democratic opposition forces, his highly personalized style of rulership, built partly on repression and partly on extensive patronage networks, his scandalous squandering of the Congo's wealth, his megalomaniac obsession with grandiose development schemes at the expense of public goods for the masses, and his pathetic *sauve-qui-peut* attitude in the face of the relentless march of the AFDL on Kinshasa were critical factors in the ultimate collapse of his Bula Matari kingdom.

Herbst's thesis, that failure is traceable to the generalized inability of African states to control their hinterland effectively, owing to the artificiality of state boundaries combined with low population densities, raises questions about whether the weakness of the state (as defined in terms of its ability or inability to raise taxes, to provide public services, or to protect its citizens) can conceivably be treated as a constant.[10] The convenient *ceteris paribus* qualifier does not take us very far in our quest for explanation. Even where the inability of the state to "broadcast power," to use Herbst's terminology, is patent, as in the Mobutist state, the significance of intervening variables cannot be excluded.

Just as we need to recognize that not all state systems are equally vulnerable, it is no less important to avoid the trap of brute functionalism. In an otherwise inspiring essay, Zartman makes surprisingly short shrift of what others have termed "critical junctures," or decisive events, on processes of state collapse. His use of metaphors is revealing: "What is notable in these scenarios (of state collapse)," he writes, "is the absence of clear turning points, warning signals, thresholds or pressure spots.... The slippery slope, the descending spiral, and the downward trend are the mark of state collapse rather than deadlines and triggers."[11] The least that can be said of this curiously ahistorical construction is that it is difficult to reconcile with the evidence at hand (not unlike trying to explain the collapse of the French monarchy without reference to the seizure of the Bastille, the Tennis Court Oath, or the flight to Varenne). Elsewhere Zartman asks, "Why do states collapse?" Because, we are told, "they can no longer perform the functions required for them to pass as states" (not unlike explaining the death of a patient by saying that he/she could no longer perform the functions required to stay alive).[12]

If triggering events, thresholds, or critical junctures cannot be ignored, neither can the long-term forces of decay and decomposition be dismissed. It is anybody's guess how much longer the Congolese state could have lasted had it not been for the decisive blows administered by the Rwandan assault against refugee camps in October 1996; what is beyond question is that by 1996 the Congolese state was already a pushover, thoroughly undermined by its longstanding prebendal involution, declining legitimacy, and the near disintegration of its armed forces. The crisis of 1996 was the triggering event that brought the state to its knees.

The Regional Context

State collapse is contagious. Although the seeds of failure are inseparable from failed leadership, the risks of disintegration are significantly greater where the proximity of a collapsing state threatens to contaminate its neighbor. Just as the civil war in Liberia has decisively hastened the collapse of Sierra Leone (and vice versa), the flow of refugees generated by the continuing civil strife in Sierra Leone poses a clear and present danger to Guinea. Nowhere, however, is the contagiousness of collapse more dramatically illustrated than in the rapid spread of ethnic violence from Rwanda to eastern Congo in the aftermath of the Rwandan genocide. Of the many unanticipated consequences of that bloodbath, none has had more profoundly destabilizing consequences than the massive exodus of over one million Hutu refugees across the border into the Kivu provinces of eastern Congo.

To grasp the spin-off effects of the Rwandan carnage, attention must be paid to several features common to the Great Lakes region (Rwanda, Burundi, Uganda, and eastern Congo). One is the absence of coincidence between ethnic and geographic maps. The presence of Tutsi and Hutu communities in Uganda, Tanzania, and eastern Congo bears testimony to the arbitrariness of state boundaries. Although many peoples arrived during and after the colonial era, their presence reaches back to precolonial times. It is estimated that there are approximately ten million people speaking Kinyarwanda in the Great Lakes region, and fifteen million if Kirundi (a language closely related to Kinyarwanda) is included in the total. In North Kivu alone, about half of the total population of some 3.5 million were identified as Kinyarwanda-speaking in 1993, and of these, about 80 percent were Hutu and 20 percent Tutsi. The significance of this regional ethnic configuration is best captured by Huntington's concept of "kin country syndrome," a situation in which ethnic fault lines tend to replicate each other across national boundaries, thus creating a deadly potential for conflict to expand and escalate.[13]

Another major characteristic is the very high population density and resulting pressure on land throughout the region. Rwanda claims the highest population density in Africa, with Burundi and North Kivu close behind. With an estimated one million people in the late nineteenth century, Rwanda claimed 7.6 million on the eve of the genocide and an average of 336 inhabitants per square kilometer. The figures for North Kivu indicate similar densities in the high-lying areas of the Congo-Nile crest. It is not a coincidence that the most densely populated areas—Masisi and Rutshuru—are also the places where the most intractable land disputes have arisen.[14] Herbst described a very different situation for most of precolonial Africa: "In pre-colonial Africa, land was plentiful and populations thin on the ground. As a result there were few areas where territorial competition was the central political issue because land was plentiful. Control over territory was often not contested because it was often easier to escape from rulers than to fight them."[15] The land issue in North and South Kivu has been, and remains, at the heart of ethnic violence through much of the region.

A third factor relates to the presence of sizable refugee populations from neighboring states. The process began in Rwanda in the early 1960s, when tens of thousands of Tutsi refugees sought asylum in Uganda (70,000), Burundi (60,000), and eastern Congo (22,000). A nightmarish cycle of tit-for-tat ethnic violence followed the crossborder raids of armed refugees into Rwanda, culminating in the massacre of thousands of Tutsi civilians in 1963. That, in turn, caused a further exodus of Tutsi refugees to neighboring states. In Burundi (which, unlike Rwanda, acceded to independence under Tutsi rule), the heightening of the tension caused by the presence of Tutsi refugees from Rwanda reached a boiling point in 1972, with the genocidal massacre of at least 100,000 Hutu (some say 200,000) at the hands of the all-Tutsi army, again causing the exodus of tens of thousands of Hutu refugees to Rwanda, Tanzania, and eastern Congo (South Kivu).[16]

The most devastating illustration of "refugees as vectors of violence" occurred in eastern Congo in the wake of the Rwandan genocide, in 1994, when 1.2 million Hutu refugees poured across the border into North and South Kivu. As many as 100,000 consisted of *Interahamwe* militias and remnants of the FAR. There was no precedent in the history of the region for such a massive irruption of armed refugees into a host country or for the seriousness of the threats that they posed to their country of origin. Such exceptional circumstances brought forth an exceptional response from the Rwandan government in the form of a surgical preemptive strike against the refugee camps. The destruction of the camps by the RPA in October 1996 marked a watershed in the decomposition of the Mobutist state. Besides triggering the virtual disintegration of the Congolese Armed Forces (FAC), the search and destroy operations conducted by the RPA quickly snowballed into a popular crusade against Mobutu.[17]

From Integral State to Shell State: The Costs of Self-Cannibalization

Intimations of the mortality of the Zairian state were felt long before its downfall. Failure is a relative concept, and so also, are the challenges posed to a failed state. From the beginning, Mobutu's rule embodied a neopatrimonial polity. The extreme personalization of authority built around the presidential palace had as its corollary a systematic effort to thwart the development of a responsive and efficient bureaucracy. At no time was an effective institutional mechanism forged for resolving licts among competing constituencies. The scale of the challenges posed by the end of the Cold War was more than could be handled by the "lame Leviathan." By the early 1990s, lameness had given way to utter paralysis.[18]

For years after Mobutu's second coming in November 1965, the Zairian state tried to project the image of an all-embracing, hegemonic apparatus, dedicated to transforming the institutions of the state into an engine of development. What Young calls the "integral state" was the ideological hallmark of Mobutu's autocracy.[19] On closer inspection, a different reality emerges. Control over the civil society, though ostensibly mediated through the ruling party—the MPR—involved the extension of clientelistic nets to all sectors of society, including the army. As in every patrimonial state, the Mobutist state owed its stability to its capacity to "service" the networks; patronage was the indispensable lubricant of the state machinery. Eventually, however, the lubricant ran out and the Mobutist machine was brought to a near standstill. By 1975, Mobutu was faced with a catastrophic decline of his sources of revenue. Copper prices plummeted, debt servicing increased drastically, and the megalomaniac projects destined to usher in economic prosperity—the Inga-Shaba power line, the Makulu steel mill, the Tenge-Fugurume copper mines—proved unmitigated disasters. The inability of the Mobutist state to generate a volume of rewards consistent with its clientelistic ambitions is the key element behind its rapid loss of legitimacy.

With the end of the Cold War, the integral state came to look more and more like a "shell state."[20] The erosion of state capacity increased in proportion to Mobutu's growing inability to keep up the flow of external funding from donors, leading in turn to a further shrinkage of patronage networks. The result set in motion a process of involution centered around a handful of venal, rent-seeking cronies. What Young described as "self-cannibalization" vividly captures the hollowing out of state institutions under Mobutu's prebendal rule.[21]

For a quarter of a century, the Mobutist state was able to compensate for its lack of internal legitimacy by drawing huge dividends from its international status as the United States' staunchest ally in Africa. As has been noted time and again, what one French official described as "a walking bank account in a leopard-skin cap," was a creature of the Central Intelligence Agency. The end of the Cold War sharply increased the Congo's international isolation and legitimacy deficit; bartering its anticommunist credentials for external assistance was no longer a feasible option. Just as Mobutu owed his rise to power to the penetration of East-West rivalries in the continent, the collapse of the Zairian state must be seen as a casualty of the end of the Cold War.

Trajectories of Collapse: Thresholds and Triggers

By any of the conventional yardsticks—declining institutional performance, military indiscipline, harassment of civilians, inability to collect taxes, and governmental spending on public services, notably health and education—Zaire in the early 1990s stood at the top of the list of Africa's failed states. By then, three basic indicators of failure mapped out the road to collapse: (1) a sharp decline of institutional capabilities, matched by a corresponding lack of responsiveness to the demands of the citizenry for "more democracy"; (2) widespread indiscipline and looting of private property by the armed forces and the police; and (3) major eruptions of civil violence, notably in Shaba (1992–93) and North Kivu (1993).

Each of the foregoing in turn draws attention to certain critical junctures or thresholds in the decomposition of the state: (1) the (dis)organization of the CNS in 1991 and the rise of multiparty competition; (2) the looting sprees of the army and presidential guard in 1993, marking the virtual dissolution of the state's "legitimate monopoly of force"; and (3) the North Kivu emergency of 1993.

The CNS and the Aborted Transition to Multiparty Democracy

Yielding to domestic and international pressures, in April 1990, Mobutu formally announced the advent of "political reform" and the opening of multiparty competition; a year later the CNS met in Kinshasa to lay the constitutional groundwork for multiparty democracy. Bringing together some 3,400 representatives of political parties and members of the civil society, the aim was to lay the groundwork for a reconfiguration of the state, but as one observer noted, "It dramatically accelerated its disintegration."[22]

The conference made clear Mobutu's determination to use "divide and rule" strategies to pull the rug from under feet of the main opposition forces, notably Tshisekedi's Union Démocratique pour le Progrès Social (UDPS). His talent for buying off members of the opposition and bankrolling the birth of friendly factions led to a phenomenal proliferation of political parties. More than 200 parties were registered at the end of the year. Meanwhile, the volume of cash funneled into floating satellite parties translated into a further shrinking of public spending on social services, while seriously compromising the chances of a broad consensus among participants to the conference.

The imperative of "divide and rule" inexorably encouraged the rise of local and regional fiefdoms and the entrenchment of pro-Mobutu forces in some provincial arenas, as in Shaba, where Karl I. Bond's UFERI soon emerged as the staunchest opponent of Tshisekedi's UPDS; and in South Kivu, where pro-Mobutu politicians, mostly of Bembe origins, took systematic steps to denigrate and deny rights of citizenship to long-established communities of ethnic Tutsi—the so-called Banyamulenge. The same scenario could be seen in North Kivu where Tutsi fifty-niners were openly branded as "foreigners" working hand-in-hand with FPR guerrillas in neighboring Rwanda. Under the pretense of the "géopolitique" argument set forth by Mobutu's client parties—whereby positions of authority in the provincial administration should be reserved for those originating from that province—"indigeneity" was now brandished as the key priority of provincial reconfigurations.

Competition between pro- and anti-Mobutu parties led to violent ethnic eruptions in Shaba and North Kivu. In Shaba, the efforts of the pro-UFERI governor to consolidate his grip on provincial institutions took the form of systematic pogroms against the Kasaian populations, mostly Luba immigrants suspected of sympathies for the Kasaian-led UPDS. Hundreds were killed at the hands of the UFERI *jeunesse* groups, while thousands fled to Luba-dominated areas of the Kasai province.

Significantly, ethnic cleansing of Luba immigrants occurred shortly after Mobutu dismissed Tshisekedi, the Kasaian-born UDPS leader, from the prime ministership in October 1991. His tenure in office lasted exactly six days and came to an abrupt end after he insisted on controlling the Central Bank. Tshisekedi's dismissal only increased his popularity among Luba elements, in turn prompting UFERI to unleash a campaign of indiscriminate violence against the immigrant communities of southern Katanga.[23]

In North and South Kivu, neither ethnic Tutsi nor Banyamulenge were able to gain representation in the CNS, causing serious tensions vis-à-vis the self-proclaimed "native Congolese."[24] In May 1993, North Kivu exploded, with ethnic violence sweeping across several rural localities. By willfully encouraging ethnic confrontations as a means of controlling the forces released by the CNS, Mobutu created the very conditions that accelerated failure. Not only did the apparatus of the state prove utterly incapable of mediating the competing claims of social actors, the army virtually disintegrated.

The Failure of the Security Forces

In the catalogue of afflictions suffered by the state, none looms larger than the appalling performance of the Zairian armed forces; its "rabble" character remained almost constant throughout the Mobutu years. The history of Zaire demonstrates—and this is even more cruelly evident in the case of Laurent Kabila's DRC—is the inability of the regime to make an effective use of its security forces to deal with the threat of regional, externally supported insurrections.

Like the state itself, the FAZ can best be seen as a political machine lubricated by strong doses of corruption, clientelism, and ethnic favoritism. Numbering approximately 150,000 in 1993, Mobutu's army consisted of two core units, the DSP and the GC, headed respectively by his brother-in-law, General Etienne Nbgale Kongo Nzimbi and General Philemon Kpama Baramoto, both of Ngbandi origins like Mobutu himself. Approximately half of the sixty-two FAZ generals came from Mobutu's region (Equateur), and one third were of Mobutu's Ngbandi. They were overwhelmingly concentrated in the DSP and the GC. Recruitment into the higher ranks can best be described as a patronage operation designed to reinforce the loyalty of the officer corps to the supreme patron. Kinship played a key role in strengthening loyalty, and merit and competence were of secondary importance to personal devotion to Mobutu. In return for their political loyalty, the army high command was given a free hand to engage in lucrative commercial activities. Some were involved in smuggling operations, and others sold military equipment, spare parts, and military fuel on the black market. Embezzling the salaries intended for the troops was a standard practice among officers, a fact that goes a long way toward explaining the exactions and indiscipline of the troops.

Already in 1964–65, during the Muleliste insurrection in eastern Congo, the poor performance of the Congolese army had been made painfully clear. Had it not been for the assistance proffered by South African and European mercenaries (and the bombing missions flown by Cuban exiles in the pay of the CIA) Mobutu's second coming, in November 1965, might not have materialized. Again, only through the timely intervention of French and Moroccan troops during the Shaba I and Shaba II insurrections, in 1977 and 1978, was the Mobutist state saved from its self-inflicted doom.

The danger posed by the absence of an even minimally disciplined army was dramatically revealed during the looting sprees that swept across the country from 1991 to 1993. Resentful of not being paid salaries comparable to those of the CNS delegates and further angered by the refusal of local traders to accept Mobutu's worthless banknotes, bands of soldiers in September 1991 went on a rampage in Kinshasa, stealing and killing anyone who stood in their way. The same scenario unfolded in Lubumbashi in October 1991; in Mbanza-Ngungu in January 1992; in Mbandaka in September 1992; in Goma in December 1992; in Kisangani, Goma, and Rutshuru in January 1993; and in Lisala in August 1993. In each locality, millions of dollars worth of property were destroyed by rampaging soldiers. The extensive pillages brought into sharp relief the extreme fragility of a security apparatus largely built on ethnic clientelism and the degree to which the absorption of financial wealth by the Mobutu clique conspired to destroy the army's morale and heighten its indiscipline.

By 1993, the FAZ was spinning out of control. Facing the prospect of Mobutu running out of cash, bitter rivalries emerged among different factions of the officer corps—notably between the Mbudja and Ngbandi sub-groups—headed respectively by Generals Bumba and Babia. As the latter's faction eventually gained the upper hand, the security forces came increasingly under the control of the all-Ngbandi "gang of four"; Generals Mavua, Eluki, Baramoto, and Nzimbi; respectively minister of national defense, chairman of the chiefs of staff, commander of the GC, and head of the DSP. By 1996, the "gang of four" had become a collective loose cannon, and Mobutu was at the mercy of his generals.

What one observer referred to as "the 'western' of the Generals and the birth of factions and godfathers," marked the unraveling of the FAZ. "Unfortunately Mobutu failed to read the message sent by the mutinous troops. The latter were simply fed up with the mafia operating within the army. The troops were paid irregularly, poorly fed, poorly led, while their commanding officers were abusively swelling the size of their units and embezzling their salaries with impunity."[25] To compensate for their unpaid salaries, the officers gave their troops a blank check to ransom and loot; meanwhile the loyal clienteles built around the Ngbandi-dominated DSP proved just as adept in engaging in plunder and theft. When the time came to take on Kagame's "refugee warriors" and their Congolese allies in the east, in October 1996, all that Mobutu could summon was a band of armed thugs masquerading as an army.

The Kivu Emergency: 1993–96

Long before the attacks on the refugee camps, in October 1996, North Kivu had become a calabash of seething political and ethnic tensions, for which Mobutu bears much of the responsibility. By first favoring the Tutsi community, and more specifically the first generation of "fifty-niners," against "native Congolese" and then turning against them, and by declaring all Banyarwanda foreigners and denying them the rights of citizenship, Mobutu sowed the seeds of his own undoing.[26]

The roots of the Kivu crisis center on land issues. These issues are traceable in part to the legacy of Belgian policies, and in part to the critical role played by one of Mobutu's most trusted advisers and chief of staff, Bisengima, a Tutsi "fifty-niner." Land hunger in the Kivu would have never reached such critical dimensions had it not been for (1) the long-term effects of Belgian policies in "facilitating" the immigration of tens of thousands of Rwandan families to North Kivu to meet the labor demands of European planters, along with the designation of hundreds of thousands of acres as "vacant lands" in order to turn them into protected parklands; and (2) the crucial role played by Tutsi refugees from the Rwandan revolution (1959–62) in appropriating large tracts of land at the expense of the "indigenous" communities. This is where Bisengimana—himself, like many of his kinsmen, one of the largest landowners in the Kivu—bears considerable responsibility in heightening tensions between the Banyarwanda and the native Congolese.

By 1981, the land problem and the nationality question had become both sides of the same coin. Citizenship rights meant the right to vote and the right to buy land. Until then, the Banyarwanda could exercise both, thanks to a 1972 law pushed through parliament at the request of Bisengimana. By 1977, he had fallen out of grace, and anti-Banyarwanda sentiment was growing throughout the region. The nationality law of 1981, in effect, withdrew citizenship rights from all Banyarwanda, including those whose roots in the Kivu went back to precolonial times. From then on, citizenship only applied to "those persons who could show that one of their ancestors was a member of a tribe, or part of a tribe, established in the Congo prior to 1908," when the Congo ceased to be a "Free State" and became a Belgian colony.[27] Behind the palpable ineptitude of this stipulation lay a clear intention collectively to deprive all Banyarwanda of their citizenship.

Although some Banyarwanda had hoped that the nationality issue would be resolved at the CNS, this was not to be the case. The party delegations representing the interests of the "foreigners" were refused admission to the conference; the civil society delegates likewise. The "géopolitique" argument received widespread support among the majority of the participants, thus ratcheting up the ethnic temperature in eastern Congo.

The tensions over the nationality issue came to a boil in May 1993 when anti-Banyarwanda violence suddenly erupted in Masisi and Walikale (North Kivu), causing an estimated 10,000 deaths (mostly Hutu) and the displacement of some 250,000 people. Although the evidence concerning the immediate circumstances of the rioting is sketchy, certain basic facts are reasonably clear. "Violence was directed against all Banyarwanda irrespective of their ethnic identity (Hutu or Tutsi); it was instigated by indigenous "tribes" (Hunde, Nande, and Nyanga), assisted by Mai-Mai and Bangilima warriors; the killings occurred in response to a widespread campaign of civil disobedience organized by the Magrivi, a pro-Hutu *mutuelle*, in large part directed against indigenous traditional authorities"—the latter suspected of being in league with Tutsi landowners.[28]

Hutu-Tutsi tensions had yet to reach the point of no return. For a while this surge of xenophobic violence caused the two ethnic fragments of the Banyarwandan community to develop closer ties. Some spoke of an emergent "Hutu-Tutsi coalition." The least that can be said is that it proved extremely short-lived. Already many young ethnic Tutsi in both North and South Kivu had gone over to the FPR and were actively engaged in the civil war next door, causing suspicions of "disloyalty" among local politicians. With the capture of power in Rwanda by the FPR in July 1994, followed by the huge flood of Hutu refugees into North Kivu, the stage was set for a major reshuffling of ethnic alliances. From then on, the Hutu-Tutsi split emerged as the critical frame of reference in Kivu politics; only to be supplanted, after the destruction of the camps in 1996, by a growing polarization between "Tutsi"—the all-encompassing label designating Rwandan Tutsi, descendants of the early migrants to North Kivu, the fifty-niners, and the long-established Banyamulenge communities of South Kivu—and "native" elements. The turning point came on October 7, 1996, when the South Kivu governor urged all Tutsi to leave the country within a week or face "appropriate" sanctions. A week later the RPA troops unleashed the full force of their assault on the refugee camps.

The 1996 Watershed: From Zaire to DRC

The nemesis visited upon the refugee camps radically altered not just the political landscape in eastern Congo, but the fate of the successor state. With the emergence of Laurent Kabila at the head of the AFDL, the stakes were raised far beyond the immediate objective of eliminating the threats posed to Rwanda by armed refugee groups; the aim was to wrestle the Mobutist monster to the ground and make the whole of the Congo safe for Rwanda. The first was achieved with relative ease by Kagame's troops, though at a horrendous cost in refugee lives; the second proved immensely more difficult.

Orchestrated by Kagame, assisted by troops from Rwanda, Uganda, and Angola, and applauded by almost every nation on the continent, the AFDL campaign against Mobutu was harnessed to a common will—to overthrow dictatorship and prepare the ground for democracy. The Rwandan army played a decisive role in the undoing of Mobutu.[29]

There are few parallels for the popular legitimacy of a self-styled revolutionary leader soaring and collapsing in such a brief interval. Laurent Kabila's ineptitude in handling the demands of civil society must be seen as one of the main reasons behind his plummeting popularity in the months following the fall of Kinshasa. Another factor stemmed from his overwhelming military and political dependence on Banyamulenge and Rwandan elements.

That Laurent Kabila would not stand as the apostle of democracy was made clear in his inaugural speech, on May 29, 1997. The CNS was ruled out as the basis for a new constitutional order; it belonged to a Mobutist past that had to be rejected completely. So, too, were opposition political parties. If any doubts remained about Kabila's dictatorial dispositions, these were quickly dispelled by the arrest and incarceration of dozens of civil society leaders and journalists in the months following his inauguration. True to his paleo-Marxist nurturing, in 1999 Kabila dissolved the AFDL and established People's Power Committees (PPCs) aimed at giving power to the masses—a thinly veiled attempt to place police informants in strategic positions so as to have opponents arrested. Ominously, on November 14, 1999, he authorized the PPCs to carry weapons, an operation supervised by the People's Self-Defence Force (FAP), a private militia officially said to be an extension of the army. On the eve of the millennium, the DRC had all the earmarks of a police state. Summarizing the parallel with Mobutu's Zaire, Oleghankoy—who first rallied to and then promptly defected from the RCD-Goma—commented, "Kabila and Mobutu are like Pepsi and Coca-Cola: you can't taste the difference."[30]

Nor could this "Mobutisme sans Mobutu" syndrome leave the international community indifferent, least of all the United States. Secretary of State Madeleine Albright's visit to Kinshasa in December 1997 turned out to be a near-disaster as Laurent Kabila took advantage of a press conference to come down hard on the opposition, ending his tirade with a mocking smile and a cynical "Vive la démocratie!"[31] Whereas other donors remained equally wary of providing financial assistance, the United Nations became involved in a long and inconclusive struggle with Kabila over the fate of tens of thousands of Hutu refugees allegedly killed by AFDL and Rwandan troops in the course of their exodus. The UN investigatory commission headed by Special Rapporteur Roberto Garreton ran into endless problems. Following one complication after another, in March 1998, a year after it had been appointed, the Garreton commission left Kinshasa, empty-handed.

Laurent Kabila's stonewalling could not have made clearer his utter dependence on Kigali. Whatever evidence there is about the circumstances surrounding the massacre of refugees suggests that the RPA was far more involved than the AFDL. In blocking the work of the commission, Kabila was evidently taking his marching orders from Kigali.

If further proof were needed, one could point to the growing influence of certain key Rwandan and Banyamulenge personalities in his entourage: James Kabarehe, Kagame's army chief of staff; Bizima Karaha, the minister of foreign affairs; Deogratias Bugera, the minister of presidential affairs and former secretary general of the AFDL; and Moise

Nyarugabo, his personal secretary (the last three would eventually surface as key members of the RCD-Goma). Nor could one fail to notice the commanding presence in Kinshasa of many Tutsi-looking, Kinyarwanda-speaking elements. As anti-Tutsi feelings intensified in the capital, Kabila could not be seen otherwise than as a stooge of Kagame. As 1997 drew to a close, the choice he faced was either to hang on to his Rwandan protectors and suffer an even greater loss of legitimacy, or to free himself of their embrace and face the consequences. By mid-1998 Kabila had made his choice—and the consequences proved fatal to his regime.

The Road to Hell: The 1998 Rebellion and its Aftermath

The crunch came on July 27, 1998, with Laurent Kabila's announcement that all foreign troops would be expelled from the DRC. The next day, six planeloads of Tutsi and Banyamulenge troops hurriedly flew out of Kinshasa, leaving hundreds of others to their own devices.[32] Meanwhile, hundreds of Tutsi residents of Kinshasa (and not a few Tutsi-looking Africans) were massacred by what was left of Kabila's army and angry mobs of Congolese. By yielding to the mounting anti-Tutsi sentiment, the Congo's new king turned the kingmakers into his bitterest enemies.

Kagame's sense of outrage struck a responsive chord among several Congolese opposition figures whose distaste for Kabila exceeded their grievances against the Rwandans. The crisis gave them a unique opportunity to turn the tables on Kinshasa. Like Kabila in 1996, they knew that the road to Kinshasa passed through Kigali; like Kabila they quickly realized the need for a homegrown, authentically Congolese vehicle to lend credibility to their plans. Thus the Rassemblement Congolais pour la Démocratie (RCD) came into existence in Kigali on August 16. By then, a full-scale rebellion was already under way in eastern Congo; in Kinshasa, the FAC braced for a decisive confrontation with Kagame's troops.

In early August, with an unerring aim for the jugular, Kagame airlifted some 600 troops from Goma to Kitona, a major military airbase about 200 kilometers west of Kinshasa. There they joined the local FAC garrison (then undergoing "re-education"). The key towns of Moanda and Matadi were seized almost immediately. By August 17, the huge hydroelectric dam at Inga was under rebel control. By a flick of the switch, Kinshasa was plunged into darkness, and its water supply cut off. Then, precisely when Kinshasa seemed about to cave in, Angola saved the day. On August 22, an estimated 3,500–4,000 Angolan troops surged from the Cabinda enclave and with tanks and heavy artillery, attacked Kagame's men from the rear. Fleeing the Angolan assault from the west, on August 26 Kagame's men made a last-ditch effort to seize Kinshasa, only to concede defeat.

Despite its setback in the west, the rebellion quickly picked up momentum in the east. After the recapture of Kisangani by the Rwandan army, rebel troops struck out north and west and with the backing of the Ugandan army, took one town after another: Bunia, Buta, Bumba, Isoro, and Aketi.[33] With the fall of Kindu, the capital of the Maniema, on October 12, the rebellion scored a major victory. Besides giving the rebels and their Rwandan allies free access to the mineral resources of the region, the path was now cleared for a further advance south towards Kasongo, Kabalo, Kabinda, and the diamond-rich Kasai province.

1998: A Replay of 1996?

On the surface, the 1998 rebellion had all the earmarks of a replay of the 1996 anti-Mobutist insurrection. In both instances, the initiative came from Kigali, with the support of Kampala. The points of ignition, logically enough, were Goma and Bukavu, with the Banyamulenge acting as the spearhead of the rebellion. The insurgents had relatively little in common besides their shared aversion to the Kinshasa regime.

In 1998, however, Angola switched sides, a critical difference. The key to this decisive turnaround lies in the Angolan civil war. All too aware of the absolute necessity of retaining Laurent Kabila's support in his fight against Jonas Savimbi's Uniao Nacional para a Independencia Total de Angola (UNITA) and seeking to destroy their rear bases in the DRC, Angolan President Eduardo Dos Santos did not hesitate to throw his weight behind Kabila. Had he acted differently, the DRC probably would no longer exist.

In 1998, as in 1996, the senior partner in the coalition became the source of enduring hatred among the insurgents, but with different implications. The pattern of alliances stitched together from Kigali was far more fragile than in 1996. In late 1998, thoroughly exasperated by Kigali's efforts to control the RCD, Ernest Wamba dia Wamba, an exiled academic of Bakongo origins, decided to set up his own rebel faction—the RCD-Bunia—and turn to Uganda for support. Equally distrustful of Rwanda's intentions, a third rebel movement emerged in Equateur Province, the Congo Liberation Movement (CLM), led by Jean-Pierre Mbemba, son of a well-known businessman and former supporter of Mobutu.

Seemingly endless factional struggles have since plagued each rebel movement. The most violent, in late 2000, virtually ripped apart the RCD-Bunia when a dissident faction led by Mbusa Nyamesi turned against Wemba and forced him to seek refuge in Uganda.

Not only has anti-Rwandan sentiment driven a deep wedge between the two wings of the RCD, but also between their external sponsors, Rwanda and Uganda. Competition between their respective clients over access to the Congo's mineral wealth is one of the underlying factors behind the trial of strength between the UPDF and the RPA for control of Kisangani. In August 1999, following an armed confrontation between two RCD factions, Rwandan and Ugandan troops jumped into the fray and for four days fought each other tooth and nail on behalf of their respective allies in Kisangani, leaving some 200 soldiers and civilians dead. An even bloodier confrontation erupted in May 2000, and for much the same reasons, resulting in the death of an estimated 1,000 local residents. Many more were left wounded and homeless.

The battle for Kisangani is more than a case of external patrons reluctantly drawn into a factional struggle. More than anything else, it reflects a deadly rivalry for the rich deposits of gold, diamonds, and coltan (columbite-tantalite ore, used in the manufacture of cell phones, computers, and jet engines) of eastern Congo. Since 1996 the stakes involved in the struggle have changed dramatically. As is now becoming increasingly clear, the security imperative invoked by Kigali in 1996 is of secondary importance to the huge profits drawn by Rwanda and Uganda from the plunder of the Congo's mineral resources.[34] Not all of this wealth ends up lining private pockets; much of the war effort is in a large part financed by exports from eastern Congo.

Except for the Kivu, where violence has remained constant, and constantly horrendous, and the killings of tens of thousands of fleeing Hutu refugees by the RPA, the 1996 insurrection did not involve major bloodshed among Congolese. The same cannot be said of the 1998 rebellion. The cost in human lives remains without precedent. Both sides are responsible for unspeakable atrocities against civilian populations. The slaughter of Tutsi in Kinshasa and Lubumbashi (in the name of what some government-controlled media referred to as the Hamitic threat to Bantu people) has been matched by the innumerable revenge killings committed by Rwandan troops against the civilian communities of North and South Kivu.

A major source of violence stems from the incessant attacks launched by the Mai-Mai militias against RPA soldiers and their RCD allies, in turn bringing devastating retaliatory strikes against civilians. Cases in point include the massacres in Kasika (South Kivu) in August 1998, when more than 1,000 Congolese were killed at the hands of the RPA or Banyamulenge soldiers, and in Makobola (also in South Kivu) in January 1999, when an estimated 500 villagers were wiped out in similar circumstances. Similar atrocities were reported in Ngenge, Kalehe, Kilambo, Lurbarika, Luberezi, Cidaho, Uvira, Shabunda, Lusenda-Lubumba, Lulingu,

Butembo, and Mwenga, where in November 1999, fifteen women are said to have been buried alive after being tortured. The overall picture conveyed by Garreton's 1999 report to the UN Human Rights Commission is one of unmitigated horror. Between December 1998 and November 1999, some thirty-five cases of massacres of civilians were reported as reprisals for Mai-Mai attacks against RPA soldiers and/or their RCD allies, causing thousands of casualties, all of which were at first denied by the RCD and later acknowledged as "unfortunate mistakes."[35]

The Hema-Lendu Tragedy

Just as lethal in its effects is the extension of the Hutu-Tutsi conflict to areas inhabited by populations sharing cultural affinities with Tutsi and Hutu. The most dramatic illustration of the phenomenon occurred in a remote corner of the newly created Kibali-Ituri province, near Bunia, in June 1999, when violent clashes suddenly erupted between Hema and Lendu, resulting in an estimated 10,000 people killed and over 50,000 displaced.

The Hema are pastoralists who have much in common, culturally, with the Tutsi of Rwanda and Burundi, the Banyamulenge of eastern Congo, and the Hima of the Ankole district in Uganda. The Lendu, in contrast, are settled agriculturalists and hunters. Despite long-standing tensions between them, the savagery that has attended recent clashes is unparalleled in their history. The most recent flare-up, in January 2001, transformed the area in and around Bunia into a human abattoir. Graphic descriptions of the atrocities committed by both sides were reported in the press. One observer commented on how the head of a young boy was hacked off and then "skewered on the tip of a spear and paraded on the back of a pick-up truck while soldiers on the truck sang a soccer song."[36] Although the exact number of lives lost will never be known, there is general agreement that the spark that ignited the killings was a dispute over land in Djugu, involving Hema claims over a farm owned by Lendu. Soon, the conflict took on ominous proportions. According to a humanitarian source, "It has now become a conflict over power and money. The presence of various Congolese and foreign armed groups, the easy availability of weapons, the war-ravaged economy, and a rise in 'ethnic ideology' in the area have provided dangerous fodder for the conflict's rapid extension and ferocity."[37] More specific circumstances also played a role, notably the decidedly pro-Hema attitude of the provincial governor, Adele Mugisha, herself a Hima from Ankole. Her ethnic sympathies seem largely responsible for her decision to authorize elements of the UPDF to back local Hema militias in their efforts to drive the Lendu from their land.

In addition to its terrible cost in human lives, the Hema-Lendu strife has had a profoundly disruptive impact on the intramural struggle going on within the RCD-Bunia. While Wamba dia Wamba cast his lot with the Lendu, his vice-president, John Tibasima (a Hema), and prime minister, Mbusa Nyamwesi (a Nande), both tended to support the Hema. After a violent fire fight between the rival subfactions, Wamba was hastily summoned to Kampala and urged to resign from the presidency of the movement, thus paving the way for the merger of the Nyamusi-Tibasima faction with Bemba's MLC, now renamed the Congolese Liberation Front (CLF). Despite the hopes raised by the Hema-Lendu peace accord brokered by the CLF in February 2001, ethnic killings continue unabated through much of the Ituri province. In February 2000, attacks by Lendu militias left 200 people dead and thousands displaced in a Hema village north of Bunia, prompting HRW to urge the UN Secretary General to immediately send more military and civilian observers to the strife-torn Ituri province, a call that at the time of this writing (March 2002), has yet to be heeded.

The Banyamulenge: Ethnic Cleansing Waiting to Happen?

Next in line on the list of "minorities at risk" are the Banyamulenge of South Kivu, whose fate, like that of the Hema and Lendu, is deeply intertwined with the politics of foreign-linked factionalism—in this case the RCD-Goma. Although the term Banyamulenge is often used indiscriminately to refer to all ethnic Tutsi in North and South Kivu, they form a group apart, whose history is rooted in the mists of precolonial history.[38] The date of their migration into the region is a matter of controversy, but most historians would agree that they settled in the high-lying plateau of the Itombwe long before the advent of colonial rule. As such they have every right to claim Congolese citizenship. Their ethnic profile is Tutsi, their language is Kinyarwanda, their traditional homeland is the Itombwe plateau, but they all insist, with reason, that their national identity is Congolese. This is what many of their Congolese neighbors contest, arguing that they are Tutsi who recently entered the country from Rwanda and that Rwanda is where they belong.[39]

The fight over citizenship rights masks a conflict over memory. Selective memory, or selective forgetting, only serves to harden the edges of ethnic enmities. Each side sees itself as a victim of the other. Central to the collective memory of the Banyamulenge is the story of their precolonial migrations, a well-established historical fact that their Congolese opponents strenuously contest. While the latter reproach them for their involvement on the side of Kinshasa during the 1964 Muleliste rebellion, the Banyamulenge retort that they initially joined forces with the rebels and only switched sides after seeing their cattle stolen and slaughtered to feed the rebel army.[40] When reviled for sending their young men to fight with the FPR as early as 1981, they argue that they had few other choices given that they were treated as foreign interlopers in their own land and denied citizenship rights. When questioned about their involvement in the destruction of refugee camps in South Kivu in late 1996 and their subsequent rallying to the AFDL, they are quick to respond that they were pushed into the arms of the Rwandans by the threats posed to their people; few indeed have forgotten the withering verbal attacks of the Uvira Zone Commissioner, Shweka Mutabazi, in July 1996, encouraging the "authentic" Congolese to "hunt down the Banyamulenge snake." Nor have they forgotten the request of a leading human rights group—ironically labeled the Collectif d'Actions pour le Développement des Droits de l'Homme (CADDHOM—to the governor of south Kivu to expel "as quickly as possible" these "Rwandan immigrants" who show "no respect for the laws and authorities of this country." But if anything is forever etched in their collective memory, it is the wanton killing of hundreds of Banyamulenge in Kinshasa and Lubumbashi in the wake of the 1998 war when the Kabila government declared open season on them. For many of their enemies, however, the one layer of memory that eclipses all others is the auxiliary role played by the Banyamulenge in making the Kivu a colony of Rwanda.

While grappling with a past that evokes conflict and hatred on both sides, the Banyamulenge are faced with hard choices: either to cast their lot with the RCD-Goma and enjoy the continued protection of the RPA or to distance themselves from both in the interest of national reconciliation. Several leading Banyamulenge leaders have chosen the first option, notably Azarias Ruberwa, currently secretary general of the RCD-Goma, and Bizama Karaha, serving as minister of the interior. Others, arguing that they have been all along "instrumentalized" by Rwanda, insist that there is no other solution to the Kivu crisis than to combat Rwandan expansionism and seek a modus vivendi with the people of the Kivu, north and south. This is the position taken by Manasse Ruhimbika (aka "Muller"), head of the FRF. Founded in Uvira in January 2000, the FRF summed up its key objective in a letter of January 20, 2000, to the UN secretary general: "In the face of this double threat—extermination by the Kabila government or instrumentalisation by the allies of the RCD-Goma—the Congolese Tutsi, in concert with other peace-loving Congolese, have taken the decision to organize themselves into a movement ("collectif") designed to negotiate a peace agreement in eastern Congo between the Congolese Tutsi and their neighbors."[41] Since then Banyamulenge politics have become more complex, with the emergence of a guerilla movement in the Itombwe led by a certain Masunzu, determined to hold his ground against both the RCD-Goma and the Rwandans. The net result of the leadership crisis faced by the Banyamulenge has been to split their movement into a host of warring factions.

The dilemma facing the Banyamulenge remains unchanged; however, if and when the Rwandan occupying forces are withdrawn from eastern Congo—a key objective of the Lusaka accords—what are the guarantees that they will not be the target of a wholesale massacre by the self-styled "authentic" Congolese, or that they will not be forcefully expelled to Rwanda? There is little question that the overwhelming dependence of the RCD-Goma on Rwanda has been the source of major discord among the Banyamulenge, but what is one to make of Rwanda's argument that they are the only safety net available to their kinsmen in North and South Kivu?

Managing conflict within their respective client factions is a burden which both Kagame and President Yoweri Museveni must bear, and so far neither can claim much success. The same could be said of Laurent Kabila as he vainly tried to impart some degree of internal cohesion and coordination to a congeries of semi-autonomous satellites—Mai-Mai warlords, *interahamwe* bands, and FDD militias—while at the same time fending off plots, real or imagined, within his own politicomilitary apparatus. In the end, Kabila failed on both counts.

What is beyond dispute is that in his three and a half years in office, Laurent Kabila outdid Mobutu in taking his country into the abyss. Measured by the familiar yardsticks of the Mobutu dictatorship—extreme personalization of power and nepotism, corruption and rent seeking, neglect of public services, and indifference to the demands of the civil society—his performance is arguably even worse than that of his predecessor. Although Mobutu must bear full responsibility for sponsoring the collapse of the state, Laurent Kabila's ineptitude is what precipitated its dismemberment. Whereas Mobutu refused to share power while resisting the breakup of the state, Laurent Kabila "preferred sharing the country to sharing power."[42] His early aura of legitimacy as the man who toppled Mobutu was mortgaged at the outset by his heavy dependence on his Rwandan backers, but this factor is not enough to explain his inability to build up the power base required to challenge his former allies. At no time was a serious attempt made to come to terms with the opposition, give voice to the civil society, reorganize the army into a viable fighting force, or reallocate the country's resources with an eye to the crying needs of the rural sectors. His style of governance was that of a warlord, not of a statesman; reminiscent in many ways of "the methods of leadership he practiced as a militia leader in Fizi-Baraka or while running his many Tanzanian businesses."[43] For all his avowed enmity to the

Mobutist dictatorship, Laurent Kabila's ramshackle regime was an institutional clone of its predecessor.

Enter Kabila *Fils*

"Despite widespread discontent with his rule, Kabila's regime is not threatened by internal unrest, or even a coup."[44] Less than a month after the publication of this upbeat assessment in an otherwise excellent report by the ICG, Laurent Kabila was shot dead by one of the child soldiers (*kadogo*) in charge of his security. The exact circumstances of the assassination are still murky. What were the assassin's motives? Was the hand that pulled the trigger guided by Angolans? If so, why? What is the connection between Laurent Kabila's order to execute Masasu Nindaga, one of his key lieutenants in the Katanga, on November 27, 2000 and the kadogo's bullet? One can only venture the most tentative answers. The most plausible hypothesis points to a convergence of two separate sets of factors. The decision to eliminate Kabila most probably came from Dos Santos or his Chief of Staff, General Jogo Baptista de Matos; according to a well-informed source, the kadogo, one of several involved in the assassination, was the instrument chosen by the Angolans.[45] But compliance would not have been forthcoming had it not been for Laurent Kabila's callous indifference to the kadogos' fate while fighting the RPA and its domestic allies. In brief, the kadogos and the Angolans had different sets of grievances, yet they both converged on the same target.

The growing frustration of the Angolans stemmed in part from the extraordinary inefficiency of the Laurent Kabila establishment in getting its act together on the battlefield and in building a viable power base in Kinshasa. Nepotism and corruption were another source of disillusion. The last straw came when Dos Santos realized that Laurent Kabila was conniving with UNITA rebels—via a group of Lebanese intermediaries based in Kinshasa—in channeling into his hands the benefits of illicit trade in diamonds. This realization in turn explained the gunning down, gangland-style, of the eleven Lebanese involved in the diamond deals, along with their immediate relatives, in the days immediately following Kabila's assassination. The order to kill the Lebanese came from Colonel Eddy Kapend, Kabila's aide-de-camp, these confirming his pro-Angolan leanings. A Lunda from the Katanga, like General Yav Nawesh, Kapend was seen by the Angolans as their safest ally in their fight against Movimento Popular de Libertação de Angola (MPLA) penetration into the Katanga. Significantly, Kapend and Yav are now in jail, a move suggestive of Joseph Kabila's determination to resist manipulation by the Angolans.

The kadogos' unhappiness with Kabila is easy to understand; poorly trained, poorly fed, and seldom paid, most of them were used as cannon fodder against Rwanda's crack units in the Katanga. Hundreds were killed while fighting RPA and RCD soldiers on the eastern front. Many felt outraged upon learning of the execution of their beloved "patron," Masasu Nindaga, in November 2000 near Pweto (Katanga). Kabila's first chief of staff and former leader of the Mouvement Révolutionnaire pour la Libération to Congo (MRLC) and one of the four original parties that formed the AFDL, Nindaga was from the Kivu region like the vast majority of the kadogos; his father was a Mushi and his mother a Munyamulenge. His political credentials notwithstanding, his maternal ties were enough to raise doubts about his loyalty to the AFDL, and in November 1997, Kabila had him arrested; he was not released until April 2000 after an amnesty was declared. Once again suspected of conniving with the Tutsi enemy, he was arrested and executed on November 27, 2000, on the eve of the Pweto battle, which saw the routing of Laurent Kabila's army at the hands of the RPA and RCD troops and the flight of an estimated 10,000 kadogos into Zambia.

Although the succession leaves many important items of contention unresolved, so far the performance of Kabila *fils* is not nearly so negative as had been initially foreseen. No sooner was the new incumbent anointed than the strongest doubts were expressed within and outside the Congo about his ability to lead his country out of the mess inherited from his father. Commentators pointed to his youth, his lack of experience, his poor French, and his unfamiliarity with the arcane politics of Kinshasa, all of which presumably disqualified him for the job.[46] Nonetheless, his achievements, modest as they are, call for a more nuanced assessment. Where his father made a mockery of the Lusaka accords, consistently resisted calls to negotiate with the rebels and their allies, and heaped scorn on the UN-appointed facilitator, Joseph Kabila has shown himself surprisingly receptive to their implementation. Masire was called back to the Congo, the ban on political parties was lifted, preparations are under way for a national dialogue, and as a significant sign of good will, Kagame and Museveni began to pull back their troops. Furthermore, the impression Joseph Kabila has made on his interlocutors during visits to European capitals and Washington has been generally favorable. More importantly he has made every effort to distance himself from the old-guard politicians surrounding his father, as well as from his Angolan allies. Nonetheless, one can hardly overlook the constraints imposed by his father's legacy on his ability to reconstruct the Congolese state.

The troubled circumstances of Joseph Kabila's rise to power throw into stark relief two obvious handicaps: his dependence on external patrons, especially Angola, and the collapse of his army. In the absence of an army worthy of the name, reliance on Angolan and Zimbabwean troops is his only option. The price to be paid is a continued abdication of his sovereignty, not only because of the limits thus placed on his strategic options, but because it provides justification for the presence of Rwandan and Ugandan troops in eastern Congo. Withdrawal is a two-way street, and there is little evidence that the limited pullback of Rwandan and Uganda troops was matched by similar moves by his allies.

The kadogo factor raises other problems. Besides being a metaphor for the appalling inefficiency of the Congolese army, it could also become a synonym for further unrest. With tens of thousands of child soldiers left to their own devices, most of them thoroughly disillusioned, when not facing starvation and death, the prospect of a massive influx of kadogos back to their home provinces (North and South Kivu) and into the Mai-Mai nets is by no means to be excluded. Were the kadogos' shift of allegiance to materialize on a substantial scale, the result would be to ratchet up the threats posed to Rwanda and give Kagame further reasons for maintaining a military presence in eastern Congo. Yet security is not the only reason for the occupation of North and South Kivu. The enormous profits derived from the exploitation of the region's mineral wealth, and the variety of interested parties on the receiving end of the line, are not the least of the obstacles in the way of the implementation of the Lusaka accords.

The "Continuation of Economics by Other Means"

Keen's twist on the Clausewitzian aphorism focuses attention on the relationship between violence and economics, between the vicious struggle going on among parties to the conflict as they try to extract maximum benefits from the Congo's mineral resources, and on the role of foreign buyers overseas.[47]

Consider the following incident, one among many never reported in the media. On November 7, 2000, a group of Mai-Mai commandeered a Ugandan pick-up truck loaded with $70,000 worth of coltan coming from Manguredjipa, a small locality in the northeast of the DRC near the Ugandan border. The following day a group of UPDF soldiers, accompanied by a tank, was sent to neighboring villages in hope of recovering the loot. As they came to Kikere, where a wedding was taking place, they opened fire on the assembled crowd near the church, killing seventeen; one house nearby was set on fire, while others were emptied of all furniture. A total of thirteen people were reported burned to death; a number of villagers, including women and children, were taken prisoners and sent to jail in Rughenda. Thirty people, including three Mai-Mai, were said to have been killed.[48]

The killings in Kikere are cruelly emblematic of what Jackson describes as "the perniciously symbiotic relationship between economic activity and violence." As he observes, "Violence provides the cover for the economic exploitation of the Kivus by elites at home and in neighboring Rwanda. In turn, part of the massive economic profits underwrites the violence of the actors."[49] The "incident" also raises important questions about other foreign participants, unknown to the people of Kikere. Rwandan and Ugandan invaders would have few stakes in the conflict, were it not for the willingness of Western corporate interests to act as their business partners, or better still, as their partners in crime.

A complex chain of transactions and intermediaries link the local diamond and coltan miners to trading posts in Kisangani, Goma, and Bukavu and from Kigali and Kampala to foreign business interests in Europe and the United States. The last play a dominant role in channeling profits into African hands. Rwanda, not exactly known for its diamond production, now has several diamond marketing agencies (*comptoirs*). Uganda, likewise, has exported millions of dollars worth of gems in the last few years. Museveni's half brother, General Salim Saleh, has a major stake in the weekly shipment of gold from the Office des Mines d'Or de Kilo-Moto and the Société Miniere et Industrielle du Kivu (Sominki). According to one eyewitness account, "In Kilo-Moto the Ugandans have kicked out all Congolese; every Tuesday and Friday a Ugandan jet lands In Durba and takes the loot to Kampala."[50] Nor are Rwanda and Uganda the worst offenders. Zimbabwe is deeply involved in the same sort of transactions.

Particularly damning are the findings of the 2001 UN report on the illegal exploitation of natural resources in the DRC.[51] The report laid to rest the notion of security imperatives as the sole or primary reason for the presence of RPA and UPDF forces in the Congo. In a wealth of information collected in the course of an extended visit to eastern Congo, Rwanda, and Uganda, the authors conclusively implicated top-ranking officers from Rwanda and Uganda in the looting of natural resources, the huge profits derived by their respective client factions in the Congo, and the deep involvement of Western and non-Western corporate interests in the export of coltan and other commodities, including timber, ivory, gold, diamonds, and coffee.

The same report describes Presidents Kagame and Museveni as "the godfathers of the illegal exploitation of natural resources and the continuation of the conflict in the DRC."[52] It draws attention to the close ties between the Rwandan president and "the business community operating in the DRC, the army and the structures involved in the illegal activities." (In eighteen months, Rwanda is estimated to have made $250 million in profits from the export of coltan alone.) As for Museveni, "when he appoints the very people who carry out criminal activities, and when his family members get away with criminal activities, it becomes overwhelming that the president has put himself in the position of accomplice." The subaltern individual actors identified as playing a crucial role in "providing support, entertaining networks or facilitating the exploitation of natural resources" include, on the Uganda side, Museveni's brother, Salim Saleh; Saleh's wife; General James Kazini, former Chief of Staff of the UPDF; and Colonel Tikamanyire. On Rwanda's side, the names most frequently mentioned are those of Colonel James Kabarebe, former Chief of Staff of the RPA; Tibere Rujigiro, a key member of the RPF; and Aziza Kulsum Gulamali, described as a "unique case," in part because of her uncanny ability to survive the shifting sands of factional realignments. After serving as a major business partner of the FDD, the Burundi-based Hutu rebel faction, she is now heavily involved in coltan, gold, and ivory trafficking on behalf of the Rwandans and their RCD ally in Goma.

The importance of these "facilitators" cannot be overemphasized. Through their close personal contacts with the leadership of the Congolese rebellions, they act as the privileged intermediaries between the local factions and their external patrons. Many are major shareholders in the companies created to siphon off mineral and timber resources. A case in point is the Victoria Group, owned by Museveni's son, Muhoozi Kainerugabe, and Museveni's sister-in-law, Jovia Akandwanaho. The Group deals in diamonds, gold, and coffee; has buyers in every major locality in the Orientale Province; and pays taxes to Bemba's MLC. Or take the case of Trinity, described as a fictitious company and a conglomerate of various businesses owned by Salim Saleh and his wife; the "manager" of the company is none other than Ateenyi Tibasima, second vice-president of the RCD-ML. A similar pattern emerges on the Rwandan side. Rwanda Metals and Grands Lacs Metals both deal in coltan, both have close ties to the RPA, and their shareholders include RPA officers, as well as RCD politicians. "A myriad of small companies were created and their shareholders are invariably powerful individuals in the Rwandan nomenklatura or RCD structures." Where Rwanda differs from Uganda is in the closer integration of its business interests with its client faction in eastern Congo and the presence of a "financial bridge" between them and the Kigali-based Banque du Commerce, du Développement et de l'Industrie (BCDI). "This financial bridge is statutory; indeed, the RCD statute indirectly recognizes the role of Rwanda in overseeing the finances of the movement and its participation in decision-making and control/audit of finances."[53]

Though receiving less attention than Uganda or Rwanda, Zimbabwe's participation in the looting is amply chronicled. Much of Mugabe's war effort is sustained by the profits derived from mining concessions and joint ventures with Congolese companies. Among Zimbabwean companies doing business in the Congo, pride of place goes to the state-owned Zimbabwe Defense Industries (ZDI), run by retired military officers and party officials, and Zvinavashe Investment, a holding company owned by Maj. Gen. Vitalis Zvinavashe, the head of Zimbabwe's military and commander of the joint southern African forces fighting in the Congo.[54] A major source of profit for the Zimbabweans is the copper parastatal, Générale des Carrières et des Mines (Gécamines), now managed by Zimbabweans; another is Société Miniere de Bakwanga (MIBA), which holds a virtual monopoly on diamond extraction in the Kasai. To procure Zimbabwe's military support, a large portion of the Gécamines mining rights were transferred to a Zimbabwean company, Ridgepoint, without compensation. In a similar arrangement, diamond mining concessions were transferred from MIBA to the Zimbabwean Defense Forces (ZDF), until it became apparent that the recipient did not have the required capital or technical skills to draw maximum advantage from the deal. It was at this point that the controversial mining start up, Oryx Zimcom, with a $1 billion, twenty-five-year concession in the DRC, entered into a joint venture with COSLEG, a Zimbabwean company, and MIBA to provide the needed expertise.[55] The pattern that emerges from these transactions is one of a tight imbrication of private and corporate interests, with the major shareholders in COSLEG being none other than top-ranking Zimbabwean army men and politicians. As of July 2000, as many as 500 Zimbabwean companies were said to operate in the DRC as a result of insider deals between Mugabe and Kabila.

Not the least significant of the findings of the UN report is the active participation of Western and non-Western corporate interests in the import of the Congo's mineral wealth. Out of a sample of thirty-four companies importing minerals from the DRC, thirteen are based in Belgium, five in Germany, another five in Holland, two in Great Britain, one in Russia, one in India, and another in Malaysia. Reflecting on such unprecedented plundering of the Congo's wealth, one commentator wrote: "The Congo has become a carcass being chewed at by its elite and its neighbors. They have looted and sold its natural resources on a scale without precedent. This, with the direct or tacit complicity of pious governments and corporations around the world."[56]

If the presence of foreign armies in the DRC brings to mind the "soldier without border phenomenon," its counterpart is the smuggler, for whom borders are a necessary condition of trade. Secret shipments of arms to the region come from many sources, some in South Africa, others from as far as Bulgaria, described by one observer as "the arms bazaar for rebels and terrorist organizations of every political, ethnic and religious persuasion, including the Hutu militia who were responsible for mass killings in Rwanda."[57] Whereas the Bulgarian state marketing agency, Kintex, along with the country's largest arms manufacturer, Arsenal, are reported to have sold weapons to Hutu militias, much of Joseph Kabila's military hardware comes from ZDI. In short, much of the DRC has become a free trade area for arms merchants, drug traffickers, gold and diamond smuggling, and plain thugs; transforming the region into a prime example of a criminalized economy.[58]

The Essence of Failure

"Victims of their own wealth" is the title of a recent Canadian newspaper article on the war in the DRC.[59] Suggestive as it is, greed is not the only force driving local factions to turn against each other; despair is the price paid by the Congolese for the greed of their neighbors. None of the huge profits extracted from the Congo is ploughed back into the local economy. The result has been the utter collapse of infrastructures and the near evaporation of social services. The school system is in a shambles, and the few schools that still operate are hardly enough to meet the growing demand for education or professional training. As Garreton reported in 1999, "In Kisangani schools are open only a few days a week, while other have been closed; school enrollment has declined to alarming levels, and since students cannot be reunited with their families, some have ended up joining the army."[60]

For younger generations of Congolese, joining one Mai-Mai faction or other offers the only hope of salvation. The phenomenon lies at the heart of factional violence sweeping across North and South Kivu. As Vlassenroot showed, the social marginalization of youth is the single most important underlying factor behind the proliferation of armed militias collectively referred to as Mai-Mai.[61]

While there can be no doubt about their intense hatred of the foreign invader, the youth's willingness to engage in factional violence must be seen as a rational option where professional chances are almost nil. Confronted with a situation where traditional safety nets have disintegrated, and in the absence of meaningful employment alternatives, joining the Mai-Mai becomes a "viable employment option." Analyzing the circumstances that led to the flowering of the militias, Vlassenroot traces their birth to the emergence of "marginalized youngsters and school dropouts [who] formed groups of under-age combatants acting against every representative of modern political authority." Whether named Kasindiens, Bangilima, Katuku, Batiri, Simba, or Mai-Mai, he writes, "these are nothing more than different names for the same phenomenon."[62] They are the political expression of a diffuse sense of hopelessness in the face of social and economic circumstances that are totally beyond their control. For many, recourse to magic is the only source of psychic reassurance. Belief in their own invulnerability, through the intercession of witch doctors, provides the clearest symbolic link to their 1964–65 Mai-Mai predecessors. Like the Mai-Mai of the Muleliste rebellion, their strategies are dictated by short-term interests, and so, also, their tactical alliances. All share the conviction that they owe their misery to the invasion of their country by foreign armies. The conditions created by looting Kivu's economy drives them to seek redemption in violence. The perverse effects of the global economy have summoned back into existence some of the most intractable forces encountered in the continent: warlordism fueled by immiseration and xenophobia.

What Paths to Reconstruction?

As if driven by a desire to avoid his father's mistakes, Kabila the younger did more in his first six months to move the peace process forward than Kabila, the elder, did in three years. Although the full implementation of the Lusaka accords is still distant, on several key issues substantial progress has been registered. The principle of an inter-Congolese dialogue has been accepted, along with Masire's presence in Kinshasa. In a move that goes far beyond the terms of the Lusaka accords, Rwanda pulled back its troops some 125 miles from its frontline position at Pweto (Katanga); Uganda followed suit, withdrawing some 1,500 troops from Buta (Orientale Province) in the north. Meanwhile, the UN Mission in the Congo (MONUC) deployed some 3,000 peacekeepers in the buffer zone separating the combatants. Further contributing to the relaxation of tension was Joseph Kabila's stated willingness to give serious attention to Rwanda's security concerns.

Between the revival of the Lusaka accords and the reconstitution of Congolese statehood lies a huge distance and some formidable hurdles: the restoration of a legitimate government, the reassertion of Congolese sovereignty, and the reconstruction of a disciplined and efficient military. All three are closely interrelated. None can be resolved without peace, yet the terms on which peace is arrived at will spell the difference between success and failure.

For Lusaka to succeed, the process must begin with a cease-fire agreement, continue with the concomitant withdrawal of all foreign troops and the deployment of UN peacekeepers, move on to the disarmament of "negative forces" (i.e., *interahamwe* and Mai-Mai), and reach its conclusion with the installation of a transitional government brought into existence through an inter-Congolese dialogue. The logic of this scenario, compelling as it is, makes unduly short shrift of the realities on the ground. Neither Kinshasa nor the UN have the capacity to bring the "negative forces" under control, and as long as Kigali can legitimately claim that they pose a threat to its security, their presence in the Kivu serves as a convenient pretext for the continuation of war by other means. The same is true of Uganda, even though the threat posed by the Alliance of Democratic Forces (ADF) to its security is benign compared to the Mai-Mai and *interahamwe*. Although Angola and Zimbabwe both derive substantial material benefits from their involvement, for Luanda, strategic considerations are rather more significant.

Given the obstacles in the way of restoring territorial sovereignty, one must give serious consideration to the alternative path explored by Herbst: the decertification of the Congolese state through a redrawing of its geographical boundaries.[63] Concretely, doing so would translate into the international recognition of new territorial entities, corresponding roughly to the areas presently under the control of rebel and foreign forces. North and South Kivu would thus become a separate state, and the broad swathe of territory, running from Bunia in the east to Gbadolite in the west, would form another independent entity. The Congo would thus morph into three states (or possibly four if the Bunia-based RCD decided to go it alone). Whether the breakaway states would provide a more appropriate formula for resolving the Congo's woes is very doubtful, however. To begin with, none of the domestic rebel factions are willing to settle for less than the capture of power in Kinshasa; secession is simply not part of their agendas, at least for the time being. Furthermore, as far as eastern Congo is concerned, Rwanda would not be prepared to recognize the breakaway state unless it had the option to exercise substantial military and economic control over the area, a situation likely to arouse the fiercest opposition not only from "native" Congolese but from a great many Banyamulenge, who feel that they have been "instrumentalized" by Rwanda. Another major drawback is that the creation of smaller state systems does not in itself guarantee internal harmony. The shrinking of political arenas may do little more than displace the focus of conflict without enhancing the mediating capacity of the breakaway state, or it may create new sources of tension between pro- and anti-secessionist forces. Herbst's contention that "it is hard to see that the creation of smaller units is inherently bad" is not inherently wrong; in the case of the Congo, however, it is less than ideal. Not out of reverence for the old Belgian slogan—"*Congo uni, Congo fort*"—but because of the potential for renewed conflict that such an arrangement would create, the intense rivalries likely to arise over the hoarding of the Congo's wealth by the richest states (North and South Kivu), and because of the likelihood of continued hegemony by Rwanda, and possibly Uganda, over the newly created states.

There is no magic formula for the reconstruction of a Congo state, only tentative, piecemeal measures, designed to limit the costs of anarchy and facilitate the step-by-step implementation of the Lusaka accords. For all its drawbacks, Lusaka offered the most hopeful solution. Yet, to become reality, the accords needed strong support from the international community. Such support recognized that a proper sequencing of initiatives is of crucial importance if they are to be workable, that nothing constructive can be accomplished unless a modicum of peace is achieved, and that peace in turn requires a far heavier investment in the deployment of peacekeepers, as well as the strongest pressures upon international and non-state actors to induce compliance with the peace process.

There are also lessons to be learned from the past. After the near disintegration of the Congolese state in 1965, the recipe for reconstruction included three major ingredients: (a) the appointment of a strongman at the helm, (b) massive infusions of financial and technical assistance, and (c) the reorganization of the armed forces. Although the strongman turned out to be an unmitigated disaster for the country, there is little question about Mobutu's role in restoring stability. But as history demonstrates only too well, long-term stability requires legitimacy, and this is even more true today than in the 1960s.

The immediate priority in today's Congo is the reconstitution of a legitimate state system within the limits of its present boundaries; only then can one envisage moving on to the next stages, namely, the reassertion of territorial sovereignty, the creation of a viable military force, the neutralization of "negative forces," and the expansion of political participation.

Only the wildest optimist would pretend that peace is around the corner. Deep and lasting hatreds have been sown among the people of the Congo toward foreign invaders and their domestic allies, and these suspicions will not go away any time soon. Nor will the potential for a resumption of hostilities vanish overnight.

Chapter 15
The Tunnel at the End of the Light

For those of us old enough to remember what in the 1960s was known as "the Congo crisis"—soon to become the "endless crisis"—the tragic singularity of the present conjuncture is perhaps less apparent than some of the contributions to this volume might suggest. No one who lived through the agonies of the Congo's improvised leap into independence—followed by the swift collapse of the successor state and the breakup of the country into warring fragments—can fail to note the analogy with the dismemberment of the Mobutist state in the wake of the 1998 civil war. Then as now, the former Belgian colony was faced with a crisis of stateness of huge proportions. The challenges confronting the international community today are in a sense remarkably similar to what they were in the early 1960s: (a) how to reconstruct a broken-backed polity; (b) how to rebuild an army reduced to a rabble by the emergence of armed factions; and (c) how to revitalize basic human services and ensure a minimum of security and economic self-sustenance—in short, how to restore the legitimacy, territorial integrity, and internal sovereignty of the state. These are the daunting challenges facing the international community. This is not meant to suggest that history repeats itself, only that historical perspectives can offer important clues to an understanding of the present.

A Legacy of Exceptionality

There is no need to invoke *Heart of Darkness* to acknowledge the enduring legacy of the Congo's historical exceptionality. The latter, according to James Coleman and Ndolamb Ngokwey, is "insistently defined by superlatives."

Few other countries have suffered a precolonial capitalist exploitation so harsh, predatory, socially disorganizing, and unrestrained; a colonial system of bureaucratic authoritarianism so massive, deeply penetrative, paternalistic, and insulated from external monitoring; a democratic experiment immediately before independence of such fleeting brevity and politicized ethnicity; an indigenous leadership so denied of experience and unprepared for independence; an imperial evacuation so precipitate and ill-planned; an initial postcolonial period of such Hobbesian chaos, secessionism, and external manipulation; and the subsequent postcolonial agony of a protracted and seemingly interminable personalistic and patrimonial autocracy by one of Africa's most durable presidential monarchs.[1]

To this litany of woes must be added the staggering human losses recorded by the International Rescue Committee: since 1998 an estimated three million lives have been wiped out, which in comparative terms is roughly the equivalent of the casualties sustained on 9/11 on a daily basis for three consecutive years.

Reflecting on "the Congo distaster," Colin Legum observed in 1960: "Twice in its recent history—in the 1880s and again in 1960—the Congo became a threat to world peace. It is obviously a country to watch."[2] Where the current crisis differs from its immediate postindependence antecedent is that it no longer poses a threat to world peace, only to the people of the Congo. In the early 1960s, the United States and Belgium did indeed keep a close watch on developments in the Congo, to the point of being complicit in the murder of Patrice Lumumba, then seen as the most threatening vector of Soviet penetration into the heart of the continent. Cold War responses to the Muleliste insurgency of 1964–65, when nearly half of the country ended in rebel hands, ensured the swift reconstruction of the Congolese state under the auspices of Western patrons. Had it not been for the timely intervention of South African and European mercenaries and the bombing missions flown by Cuban pilots in the pay of the CIA, Mobutu's second coming on November 25, 1965 might not have materialized. With the end of the Cold War, the huge mineral resources of the Congo ceased to be seen as a major stake in East-West rivalries; and for a while, a light was seen to flicker at the end of the tunnel. But Zaire's "intransitive transition," as Gauthier de Villers and Jean Omasombo Tshonda explain,[3] soon dispelled all illusions about the likelihood of a quick exit. For some thirty years, Cold War priorities helped consolidate the grip of Mobutu's dictatorship; its termination, in the wake of the Rwanda-sponsored AFDL crusade, transformed the "Mobutu or chaos" alternative into a self-fulfilling prophecy.

The chaos scenario was by no means foreordained, however. It was the unintended consequence of the strategic options that framed U.S. policies for over thirty years. As Michael Schatzberg prophetically warned some twelve years ago, it was the unshakeable conviction of U.S. policymakers that there was simply no alternative to supporting Mobutu that made it happen: "Paradoxically, by supporting uncritically Mobutu's rule and affirming his 'indispensability,' U.S. policy is contributing to the chaos it has always sought to avoid. The real threat to tranquility in central Africa is neither the Libyans in the north nor the Cubans in the south, but the inherent instability of Mobutu's tyranny."[4] Even as late as 1991, when the National Sovereign Conference got underway, there was little indication of a change of heart in Foggy Bottom. As the unrepentant Chester Crocker told Michela Wrong, "If we had tried to attach 1990s governance conditionalities to Mobutu, we would have been calling for his overthrow."[5] One wonders in retrospect whether Mobutu's overthrow by "governance conditionalities," assuming that such a scenario could not be avoided, would have had more disastrous consequences for the people of the Congo than his violent ouster by a coalition of insurgents led by the Rwandan army.

Foreign-Linked Clientelism

Today's crisis unfolds in a radically different international context. At stake are the strategic, political, and economic interests of five African countries, namely, Rwanda, Uganda, Burundi, Angola, and Zimbabwe, each seeking to draw maximum advantage from the near collapse of the Congo state, and this with the direct or tacit complicity of local actors. The complex texture of the crisis, involving shifting alliances and conflicting agendas, are nowhere more brilliantly dissected than in Filip Reyntjens's classic work on the war in the Great Lakes, appropriately subtitled *Alliances mouvantes et conflits extraterritoriaux*.[6] One is tempted to see a "geopolitical schadenfreude," to use Michael Hirsh's phrase, in the ruthlessness with which the Congo's failed state syndrome is being exploited by its neighbours.[7] As one observer tersely put it, "The Congo has become a caracass being chewed at by its elite and its neighbours."[8] But as the chapters in this book demonstrate, the metaphor hardly does justice to the convoluted dynamic at work in the current drama. The sheer number of political actors involved, domestic and foreign, together with the fluidity of the regional political fields and the seemingly endless proliferation of factions generated by the constant recalculation of costs and benefits adds up to a picture of staggering complexity.

A key factor behind the disintegration of the Congolese state lies in the convergence of short-term interests between different sets of Congolese politicians and their foreign allies, in short, in foreign-linked clientelism. The key players are well known. The dominant faction in the east, the RCD, is heavily dependent on Rwanda militarily, and Rwanda, in turn, uses the RCD as the spearhead of its economic and political penetration in eastern Congo. The MLC, while casting about for a rapprochement with Kinshasa, has yet to sever its ties with Uganda, and many of the smaller factions operating in the northeast can best be described as satellites of Kampala. As for the Kabila government, there can be little question about the crucial role played by Angola and Zimbabwe in ensuring its security or, for that matter, about the handsome dividends, economic and strategic, reaped by each state in return for their military presence on the ground.

But this only tells part of the story. Managing patron-client ties is a complicated task, all the more so in situations of chronic conflict and violence, and where presumptive patrons are competing with each other for the allegiance of local clients. Perceptions of costs and benefits are by no means fixed once and for all. Today's loyal clients may end up being tomorrow's enemies. A mutually profitable relation may suddenly dissolve into factional dissidence or worse. The seemingly endless defections suffered by the RCD speak volumes for the inherent fickleness of client networks (of the fifty original founding members, only twenty are still formally affiliated with the movement). For the most recent and dramatic illustration of the phenomenon, one only needs to turn to Koen Vlassenroot's painstaking analysis of the internal tensions that have plagued the relations between the Banyamulenge and the RCD leadership, and among different Banyamulenge leaders, culminating in the dissidence of the Masunzu faction and the joint intervention of the RPA and RCD troops.[9]

Changing Partnerships

The case of the Banyamulenge brings into focus just how fragile local alliances can be when the demands made by the senior partner exceed the benefits expected by client factions: at the root of many Banyamulenges' unhappiness with their Rwandan ally is the strong suspicion that they have been "instrumentalized" by Kigali; that the price they paid in fighting Kabila's troops in 1998 far exceeded the rewards to which they felt entitled. It is hard to imagine, in the light of the violent confrontations that took place in 1999 and early 2002 between RPA soldiers and Banyamulenge, that the latter were Kigali's closest ally in 1997 and 1998. The sense of frustration shared by many Banyamulenge must be seen against the background of the changes taking place on the ground. Back in 1996–97, faced with repeated threats from local Mobutist politicians, they needed little prodding to join the Rwandans and their AFDL allies in their fight against Mobutu; from 1998 onward, however, their growing resentment of the Rwandan tutelage, coupled with Kigali's insistent demands that they leave their traditional homelands in south Kivu and return to Rwanda en masse, fundamentally altered the terms of the partnership.

If fluidity and fragmentation are indeed key characteristics of the Banyamulenge political field this is also true of the Mai-Mai militias of north and south Kivu; with much the same adverse consequences for the presumptive patron, in this case Kinshasa. Ironically, precisely when a major anti-Rwandan dissidence erupted among the Banyamulenge in 2002, a similar phenomenon, albeit on a much lesser scale, was taking place among the Mai-Mai, with some factions turning against Kabila to join the RCD, others joining hands with Masunzu's "rebels." Here again the context is the key. As preparations for the Inter-Congolese Dialogue (ICD) got under way, and with the RCD eager to meet the demands of the civil society on its own terms, some Mai-Mai warlords did not hesitate to cut a deal with their former enemy.

The Congolese version of Jean-Francois Bayart's "l'Etat-rhyzome" is conspicuous for its inability to effectively control its offshoots.[10] The farther away from the capital, the weaker the networks, and the more complicated the brokerage between the Kinshasa-based patron and its provincial clients. And the same is true, of course, of the clientelistic links reaching out from Kampala and Kigali to the rebel factions in the Ituri, Orientale, and Kivu provinces. The RCD, Kigali's most faithful client in North and South Kivu, appears to have lost what little legitimacy it may have enjoyed. The movement is currently split into six break-away factions.[11] The Rwandan loyalists (RCD-Goma), meanwhile, continue to be the target of unmitigated hatred on the part of many Congolese, including a substantial segment of the Banyamulenge community.

Factionalism and Ethnicity

Factionalism cuts across ethnicity, but ethnic loyalties or sub-loyalties persist through the thick and thin of factional struggles and are often manipulated for political advantage. Their overlap adds another element of complexity to power equations. A useful point of entry into this conceptual minefield is Crawford Young's characterization of ethnicity as a "subjective" and "contextually shifting phenomenon";[12] only by taking into account the dramatic changes in the regional context can one begin to understand the sudden eruption of ethnic hatreds at specific historical moments, most prominently in the aftermath of the Rwanda genocide, and at the beginning of the 1998 civil war.

Despite the continuing factional sideshows, to this day Hutu-Tutsi polarities remain the basic referential frame, among a large segment of the Congolese population, for identifying friends and enemies. Whether ethnic identities in fact correspond to these labels is immaterial; all that is needed is for certain basic cultural or physical markers to be perceived as indicators of Tutsiness or Hutuness. Countless Tutsi-looking Congolese, and not a few Africans from other states, were ruthlessly assaulted and murdered by Congolese mobs in the wake of the August 1998 crisis. Tens of thousands perished in 2000 and 2001 when Lendu turned against

Hema, and vice versa, in the Ituri province. Even though neither group clearly fits the Hutu-Tutsi frame, the agricultural (Lendu) versus the pastoralist (Hema) dichotomy was enough to legitimize mutual destruction.

The case of the Banyamulenge is even more telling, given that they constitute a distinct cultural entity in south Kivu, whose roots are traceable to precolonial times. Even though they see themselves as Congolese and firmly reject intimations of being Rwandans, to this day many "native" Congolese do not hesitate to vehemently challenge their claims to being bona fide Congolese citizens. Widely perceived as Rwandan Tutsi in disguise, the Banyamulenge, writes Vlassenroot, are seen as "arrogant aggressors, occupying their provinces, exploiting their mines and killing their children."[13] Ultimately, the fate of the Banyamulenge hangs on the issue of citizenship, and this is true also of tens of thousands of ethnic Tutsi in north Kivu, who settled in the province before or during colonial rule. Unless their claims as citizens are recognized, the prospects for peace will remain in doubt. Whether Tutsi communities indigenous to the Congo would be able to survive an eventual withdrawal of the Rwandan army is anybody's guess.

War and Plunder

No less problematic, however, is the likelihood of a Rwandan pull-out. Kigali's security concerns are increasingly eclipsed by the huge benefits drawn from the exploitation of the Kivu's mineral wealth. What began as a free-for-all stealing of cash and private property in the months immediately following the 1998 conquest of eastern Congo by Uganda and Rwanda, gave way a year later to a more "systematized exploitation" of mineral resources. Though both are bereft of diamond deposits, "over the last few years Rwanda and Uganda have exported diamonds worth millions of dollars. . . . While the combined diamond exports of Uganda and Rwanda more than double from 1998 to 2000, exports from the Democratic Republic of Congo (DRC) were halved."[14] It is from the extraction of coltan, however, that Kigali derives much of the financial wealth needed to prosecute its military operations in eastern Congo. Quoting from the UN *Report of the Panel of Experts on the Illegal Exploitation of Natural Resources*, Ingrid Samset notes that in a period of eighteenth months, from 1999 to 2000, Rwanda is believed to have earned "a stunning $250 million."[15] During the same period, we are told, Rwanda was able to double its military expenditures.

The wholesale plunder of the Congo's mineral wealth is what enables both Rwanda and Uganda to sustain their war effort at minimal cost; in effect, the Congolese are supporting the financial burden of their own occupation by foreign armies. This said, it is noteworthy that Rwanda's total cash earnings from its imperial thrust far exceed the aggregate cost of its military activities in the region, thus bringing to Kigali a "massive economic surplus." It is difficult to avoid the conclusion that by turning a blind eye to the profits drawn from the looting of the Congo's wealth, the international community—meaning not only the European Union and the United States, but the World Bank and the International Monetary Fund—is tacitly encouraging a colonial enterprise in the best tradition of European imperialism.

If Rwanda is the worst offender, it is by no means the only one. Zimbabwe and Angola are also on the receiving line of diamond concessions (though Zimbabwe substantially more so than Angola); and in return for Zimbabwe's military "cooperation," the Gecamines, the key parastatal on the copperbelt, has transferred a large portion of its mining rights to a Zimbabwean company run by Mugabe's henchmen in the state-owned ZDI.

It is hardly surprising that the presence of foreign armies on Congolese soil should generate widespread resentment of the occupants. Nowhere is this more dramatically evident than in eastern Congo, where hatred of Rwanda, and by implication of all Tutsi, domestic or foreign, has taken on alarming proportions. Bishop Kataliko's lament that "the Congolese people are obliged to resist because our riches are being looted by foreign powers with the complicity of a Congolese elite" is no empty jeremiad. Here as elsewhere "to the victors go the spoils," but at least some of the spoils end up in local hands. The trickle-down effect of exploitation translates into complex mechanisms of extraction and redistribution. A new type of informal economy is developing around coltan extraction, funneling profits from the diggers to the intermediaries, from the intermediaries to the foreign-manned comptoirs, and from the comptoirs to Kigali and beyond. "Coltan fever," writes Stephen Jackson, has "rapidly dollarised many relatively remote rural areas," while generating a host of secondary activities linked to the new economy—prostitution, brewing and shebeens, and petty commerce of all varieties.[16] Tempting though it may be to conclude that there is mutual advantage in profit sharing, this is hardly supported by the evidence painstakingly gathered by Jackson. The get-rich quick mentality fostered by coltan fever has reversed traditional agricultural trading patterns, causing serious shortages of staple foods. The sharp drop in the price of coltan, from $150 to $25 a kilo, coupled with Rwanda's reliance on Hutu prisoners to do the digging, has intensified competition and led many prospective diggers to find alternative sources of employment by joining the Mai-Mai militias. Notwithstanding the taxes levied by Rwanda and its RCD ally on coltan and diamond sales, little or nothing of this revenue is ploughed back into social infrastructures; and for every Congolese who stands to profit from the trade, ten others are falling through the cracks.¹⁷ As Koen Vlassenroot has persuasively argued, the growing marginalization of the Congolese youth is certainly a key element behind the Mai-Mai phenomenon; in the absence of alternative sources of employment, and with no safety net left in the traditional society, joining the militias becomes the only rational option. "There is a clear link," he writes, "between this new political violence and the nature of the postcolonial state, which, lacking the mechanisms to bind its citizens to the social order, produced thousands of marginalized young people."¹⁸

Citing David Keen's twist on the Clausewitzian axiom that "war is a continuation of economics by other means," Jackson shows the circular relationship between war making and profit making, one relentlessly reinforcing the other. The result has been to "elevate violence in a vicious circle of conflict based rapine: profits increasingly motivate the violence, violence makes the profits possible."¹⁹ One only needs to recall the bloody confrontations between Rwanda and Uganda over access to diamond deposits in and around Kisangani, and the similarly violent encounters between Jean-Pierre Bemba's MLC and the Nyamwesi wing of the RCD, to appreciate the point. For a more recent account of how greed and violence intersect, one can do no better than quote from the UN *Interim Report of the Panel of Experts on the Illegal Exploitation of Natural Resources* of May 2002:

In the area of the northeastern DRC where two battalions of Ugandan troops are still stationed, violent armed conflicts have primarily been among the three Uganda-backed Congolese rebel groups that dominate the northeast-MLC, its purported ally RCD-National and RCD-ML. Some of these rebel armies have been reinforced at times by highly fluid alliances with what have been described as Mai-Mai groups. In some areas Ugandan soldiers also intervened. Battles were fought over Buta, Isoro, Watsa, Bafwasende and Bunia, all endowed in varying degrees with deposits of gold, diamonds, coltan or cassiterite as well as stands of timber. . . . Control of precious resources and customs and tax revenues, all vital to the consolidation of the highly commercialized power bases of certain individuals and groups, have repeatedly fueled these battles. Over the course of three and a half years of conflict, various armed groups have clashed over these economically strategic areas, trading control back and forth among them.²⁰

The same source leaves the reader with few illusions about the human toll:

Reports and testimonies indicate that civilian populations have suffered greatly as a result, with casualties, forced displacements, increased food insecurity and malnutrition. A state of generalized insecurity reigns in many areas in the Orientale Province and the Kivus, as bands of youthful 'soldiers' or free-floating militias attack, loot and burn villages and fields. . . . In some areas entire communities have been forcibly displaced by armed forces so they can take control of resource-rich zones or the access roads for those zones. Military forces and militias have reportedly evicted local artisanal diggers in order to seize production or take control of informal mining sites. Other serious human rights violations, including killings, sexual assaults and abuse of power for economic gain have been reported as directly linked to military forces' control of resource extraction sites or their presence in the vicinity of such sites.[21]

How are people to survive in such a Hobbesian universe? Many do not. And yet, where circumstances are not so lethal, as in Kinshasa and Lubumbashi, the Congolese have invented their own techniques of survival.

Survival Techniques

Kinshasa is one of several arenas where informal coping mechanisms flourish in conditions of utter despair and rampant poverty. Keeping body and soul together requires treasures of ingenuity. "Getting by," or *la débrouille*, covers a wide spectrum of activities and stratagems, hustling and peddling, wheeling and dealing, whoring and pimping, swapping and smuggling, trafficking and stealing, brokering and facilitating—in short, making the most of whatever opportunities arise to avoid starvation. Conventional categories are of little help to map out the new urban jungle. Consider the following sample of the emergent lexicon: *dare-dare* or *businesseurs* (street peddlers), *Tchadiens* (hawkers who cry out the destinations of taxi-buses), *cambistes* (money changers), *moineaux* (street children making a living from begging), to which might be added the *tolekistes boyomais* (operators of cyclo-taxis), *shayeurs* (market peddlers) and the ubiquitous *ndumba* (prostitutes) looking for *ya'soda* (partners)—all of them representative of an ever-growing aggregate of *conjoncturés*, all of them victims of the "conjuncture." Equally suggestive of the hardships of everyday life are the expressions that have gained currency to describe what it takes to make ends meet: *kupikanisha* or *kukombanisha* (to fight), *kupika sando* (hitting with a hammer), *kujikikapika* (to exert oneself), *kuboce* (to work hard), *kutwanga kisu* (to lie), and so forth. As the authors point out, there are tacit rules and understandings to be observed, a sort of moral economy of *la débrouille*. It is immoral to steal from a *maskini wa Mungu* (God's poor), but the phrase *ni bya l'Etat* (it belongs to the state) is enough to legitimize stealing public property. Theodore Trefon makes much the same point: "There is order in the disorder. Function and dysfunction overlap. This applies to all social and political levels, ranging from neighbourhood, professional or ethnic associations and networks to the level where political decisions are made."[22] Clearly, neither Kinshasa nor Lubumbashi fit the image of Hobbesian anarchy—unlike many parts of eastern Congo. But neither do they fit into the mold of a vibrant and responsive civil society.

A Janus-Faced Civil Society

In today's Congo the civil society is both part of the problem and part of the solution. Its Janus-faced quality tells us why: at one end of the spectrum lurks the satanic face of the civil society—the face of the génocidaires and the rapists, the armed bands and the militias, the poachers and murderers, and the camp followers and the smugglers; at the other end shines the engaging face of humanitarian NGOs, church groups and voluntary associations, and a whole array of organizations dedicated to denouncing abuses, fostering grassroots solidarities, and assisting the weak and the destitute. Between them a cruel dialectic is unfolding, pitting the forces of hope against the forces of desperation and revenge. Jean-Francois Ploquin correctly emphasizes the potential for renewal inherent in the civil society: "By maintaining a free flow of communication, by putting pressure on the authorities to engage in a dialogue, by drawing attention to other modes of expression than recourse to force, by weaving links between urban and rural populations and their elites, by working towards the harmonization of differing viewpoints, by denouncing oppression and the looting of resources, by resisting attempts at balkanization, and by reminding international actors of their obligations, civil society actors fulfill a function that is all too often set aside by the political class."[23] Whether this potential can become reality is another matter. A key problem confronting almost every CSO—including those which are most conspicuously lacking in civility—is that they rarely define their interests in relation to the state, such as it is, but in relation to the conflicts raging among different fragments of the Congolese state. Their stand on behalf of, or in opposition to one faction or another or their foreign patrons, threatens their autonomy, erodes their credibility, and weakens their capacity to serve as an effective vehicle for economic and political reform.

What Next?

If reform is unlikely to materialize from the womb of the "*forces vives,*" can it conceivably emerge from an inter-African dialogue—or from what Wamba dia Wamba, a key participant in the Lusaka negotiations, once described as "palaver as a practice of self-criticism," or to put it in his own inimitable phrasing "la palabre comme pratique de la critique et de l'autocritique sur le plan de toute la communauté"?[24] Will the Pretoria agreement between Kabila and Kagame, on July 30, breathe a new life in the Lusaka accords and chart a new course toward peace?

The joker in the pack will not be easily exorcised, for the reasons noted above. Furthermore, some of the key provisions outlined in the

Pretoria pact leave one to wonder whether, in the words of *The Economist* of July 27, 2002 it is little more than "a ploy in a well established game of bluff." Indeed, one wonders by what miracle Kabila's army could round up and disarm some 5,000 Hutu "rebels." Even if the mandate of the UN Mission to the Congo were altered for that purpose, it would take far more than 16,000 UN troops to do the job. Whether South African troops could be trained and deployed in time to assist Kabila's army is a moot point.

The broader context of factional struggles in eastern Congo has sown the seeds of a conflict that will persist for a long time to come. The deep fractures engendered by years of ethnofactional strife will not go away any time soon. Even in the best of circumstances, in the unlikely event of a total Rwandan pull-out, the fate of the Banyamulenge will remain uncertain at best; Masunzu's dissidence notwithstanding, many feel that the protective shield of the RPA is their best guarantee against retaliatory massacres by "native" Congolese. Meanwhile, the "pax Rwandana" generates its own perverse effects, creating the very threats to the Banyamulenge community that help legitimize the intervention of Rwandan proxies in eastern Congo.

"Diplomacy without power is feeble, and power without diplomacy is destructive and blind," wrote Hans Morgenthau. The Congo crisis has experienced both. There are reasons to doubt that an appropriate mix of power and diplomacy will emerge from the Pretoria accords. Even though they raised a glimmer of light at the end of the tunnel, the most likely alternative for the foreseeable future is the tunnel at the end of the light.

Chapter 16
From Kabila to Kabila: What Else Is New?

Reflecting on the merits of electoral democracy in the Congo, one of the least memorable characters in John Le Carré's novel *The Mission Song* makes his point with characteristic bluntness: "Elections won't bring democracy, they'll bring chaos. The winners will scoop the pool and tell the losers to go fuck themselves. The losers will say the game was fixed and take to the bush. And since everyone voted on ethnic lines anyway, they'll be back to where they started and worse."[1] Expletive aside, Skipper's assessment encapsulates many of the concerns of the international community in the aftermath of the Congo's first free multiparty elections since 1965.

What is the likelihood of renewed unrest when electoral triumph translates into a winner-takes-all outcome? Could it be that exclusion will pave the way for the reactivation of new pockets of insurgency? How much credence should be given to the accusations of massive electoral fraud directed at Kabila's camp? And if electoral processes, however free and fair, are no guarantee that peace will ensue, is this a sufficient reason for dismissing the significance of this first step in the direction of democracy?

If the answers are still speculative, there can be no doubt that the new government faces a challenge of enormous proportions when one considers its limited capacity to construct a viable state system. How to restructure the security apparatus, transform the country's huge mineral wealth into new opportunities for economic development, and lay the foundation for a reasonably effective justice system are issues that lie at the heart of any attempt to consolidate the transition. Some of these constraints are a legacy of the past; others are directly traceable to the flaws brought to light by the transition process.

The Leap into Multiparty Democracy

Few would deny that the 2006 elections must be seen as a turning point in the Congo's faltering march towards democratic governance.[2] Besides legitimizing Joseph Kabila's succession to the position of his assassinated father, they have drastically redefined the rules of the game, moving the chessboard from a lame power sharing deal to the trappings of democratic governance. They have created a new public space for formulating and implementing policy, where the provinces are intended to play a significant role. After a decade of mayhem in the wake of Mobutu's demise, the first competitive elections held in forty-one years hold the promise, however fragile, of a long-awaited turnaround.

Following a bitterly contested two-stage presidential poll on July 30 and October 29, on December 6, 2006, Joseph Kabila became the first democratically elected president since independence, with 58 percent of the popular vote in the runoff, as against 42 percent to his nearest opponent, Jean-Pierre Bemba. Thus came to an end the long drawn-out transition process set in motion by the so-called Global and Comprehensive Peace Agreement of December 2002, later institutionalized through the power sharing formula hammered out in 2003.

For the relatively smooth unfolding of the operational side of the elections, much of the credit goes to the Independent Electoral Commission (IEC)[3] and its president, the Abbé Apollinaire Malu-Malu, in meeting the staggering logistical challenge involved in setting up some 50,000 polling stations, registering twenty-five million voters, recruiting thousands of poll watchers, making sure that ballot papers (six broadsheet-size pages each) would reach their destination in time, and managing the flow of some 1,200 election observers. Outside assistance also helped. In addition to the $500 million electoral subsidy from the international community, the presence on the ground of some 17,000 UN peacekeepers, beefed up by an additional 1,400-person EU contingent (Eurofor), proved crucial in preventing partisan clashes from getting out of hand.

Attesting to the competitiveness of the first round of the presidential poll—held jointly with the race for parliament on July 30—thirty-three aspirants ran in the first round. Some 9,700 candidates fought for a seat in the National Assembly, consisting of 500 members. Competition was equally high for representation in the eleven provincial assemblies, whose principal, constitutionally mandated responsibility is the election of eleven provincial governors and 108 senators. Seventy-eight parties, out of 267 formally registered, presented slates of candidates for a total of 632 seats, later to be joined by fifty-eight co-opted members. Although the rate of voter participation varied widely from one province to the next—ranging from 90 percent in South Kivu to 39 percent in Kasai Oriental in the first round, and 80 percent in Maniema and South Kivu to 42 percent in Kasai Oriental in the second round—the overall impression is one of high voter participation. Out of a total of 25.4 million registered voters, eighteen million voted during the first round of elections and only slightly less during the second round.

Although the voting was by no means exempt of fraud, the consensus of opinion among observers is that these irregularities did not substantially alter the results. Delegates from the African Union (AU), the Economic Community of Central African States (CEEAC), and the South African government were unanimous in saying that "the incidents and irregularities noted were not so extensive as to cast doubt on the credibility of the vote," an assessment also shared by the International Committee for Support of the Transition (better known by its French acronym, CIAT). CIAT Chair and head of the MONUC, William Swing candidly admitted that "even for [him], a congenital optimist, the elections were better than [his] wildest expectations."[4] A very different assessment, however, emerges from the UN report on the human rights situation during the transition: throughout this period, from July to December 2006, "Congolese authorities often violated the right to freedom of assembly and ordered the breaking up of elections-related demonstrations, on a selective basis, whether or not these demonstrations threatened public order.... [Since the beginning of the campaign] there was a marked increase in politically motivated arbitrary arrests, especially in the capital. Summary executions and enforced disappearances were also documented."[5]

Bemba's party was not the least vocal in denouncing electoral fraud. No sooner were the results of the first round announced than violent scuffles erupted in Kinshasa between it and Kabila's, resulting in twenty-three people killed, forty-three wounded, and the destruction of Bemba's personal helicopter. Almost as pregnant with disaster was the scenario that came to pass three months later, with Bemba's blowhards venting their anger against the supreme court—held responsible for validating Kabila's victory—sending magistrates scurrying for cover while UN armored vehicles fired warning shots at the protesters. Although at first refusing to concede defeat, in the end he felt he had no other choice but to recognize, albeit grudgingly, Kabila's victory.

Regional Polarization

The east-west divide is the most notable characteristic of the electoral map revealed by the presidential race. With the bulk of Kabila's support concentrated in the eastern provinces, and Bemba's in the west—most notably in the capital, where his electoral coalition won over 68 percent of the vote—the obvious conclusion was that the new government would operate in a distinctly hostile environment. This was dramatically confirmed during the extremely bloody confrontation of March 22–23 between Bemba's private militia and the security forces, resulting in the deaths of hundreds of people. This, as we shall see, marks a turning

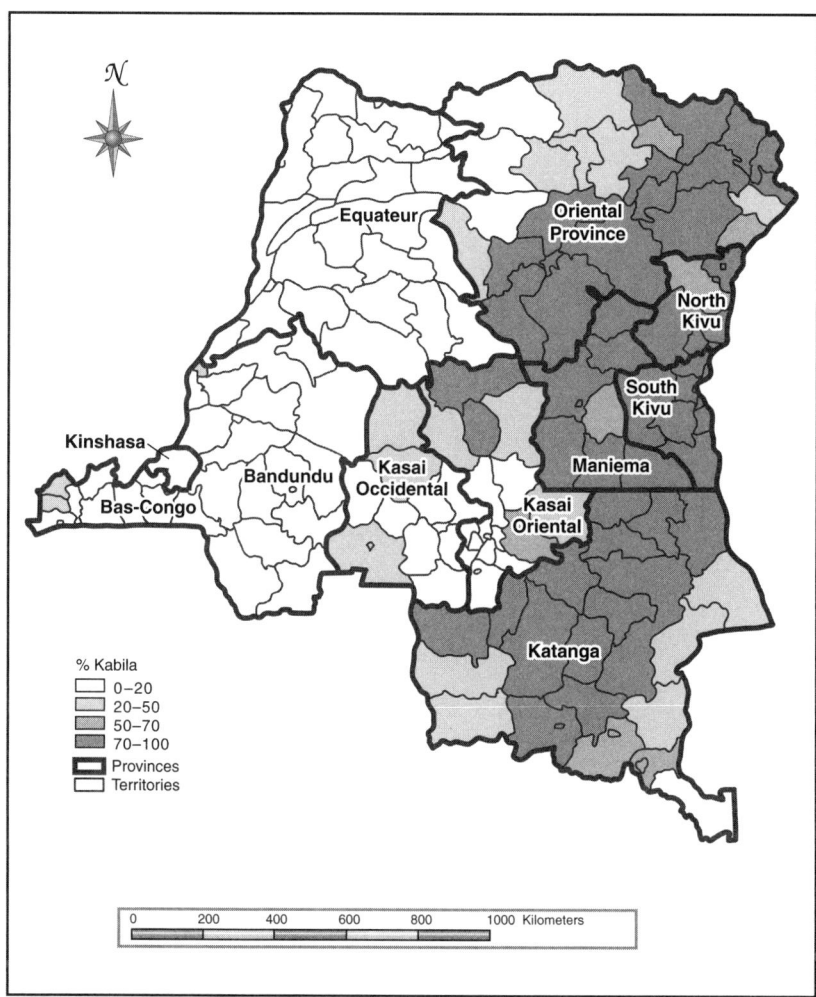

Map 6. Presidential elections, first round: Distribution of Kabila's electoral support. Reproduced from L. de Saint-Moulin and E. Wolff, "Cartes et documents: Les resultants de l'election presidentielle en RDC," *Belgeo*, no. 4 (2006): 465–72, by permission of the authors.

point in the efforts of the presidential majority to consolidate its grip on the emergent polity.

The political fault line between east and west is inscribed in part in the gravitational pull of regional loyalties. While ethnic ties did play a part in specific areas in shaping electoral configurations, regionalism proved even more decisive. It is certainly the key factor in explaining

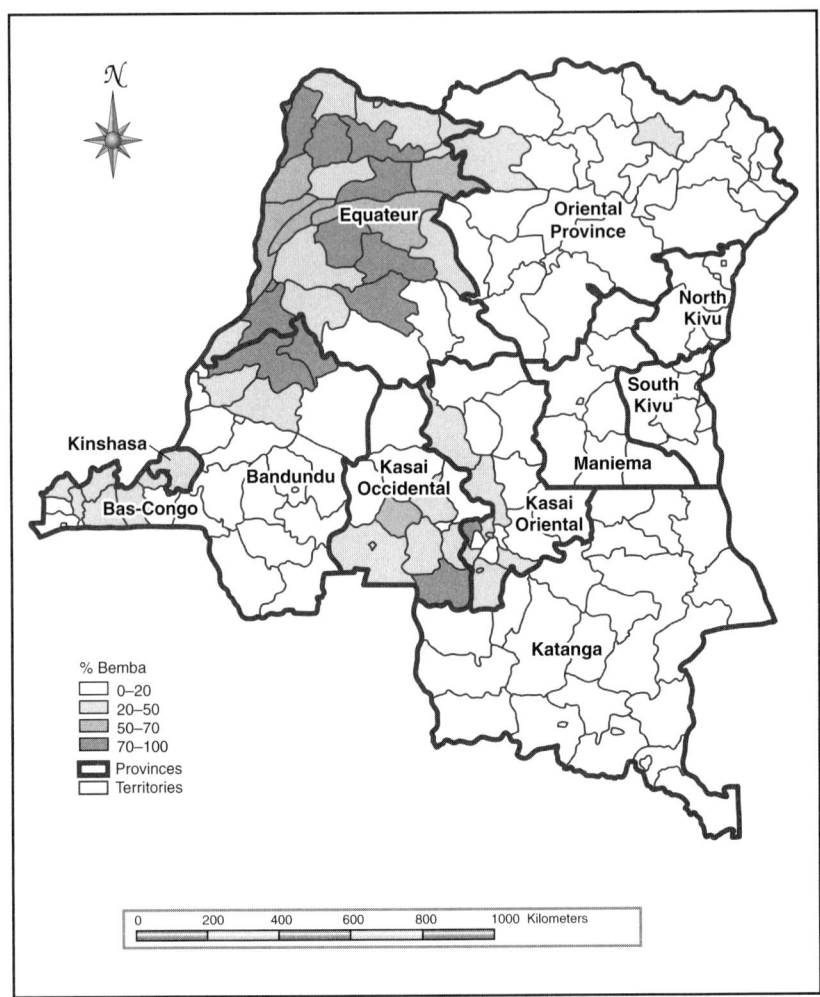

Map 7. Presidential elections, first round: Distribution of Bemba's electoral support. Reproduced from L. de Saint-Moulin and E. Wolff, "Cartes et documents: Les resultants de l'election presidentielle en RDC," *Belgeo*, no. 4 (2006): 465–72, by permission of the authors.

Bemba's landslide scores in the Equateur and Bas Congo provinces, sweeping respectively 97 and 74 percent of the vote.

Unlike Kabila, a Swahili speaker, Bemba's fluency in Lingala (i.e., the language of the Bangala) and adeptness at projecting politically loaded musical themes into his campaign—such as the wildly popular

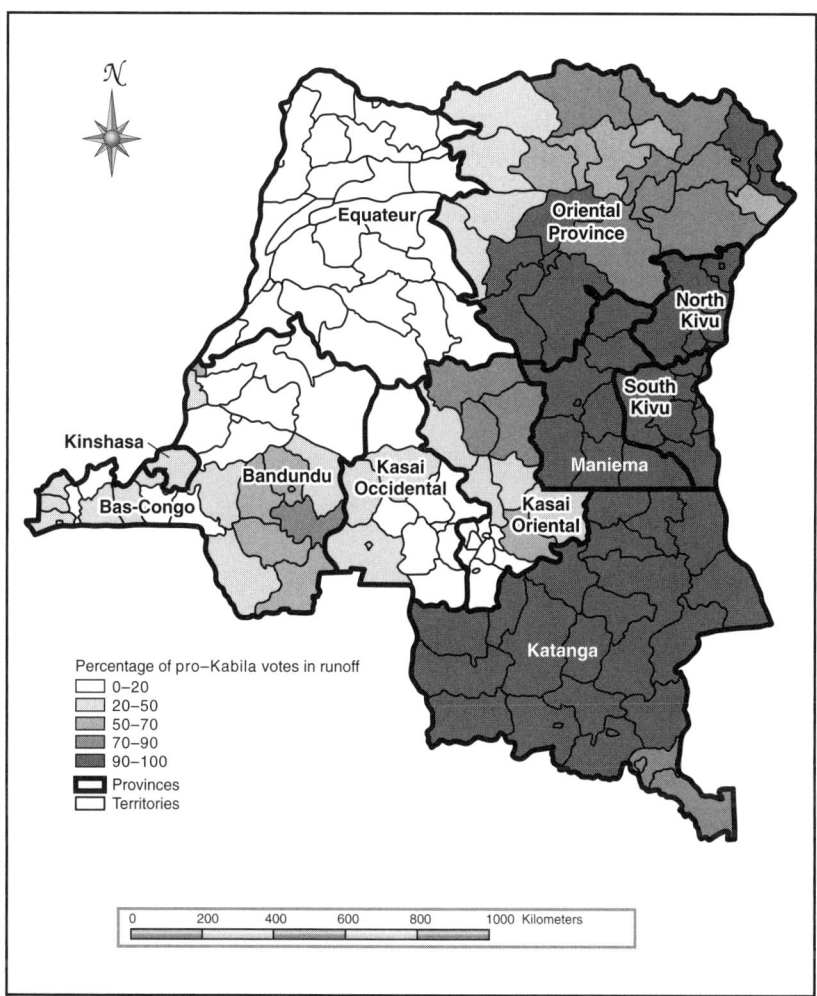

Map 8. Presidential runoff: Distribution of Kabila's support. Reproduced from L. de Saint-Moulin and E. Wolff, "Cartes et documents: Les resultants de l'election presidentielle en RDC," *Belgeo*, no. 4 (2006): 465–72, by permission of the authors.

"*Aza mwana Congo*" ("He is a son of the Congo")—earned him immediate and enthusiastic support among the Bangala populations of Kinshasa and Bangala-related communities of the Equateur, his native province. To this must be added his adroit manipulation of the nationality issue—referred to locally as *Congolité*—as a means of casting aspersions on Kabila, repeatedly tagged as a *mupaya* (foreigner) in the

Bemba-controlled media, in contrast with the Gemena-born *mwana mboka*, the native son.⁶ Nonetheless, neither *Congolité* nor *ethnicité* is sufficient to account for Bemba's surge of popularity in Kinshasa. His family and business connections were critical assets. As the son of Jeannot Bemba Saolana—one of Mobutu's most trusted and richest collaborators, and duly rewarded for his services in managing his patron's agro-business interests in Equateur—Bemba inherited a huge fortune and a vast array of strategic connections in Kinshasa's business community. Much of his campaign financing, not to mention the costs of his protection unit, better seen as a 300-strong mercenary force, stems in part from his ownership of a large number of lucrative enterprises⁷ and in part from the wealth derived from his appropriation of mineral resources during his years in the bush as President Museveni's erstwhile client-warlord.

Kabila's electoral triumph, on the other hand, is inscribed in a broader swath of regional support, running from Katanga in the south to Maniema, South Kivu, North Kivu, and Orientale Province in the north. Scores ranged from 98 percent in North and South Kivu to 93 percent in Katanga, his native turf. Here again, ethnicity hardly tells the whole story. That he happens to be viewed as the incarnation of popular resistance to Rwanda's hegemonic ambitions is the key to an understanding of his widespread popularity among the populations of the east. The solid support gained by Azarias Ruberwa among the Banyamulenge and other rwandophones of North Kivu is the major exception to the rule, but the modest gains achieved by his RDC at both the provincial and national levels does not alter the overall picture. Although picking up one fourth and one third of the votes respectively in Kasai Occidental and Kasai Oriental, it is in the east, the most densely populated and wealthiest region, that Kabila's victory achieved landslide proportions.

In different circumstances, the Kasai region—the bastion of the proverbially enterprising Luba people—would have voted overwhelmingly for Etienne Tshisekedi's UDPS. The disqualification of Mobutu's long-time opponent and outspoken Luba activist—following his decision to boycott the transition process after being left out of the 2003 power sharing agreement—turned out to be to Bemba's advantage in the first round, only to shift decisively to Kabila's in the second round. In the absence of Tshisekedi's candidacy, and because he encouraged his followers to abstain from the vote, the alternative Luba candidate, Oscar Kashala, until then virtually unknown to voters, only made modest gains in the Kasai, yet managed to emerge among the five remaining candidates in the second round, along with Antoine Gizenga and Mobutu's son, Francois Mobutu Nganza.

Gizenga's Comeback

As the third-biggest vote getter, with 2.2 million votes and thirty-four deputies, the appointment of Gizenga to the prime ministership on December 30 was not totally unexpected. Nonetheless, the re-emergence of the aging leader of the Parti Lumumbiste Unifié (PALU) on the political scene, after spending twenty-five years in exile, mostly in eastern bloc countries, caught many observers by surprise. Only very few today remember his early political career as the head of the notoriously hard-line Parti Solidaire Africain (PSA),[8] whom Lumumba appointed as his vice-premier in the fist post-independence government. His image at the time was that of an impenitent communist sympathizer, and the ubiquitous presence at his side of the mysterious Madame Blouin—a Brazzaville born *métisse* rumored to be closely associated with Sékou Touré's Parti Démocratique de Guinée (PDG), once dubbed as Gizenga's "black pasionaria"[9]—did little to diminish his reputation as a dangerous proxy for Soviet influences in the Congo. His radical aura still clings to his name. Perhaps more than anything else, his reentry on the political scene reveals the radical streak that runs through a major segment of the population. Today the 81-year-old patriarch stands as a living symbol of the Lumumbist heritage.

Rather than his leadership skills or ability to mesmerize crowds, Gizenga's comeback is also a commentary on his Pende background and strong ethnoregional roots in Bandundu, where he scored a stunning victory, and in part a reflection of his impeccable Lumumbist credentials and continuing reputation as an ardent defender of a radical brand of nationalism. In today's political context he stands as the embodiment of a widely shared revulsion against the threats posed to the Congo's sovereignty by its neighbors. Against a political class known for its venality, he projects an image of incorruptibility. His principled commitment to the restoration of Congolese sovereignty is seen by many as the quality most needed to lead the Congo out of the morass of civil strife and endemic poverty. The question in the minds of many observers is whether his political resurrection will measure up to the formidable challenges ahead. Not the least will be to lend a measure of internal cohesion to his government—a hydrocephalic monster consisting of sixty members (six ministers of state, thirty-four ministers, and twenty vice ministers) belonging to fourteen parties.

A Fragmented Parliamentary Arena

Tempting as it is to stress the significance of regional polarization, the sheer number of parties represented in parliament points to a very different trend. Out of the 267 parties registered, 70 obtained seats. To this must be added scores of candidates who ran on independent lists, of whom 63 won seats, including 17 in Katanga.

The parallel with the May 1960 elections on the eve of independence is unmistakable and for much the same reasons. The immensity of the country, the geographical dispersion of its urban centers, the diversity of its ethnic configurations, along with the intensity of the electoral competition and inability of the candidates to offer a meaningful choice to the electorate other than one based on region and ethnicity—all of these came into play. Crawford Young's description of the party landscape in 1960, when "each provincial capital produced its own flowering of parties, which then extended into the rural hinterland, seeking as a natural clientele the groups related to the party leadership,"[10] is just as relevant today as it was on the eve of independence.

As in 1960, the coalescence of smaller parties around a politically dominant partner has been a key characteristic of the pre-electoral jockeying for position. Thus, the winning presidential coalition, the Alliance pour la Majorité Présidentielle (AMP) is a collection of some thirty parties gravitating around Kabila's core group, the Parti Populaire pour la Reconstruction et le Développement (PPRD), the instrument forged by Kabila *père* to tighten his grip on what was left of the state. Similarly, although his MLC forms the nucleus of Bemba's Union pour la Nation (UN), formerly known as the Regroupement des Nationalistes Congolais (RENACO), the latter includes twenty-four smaller parties. To further complicate matters, some of these coalition partners are themselves aggregates of minor political groups, thus resulting in a complex pyramid of satellites and sub-satellites. A prime example is Kabila's major ally in the east, the Mouvement Social pour le Renouveau (MSR), which operates as a roof organization for a wide variety of local groupings, many drawn from the civil society: with 30 deputies in parliament—against 35 for PALU, 70 for the MLC, and 110 for the PPRD—the MSR is the fourth-largest party represented in the national assembly.

Although the Kabila camp can count on the support of a comfortable majority, including thirty-four deputies affiliated with PALU, the AMP remains an extremely fragile edifice, vulnerable to shifting political loyalties. Like its UN opponent, it has yet to become a solid political machine. Looking back at the precedent of the 1991 NSC—notable both the proliferation of parties and their fickleness—the prospects for a stable governing coalition are very much in doubt.

In the Senate, consisting of 108 members indirectly elected by the eleven provincial assemblies, the AMP claims a majority of fifty-five seats, of which twenty-one are held by the PPRD, against fourteen for the MLC. Albeit to a lesser degree than the National Assembly, the upper chamber remains deeply fractured along party lines. The most notable exceptions are the twenty-six "independents," among whom are found a large number of "dinosaurs," whose roots go back to the Mobutist era.[11] Most can be counted on to cleave to their time-honored clientelist strategies.

The legislature will likely emerge as the most congenial habitat for what Christopher Clapham aptly called "the clientelism of representation," that is, as the hub for "the formation of clientelist networks extending across the entire political community."[12] In such a context, representatives often act as the brokers through whom benefits can be funneled into the hands of provincial patrons, who in turn will use them to build their local clienteles.

The Costs of Political Exclusion

In one major respect, the prediction voiced by Le Carré's Cassandra has become reality: the winners have indeed "scooped the pool," leaving the opposition empty handed. The curse of exclusion is not a new phenomenon. It was already discernible in 2003, after the reshuffling of the cards at the Sun City inter-Congolese dialogue, when many of the faction leaders in Ituri and elsewhere found themselves left out of the game, with dire consequences for the region. Today, however, the extent of Kabila's control of the new institutions makes it even more of a menace. That Bemba, the main opposition candidate who won 42 percent of the vote in the second round of the presidential race, should end up with not a single seat in the government, only one governorship out of eleven, and not a single chairmanship of parliamentary committees, carries ominous implications.

Post-electoral clashes in pro-Bemba constituencies attest to the anger of the opposition as it realized it would be left empty handed. On February 1, the Bas Congo province, Bemba's stronghold, was the scene of a violent confrontation between the pro-UN Bundu dia Kongo sect and AMP supporters, resulting in 137 deaths, according to the MONUC. Although the verdict of the provincial Court of Appeals called for new elections, the decision was reversed by the notoriously pro-Kabila Constitutional Court, thus confirming the nomination of the AMP candidate, Simon Mbaki Batshia. Again, Kinshasa was the scene of widespread unrest after the election of an AMP governor by what many thought to be similarly dubious methods, but not until March did the capital experience bloodshed on a frightening scale.

The spark that ignited the crisis came from Bemba's refusal to comply with the request of the government to integrate his militia into the FARDC. The fighting lasted through March 22–23, causing anywhere from 200 to 500 deaths. Jason Stearns, a seasoned observer, called it "one of the worst outbreaks of violence in Kinshasa's history."[13] Bemba, at his wit's end, found refuge in the South African Embassy; not until April 11 was he and his family allowed to leave for Portugal, officially to seek "medical treatment." The headline in the newspaper *L'Avenir*— "UN decapitated following the unfortunate events in Kinshasa"[14]—aptly summed up the immediate consequence.

The pro-Bemba constituencies were not the only ones to experience the costs of exclusion. Tshisekedi's UDPS in the Kasai region and Azarias Ruberwa's RCD in North Kivu were the principal losers. Thus among the many communities virtually denied participation in government were, in addition to the broad assemblage of Lingala-speaking communities of the northwest, many of the Luba people of the Kasai, and more importantly, the Tutsi of North and South Kivu. Together the number of voters ending up on the losing side of the electoral equation could well add up to nearly half of the electorate.

The consequences of exclusion were made dramatically clear in the months following the elections. North Kivu is where the threat to stability arising from the electoral demise of the Tutsi community emerged in full light. While the RCD gained only seven seats in the in the national legislature, not a single Tutsi made it into the provincial assembly, and only one became a provincial minister. The Nande and Hutu candidates, on the other hand, were generously represented in national and provincial assemblies. In these circumstances, one can better understand the surge of popularity of a Laurent Nkundabagenzi—better known as Nkunda—among the Tutsi of North Kivu, notwithstanding his record as one of the most brutal warlords of the region. As the self-proclaimed defender of Tutsi rights, he is widely seen as the most credible candidate to uphold their claims to recognition as a minority at the mercy of a tyrannical majority. So far from tarnishing his image, the brutal offensives carried out by his movement against non-Tutsi civilian populations in October 2007, resulting in hundreds of thousands of displaced persons, has only reinforced his appeal. His incessant propaganda against non-Tutsi, whom he accuses of harboring genocidal plans, has contributed in no small way to create a sense of paranoia among his supporters, thus exacerbating intercommunal tensions throughout the province and beyond. As North Kivu appears to totter on the brink of a wider conflict, Kabila's army has demonstrated its appalling incapacity to bring a modicum of peace to the region. So, far from being a solution, Kabila's security forces are a large part of the problem.

The Heritage of Neo-Patrimonial Rule

Democratic transitions are inseparable from the authoritarian baggage inherited from previous regimes. The Congo is no exception. The

Mobutist state has left an enduring imprint on the fabric of [...]
It has institutionalized a culture of corruption and clientelism th[...]
tinues to influence public attitudes to authority as much as it shapes the rulers' attitude to the public. Clientelism in its manifold manifestations, internal and external, is indeed a key feature of Congo politics. It is inherent in what the late Jean-François Médard described as "neo-patrimonial" rulership,[15]—a hybrid system where the logic of personalized ties thoroughly penetrates legal-rational institutions—a system in which the public and private spheres are but two sides of the same coin, where the exchange of self-serving favors is the norm, where connections and cash are the currencies of power and influence, and with the ruler cast in the role of a superpatron dexterously handling carrots and sticks. This clientelist legacy has largely survived through the ten-year interval between the demise of Mobutu and the advent of competitive elections.

The rise of Laurent Kabila—first as Kagame's cat's paw, then as his bitterest enemy—was seen by many as emblematic of a fundamental break with the Mobutist era. This misreading of the evidence was made clear by the way journalists and U.S. officials referred to the newcomer as one of the refreshingly virtuous "new leaders" thrown up by the revolutionary upheavals of the mid-1990s.[16] A closer look at the Kabila interlude suggests a different take. His power base was constructed on nepotism, cronyism, and the selective allocation of prebends—mostly in the form of cash, real estate, and juicy corporate contracts. The rallying of prospective allies in the countryside proceeded from the same logic—the extension of material benefits for political support. At no time did his modus operandi constitute a significant departure from previous practice—save for his more frequent recourse to indiscriminate brutality.

The rise to power of Kabila fils as the handpicked successor to his father in January 2001, opened a new chapter in the Congo's tortuous saga. Many important breakthroughs were registered during the six years that he served as interim president. Among his more notable achievements were the ICD at Sun City (2002), the subsequent troop withdrawal agreements concluded with Rwanda and Uganda, the power sharing arrangement designed to accommodate the claims of the two principal rebel movements—Bemba's MLC and Ruberwa's RCD—by handing them two of the four vice-presidencies, the adoption of a new constitution, and the organization of multiparty elections. Where his father consistently dragged his feet on the implementation of the Lusaka accords (July 1999), he ended up being the person most directly responsible for putting them into effect.

These are no small accomplishments. Closer scrutiny, however, suggests a more sober assessment. His years in office had little impact on the civil strife ravaging much of the eastern provinces. Whether looked at from the standpoint of the proliferation of armed militias; the crescendo of rape and sexual torture inflicted on thousands of women; or the continuing incursions of Rwandan soldiers and recurrent attacks against civilians mounted by the Rwanda-backed rebel leader Laurent Nkunda, resulting in the massive displacement of civilians; the overall picture is one of undiminished rural unrest, accompanied by appalling levels of poverty, disease, and malnutrition.

Thus to view his interim presidency as the harbinger of a definitive turnaround strains credulity. The inability of the transition government to cope effectively with the aftereffects of civil war is the legacy of a neo-patrimonial system incapable of promoting reform, much less of reforming itself. That much can be gathered from the picture drawn by Thierry Vircoulon of the "presidential space" on the eve of the elections: "a shadowy government inhabited by a slew of personal militias, secret emissaries and family clans, all positioning themselves in a climate of permanent conspiracy, jockeying for power and *affairisme*."[17]

The transitional government—based on the so-called 4 + 1 formula, that is, one president and four vice-presidents—did not signal a departure from the neo-patrimonial syndrome as much as it created four separate structures for the efflorescence of patron-client ties. Behind the façade of power sharing, emerged a fragmented pattern of neo-patrimonialism strikingly reminiscent of the situation described by Michael Bratton and Nicolas van de Walle: "When the supremo 'sub-contracts' executive functions to subordinate barons, power is divided and decisions are made only after a degree of competition and bargaining among the powerful. But because these patrons recruit clients and operate state agencies as personal fiefdoms, they tend to reproduce varieties of neo-patrimonialism rather than another genus of regime."[18]

Competition among the vice-presidential barons was certainly a major source of tension in the transition government. But so was competition and discord between barons and their subordinates. This was conspicuously the case among Bemba's clients, as shown by the defection of two of the MLC's most talented political figures, Antoine Ghonda and Olivier Kamitatu; the first briefly served as Kabila's Minister of Foreign Affairs in 2003 and the other as president of the transitional parliament. Others followed or preceded them, such as José Endundo Bononge, ex-minister of public works, Valentin Senga, ex-minister of agriculture, and Samuel Simene, ex-vice minister of finance. In addition to demonstrating the fragility of vice-presidential fiefdoms, the result has been to further the trend toward fragmentation as many of the dissidents ended up organizing their own political formations.

The persistence of the neo-patrimonial nexus explains why so little was done to lay the foundation of an effective state system. The costs of structural reforms were too high compared with the benefits derived by the ruling elites. Giving up their private wealth and privileges for the sake of a distributive logic based on merit and performance would be tantamount to political suicide. In such conditions, the distribution of state resources is limited the privileged few: "The state's resources are distributed to the 'insiders' of the system, so much so that the state itself becomes the captive of the governing elites."[19] In today's Congo, however, the governing elites are not the only ones to cash in on the privatization of the state: just as in the past, much of the country's mineral wealth has been appropriated by rebel factions, and this is still the case today. Furthermore, although the mining sector is officially under the control of the state, Kabila's courtiers, taking their cue from their Mobutist predecessors, have strenuously resisted public scrutiny. Despite reports of the government's intention to review all mining contracts with foreign companies, the lack of transparency surrounding the review process raises the strongest doubts about the likelihood of a significant change in the clientelist appropriation of mineral resources.

The Challenges Ahead

In the years ahead the government will face a number of enduring challenges at many levels, all interrelated. Just as the security problem is linked up with the failure of military integration, the latter is rooted in the persistence of armed factions and rampant corruption within the higher echelons of the army. And although human rights violations are inseparable from the rise of intercommunal tensions, both have a great deal to do with the dysfunctions of the transitional justice system. As for the issue of economic governance, it brings into sharp relief the problems raised by the appropriation of mineral resources by militias and the carryover of clientelism into the public sphere.

The appalling performance of the army during the transition provides a logical point of entry into this vortex. Today, as in the Mobutu years, the army is one of the worst perpetrators of human rights violations. Typical of the countless abuses committed by the FARDC is what happened in Bunia only days after the elections: "Soldiers protesting unpaid bonuses fired guns and hand grenades, looted shops and homes around Bunia, and raped the daughter of a World Food Program worker in a nightlong rampage."[20] According to the previously cited UN report on the human rights situation during the elections, FARDC brigades "continued to be responsible for summary executions, torture and rape, as well as arbitrary arrests and intimidation of civilians exercising their political rights. . . . FARDC soldiers, who are ill-equipped largely unpaid and unfed, continued to live on the back of the population, harassing civilians and extorting their goods."²¹ Other security units, such as the Republican Guard, as well as the intelligence agency, the widely feared Agence Nationale de Renseignement (ANR), are also cited as major perpetrators of abuse against civilians.

Writing in the early 1960s, a close observer of the Congolese scene described the Armée Nationale Congolaise (ANC) as "the principal creator of havoc in the country,"²² a characterization that applies equally well to the FARDC. The "military as a rabble" is a theme that runs throughout the country's history since the early days of independence. The situation we described in our 1993 report to USAID—"the dominant trend in the security situation has been from repressive actions directed against regime opponents to something approximating organized anarchy" (see Chapter 12)—finds an echo in the litany of ills reported in a recent UN report: "FARDC remains fragile because of weak command and control; high levels of corruption; poor operational planning and tactical skills; poor administrative and logistical capacity to oversee deployment, payment, sustenance and equipping of troops; very limited training capacity; and questionable loyalty on the part of some troops."²³ How to transform the "principal creator of mayhem" into something resembling a professional army is the key challenge facing the Kabila government.

Today, as under Mobutu, corruption is rife in the armed forces. Corrupt practices range from the deliberate inflation of registered soldiers to the appropriation of salaries by commanding officers, arbitrary promotions, and over-invoicing of operational costs. In 2005 alone, according to well-informed observers, "More than $3 million were stolen from the army payroll."²⁴ But perhaps the worst offenders were found in the higher reaches of government, as shown by the enormous profits derived by Bemba during the crisis of November 2005, following the infiltration of Rwandan troops into North Kivu. The transport of some 10,000 troops to the east on cargo planes owned by Bemba is said to have cost the government millions of dollars, most of it ending up in Bemba's pockets. Despite the lucrative contracts signed for the transport of food and fuel, little of either reached their intended destination; causing the troops to go on a rampage; looting, killing, and raping the civilians they were supposed to protect. An estimated ten million dollars vanished in the course of these highly profitable transactions.²⁵ It is hard to think of a more striking illustration of "the profits of violence" generated by the breakdown of law and order.²⁶

The many setbacks, met by efforts to integrate armed factions within the regular army, bear witness to the tenacity of personal ties between warlords and their rank and file combatants. Attempts to buy off warlords by repositioning them as officers in the FARDC proved utterly counterproductive. Only weeks after his promotion to the rank of colonel in the

FARDC, Peter Karim, a notoriously brutal militia leader and head of the Front des Nationalistes et Intégrationnistes (FNI), suddenly resurfaced in Ituri to resume his command of some 2,000 militiamen. In compliance with a similar accord, signed in November 2006, two other Ituri warlords, Mathieu Ngojolo and Cobra Matata, identified with the MRC and the Front de Résistance Patriotique de l'Ituri (FRPI), respectively, also agreed to rejoin the FARDC, lay down their arms, and begin disarming their 5,000-strong militias, yet by January 2007 only 300 had effectively surrendered.[27] As much as a commentary on the failure of integration strategies, the failure of the ralliements points to more fundamental issues—the scarcity of civilian jobs to meet the exigencies of demobilization-cum-reinsertion, the attractiveness of alternative sources of employment offered through the illicit exploitation of mineral wealth, and the residual loyalty of the troops to their ethnic commanders; not to mention the host of administrative difficulties faced by the National Disarmament Commission (CONADER).[28]

How the failure of integration helped fuel intercommunal tensions is nowhere more painfully evident than in the fiasco following the deal negotiated by Kabila and Nkunda in December 2006. The aim was to bring Nkunda's forces into the FARDC through a process of mixage: accordingly, Nkunda's eighty-first and eighty-third brigades joined FARDC troops to form mixed brigades (Alpha, Bravo, Charlie, Delta, Echo); these in turn were expected to mount a concerted assault against FDLR units. The clean-up operations, in April and May 2007, led to a total disaster. While the FDLR pulled back to safer locations, "the attackers, often led by Tutsi officers, used brutal counterinsurgency tactics," according to an ICG report; in one locality "at least 30 civilians were killed and many raped or injured, usually after accusations of complicity with the FDLR."[29] In several other localities, the mixed brigades were reported to have killed scores of civilians. By early May, the mixage experiment dissolved into warring factions, mostly along Hutu (or native Congolese) versus Tutsi lines, and Nkunda formally announced on local television that "the mixage process was over, because the government had not been sincere in implementing the agreement."[30] The immediate result was a ratcheting up of Hutu-Tutsi polarities throughout the province.

The inability of the army to bring the Hutu militias under effective control provides Kigali with a convenient pretext for military intervention, directly or indirectly. There is little question that the Hutu-dominated FDLR poses a clear and present danger to Tutsi and other communities. Numbering anywhere from 6,000 to 7,000 and consisting of a fair number of *interahamwe*, many operating in tandem with Mai-Mai militias and Hutu elements indigenous to the DRC, the FDLR are responsible for horrific human rights violations. They have played a major role in fueling ethnic hatreds and will likely continue to do so for the foreseeable future.

Concerns over the threat they pose to Rwanda's security, however, are wildly exaggerated. Continued access to the Congo's economic wealth is where Rwanda's long-term interests lie. The importance of the Congo connection is reflected in the blueprint of the Rwandan government, which, we are told, "has even established a 'Production section' responsible for the exploitation and trade in Congolese resources, as part of the Congo desk in its External Section Organization."[31] Irrespective of the generous assistance of international donors, only by taking into account the substantial profits derived from the systematic exploitation of the Congo's mineral resources can one begin to understand the remarkable rate of economic growth enjoyed by Rwanda over the last few years, as well as its capacity to sustain the fiscal burden of one of the largest, best-trained armies in the region. It is hardly an exaggeration to say that the Congo financed its own occupation, in partnership with local Congolese entrepreneurs, interlopers, and militia groups. Central to an understanding of the resilience of Rwanda's economic tutelage are the powerful vested interests built over the years through a variety of intermediaries indigenous to the Congo. How to break the hold of the middlemen managing the *comptoirs* and redirect the flow of benefits into the coffers of the state (such as it is) is not the least of the problems confronting the new government.

If Kabila's army is incapable of dealing effectively with the FDLR, it is also no match for Nkunda's militias. The rapid expansion of Nkunda's rebel organization bears testimony to the FARDC's impotence as a constabulary. The political wing of his movement is now officially labeled Congrès National pour la Défense du Peuple (CNDP), following "a meeting attended by members of the public, senior military commanders and politicians of the rebel movement in Masisi" in July 2006.[32] The newly founded party is said to have offices in many of the areas under his control; it has its own radio station (Radio Umoja), broadcasting news in Kinyarwanda, Swahili, and French; and it also has informal links with the Tutsi refugee camps inside Rwanda, many of which serve as recruiting grounds for his army. Kagame's backing is not the least of the many assets in Nkunda's hands.

Just how much of a threat Nkunda poses to the nascent Congolese state, and more directly to the civilian populations of North Kivu, is tragically illustrated by the wanton killings unleashed by his militia against the populations of Masisi in October 2007, in the wake of the collapse of the mixage experiment. There are indeed few precedents for the scale and sheer savagery of human rights violations committed by all sides in the conflict. In addition to massive human displacements (750,000 for

Kivu alone) and hundreds of civilians killed and raped, as some have noted, the conflict has metastasized into a wider phenomenon, threatening to morph into a larger, crossborder confrontation.

Although responsibility for the atrocities against civilians is widely shared, there is a sense in which the Nkunda faction stands as a peculiarly noxious phenomenon. Quite aside from the substantial military and logistical support he gets from Rwanda, Nkunda claims a degree of visibility—and credibility—unmatched by other warlords. His professional background is instructive. Before emerging as a leading figure in the RCD, he fought in Rwanda alongside Kagame's RPF, and then in the Congo in 1996 and 1998. His role in organizing the bloody repression of the anti-RCD insurgents in Kisangani in 2002 confirmed his reputation of ruthlessness in dealing with his opponents. After declining the offer of the Kinshasa interim government to serve as a regional military governor in Kasai Oriental, he resurfaced in Bukavu in May 2004, during the brief takeover of the capital of South Kivu by his men, allegedly to protect the local Tutsi population from an impending genocide. The net result has been the death of scores of Congolese civilians in Bukavu and a sharp and immediate rise of anti-Tutsi sentiment among the non-Tutsi resident population. To this day, Nkunda's notoriety rests on his apparent indifference to massive human rights violations, as long as these are inflicted for the sake of protecting the rights of the Tutsi minority. It is not for nothing that he has been described as a "pyromaniac fireman."

The Nkunda episode shows the interconnectedness of the Congo's problems with regional issues. The phenomenon is by no means reducible to the uncontrolled appropriation of the country's mineral wealth by domestic and external actors. At stake in the ongoing conflict are the rights of Rwandophone minorities, primarily Tutsi, in a context that greatly enhances their vulnerability to continued political exclusion and, ultimately, to revenge. Given the extreme fragility of provincial institutions, the unreliability, if not the culpability, of the security forces and the near absence of a functioning judicial system, how to devise institutional mechanisms for the protection of minority rights is bound to remain extremely problematic.

The Dark Side of Congolese Democracy

Reflecting on the future of Yugoslavia in the 1990s, Richard Holbrook summed up the Hobson's choice facing pro-democracy advocates: "Suppose elections are free and fair and those elected are racists, fascists, separatists: that is the dilemma."[33] Putting a different construction on Holbrook's warning, suppose the men put in office through the transition consist of self-serving neo-patrimonial elites unwilling to let go of their privileges. Suppose, in other words, that the main lineaments of the Mobutist state should reappear under the guise of multiparty democracy? This is not an unlikely scenario. One only needs to consider how few changes have occurred in the modus operandi of the power-holders. The enduring hold of clientelist norms runs through much of the political system. One wonders, in these conditions, whether the move to democracy can do more than recycle the habits of the past.

There is an even darker side to the present conjuncture that brings to mind the perverse effects of democratization so compellingly analyzed by Michael Mann in *The Dark Side of Democracy*. In his book, Mann shows how, through the Burkean law of unanticipated consequences, regimes newly embarked on democracy can pave the way for the horrors of "murderous ethnic cleansing," including genocide. Reduced to its simplest expression, the argument is that in a context of ethnic pluralism, rule by the people often translates into the rule of a dominant community, thus "entwining the demos with the dominant ethnos, generating organic conceptions of the nation and the state that encourage the cleansing of minorities."[34]

North and South Kivu are obvious examples. There is in both a high potential for the calculated use of violence against the Rwandophone minorities in the name of an aggressive, nationalistic brand of *congolité*. Anti-Rwandan sentiment, amplified by the media and the distribution of anonymous tracts and nurtured by the growing xenophobia of non-Rwandophone communities of the Kivu provinces, provides fertile ground for renewed ethnic cleansing. Stephen Jackson shows how the *allochtones*, or outsiders, are being used as a foil for the claims of the *autochtones*, the sons of the soil, thus transforming the concept of autochtony into a powerful mobilizing force.[35] The degree to which the manipulation of social identities helps foster an atmosphere of paranoia is excellently captured in his commentary about the "discourse of autochtony":[36]

> Those accused of plotting the demise of the Congolese state are sometimes called allochtons, sometimes Rwandans, sometimes Rwandophones, and sometimes Tutsi. Equally, the targets of the plot are sometimes given as Congolese, sometimes as autochtons, and sometimes as a specific ethnic group, including on occasion, the same Hutu population that might otherwise be considered among the enemies. Such ambiguities pervade the discourse of autochtony, which at every level is slippery, nervous, and paranoid. It is centrally obsessed with infiltration, ruse, conspiracy, and duplicity.

The menace of ethnic cleansing is by no means a one-way phenomenon. As noted earlier, the repeated attacks mounted by Nkunda against civilians has contributed in no small way to ratchet up mutual enmities between *autochtones* and *allochtones*. Rwandan proxies of the Nkunda variety are as much of a threat to self-proclaimed "native" Congolese as are the defenders of autochtony to those native-born Rwandophones collectively suspected of serving Rwanda's interests. The danger lies in the potential for escalation inherent in the mobilizing power of the autochtony/allochtony dichotomy, pushing the boundaries of conflict upwards from the local to the regional levels. The odds are that such a situation would not leave Kagame indifferent to the fate of his kinsmen.

If only to mitigate the bleakness of such scenarios and to give credit where it is due, one can hardly overstress the decisive role played by the UN presence in preventing local outbursts from escalating into wider conflicts. Whether as a peacekeeping force, through the deployment of some 17,000 MONUC troops; as the orchestrator of the oversight, mediating, and advisory functions of the CIAT; or as a source of logistical support during the pre-electoral phase, the United Nations has been an important stabilizing factor.

Nonetheless, on a number of occasions the United Nations has fallen short of its mandate, most conspicuously of its obligation "to ensure the protection of civilians, including humanitarian personnel, under imminent threat of physical violence." The negative side of the UN coin was cruelly revealed by *The Economist* in December 2004: "Since MONUC was first deployed in 1999, it has consistently failed to keep anyone in the region safe."[37] Two years later, on the eve of the elections, Aidan Hartley described how a UN/MONUC joint military operation aimed at dislodging recalcitrant militias in Kazana (Ituri) resulted in the death of some thirty civilians. "What is happening in eastern Congo," he wrote, "is a continuing civilian catastrophe and the UN deserves a share of the blame."[38] To these sweeping criticisms might be added the much publicized involvement of MONUC troops in child-prostitution scandals;[39] the huge costs of its military, administrative, and humanitarian operations; and the unfortunate tendency of MONUC officials to ignore the political dimensions of local and regional conflicts.[40]

No single event encapsulates the performance of the UN in the Congo. For every instance of peacekeepers standing idly by while civilians were being butchered—as happened in Bukavu in May 2004—others could be cited showing courage and initiative. Some of the more positive accomplishments of the MONUC include several highly effective military interventions against militias in Ituri and North Kivu; the repatriation of thousands of combatants to Rwanda, Burundi, and Uganda; and "cordon and search" operations aimed at disarming rebel groups. Last and not least, through the MONUC, important information channels have been made available to NGOs and provincial authorities, as shown by its recent investigation of several sites in Rutshuru where mixed brigades summarily executed civilians.[41]

If the Congo elections did not turn out to be the unmitigated disaster that some had predicted, this is due in no small part to the situation of "controlled sovereignty" exercised through the international community.[42] Whether assessed in terms of diplomatic pressures (as was the case during the Lusaka conference of 1999, in the weeks leading to the Global and Inclusive Agreement of 2002), security measures, electoral support and post-electoral economic and humanitarian assistance, and the part played by international donors in ensuring a measure of stability during the transition can hardly be overemphasized. Just how much external control the new government is prepared to accept as it looks to the future, in what form, and for how long are the key questions now facing both the Kinshasa authorities and the international community.

Let us, by way of a conclusion, return to our opening quote: there is every reason to agree with the character in Le Carré's novel that "elections won't bring democracy," but to predict chaos is premature; winners have indeed "scooped the pool," but the nascent judicial, legislative, and peacebuilding institutions suggest a more useful alternative than telling the losers "to go fuck themselves"; nor is it foreordained that they will take to the bush, even though that eventuality is not to be discounted. Once again the Congo has embarked on an uncertain journey, for which there are no reliable road maps and a large pool of reckless drivers. It promises to be a rough ride but hopefully, not a fatal one.

Notes

Preface

1. International Crisis Group (ICG), *Security Sector Reform in the Congo* (Brussels and Nairobi: ICG, 2006), p. 1. A relatively small number died of direct violence—approximately 2 percent; the rest were victims of the lethal side effects of the war: disease, starvation, exposure, and the general breakdown of infrastructures.

2. One example among others: in a lead article on "The Deadliest War in the World," *Time* magazine offers the following science-fiction explanation for the outbreak of the 1998 war in the Congo: "In 1998, after Kabila got too friendly with the *interahamwe*, Uganda and Rwanda invaded the Congo again, triggering what became known as Africa's first world war." I must add in all fairness that there are notable exceptions to the rule, found for the most part in European media. The names of Marie-France Cros (*La Libre Belgique*), Stephen Smith (*Libération* and *Le Monde*), and Michela Wrong (*Financial Times*) immediately come to mind; all are known for the high quality of their reporting. See Simon Robinson and Vivienne Walt, "The Deadliest War in the World," *Time*, June 5, 2006, p. 40.

3. For a brilliant exploration of the implications of the concept, see Michael Ignatieff, *The Warrior's Honor: Ethnic War and the Modern Conscience* (New York: Henry Holt and Co., 1997), pp. 48–62.

4. Abdul Joshua Ruzibiza, *Rwanda: L'histoire secrète* (Paris: Editions du Panama, 2005).

5. For a further elaboration, see Samuel P. Huntington, *The Clash of Civilizations and the Remaking of World Order* (New York: Simon and Schuster, 1996), pp. 252–54.

6. This is the theme of Stephen Jackson's outstanding analysis, "Sons of the Soil? The Language and Politics of Autochtony in Eastern DR Congo," *African Studies Review* 49, no. 2 (2006): 95–124.

Chapter 1. The Geopolitics of the Great Lakes Region

1. For specific illustrations, see Marie-France Cros and Francois Misser, *Géopolitique du Congo* (Brussels: Editions Complexe, 2006).

2. K. Sibabibdula, "Les Nande au contact avec d'autres civilisations: Lecture de quelques vécus indicateurs," in *Les identités meurtrières: Faire face aux défis posés par*

nos murs psychologiques et idéologiques (Goma: Pole Institute, June 26, 2004), p. 84, available at poleinst@compuserve.com.

3. J.-P. Chrétien, "L'Afrique des Grands Lacs existe-t-elle ?", *Revue Tiers Monde* 27, no. 106 (1986): 266.

4. Ibid.

5. M. Mann, *The Dark Side of Democracy: Explaining Ethnic Cleansing* (New York: Cambridge University Press, 2005).

6. The expression is borrowed from Christopher Hill, *The World Turned Upside Down* (New York: Penguin Books, 1972), p. 39.

7. According to a 1991 report by the Canadian Agency for International Development, the rate of deforestation in the Kivu region is 65,000 hectares per year. "Schéma régional d'aménagement du Kivu," ACDI, September 1991, p. 154.

8. Between July and October 2006, as many as 508 hippopotamuses and forty-eight elephants were killed by Mai-Mai militias and soldiers in and around the Virunga National Park, in eastern Congo, according to the park's head warden, Deo Mbula. According to the same source, there were 308 hippos left. "At this rate," he added, "there will be none left in a month." See "Poaching in the Congo Threatens Hippos" (Agence France Presse), *New York Times*, October 29, 2006, p. 4. How war-induced environmental degradation affects peace prospects is best captured in a recent press report about the side-effects of the vanishing hippo population of Lake Edward. Extensive poaching by various militias has resulted in the elimination of an estimated 93 percent of hippos; in turn reducing the dung-generated phyloplankton feeding the lake's freshwater tilapia, which is why the efforts of local NGOs to retool former militias into fishermen have been less than successful. As one local fisherman lamented, "Fifteen years ago we routinely hauled in 500 good-sized tilapia in one night ... even catching thirty fish now is a blessing." M. Phillips, "More Dung, Please: Vanishing Hippos Break a Food Chain," *Wall Street Journal*, November 19–20, 2005, pp. 1 and 4.

9. See Alan Moorehead's depiction of Lake Kivu, "a lovely pool of green water, set among some of the most splendid forests and mountains of all Africa," penned in 1959, and compare it with the hellish picture drawn by journalists during the cholera epidemic that broke out in the wake of the Hutu refugee exodus in 1994. A. Moorehead, *No Room in the Ark* (London: Penguin Books, 1962).

10. For the full report of the International Rescue Committee (IRC), see Richard Brennan et al., "Mortality in the Democratic Republic of Congo: A Nationwide Survey," *The Lancet*, January 7, 2006, pp. 44–51.

11. Ibid.

12. J. Hari, "A Journey into the Most Savage War in the World," *The Independent*, May 6, 2006, p. 1.

13. See J. Cuvelier and T. Raeymaekers, *Supporting the War Economy in the DRC: European Companies and the Coltan Trade* (Brussels: International Peace Information Service [IPIS], January 2002); Human Rights Watch (HRW), *The Curse of Gold, Democratic Republic of the Congo* (New York: HRW, 2005); C. Dietrich, *Hard Currency: The Criminalized Diamond Economy of the Democratic Republic of the Congo and Its Neighbours*, Partnership Africa Canada, Occasional Paper # 4, 2002.

14. F. Grignon, "Economic Agendas in the Peace Process," in M. Nest, ed., *The Democratic Republic of the Congo: Economic Dimensions of War and Peace*, International Peace Academy Occasional Papers Series (Boulder: Lynne Rienner, 2005), p. 87.

15. P. Collier et al., *Breaking the Conflict Trap: Civil War and Development Policy* (New York: Oxford University Press, 2003).

16. See J. Arnson and W. Zartman, eds., *Rethinking the Economics of War: The Intersection of Need, Creed and Greed* (Washington, D.C.: Woodrow Wilson Center Press/The Johns Hopkins University Press, 2005); K. Ballentine and J. Sherman, eds., *The Political Economy of Armed Conflict: Beyond Greed and Grievance* (Boulder: Lynne Rienner, 2003).

17. Bucyalimwe Mararo, "Le TPD à Goma (Nord Kivu): Mythes et réalités," in S. Marysse and F. Reyntjens, eds., *L'Afrique des Grands Lacs. Annuaire 2003–2004* (Paris: L'Harmattan, 2004), p. 140.

18. Lemarchand, "The Fire in the Great Lakes," *Current History* 98, no. 628 (May 1999): 196.

19. For an illuminating discussion, see M. Balibutsa, *Une archéologie de la violence en Afrique des Grands Lacs* (Libreville: Éditions du CICIBA, 1999), pp. 246–444. See also Jean-Pierre Chrétien, *The Great Lakes of Africa: Two Thousand Years of History*, trans. Scott Straus (New York: Zone Books, 2003).

20. James Scott, *Seeing Like a State: How Certain Schemes to Improve the Human Condition Have Failed* (New Haven and London: Yale University Press, 1998), pp. 2, 3.

21. See J-C. Willame, *Banyarwanda et Banyamulenge: Violences ethniques et gestion de l'identitaire au Kivu* (Paris: L'Harmattan, 1999).

22. For much of the information in this section, I am indebted to Etienne Rusamira, Sanson Muziri, and Manasse Muller Ruhimbika for sharing with me their views on the many issues relating to the history and politics of the Banyamulenge.

23. J. Mutambo, *Les Banyamulenge* (Limete: Imprimerie Saint Paul, 1997), p. 26.

24. As if to give credence to the worst stereotypes about the Tutsi's ingrained deceitfulness and dissimulation, Kagame consistently denied having anything to do with the 1996 invasion; only months later, in an interview with John Pomfret, did he finally admit Rwanda's role in planning and directing the rebellion leading to Mobutu's overthrow. See J. Pomfret, "Rwanda Led Revolt in Congo," *Washington Post*, July 9, 1997, p. 1.

25. Referring to the violent confrontations that took place in Bukavu and Gatumba (Burundi) in 2004, a recent International Crisis Group (ICG) report notes that "the crises illustrate that the notion of besieged Tutsi and Hutu communities is still used to justify military action against the transitional government by both Congolese dissidents and the Rwanda government." ICG, *The Congo's Transition Is Failing: Crisis in the Kivu* (Brussels and Nairobi: ICG, 2005), p. 11.

26. The extent to which Uganda's politics of indigeneity translated into exclusionary policies and practices directed against Banyarwanda, and thus played a key role in clinching the FPR's decision to invade Rwanda, is excellently discussed by M. Mamdani, *When Victims Become Killers* (Princeton: Princeton University Press, 2001), pp. 159–84.

27. See Lemarchand, "Le génocide de 1972 au Burundi: Les silences de l'Histoire," *Cahiers d'Etudes Africaines* 167, XLII-3, 2002, pp. 551–67.

28. There were, however, notable exceptions, such as Barthélémy Bisengimana, who served as Mobutu's chief of staff from 1965 to 1977.

29. N. Ndimubanzi, "La question identitaire au Bwisha (Rutshuru, Nord-Kivu): Le point de vue de l'histoire," in *Les identités meurtrières*, p. 64.

30. Bucyalimwe Mararo, "Kivu and Ituri in the Congo War: The Roots and Nature of a Linkage," in S. Marysse and F. Reyntjens, eds., *The Political Economy of the Great Lakes Region in Africa* (New York: Palgrave, 2005), pp. 190–222.

31. According to one interpretation, it all started in the village of Ntoto in the Walikale territory, a hundred kilometers west of Goma, with the massacre of a crowd of Banyarwanda by armed Nyanga youth on March 20. About fifty were reported killed. See J. B. Murairi Mitima, *Les Bahunde aux pieds des volcans Virunga (R.D Congo)* (Paris: L'Harmattan, 2005), p. 174.

32. See F. Reyntjens and S. Marysse, eds., *Conflits au Kivu: Antécédents et Enjeux* (Antwerp: University of Antwerp, Centre for the Study of the Great Lakes Region of Africa, 1996); P. Mathieu, P-J. Laurent, and J-C. Willame, eds., *Démocratie, enjeux fonciers et pratiques locales en Afrique* (Paris: L'Harmattan, 1996); P. Mathieu and J-C.Willame, *Conflits et guerres au Kivu et dans la région des Grands Lacs* (Paris: L'Harmattan, 1999).

33. In an otherwise excellent analysis, the author of a recent ICG report refers, bizarrely enough, to "the separate units called 'Gishare,'" under which "the immigrant communities were administered, with Tutsi chiefs ruling over Hutu subjects," ICG, *The Congo Transition Is Failing*, p. 8. Just as fanciful is the notion of "ethnic purges in the 1950s in neighboring Rwanda," and the contention that "in 1972 Mobutu bestowed citizenship in blanket fashion on all Rwandan immigrants." Ibid. This is as close as one gets to science fiction in any of the recent ICG reports on the Great Lakes. For a useful corrective, see J-B. Murairi Mitima, *Les Bahunde*, pp. 163 ff.

34. *Population du Kivu. Résumé* (typescript). From the author's files.

35. Interview with N. Matetsa, Goma, August 21, 1993.

36. Thierry Vircoulon, "L'Ituri ou la guerre au pluriel," *Afrique contemporaine* 215, no. 3 (2005): 131.

37. See K. Vlassenroot, "Identity and Insecurity: The Building of Ethnic Agendas in South Kivu," in R. Doom and J. Gorus, eds., *Politics of Identity and Economics of Conflict in the Great Lakes Region* (Brussels: VUB Press, 2000), pp. 268–88, and "Land and Conflict: The case of Masisi," in Vlassenroot and Raemaekers, *Conflict and Social Transformation in Eastern DR Congo* (Ghent: Academia Press, 2004), pp. 81–101.

38. D. Keen, "The Economic Functions of Violence in Civil Wars," *Adelphi Papers*, no. 320, cited in Vlassenroot, "Identity and insecurity," p. 284.

39. *Conflits au Kivu: Antécédents et Enjeux*, pp. 23, 25. Unsurprisingly, the deputy responsible for sponsoring the bill was a Nande from North Kivu, Denis Paluku, who also happened to be a member of the political bureau of the ruling Mouvement Populaire de la Révolution (MPR). Paluklu served as governor of North and South Kivu before ending up as governor of Katanga (then known as Shaba).

40. M. Ruhimbika, *Les Banyamulenge (Congo-Zaire) entre deux guerres* (Paris: L'Harmattan, 2001), p. 30.

41. For the full text of the resolution, see ibid., pp. 203–11.

42. Ibid., p. 31.

43. See the outstanding contribution of Olivier Lanotte, *Congo: Guerres sans frontières* (Bruxelles: GRIP, Éditions Complexe, 2003) and F. Reyntjens, *La guerre des Grands Lacs: Alliances mouvantes et conflict extra-territoriaux en Afrique Centrale* (Paris: L'Harmattan, 1999).

44. The concept of spoiler is borrowed from S. J. Steadman, "Introduction," in Steadman, D. Rothchild, and B. Cousens, eds., *Ending Civil Wars: The Implementation of Peace Agreements* (Boulder: Lynne Rienner, 2002). The author writes: "My research tried to add to the differentiation among cases of civil war termination by putting forth a typology of spoilers, based on their position in the peace process, number of spoilers, their intent and whether the locus of spoiling behavior lies with the leader or followers of the party" (p. 12).

45. ICG, *Congo's Elections: Making or Breaking the Peace* (Brussels and Nairobi: ICG, 2006), p. 14, note 97. Except where otherwise indicated, all other quotes in this section are from this same source.

46. Human Rights Watch, *War Crimes in Kisangani: The Response of Rwandan-Backed Rebels to the May 2002 Mutiny* 14, no. 6 (August 2002): 2.

47. Samuel Huntington, *The Clash of Civilization and the Remaking of World Order* (New York: Simon and Schuster, 1996), p. 272.

48. See Marina Rafti, "Crumbling in Exile: The Changing Nature of the Rwandan Opposition," in S. Marysse and F. Reyntjens, eds., *L'Afrique des Grands Lacs, Annuaire 2004–2005* (Paris: L'Harmattan, 2005), pp. 95–118.

49. Gérard Prunier "Rebel Movements and Proxy Warfare: Uganda, Sudan and the Congo," *African Affairs* 103, no. 412 (2004): 368.

50. A. Mwaka Bwenge, "Les milices Mai-Mai à l'est de la République du Congo: Dynamique d'une gouvernementalité en situation de crise," *Revue Africaine de Sociologie* 7, no. 2 (2003): 23.

51. Huntington, *The Clash of Civilizations*, p. 252.

52. M. Weiner, *The Global Migration Crisis: Challenge to States and to Human Rights* (New York: Harper's Collins, 1995), p. 137. See also Weiner, "Bad Neighbors, Bad Neighborhoods: An Inquiry into the Causes of Refugee Flows," *International Security* 21, no. 1 (Summer 1996): 5–42.

53. G. Loescher, "Refugee Movements and International Security," Adelphi Paper No. 268 (London: International Institute of Strategic Studies, 1992).

54. Weiner, *The Global Migration*, p. 137.

55. Béatrice Umutesi, *Surviving the Slaughter: The Ordeal of a Rwandan Refugee in Zaire* (Madison: University of Wisconsin Press, 2004); see also Lemarchand, "Bearing Witness to Mass Murder," *African Studies Review* 48, no. 3 (2005): 93–101.

56. The expression is Howard Adelman's in his highly biased interpretation of the refugee problem, H. Adelman, "The Use and Abuse of Refugees in Zaire," in S. J. Steadman and F. Tanner, eds., *Refugee Manipulation: War, Politics and the Abuse of Human Suffering* (Washington, D.C.: Brookings Institution Press, 2003), p. 120. For a persuasive, well-documented counterargument, see Reyntjens, *La guerre des Grands Lacs*, pp. 100–142 and J. P. Godding, *Réfugiés rwandais au Zaire: Sommes-nous encore des hommes?* (Paris: L'Harmattan, 1997).

57. See Reyntjens, *La guerre des Grands Lacs*, p. 76 and "The Privatistion and Criminalisation of Public Space in the Geopolitics of the Great Lakes Region," *Journal of Modern African Studies* 43, no. 4 (2005): 587–607.

58. Lanotte, *Congo*, p. 173. For much of the information in this section, I am indebted to his outstanding contribution. See esp. pp. 159–96.

59. See Reyntjens, "The Privatization and Criminalisation of Public Space," p. 591.

60. H. French, *A Continent for the Taking: The Tragedy and Hope of Africa* (New York: Knopf, 2004).

61. Notably Bizima Karaha, Deogratias Bugera, Moise Nyarugabo, and Benjamin Serukiza, all of whom held important positions in the bogus government set up by the RCD immediately after its creation in 1998. See Lanotte, *Congo*, p. 76.

62. ICG, *The Kivus: The Forgotten Crucible of the Congo Conflict* (Brussels and Nairobi: ICG, 2003), p. 13.

63. Ibid.

64. Thanks to the pioneering research of Koen Vlassenroot and Frank Van Acker; see in particular their excellent article, "Les 'Mai-Mai' et les functions de

la violence milicienne dans l'est du Congo," *Politique Africaine*, no. 84 (December 2001): 103–16. See also Mwaka Bwenge, "Les milices Mai-Mai à l'est de la République du Congo: Dynamique d'une gouvernemantalité en situation de crise," pp. 20–34.

65. Examples include the JUFERI in the Katanga, a youth brigade identified with the anti-Kasaian Union des Fédéralistes et Républicains Indépendents (UFERI); in North Kivu, the MAGRIVI (Mutuelle des agriculteurs des Virunga) and the ACOGENOKI (Association coopérative des groupements d'éleveurs du Nord Kivu), identified respectively with the Hutu and Tutsi communities; in South Kivu, the Groupe Milima (after the Swahili term for "mountain") founded by Ruhimbika to represent the interests of the Banyamulenge.

66. Ruhimbika, *Les Banyamulenge*, pp. 106–7.

67. Vlassenroot and Van Acker, "Les'Mai-Mai,'" p. 109.

68. Ibid., p. 113.

69. JUSTICE-PLUS, Organisation de Vulgarisation et de Défense des Droits de l'Homme, *Ituri: La Violence au delà du clivage ethnique*, December 2003, p. 2. For a similar interpretation, see Vircoulon, "L'Ituri.'"

70. C. Tilly, "War Making and State Making as Organized Crime," in P. Evans, D. Rueshemeyer, and T. Skocpol, eds., *Bringing the State Back In* (Cambridge and New York: Cambridge University Press, 1985), p. 170.

71. Reyntjens, "The Privatization and Criminalisation of Public Space," p. 592.

72. Nest, "The Political Economy of the Congo War," in *The Democratic Republic of Congo: Economic Dimensions of War and Peace*, p. 47.

73. To quote from a 2005 ICG report, "Between January and August 2004, 1,70 tons of cassiterite was flown out of Walikale. At the current world price, this amounts to between $12 and $17 million. Most of the profits are made by the dealers in Goma and Bukavu. . . . Much of the ore was processed across the border in Gisenyi, at a smelter operated by the South African Metal Processing Association (MPA). MPA is associated with an individual who has in the past been a substantial backer of the RPF." ICG, *The Congo's Transition Is Failing*, p. 14.

74. Grignon, "Economic Agendas in the Peace Process," in Nest, ed., *The Democratic Republic of Congo*, p. 80.

75. Mararo, "Le TPD à Goma (Nord Kivu): Mythes et réalités," *L'Afzique des GrandsLacs: Annuaire 2003–2004*, p. 160.

76. Tull, "A Reconfiguration of Political Order? The State of the State in North Kivu (DR Congo)," quoted in Mararo, "Le TPD à Goma," *L'Afzique des GrandsLacs: Annuaire 2003–2004*, p. 159.

77. Interview with Roger Bashali Nsiyi, Antwerp, July 2003.

78. C. V. Wedgewood, *The Thirty Years War* (New York: The New York Review of Books, 2005), p. viii.

Chapter 2. The Road to Hell

1. Paul Collier, *Economic Causes of Civil Conflict and their Implications for Policy* (Washington, D.C.: World Policy Research Paper, 2000), p. 4.

2. Jean-Francois Bayart, Stephen Ellis, and Béatrice Hibou, *La Criminalisation de l'Etat en Afrique* (Paris: Editions Complexe, 1997).

3. Jeffrey Herbst, *States and Power in Africa: Comparative Lessons in Authority and Control* (Princeton: Princeton University Press, 2000).

4. Samuel Huntington, *The Clash of Civilizations and the Remaking of World Order* (New York: Simon and Schuster, 1996), p. 272 ff.

5. René Lemarchand, *Rwanda and Burundi* (London: Praeger and Pall Mall Press, 1970).

6. André Guichaoua, *Le Problème des Réfugiés Rwandais et des Populations Banyarwanda dans la Région des Grands Lacs* (Geneva: UN High Commissioner for Réfugees, 1992), p. 17.

7. Lemarchand, *Burundi: Ethnic Conflict and Genocide* (New York: Wilson Center Press and Cambridge University Press, 1995).

8. Gérard Prunier, *The Rwanda Crisis: History of a Genocide* (London: Hurst and Co., 1997)

9. Jean-Claude Willame, *Banyarwanda et Banyamulenge* (Paris: L'Harmattan, 1997).

10. Filip Reyntjens, *La Guerre des Grands Lacs* (Paris: L'Harmattan, 1999).

11. Lemarchand, "Patterns of State Collapse and Reconstruction in Central Africa: Reflections on the Crisis in the Great Lakes Region," *Afrika Spectrum* 32, no. 2 (1997): 173–93. See also Reyntjens, *La Guerre*.

12. Reyntjens, "Les mouvements armés de réfugiés rwandais: Rupture ou continuité?" in G. Thoveron and H. Legros, eds., *Mélanges Pierre Salmon* (Brussels: Institut de Sociologie de l'Université Libre de Bruxelles, 1992), pp. 170–82.

13. Reyntjens *Laguerre*, and Lemarchand, *Rwanda and Burundi*.

14. Mahmood Mamdani, *When Victims Become Killers: A Political Analysis of the Origins and Consequences of the Rwanda Genocide* (Princeton: Princeton University Press, 2003).

15. Simon Turner, "Representing the Past in Exile: The Politics of National History among Burundian Refugees," *Refuge* 17, no. 6 (1998): 22–28.

16. International Crisis Group. *Burundian Refugees in Tanzania: The Key Factor to the Burundi Peace Process* (Brussels and Nairobi: ICG, 1999).

17. Ibid.

18. Collier, *Economic Causes*, p. 1.

19. Ibid., p. 3

20. Bayart, Ellis, and Hibou, *La Criminalisation*.

21. Herbst, *State, and Power*, p. 272.

22. Crawford Young, *The African Colonial State in Comparative Perspective* (New Haven: Yale University Press, 1994).

Chapter 3. Ethnicity as Myth

1. John Lonsdale, "The Moral Economy of Mau Mau," in Bruce Berman and John Lonsdale, eds., *Unhappy Valley: Violence and Ethnicity* (London: James Currey, 1992), p. 466

2. John Lonsdale, "Moral Ethnicity and Political Tribalism," in Preben Kaarsholm and Jan Hultin, eds., *Inventions and Boundaries: Historical and Anthropological Approaches to the Study of Ethnicity and Nationalism* (Roskilde: Roskilde University, 1994), p. 132.

3. Lonsdale, "The Moral Economy of Mau Mau." *Unhappy Valley: Violence and Ethnicity*, p. 467.

4. Charles W. Anderson, Frederick von der Mehden, and Crawford Young, *Issues of Political Development* (Englewood Cliffs, N.J.: Prentice-Hall, 1976), p. 32.

5. William Finnegan, "The Invisible War," *New Yorker*, no. 25 (January 1999): 60.

6. R. Atkinson, "The Evolution of Ethnicity among the Acholi of Uganda: The Precolonial Phase," *Ethnohistory* 36, no. 1 (1989): 21.

7. Ruddy Doom and Koen Vlassenroot, "Kony's Message: A New Koine? The Lord's Resistance Army in Northern Uganda," *African Affairs*, no. 98 (1999): 5.

8. Eric Hobsbawn and Terence Ranger, *The Invention of Tradition* (Cambridge: Cambridge University Press, 1983).

9. Terence Ranger, "The Invention of Tradition Revisited: The Case of Colonial Africa," in Preben Kaarsholm and Jan Hultin, eds., *Inventions and Boundaries: Historical and Anthropological Approaches to the Study of Ethnicity and Nationalism*, p. 25.

10. Marcel d'Hertefelt, "Mythes et idéologies dans le Rwanda ancien et contemporain," in J. Vansina, R. Mauny, and L. V. Thomas, eds., *The Historian in Tropical Africa* (London: Oxford University Press, 1964), pp. 219–38.

11. Lemarchand, *Rwanda and Burundi* (London: Pall Mall, 1970), p. 24.

12. M. I. Finley, *The Use and Abuse of History* (New York: Viking Press, 1980), p. 13.

13. Ibid.

14. Jacques Maquet, *The Premise of Inequality in Ruanda* (Oxford: Oxford University Press, 1961).

15. Edith Sanders, "The Hamitic Hypothesis: Its Origins and Functions," *Journal of African History* 10, no. 4 (1960): 521–32.

16. C. G. Seligman, *Races of Africa*, reprint of 1922 ed. (Oxford: Oxford University Press, 1988), p. 141.

17. Diedrich Westerman, *The African Today* (Oxford: Oxford University Press, 1931), pp. 25–26.

18. Ian Linden, *Church and Revolution in Rwanda* (Manchester: Manchester University Press, 1977), p. 165.

19. Alexis Kagame, *Le Code des institutions politiques du Rwanda pré-colonial* (Bruxelles: Institut Royal Colonial Belge, 1952).

20. Rev. Père Pagès, *Au Ruanda sur les bords du lac Kivu, Congo Belge: Un royaume Hamite au centre de l'Afrique* (Bruxelles: Falk, 1933).

21. Alexis Kagame, "Le code ésotérique de la monarchie," *Zaire*, no. 4 (1947): 363–86.

22. Claudine Vidal, *Sociologie des passions* (Paris: Karthala, 1991), p. 52.

23. Jan Vansina, *L'évolution du royaume du Rwanda des origines à 1900* (Bruxelles: Académie Royale des Sciences d'Outre Mer, 1962).

24. Catherine Newbury, *The Cohesion of Oppression* (New York: Columbia University Press, 1988) and "Ethnicity and the Politics of History in Rwanda," *Africa Today* 45, no. 1 (1998): 7–24.

25. Ben Halpern, "Myth and Ideology in Modern Usage," *History and Theory*, 11, no. 1 (1961): 137.

26. Fidèle Nkundabagenzi, *Rwanda Politique* (Bruxelles: CRISP, 1962), p. 34.

27. Paul Veyne, *Did the Greeks Believe in Their Myths? An Essay on the Constitutive Imagination* (Chicago: University of Chicago Press, 1988), p. xii.

28. Jean-Pierre Chrétien, *Rwanda: Les médias du genocide* (Paris: Karthala, 1995).

29. Lemarchand, *Burundi: Ethnic Conflict and Genocide* (Cambridge: Cambridge University Press; New York: Woodrow Wilson Center Press, 1996).

30. Ibid., pp. 20–23.

31. Liisa Malkki, *Purity and Exile: Violence, Memory and National Cosmology among Hutu Refugees in Tanzania* (Chicago: University of Chicago Press, 1995), cited in Lemarchand, *Burundi*, p. 20.

32. Cited in Chrétien, *Rwanda*, pp. 110–11.

33. Ibid., pp. 141–42.

34. Ibid., p. 59.
35. Ibid., pp. 103, 147.
36. Ibid., p. 165.
37. Ibid., p. 111.
38. Ibid.
39. Ibid., p. 141.
40. Ibid., p. 366.
41. Roger Cohen, *Hearts Grown Cruel: Sagas of Sarajevo* (New York: Random House, 1998), p. 169.
42. Emmanuel Murangira, "Le Rwanda dans ses frontières anciennes et actuelles," *Traits d'Union-Rwanda*, no. 24 (1997): 22–25.
43. Vansina, *L'évolution du royaume Rwanda dès origines à 1900,* and Ferdinand Nahimana, *Le Rwanda: Emergence d'un état* (Paris: L'Harmattan, 1993).
44. David Newbury, "Irredentist Rwanda: Ethnic and Territorial Frontiers in Central Africa," *Africa Today* 44, no. 2 (1997): 216.
45. Ibid., p. 217.
46. Jean-Claude Willame, *Banyarwanda et Banyamulenge: Violences ethniques et question de l'identitaire au Kivu* (Paris: L'Harmattan, 1997). For an insider's account of Banyamulenge politics by a leading critic of Rwandan policies in the Congo, see Manasse Muller Rhimbika, *Les Banyamulenge (Congo-Zaïre) entre deux guerres* (Paris: L'Harmattan, 2001).
47. Sanders, "The Hamitic Hypothesis," p. 531.
48. Lara Santoro, "Congo Leader Urges Nazi-Style Tactics against Tutsi," *Christian Science Monitor*, September 2, 1998.
49. Leszlek Kolakowski, *The Presence of Myth* (Chicago: University of Chicago Press, 1972), p. 104.

Chapter 4. Genocide in the Great Lakes

1. See "Democratic Republic of the Congo: What Kabila Is Hiding. Civilian Killings and Impunity in Congo," Human Rights Watch/Africa and Fédération Internationale des Droits de l'Homme (FIDH) (Washington: October 1997), p. 39, and Physicians for Human Rights (PHR), "Investigations in Eastern Congo and Western Rwanda," *PHR Report,* July 16, 1997, p. 18. For further evidence, see the special issue of *Dialogue*, "Les réfugiés Rwandais: Le drame persiste," no. 198 (May–June 1997).
2. Between 1993 and 1996, the following NGOs, international organizations, and research institutes have all been involved, in one way or another, in seeking solutions to the Burundi crisis: the African-American Institute (Washington), International Alert (London), the International Peace Academy (New York), the United States Institute of Peace (Washington), Codesria (Dakar), the Scandinavian Institute of African Studies (Uppsala), Newick Park Initiative (London), Physicians for Human Rights (Boston), Human Rights Watch/Africa (Washington), the Institut des Droits de l'Homme (Montpellier), Coopération Internationale pour la Democratic (Montpellier), Stiftung Wissenschaft und Politik (Ebenhausen), Centre National pour la Cooperation au Developpement (Brussels), the Danish Burundi Committee (Copenhagen), and Aktion Courage (Bonn).
3. Stephen Weissman, "Living with Genocide," *Tikkun* 12, no. 4 (1997): 53–70.

4. A notable exception—along with our report to the London-based Minority Rights Group—was the 1973 report published by the Carnegie Endowment for International Peace, whose title—"Passing By"—accurately captured the degree of concern of the international community in the face of massive human rights violations. Illustrative of the very low priority accorded human rights issues at the time is the mildness of the protest note delivered by Western embassies to President Michel Micombero: "As true friends of Burundi we have followed closely with anxiety and uneasiness the events of the last few weeks. Thus we are comforted by your having constituted groups of wise men (elders) to pacify the country, and by the commands which you have given, to repress arbitrary actions and groups, the private vengeances and excesses of authority" (quoted in Weissman, "Living with Genocide" p. 55). Seldom has diplomatic double-talk served to conceal a more hideous reality. See also Lemarchand and David Martin, *Selective Genocide in Burundi* (London: Minority Rights Group, 1974).

5. René Lemarchand, *Burundi: Ethnic Conflict and Genocide* (Washington, D.C. and New York: Woodrow Wilson Press and Cambridge University Press, 1995), p. xv.

6. Ibid., p. 144 ff.

7. James Gasana, "Factors of Ethnic Conflict in Rwanda and Instruments for a Durable Peace," in Gunther Bachler, ed., *Federalism against Ethnicity?* (Zurich: Verlag Ruegger, 1997), pp. 103–26.

8. Personal communication, September 15, 1997.

9. Paul Richards, *Fighting for the Rain Forest: War, Youth and Resources in Sierra Leone* (Oxford and Portsmouth: James Curry and Heineman, 1996), p. xxiv.

10. David Apter, *Rethinking Development* (London and Beverly Hills: Sage, 1989), p. 23.

11. The worst of such atrocities were committed on October 21 in Kibimba (Gitega province) when seventy Tutsi students were burnt alive; on October 22 some ninety Tutsi were killed in Muruta (Kayanza province) on the orders of a local civil servant. In a number of cases, though by no means everywhere, there is irrefutable evidence of the involvement of local communal authorities in the massacre of Tutsi populations.

12. Lemarchand, *Burundi: Ethnic Conflict and Genocide*, p. xiv.

13. According to a Frodebu document, among a total of some 150 Hutu officials, party leaders, journalists, and priests killed by mid-1996 were thirteen deputies, six provincial governors, seven advisors to provincial governors, and eighteen communal administrators (the equivalent of mayors). During the night of June 6, 1995, twenty-seven students, all Hutu, were assassinated on the campus of the University of Burundi. Today the student body and faculty are virtually bereft of Hutu elements. There is a strong presumption that the same is true of the secondary schools that are still operational.

14. The Frodebu has consistently denied responsibility for the massacre, pointing instead to the Palipehutu or Front de Libération National (Frolinat), two of the most violent *groupuscules* spawned by the 1993 coup. To this day the evidence has yet to be produced that would incriminate one or the other of these presumptive culprits. What is beyond doubt is that the Bugendana massacre was the precipitant factor behind the coup that transferred the presidency from Sylvestre Ntibantuganya (a Hutu) to Pierre Buyoya (a Tutsi) on July 25, 1996.

15. Filip Reyntjens, *Burundi: Breaking the Cycle of Violence* (London: Minority Rights Group, 1995), p. 25.

16. Mahmood Mamdani, "Reconciliation Without Justice," *Southern African Review of Books* (November–December 1996): 3–5.

17. Mamdani, "Reconciliation," p. 4.

18. John Stremlau, *A House No Longer Divided: Progress and Prospects for Democratic Peace in South Africa*. A Report to the Carnegie Commission on Preventing Deadly Conflict (New York: Carnegie Corporation, 1997), p. 22.

19. Ibid., p. 23.

Chapter 5. The Rationality of Genocide

1. Helen Fein, "Patrons, Prevention and Punishment of Genocide: Observations on Bosnia and Rwanda" in Helen Fein, ed., *The Prevention of Genocide: Rwanda and Yugoslavia Reconsidered* (New York: The Institute for the Study of Genocide, 1994), p. 5.

2. The point is more fully developed in René Lemarchand, *Rwanda and Burundi* (London: Pall Mall Press, 1970), pp. 175–96.

3. Ibid., pp. 97–106.

4. See Shyirambere J. Barahinyura, *Habyarimana: Quinze ans de tyrannic et de tartufferie au Rwanda* (Frankfurt am Main: Edition Izuba, 1988).

5. See the extensive evidence gathered by the Association Rwandaise pour le Défense des Droits de la Personne et des Libertés Publiques (ADL) in its "Rapport sur les droits de l'homme au Rwanda, Septembre 1991–Septembre 1992," (Kigali: ADL, 1992).

6. See Lemarchand, *Burundi: Ethnocide as Discourse and Practice* (Cambridge: Woodrow Wilson Press and Cambridge University Press, 1994).

7. A chilling account of human rights violations in Rwanda is the report authored by Rakiya Omaar and Alex de Waal on behalf of the London-based African Rights, *Rwanda: Death, Despair and Defiance* (London: African Rights, 1994).

8. Fein, *The Prevention of Genocide*, p. 12.

Chapter 6. Hate Crimes

1. Philip Gourevitch, *We Wish to Inform You That Tomorrow We Will Be Killed with Our Families* (New York: Farrar, Straus and Giroux, 1998)

2. Alison Des Forges, *Leave None to Tell the Story: Genocide in Rwanda* (New York and Paris: Human Rights Watch and International Federation of Human Rights, 1999), passim.

3. Roger Cohen, *Hearts Grown Brutal: Sagas of Sarajevo* (New York: Random House, 1998), p. 169.

4. Tina Rosenberg, "A New Generation Looks at Germany's Past," *New York Times*, February 21, 1999.

5. The phrase is borrowed from Jacques J. Maquet, *The Premise of Inequality in Rwanda: A Study of Political Relations in a Central African Kingdom* (London: Exford University Press, 1961).

6. Quoted in Des Forges, *Leave None to Tell the Story*, p. 85.

7. Peter Uvin, *Aiding Violence: The Development Enterprise in Rwanda* (West Hartford: Kumarian Press, 1998), p. 103.

8. Michele Wagner, "All the *Bourgmestre*'s Men: Making Sense of Genocide in Rwanda," *Africa Today* 45, no. 1 (January–March 1998): 30.

9. Roger Winter, "How Human Rights Groups Miss the Opportunity to Do Good," *Washington Post*, February 22, 1998.
10. Des Forges, *Leave None to Tell the Story*, pp. 726 ff.
11. Gérard Prunier, "Au Rwanda, le génocide tel qu'il s'est produit," *Le Monde Diplomatique*, October 1999, p. 17.
12. Tzvetan Todorov, *Devoirs et Délices: Une vie de passeur* (Paris: Le Seuil, 2002), passim.

Chapter 7. The Politics of Memory

1. Mark Lacey, "Rwanda: There Is No Ethnicity There," *International Herald Tribune*, April 10, 2004, p. 2.
2. Paul Ricoeur, *La mémoire, l'histoire, l'oubli* (Paris: Le Seuil, 2002).
3. Stanley Cohen, *States of Denial* (Cambridge: Polity Press, 2001), p. 241.
4. Primo Levi, *The Drowned and the Saved* (New York: Vintage Books, 1989), p. 27.
5. See in particular Abdul Ruzibiza's devastating testimony, *Rwanda: L'histoire secrète* (Paris: Editions du Panama, 2005).
6. See Refugees International, *The Lost Refugees: Herded and Hunted in Eastern Zaire* (Washington, D.C.: Refugees International, September 1997).
7. Liisa Malkki, *Purity and Exile: Violence, Memory and National Cosmogony and Hutu Refugees in Tanzania* (Chicago: University of Chicago Press, 1995).
8. As reported by Matthew Green of Reuters, April 3, 2004; see www.genodynamics.com.
9. See Stephen Smith, "Révélations sur l'attentat qui a déclenché le génocide rwandais," *Le Monde*, March 10, 2004, pp. 1–3. For an English-language summary version, see Stephen Smith, "Rwandan President Implicated in Death of Predecessor by French Magistrate," *Guardian Weekly*, March 25–31, 2004, p. 31.
10. Ricoeur, *La mémoire, l'histoire, l'oubli*, p. 236 ff.
11. Eva Hoffman, "The Balm of Recognition," in Nicholas Owen, ed., *Human Rights, Human Wrongs* (Oxford: Oxford University Press, 2003), p. 296.
12. Cohen, *States of Denial*, p. 138.
13. Nigel Eltringham, *Accounting for Horror: Post-Genocide Debates in Rwanda* (London: Pluto Press, 2004), p. 97.
14. Marie-France Cros, "Portrait d'un juste," *La Libre Belgique*, April 5, 2004, p. 12.
15. Quoted by Pascal Bruckner, *La Tentation de l'Innocence* (Paris: Grasset, 1995), p. 11.
16. For a graphic description of the devastating attacks mounted by RPF troops on IDP camps, see "Rwanda: SOS pour une guerre oubliée," *La Croix*, February 25, 1992, p. 3, which quotes extensively from the report written by a group of missionaries ("Les prêtres du doyenné du Mutara crient la détresse des victimes de la guerre," February 10, 1992).
17. See Alison Des Forges, *Leave None to Tell the Story* (Washington: Human Rights Watch and Fédération Internationale des Droits de l'Homme, 1999), pp. 726–29.
18. Stephen Smith, *Le Fleuve Congo* (Paris: Actes Sud, 2003), p. 95.
19. "UN Report of the investigative team charged with investigating serious violations of human rights and international humanitarian law in the DRC," quoted in *Dialogue*, no. 206 (September–October 1998): 79.

20. Helen Fein, "Genocide by Attrition in the Sudan and Elsewhere," *The Institute for the Study of Genocide Newsletter*, no. 29 (Fall 2002): 7.
21. Claudine Vidal, "Les commémorations du génocide au Rwanda," *Les Temps Modernes* (2001): 613.
22. Rony Brauman, Stephen Smith, and Claudine Vidal, "Rwanda: Politique de terreur, privilège d'impunité," *Esprit* (August–September 2000): 155.
23. Filip Reyntjens, "Rwanda, Ten Years On: From Genocide to Dictatorship," *African Affairs*, no. 411 (2004): 199.
24. Hoffman, "The Balm of Rocognition," p. 280.
25. Pierre Nora, "Between Memory and History: Les Lieux de Mémoiré," *Representations*, no. 26 (Spring 1989): 8.
26. Hoffman, pp. 296–97.
27. Ibid. "The Balm of Recognition," p. 302.
28. Ibid., p. 281.
29. Paul Ricoeur, "Le pardon peut-il guérir?", *Esprit* (March–April 1995): 78.
30. Ibid., p. 80.

Chapter 8. Rwanda and the Holocaust Reconsidered

1. Mark Levene, "Connecting Threads: Rwanda, the Holocaust and the Pattern of Contemporary Genocide," in Roger W. Smith, ed., *Genocide: Essays Toward Understanding, Early Warning and Prevention* (Williamsburg: Association of Genocide Studies, 1999), pp. 27–64.
2. See Richard Evans, *In Hitler's Shadow: West German Historians and the Attempt to Escape From the Nazi Past* (New York: Pantheon Books, 1989); Edouard Husson, *Comprendre Hitler et la Shoa: Les historiens de la République fédérale d'Allemagne et l'identité allemande depuis 1949* (Paris: Presses Universitaires de France, 2000); and Christopher Browning, *The Path to Genocide* (Cambridge: Cambridge University Press, 1992).
3. Aristide Zolberg, Astri Suhrke, and Sergio Aguayo, *Escape from Violence: Conflict and the Refugee Crisis in the Developing World* (New York: Oxford University Press, 1989).
4. Robert Melson, *Revolution and Genocide: On the Origins of the Armenian Genocide and the Holocaust* (Chicago: University of Chicago Press, 1992).
5. Helen Fein, "Genocide: A Sociological Perspective," Special Issue, *Current Sociology* 38, no. 1 (Spring 1990): 30.
6. Bill Berkeley, *The Graves Are Not Yet Full: Race, Tribe and Power in the Heart of Africa* (New York: Basic Books, 2001), pp. 264–65.
7. Melson 1992, *Revolution and Genocide*, p. 2.
8. William F. S. Miles, "Hamites and Hebrews: Problems of 'Judaizing' the Rwandan Genocide," *Journal of Genocide Research* 2, no. 1 (2000): 112.
9. Ibid.
10. Léon Poliakov, *Le Mythe Aryen* (Paris: Calmann-Levy, 1994); Edith Saunders, "The Hamitic Hypothesis: Its Origins and Functions in Time Perspective," *Journal of African History* 10, no. 2 (1969): 521–32. I have noted elsewhere the more intriguing parallels between the Aryan myth and its Rwandan counterpart: (a) their genealogical roots are traceable to societies located *outside* the genocidal states, one to ancient Ethiopia, the other to Sanskrit civilization; (b) both were elaborated by nineteenth-century European intellectuals anxious to lend pseudo-scientific respectability to their speculations about the presumed

superiority of certain civilizations, including their own; and (c) in postcolonial Rwanda as in Nazi Germany these pseudo-scientific speculations were recast into virulently racist myths at the hands of Nazi and Hutu ideologues. For a more detailed discussion, see Lemarchand, "Where Hamites and Aryans Cross Paths: The Role of Myth-Making in Mass Murder," *Journal of Genocide Research* 5, no. 1 (March 2003): 145–48.

11. Miles, "Hamites and Hebrews," p. 112.

12. Melson, *Revolution and Gonocide*, pp. 18–19.

13. Peter Uvin, "Tragedy in Rwanda," *Environment* (April 1996): 16.

14. Jan Vansina. *Le Rwanda ancien: Le royaume Nyiginya* (Paris: Karthala, 2001).

15. Daniel J. Goldhagen, *Hitler's Willing Executioners: Ordinary Germans and the Holocaust* (New York: Vintage Books, 1997), pp. 23, 80–81. For a critical review, see Ruth Bettina Birn, "Revisiting the Holocaust," *The Historical Journal* 40, no. 1 (1997). As might have been expected, the Goldhagen thesis has found a highly receptive audience among some Tutsi intellectuals, like Sehene, for example, who writes, "All the Hutu or at least a very large number were convinced that the Tutsi deserved to die." Benjamin Sehene, *Le Piége Ethnique* (Paris: Éditions Dagorno, 1999), p. 120.

16. The Kinyarwanda term for *cockroach, inyenzi*, is a deliberate deformation of *ingenzi*, meaning "brave." The original label, used by Tutsi supporters of the pro-monarchical Union Nationale Rwandaise (UNAR) for designating the Tutsi guerrillas, back in the 1960s, was *"ingangurarugo ziyemeje kuba ingenzi,"* the name of one of king Rwabugiri's armies, meaning roughly "the brave ones in the service of the king's army." I am indebted to Emmanuel Hakizimana for this information.

17. The full text of the document is reproduced in the newspaper *Intego* (Kigali), no. 12, June 11, 1996.

18. Arno Mayer, *Why Did the Heavens Not Darken? The Final Solution in History* (New York: Pantheon Books, 1989).

19. For an excellent discussion of the glaring misconstructions of the provocation thesis applied to the Holocaust and Armenia, see Melson, *Revolution and Genocide*, pp. 10–12.

20. Christopher Browning, *Ordinary Men: Reserve Police Battalion 101 and the Final Solution in Poland* (New York: Harper Collins, 1992), p. 86.

21. Mayer, *Why Did the Heavens Not Darken*, p. 459.

22. Husson, *Comprendre Hitler et la Shoa*. See also Husson, *Une culpabilité ordinaire? Les enjeux de la controverse Goldhagen* (Paris: Presses Universitaires de France, 1997).

23. Ian Kershaw, *Hitler: 1936–1945, Nemesis* (London: Penguin Books, 2000), p. 841.

24. Yehuda Bauer, *Rethinking Genocide* (New Haven and London: Yale University Press, 2001), pp. 42, 47.

25. Ibid., p. 46.

26. Alison Des Forges, *Leave None to Tell the Story* (Paris and New York: Human Rights Watch and International Federation of Human Rights, 1999), pp. 65–91. See also Jean-Pierre Chrétien, *Rwanda. Les media du génocide* (Paris: Karthala, 1995).

27. Helen Fein, "Scenarios of Genocide: Models of Genocide and Critical Responses," in Israel Charny, ed., *Towards the Understanding and Prevention of Genocide* (Boulder, Colo.: Westview Press, 1984).

28. Lemarchand, *Burundi: Ethnic Conflict and Genocide* (Cambridge: Cambridge University Press; New York: Woodrow Wilson Center Press, 1995).

29. Ibid., pp. 75–105. It is noteworthy that most analysts of the Rwanda genocide more or less systematically shun the use of the term *genocide* to describe the 1972 Burundi bloodbath, as if recognition of the anti-Hutu genocide in Burundi might diminish the horror of the anti-Tutsi genocide in Rwanda. For example, in her definitive work on Rwanda, Alison Des Forges refers to the "slaughter of tens of thousands of Hutu by Tutsi . . . in 1972" and elsewhere to the "slaughter" of "some 100,000 Hutu." The G-word never appears in the Burundi context. Des Forges, *Leave None to Tell the Story*, pp. 65, 134.

30. Levene, "Connecting Threads," p. 37.

31. Yves Ternon, *L'innocence des victimes au siécle des génocides* (Paris: Desclée de Brouwer, 2001), p. 47.

32. Jacques Sémelin, "Qu'est-ce qu'un crime de masse? Le cas de l'ex-Yougoslavie," *Critique Internationale*, no. 6 (Winter 2000): 146.

33. Levene, "Connecting Threads," p. 37.

34. Alain Destexhe, *Rwanda and Genocide in the Twentieth Century* (New York: New York University Press, 1994), p. 13.

35. Semelin, "Qu'est-ce qu'un crime de masse?"

36. Hannah Arendt, *Eichmann in Jerusalem: A Report on the Banality of Evil* (New York: Viking Press, 1963); Raul Hilberg, *The Destruction of European Jews* (New York: Quadrangle, 1967); and Christopher Browning, "Ordinary Germans or Ordinary Men," address and response at the inauguration of the Dorot Chair of Modern Jewish and Holocaust Studies, Emory University, Atlanta, 1994.

37. Fein, "Genocide," p. 55

38. Bruce Jones, "Civil War, the Peace Process and Genocide in Rwanda," in Ali Taisier and Robert O. Matthews, eds., *Civil Wars in Africa* (Montreal: McGill-Queens University Press, 1999), pp. 53–86; and "Intervention without Borders: Humanitarian Intervention in Rwanda, 1990–94," *Millenium: Journal of International Studies* 24, no. 2 (1995): 243.

39. James Gasana, *Rwanda: Du parti-état à l'état-garnison* (Paris: L'Harmattan, 2002); and "Natural Resource Scarcity and Violence in Rwanda," a report prepared for the Swiss Organization for Development and Cooperation, 2000, pp. 131–34.

40. Des Forges, *Leave None to Tell the Story*, p. 361.

41. Vincent Ntezimana, *La Justice Belge Face au Génocide Rwandais* (Paris: Karthala, 2000), p. 42.

42. Des Forges, *Leave None to Tell the Story*, p. 137.

43. Donald Rothchild and Alexander Groth, "Pathological Dimensions of Domestic and International Ethnicity," *Political Science Quarterly* 110, no. 1 (1995): 43.

44. The term is borrowed from Christopher Browning to designate low-level génocidaires as distinct from the regular army, the presidential guard, and the prefectoral and communal cadres. Browning, *The Path of Genocide*, p. 9.

45. For a persuasive critique of the Milgram argument that obedience to orders from above is the key to an understanding of the behavior of Holocaust perpetrators, see David Mendel, "The Obedience Alibi: Milgram's Account of the Holocaust Reconsidered," *Analyse & Kritik* (October 1998): 74–94.

46. Reyntjens, "Rwanda: Genocide and Beyond," *Journal of Refugee Studies* 9, no. 3 (1996): 6.

47. Des Forges, *Leave None to Tell the Story*, p. 378.

48. Ibid., p. 379.

49. Maurice Niwese, *Le peuple rwandais un pied dans la tombe: Récit d'un réfugié étudiant* (Paris: L'Harmattan, 2001), p. 55.

50. Gasana, *Rwanda*, p. 12.

51. The widespread participation of prefects and communal councillors in the killings does not mean that these are traceable to the presence of a genocidal "strong state"; the dynamics of murder must be seen against the background of highly personalized networks headed by a handful of key "patrons" (such as Théoneste Bagosora, Tharcisse Renzaho, Joseph Nzirorera, and Fernand Nahimana, to cite but the most prominent) with multiple ramifications into local administrative cadres and the civil society. The principal vectors of death, namely, the *interahamwe*, the parties' youth wings, and the Radio et Television Mille Collines, were all part and parcel of the civil society. As the killings got under way, the state had virtually ceased to exist, and next to the president, the most visible embodiment of the state, Prime Minister Uwilingiyimana, along with several other cabinet members, had already been killed. For further details about the unraveling of the state under Habyalimana, see Gasana, *Rwanda*.

52. Helen Fein, *The Prevention of Genocide: Rwanda and Yugoslavia Reconsidered*, A Working Paper of the Institute for the Study of Genocide (New York: Institute for the Study of Genocide, 1994), p. 5.

53. Manus Midlarsky, "The Killing Trap: Genocides and Other Mass Murders" (Unpublished paper, 2000), p. 6.

54. Norman Naimark, *Fires of Hatred: Ethnic Cleansing in Twentieth-Century Europe* (Cambridge: Harvard University Press, 2001).

55. Ibid., p. 57.

56. Fein, *The Prevention of Genocide*, p. 12.

Chapter 9. Burundi 1972

1. See René Lemarchand, "Le génocide de 1972 au Burundi: Les silences de l'histoire," *Cahiers d'Études Africaines* 167 42–3 (2002): 551–67 ; and *Burundi: Ethnic Conflict and Genocide* (Oxford: Cambridge University Press; New York: Woodrow Wilson Center Press, 1995).

2. In his 500-page historical survey of the Great Lakes region, Jean-Pierre Chrétien devotes ten lines to the events of 1972 but nonetheless admits that "the huge countryside manhunt ... was a genuine genocide of Hutu elites." *The Great Lakes of Africa: Two Thousand Years of History*, trans. Scott Straus (New York: Zone Books, 2003), p. 316. Thirty-five years after the tragedy, as if to make amends for his protracted silence, the French historian teamed up with a journalist, Jean-François Dupaquier, to produce the most detailed and thoroughly documented analysis of the 1972 carnage. See Jean-Pierre Chrétien and Jean-François Dupaquier, *Burundi 1972: Au bord des génocides* (Paris: Kathala, 2007).

3. Nixon's handwritten comments in Memorandum for the president from Henry Kissinger, September 20, 1972, in "Burundi, Vol. 1," Box 735, Country files, Africa, National Security Council (NSC) files. I am grateful to Christian Desroches for sharing with me this extraordinary document.

4. Jacques Sémelin, *Purifier et détruire: Usages politiques des massacres et génocides* (Paris: Le Seuil, 2005).

5. Robert Melson, *Revolution and Genocide: On the Origins of the Armenian Genocide and the Holocaust* (Chicago: University of Chicago Press, 2001).

6. Roughly as many Tutsi were killed in the days immediately following Ndadaye's death as Hutu in the course of the repression conducted by the army, ranging from 30,000 to 50,000. The exact number of casualties on each side of

the ethnic fault line is impossible to tell. There is every reason to believe that the killings of thousands of Tutsi by Hutu was largely unplanned, even though in a number of localities Frodebu activists were involved in encouraging Hutu civilians to kill their Tutsi neighbors.

7. Chrétien and Dupaquier, *Burundi 1972*.

8. Abdul Joshua Ruzibiza, *Rwanda: L'histoire secrète* (Paris: Éditions du Panama, 2005).

9. For a commentary on Ruzibiza's autobiographical narrative as compared with another highly critical account of Kagame's role in the genocide, Pierre Péan's *Noires fureurs, blancs menteurs* (Paris: Mille et Une Nuits, 2005), see my review essay, "Controversy Within Cataclysm," *African Studies Review* 50, no. 1 (2007): 140–44.

10. In part, thanks to the rich body of information contained in the cables sent to Washington, D.C. by the U.S. deputy chief of mission, Michael Hoyt, available from the author's collection at the University of Florida.

11. U.S. embassy cables, Bujumbura, made available to this writer by Michael Hoyt, former DCM. For more of the same, see Lemarchand, "Le génocide de 1972 au Burundi," p. 557, note 10.

12. Ibid.

13. For further details, see Lemarchand, *Burundi: Ethnic Conflict and Genocide*, pp. 76–105.

14. *Le Soir*, September 16, 1967, quoted in Lemarchand, "Le génocide de 1972," p. 54, note 3.

15. See Lemarchand, *Rwanda and Burundi* (London: Pall Mall Press, 1970), pp. 344 ff.

16. Cited in Lemarchand, *Burundi: Ethnic Conflict and Genocide*, p. xiv.

Chapter 10. Burundi at the Crossroads

1. For a comparative discussion of the politics of memory in post-genocide Burundi and Rwanda, see René Lemarchand and Maurice Niwese, "Mass Murder, the Politics of Memory and Post-Genocide Reconstruction," in Simon Chesterman, Albert Schnabel, and Béatrice Pouligny, eds., *Mass Crime and Post-Conflict Peace Building* (New York: International Peace Academy, 2004). For a discussion of the circumstances of the 1972 genocide, see Lemarchand, "Le génocide de 1972 au Burundi," *Cahiers d'Etudes Africaines* 3 (2002): 551–67.

2. One of the most instructive accounts is by former president Sylvestre Ntibantuganya, *Une démocratie pour tous les Burundais*, 2 vols. (Paris: L'Harmattan, 1999); but see also Filip Reyntjens, *L'Afrique des Grands Lacs en Crise* (Paris: Karthala, 1999) and René Lemarchand, *Burundi: Ethnic Conflict and Genocide* (Cambridge: Cambridge University Press; New York: Woodrow Wilson Center Press 1995), pp. 76–105.

3. See Lemarchand, *Rwanda and Burundi* (London: Pall Mall Press, 1970), pp. 344 ff.

4. For a discussion of the relationship between exile and the "mythicohistories," see Liisa Malkki, *Purity and Exile: Violence, Memory and National Cosmology among Hutu Refugees in Tanzania* (Chicago: University of Chicago Press, 1998).

5. See International Crisis Group (ICG), *Réfugiés et déplacés au Burundi: Construire d'urgence un consensus sur le rapatriement et la réinstallation* (Nairobi: Africa Report, 2003).

6. Filip Reyntjens, "L'évolution politique au Rwanda et au Burundi," in F. Reyntjens and S. Marysse, eds., *L'Afrique des Grands Lacs, Annuaire 1997–98* (Paris: L'Harmattan, 1999), p. 74.

7. Personal interview with Pasteur Habimana, Bujumbura, October 25, 2003.

8. Howard Wolpe, "Burundi: Facilitation in a Regionally Sponsored Peace Process" (Unpublished manuscript, Washington, D.C.).

9. Fabienne Hara, "Burundi: A Case of Parallel Diplomacy," in Chester Crocker, Fen Osler Hampson, and Pamela Aal, eds., *Herding Cats: Multiparty Mediation in a Complex World* (Washington, D.C.: U.S. Institute of Peace Press, 2003), pp. 135–58.

10. Ibid., pp. 149, 150.

11. Ahmedou Ould-Abdallah, *Burundi on the Brink: 1993–1995* (Washington, D.C.: U.S. Institute of Peace, 2003), p. 73.

12. Ibid.

13. Ibid., p. 39.

14. For a detailed discussion of Arusha's unfinished business, see the excellent contribution of Véronique Parqué and Louis Marie Nindorera, "L'accord paix au Burundi: Quel avenir?" in Reyntjens and Marysse, eds., *L'Afrique des Grands Lacs: Annuaire 2002–2003* (Paris: L'Harmattan, 2003).

15. "NGO demands action on Refugees" (Arusha: Fondation Hirondelle, October 22, 2005).

16. For a fuller discussion, see Howard Wolpe and Steve McDonald, *Planning for Burundi's Future: Building Organizational Capacity for Economic Recovery. Report on the First Training Workshop Held in Ngozi (Burundi), March 11–16, 2003* (Washington, D.C.: Woodrow Wilson International Center for Scholars, 2003).

17. Fareed Zakaria, *The Future of Freedom: Illiberal Democracy at Home and Abroad* (New York: W. W. Norton, 2003), p. 20.

Chapter 11. Burundi's Endangered Transition

1. Although reliable census figures are lacking, it is generally assumed that Tutsi represent some 15 percent of the population, the Hutu 84 percent, and the Twa 1 percent.

2. In the context of this discussion, the phrase is taken as synonymous with power sharing. For a brief summary statement of consociational theory and its critics, by its foremost advocate, see Arend Lijphart, *Power-Sharing in South Africa* (Berkeley: University of California, Institute of International Affairs, 1985), pp. 83–117. For a more extensive treatment, see Lijphart, *Democracy in Plural Societies: A Comparative Exploration* (New Haven: Yale University Press, 1977).

3. Integrated Regional Information Networks (IRIN), September 5, 2006, p. 1.

4. The danger of approaching contemporary politics while ignoring the country's history is cruelly apparent in Bernard-Henry Levy's opaque account of his visit to Bujumbura, in *Réflexions sur la Guerre, le Mal et la fin de l'Histoire* (Paris: Grasset, 2001), pp. 77–97.

5. For a more sustained discussion of the 1972 tragedy, see René Lemarchand, *Burundi: Ethnic Conflict and Genocide* (Cambridge: Cambridge University Press; New York: Woodrow Wilson Center Press, 1995), pp. 76–105. The most thorough analysis of the events of 1972, published thirty-five years after their occurrence, is found in Jean-Pierre Chrétien and Jean-Francois Dupaquier, *Burundi 1972: Au bord des génocides* (Paris: Karthala, 2007).

6. Ibid., p. xi.
7. Filip Reyntjens, "Briefing: Burundi: A Peaceful Transition after a Decade of War?" *African Affairs* 105, no. 418 (2005): 117.
8. Data drawn from the World Bank development indicators for Burundi and from K. Bentley and R. Southall, *An African Peace Process: Mandela, South Africa and Burundi* (Cape Town: Nelson Mandela Foundation, 2004), p. 23.
9. Ian Fisher, "Citing Fears of Attacks, Burundi Herds 350,000 Hutu into Camps," *New York Times*, December 27, 1999, pp. 1, 6.
10. There is a striking parallel between Buyoya's regroupment policies and those of the French during the Algerian war, when, in the late fifties, nearly a million civilians were forcefully displaced and "parked" in internment camps. For further details, see Michel Rocard, *Rapport sur les camps de regroupement et autres textes sur la guerre d'Algérie* (Paris: Mille et une nuits, 2003).
11. Despite the signing of a comprehensive cease-fire agreement in Dar es Salaam on September 7, 2006, there are reasons to wonder whether it will hold.
12. Reyntjens, "Briefing," p. 118.
13. Ibid.
14. See Julien Nimubona, "Mémoires de réfugiés et de déplacés du Burundi: Lecture critique de la politique publique de réhabilitation," in André Guichaoua, ed., *Exilés, réfugiés, déplacés et Afrique centrale et orientale* (Paris: Karthala, 2004), p. 235.
15. See Lijphart, *Democracy in Plural Societies*.
16. Devon Curtis, "Interim Governments: Institutional Bridges to Peace and Democracy? Burundi and the Democratic Republic of the Congo" (Unpublished ms, 2005), p. 7.
17. For a fuller treatment of the Tutsi position in 1993, see Lemarchand, *Burundi: Ethnic Conflict and Genocide*, p. 162.
18. See Daniel Sullivan, "The Missing Pillars: A Look at the Failure of Peace in Burundi Through the Lens of Arend Lijphart's Consociational Theory," *Journal of Modern African Studies* 43, no. 1 (2005): 87.
19. Reyntjens, "Briefing," 125. This discussion is heavily indebted to his data and insights. See also International Crisis Group, *Elections au Burundi: Reconfiguration radicale du paysage politique* (Nairobi and Brussels: ICG, 2005).
20. Ibid.
21. Quoted in Paul J. Kaiser, "Lessons Learned and Strategies Employed by Enlightened Leadership: Reflections on the Case of Burundi" (Typescript, January 27, 2006), 2.
22. Ibid., p. 4.
23. HRW, *Warning Signs: Continuing Abuses in Burundi*, no. 3, February 27, 2006.
24. See www.arib.info/#Avril 06.
25. Association de Réflexion et d' Information sur le Burundi (ARIB), September 5, 2006.
26. Integrated Regional Information Networks (IRIN), September 5, 2006.
27. Ibid., June 23, 2006.
28. The arrest of Ndayizeye is all the more surprising when one recalls that he played a major role in 2003 in meeting Nkurunziza's demands for a greater share of government positions, namely four ministerial posts, fifteen seats in the National Assembly, six ambassadorships and a 20 percent representation of the CNDD-FDD personnel in public enterprises.
29. Déo Niyonzima was at one time the leader of the infamous SODEJEM—Solidarité jeunesse pour la défense des minorités—and played a key role in the

brutal ethnic cleansing of Bujumbura in March and April 1995, when hundreds of Hutu families were forced out of their homes in Bujumbura. It is widely believed that the SODEJEM was also responsible for the systematic murder of dozens of Hutu students, teachers, intellectuals, and civil servants in the months following Ndadaye's assassination.

30. Integrated Regional Information Networks (IRIN), August 2, 2006.
31. Ibid.
32. Ibid.
33. Ibid.
34. See Hermenegilde Niyonzima, *Burundi: Terre des héros non-chantés* (Vernier: Editions Remesha, 2004), pp. 369 ff.
35. In its issue of August 27, 2005, *The Economist* reported the following scene: "At a recent FDD [*sic*] victory rally, Mr. Radjabu slit a cockerel's throat and let an eagle feed on its entrails. This would be a harmless spectacle but for the fact that that the eagle and the cock are also the respective mascots of the FDD and its main competitor, Frodebu. These are risky gestures for a country just emerging from civil war" (p. 40).
36. Private communication, September 14, 2006.
37. *Burundi Réalités*, September 19, 2006.
38. Ibid., September 6, 2006.
39. For a fascinating exploration of how the trauma of the 1972 genocide has shaped the outlook and ideology of the Paliphehtu, see Liisa H. Malkki, *Purity and Exile: Violence, Memory and National Cosmology among Hutu Refugees in Tanzania* (Chicago and London: University of Chicago Press, 1995).
40. *Burundi Réalités*, January 17, 2006.
41. Interview with the author, October 5, 2003.
42. For further details, see *Iteka, Bulletin d'information*, no. 51 (July 2003): 1–6.
43. Vera Achvarina and Simon F. Reich, "No Place to Hide: Refugees, Displaced Persons and the Recruitment of Child Soldiers," *International Security* 31, no. 1 (Summer 2006): 127–64.
44. See *Comprehensive Cease-fire Agreement between the Government of the Republic of Burundi and the Palipehutu-FNL*, Dar es Salaam, September 7, 2006. The agreement was signed in the presence of three "guarantors," i.e., Yoweri Museveni, chairperson of the Regional Initiative for Peace in Burundi (RIPB); J. M. Kikwete, vice-chairperson of the RIPB; T. Mbeki, representative of the facilitating country (South Africa); and two witnesses: P. Mazimhaka, representative of the African Union, and Ambassador N. Satti, UN Special Envoy to the Great Lakes Region.
45. Integrated Regional Information Networks (IRIN), September 20, 2006.
46. Ibid.
47. Waldemar Frey and Henri Boshoff, "Burundi's DDR and the Consolidation of Peace," *African Security Review* 14, no. 4 (2005): 42.
48. Integrated Regional Information Networks (IRIN), August 16, 2006.
49. P. M. Kamungi, J. S. Oketch, and C. Huggins, "Land Access and Refugee Repatriation," *Eco-Conflicts* (African Centre for Technology Studies, Nairobi) 3, no. 2 (September 2004): 1.
50. Ibid. Concretely, this means that over 80 percent of the rural households have less than 1.5 hectares of land.
51. Integrated Regional Information Networks (IRIN), August 16, 2006.
52. Ibid.
53. Ibid.

54. Ibid.

55. It is a commentary on the potentially explosive nature of refugee issues that a key factor behind Ndadaye's assassination in 1993 had to do with conflicts over land, following the return of Hutu refugees.

56. P. M. Kamungi et al., "Land Access," p. 2.

57. Ibid.

58. See the outstanding contribution of Julien Nimubona, "Mémoires de réfugiés et de déplacés du Burundi: Lecture critique de la politique publique de réhabilitation," in André Guichaoua, ed., *Exilés, réfugiés, déplacés en Afrique centrale et orientale* (Paris: Karthala, 2004), pp. 213–45.

59. P. M. Kamungi et al., "Land Access," p. 2.

60. Willy Nindorera, "D'un Mouvement Rebelle à un Parti Politique au Burundi: Le Cas du CNDD-FDD" (Paper prepared for the project From Rebel Movements to Political Parties: Reviewing the Role of International Actors, Netherlands Institute of International Relations, Clingendael, Amsterdam, July 2006), p. 23.

61. See the interview with Minister Batumubwira in *Jeune Afrique L'Intelligent* (February 12–18, 2006), 39.

62. Anon., "Informal Trip Report," September 20, 2006.

63. Ibid.

64. For an excellent example of how to rethink development assistance in a conflict-oriented optic, see Juana Brachet and Howard Wolpe, *Conflict-Sensitive Development Assistance: The Case of Burundi*, The World Bank, Social development papers, "Conflict Prevention and Reconstruction," paper no. 27 (June 2005).

65. "Informal Trip Report," 3.

66. Ibid., pp. 4–5.

Chapter 13. Ethnic Violence, Public Policies, and Social Capital in North Kivu

1. James S. Coleman, *Foundations of Social Theory* (Cambridge: Harvard University Press, 1990) and Glenn Loury, "A Dynamic Theory of Racial Income Differences," in P. A. Wallace and A. Le Mund, (eds.), *Women, Minorities and Employment Discrimination* (Lexington, Mass.: Lexington Books, 1977). For a restatement of Putnam's argument about social capital, see Francis Fukuyama, *Trust: The Social Virtues and the Creation of Prosperity* (New York: The Free Press, 1995).

2. Robert D. Putnam, *Making Democracy Work: Civic Traditions in Modern Italy* (Princeton: Princeton University Press, 1993), p. 183.

3. Ibid., p. 184.

4. For an outstanding discussion, see Jean-Claude Willame, *Banyarwanda et Banyamulenge* (Paris: L'Harmattan, 1997).

5. Margaret Levi, "Social and Unsocial Capital," *Politics and Society* 24, no. 3 (March 1996): 45–55. See also Sidney Tarrow, "Making Social Science Work Across Space and Time: A Critical Reflection on Robert Putnam's Making Democracy Work," *American Political Science Review* 90, no. 2 (June 1996): 390–97.

6. Much of the information in this section is derived from interviews conducted in Goma in August 1993.

7. Eugene Muhima, personal interview, August 20, 1993.

8. Putnam, *Making Democracy Work*, p. 167.

9. R. Spitaels, "Transplantation de Banyarwanda dans le Nord Kivu," *Problémes d'Afrique Centrale* 2 (1953) : 110.

10. Note how James Fairhead describes the methods of the CNK: "CNK was able to corrupt local bureaucrats, African and Belgian, to secure land rights, and the ascription of land as 'vacant' came to have more to do with the impotence of representatives of the local populations in front of CNK—and the corruption of customary chiefs—than its vacancy or otherwise. Attributions of vacancy were frequently false. Land ceded to the colonials was not taken from vacant land, but right in the indigenously populated regions which were entirely saturated. Many Belgian state officials invested in plantations. Competition for the land between the cultivators and the planters was resolved in favor of those with money on their side, rather than the law. It is often 'forgotten' that such corruption, which has now come to be termed 'le mal zairois,' is a colonial legacy. Money has always spoken louder than the administration in Kivu." James Fairhead, *Food Security in North and South Kivu* (Typescript, 1989), part 1, section 2.

11. *Population du Kivu: Résumé*, Bukavu, November 17, 1959, from the author's files.

12. For an illuminating discussion of the cultural interactions between Rwanda and Hunde societies in the eighteenth century, see David Newbury, *Kings and Clans: Ijwi Island and the Lake Kivu Rift 1780–1840* (Madison: University of Wisconsin Press, 1991), especially chapters 2, 3, and 4.

13. For more details, see Willame, Banyarwanda et Banyamulenge pp. 76–99.

14. On the involvement of Tutsi refugees in the 1964 rebellion, see Lemarchand, *Rwanda and Burundi* (London: Pall Mall Press, 1970), chapter 7.

15. The phenomenon is excellently analyzed by Bucyalimwe Mararo in "Land, Power and Ethnic Conflict in Masisi (Congo-Kinshasa), 1940–1994," *The International Journal of African Historical Studies* 3 (1997): 503–38. See also his "Les Migrations Rwandaises au Kivu," in Bogumil Jewsiewicki and Jean-Pierre Chrétien, eds., *Sociétés Rurales et Technologies en Afrique Centrale et Occidentale au 20eme Siécle* (Québec: Éditions Safi, 1976), pp. 39–54.

16. Ibid., p. 30.

17. Nzabara Matetsa, personal interview, August 21, 1993.

18. Mararo, "Land, Power and Ethnic Conflict in Masisi," p. 532.

19. For a summary discussion of the 1971, 1972, and 1981 legislation affecting nationality rights, see Reyntjens and Marysse, eds., *Conflits au Kivu: Antécédents et Enjeux* (Antwerp: Center for the Study of the Great Lakes Region of Africa, 1966), p. 20.

20. Ibid., pp. 20 ff.

21. Muhima, personal interview, August 20, 1993.

22. Mararo, "Land, Power and Ethnic Conflict in Masisi," pp. 512–13.

23. For further information, see Willame, *Banyarwanda et Banyamulenge*, pp. 62–75.

24. Ibid., p. 64.

25. On post-1994 developments, see Roland Pourtier, "La guerre au Kivu: Un conflit multidimensionel," *Afrique Contemporaine* 180 (October–December 1996): 15–38.

26. Putnam, *Making Democracy Work*, p. 154.

27. Ibid., p. 182.

Chapter 14. The DRC

1. For some moving testimonies by Africans of how the ongoing civil war affects grassroots communities, see the contributions of Alphonse Maindo Mongo

Ngonga, Leonard N'Sanda Buleli, and Jacques Kabulo, in "RCD: La guerre vue d'en bas," special issue, *Politique Africaine* 84 (December 2001): 33–102.

2. Front de Libération du Congo, "Les cent premiers jours du Front de Libération du Congo," Beni, May 12, 2001, mimeo.

3. For some Belgian historians, like Jean Stengers, the absence of memories of the Congo Free State among Congolese is sufficient proof of its negligible impact on present-day developments. But this misses the point, argues Wrong in her brilliant account of Mobutu's demise:

I, too, had been surprised by how few of these horrors had ever been mentioned to me by Zairian friends. But it wasn't necessary to be an expert on sexual abuse to know it was possible to be traumatized without knowing why; that, indeed, amnesia—whether individual or collective—could sometimes be the only way of dealing with horror, that human behavior could be altered forever without the cause being openly acknowledged. The spirit, once comprehensively crushed, does not recover easily. For seventy five years, from 1885 to 1960, Congo's population had marinated in humiliation. No malevolent witch-doctor could have devised a better preparation for the coming of a second Grand Dictator.

Michela Wrong, *In the Footsteps of Mr. Kurtz: Living in the Congo on the Brink of Disaster* (New York: Harper Collins, 2001), pp. 59, 60. For an outstanding, painstakingly researched treatment of the horrors of the Léopoldian system, see Adam Hochschild, *King Leopold's Ghost* (New York: Houghton Mifflin, 1998).

4. The man Ronald Reagan referred to as "the voice of good sense and good will" was also the self-proclaimed Guide, the Messiah, the Helmsman, the Leopard, the Sun-President, and the cock who jumped on anything that moved. His full name, Mobutu Sese Seko Kuku wa za Banga, can be loosely translated as "the all powerful warrior who goes from conquest to conquest leaving fire in his wake." See Bill Berkeley, *The Graves Are Not Yet Full* (New York: Basic Books, 2001), p. 109.

5. See Ludo De Witte, *L'Assassinat de Lumumba* (Paris: Karthala, 2000).

6. The point is convincingly argued by Thomas Callaghy in his review of Wrong's *In the Footsteps of Mr. Kurtz*: "Life and Death in the Congo," *Foreign Affairs* 79 (2001): 143–49.

7. In Kinshasa, the black-market rate to the dollar reached 2.5 million in 1993; in Lubumbashi it went from twelve million to twenty-four million. See Berkeley, *The Graves*, p. 113.

8. Cited in Crawford Young, "Zaire: The Shattered Illusion of the Integral State," *Journal of Modern African Studies* 32 (1994): 247.

9. For a fuller discussion of this phenomenon, see Crawford Young, *The African Colonial State in Comparative Perspective* (New Haven: Yale University Press, 1997), pp. 1–12.

10. Jeffrey Herbst, *States and Power in Africa: Comparative Lessons in Authority and Control* (Princeton: Princeton University Press, 2000) p. 14.

11. William Zartman, "Posing the Problem of State Collapse," in William Zartman, ed., *Collapsed States: The Disintegration and Restoration of Legitimate Authority* (Boulder: Lynne Rienner, 1995), p. 9.

12. Ibid., p. 5.

13. Samuel Huntington, *The Clash of Civilizations and the Remaking of World Order* (New York: Simon and Schuster, 1996), p. 272.

14. Bucyalimwe Mararo, "Land, Power and Ethnic Conflict in Masisi (Congo-Kinshasa), 1940–1994," *International Journal of African Historical Studies* 30 (1997): 503–38.

15. Herbst, *States and Power in Africa*, pp. 37–39.

16. Lemarchand, *Burundi: Ethnic Conflict and Genocide* (New York: Cambridge University Press and Woodrow Wilson Center Press, 1995).

17. See Emizat Kisangani, "The Massacre of Refugees in the Congo: A Case of UN Peacekeeping Failure and International Law," *Journal of Modern African Studies* 38 (2000): 163–202.

18. The phrase is borrowed from Thomas Callaghy, *The State-Society Struggle: Zaire in Comparative Perspective* (New York: Columbia University Press, 1994).

19. Young, "Zaire: The Shattered Illusion of the Integral State," pp. 247–63.

20. "The Heart of the Matter," *The Economist*, May 13, 2000, p. 25.

21. Young, "Reflections on State Decline and Societal Change in Zaire" (Typescript, Madison, 1997), as quoted in Lemarchand, "Patterns of State Collapse and Reconstruction in Central Africa: Reflections on the Crisis in the Great Lakes Region," *Spectrum* 32 (1997): 184.

22. John F. Clark, "Zaire: The Bankruptcy of the Extractive State," in Leonardo Villalon and Philip Huxtable, eds., *The African State at a Critical Juncture: Between Disintegration and Reconfiguration* (Boulder: Lynne Rienner, 1998), p. 113.

23. In September 1993, I interviewed the UFERI governor, Gabriel Kyungu wa Kumwanza, who claimed that the UFERI youth groups were a "totally uncontrolled, self-recruiting group," but neglected to mention that he himself had played a key role in fanning the flames of ethnic hatred, never missing an opportunity to hold the Kasaians collectively responsible for the sufferings of the "native Katangans." Berkeley, one of the few journalists present in Katanga at the time, recalled that "in a series of public rallies and radio speeches the governor railed against the 'enemy within' the bilulu (insects in Swahili). 'The Kasaians are foreigners,' he declared. 'Their presence is an insult.'" By April 1992, in the wake of systematic attacks against their homes, hundreds of Kasaians were forced to return to their province of origin, including those who were born in Katanga. Berkeley, *The Graves* 122.

24. The history of the Banyamulenge, both extremely complex and tragic, lies outside the scope of this discussion. The term has been the source of considerable confusion because it is becoming increasingly used as an omnibus label to designate all Tutsi living in North and South Kivu. It came into usage in 1976 as a result of the efforts of the late Gisaro Muhoza, a member of parliament from South Kivu, to regroup the Banyamulenge populations of the Mwenga, Fizi, and Uvira zones into a single administrative entity. Although his initiative failed, the name stuck and by 1996 was often used by ethnic Tutsi and Congolese to designate all Tutsi residents of North and South Kivu. The Banyamulenge (literally the "people of Mulenge") are Tutsi pastoralists who live on the high-lying plateau of the Itombwe region of South Kivu; they came to this area long before the advent of colonial rule. Estimates of their numerical importance vary widely, from 30,000 to 300,000. The consensus of opinion among scholars points to some 60,000 to 100,000 as a more reliable figure. They are socially and culturally distinct from both the long-established Tutsi of North Kivu and the Tutsi refugees of the 1959–62 revolution in Rwanda (the so-called fifty-niners); indeed, many there are Banyamulenge who do not speak Kinyarwanda. Whereas many fifty-niners joined the eastern rebellion in 1964–65, the Banyamulenge did so reluctantly and then quickly switched sides (largely because the pro-Mulele Bafulero of South Kivu plundered their cattle during the rebellion). Despite assertions to the contrary, they did not form the bulk of the FPR fighters

recruited in eastern Congo, even though a few hundred joined the FPR in the early 1990s; the bulk of the fighting force from the Congo was drawn from among the sons of fifty-niners and ethnic Tutsi from North Kivu. By 1996, however, a large number joined Kabila's AFDL in eastern Congo; they suffered heavy casualties during the anti-Mobutist campaign and after the 1998 crisis, as shown by the inordinately large number of Banyamulenge widows in Bukavu. Today a number of Banyamulenge hold important positions in the RCD-Goma—including Bizima Karaha, Minister of Foreign Affairs—but it would be profoundly misleading to assume that they are all solidly behind the rebellion. Many share Muller Ruhimbika's view that they have been "instrumentalized" by Kagame, in the same way that the RDC is being manipulated by Kigali to promote Rwandan interests in the Congo. For more information, see Joseph Mutambo, *Les Banyamulenge* (Limete: Imprimerie St. Paul, 1997); Muller Ruhimbika, *Les Banyamulenge* (Paris: L'Harmattan, 2001); Jean-Claude Willame, *Banyarwanda and Banyamulenge* (Paris: L'Harmattan, 1997). For evidence of a precolonial presence of Banyamulenge in South Kivu, see Jean Hiernaux, "Note sur les Tutsi de l'Itombwe: La position anthropologique d'une population émigrée," *Bulletins et Mémoires de la Société d'Anthropologie de Paris* 7 (1965): 361–79. I am grateful to Etienne Rusamira, Sanson Muziri, and Muller Ruhimbika for sharing with me their excellent grasp of the Banyamulenge problem.

25. Honoré N'Gbanda Nambo Ko Atumba, *Ainsi Sonne le Glas! Les Derniers Jours du Maréchal Mobutu* (Paris: Editions Gideppe, 1998), p. 50. Also known as the Terminator for his role during the violent repression of "la marche des Chrétiens" on February 16, 1992, the author served as Mobutu's Special Advisor on Security from 1992 to 1997, until replaced by General Nzimbi. During these years, he served as Mobutu's key intermediary with UNITA and is widely reported to have made a huge fortune in "facilitating" the sale of Angolan diamonds for Mobutu.

26. By lumping together under the same label all Tutsi subgroups, irrespective of their date of arrival in the region, including the long-established Banyamulenge of South Kivu and those Tutsi of North Kivu whose roots went back to the early colonial and precolonial days, the 1981 nationality law had a catalytic effect on their common self-awareness as a victimized community. By stripping them of their nationality, Mobutu made them potentially receptive to the appeals of the FPR in the 1990s. Technically, the term Banyarwanda also included Hutu migrants from Rwanda; in fact, however, it came to be used increasingly to designate primarily Tutsi elements.

27. For a more detailed commentary, see Lemarchand, "Ethnic Violence, Public Policies, and Social Capital in North Kivu," Chapter 13 in this volume.

28. Ibid.

29. "Rwanda was the Godfather of the Congolese rebellion." Schatzberg's statement encapsulates the central factor behind the ensuing struggle for power leading to the 1998 crisis. Michael G. Schatzberg, "Beyond Mobutu: Kabila and the Congo," *Journal of Democracy* 18 (1997): 81.

30. Quoted in Corinna Sculer, "Slippery Slope to Humiliation," *The National Post*, August 21, 2000, p. D2.

31. See Peter Rosenblum, "Kabila's Congo," *Current History* (1997): 195.

32. This fact will neither be forgotten nor soon forgiven by many Banyamulenge survivors, who make no secret today of their profound dislike of their Rwandan "protectors," Clément Ngirabatware, personal interview, Montreal, September 2000.

33. That Kisangani was taken by Rwandan and not Ugandan troops is an important element in the background of the subsequent confrontation between Rwanda and Uganda: the standard Rwandan argument is that the capture of the city by the Rwandan army entitled them and their CRD ally to proprietary rights over the city and the mineral resources of its environs. Another source of distrust between them stems from the fact that Kampala was never informed of Kagame's decision to launch the August 1998 raid on Kitona; yet after the raid fizzled, Kagame immediately turned to Museveni to request that Ugandan tanks be sent to North Kivu. Etienne Rusamira, personal interview, Montreal, December 2000.

34 See Steven Jackson, "Making a Killing: Criminality and Coping in the Kivu War Economy," *Review of African Political Economy* 93–94 (September–December 2002): 517–36.

35. See the 1999 Report of the UN special rapporteur, Roberto Garreton, *Report on the Situation of Human Rights in the Democratic Republic of the Congo* (New York: UN, 2000), pp. 33–34. See also the devastating report of the Brussels-based NGO Rassemblement pour le Progrès, *Pour que l'on n'oublie jamais* (Brussels, 1999).

36. Ian Fisher, "Congo's War Turns a Land Spat into a Blood Bath," *New York Times*, January 29, 2001, p. 6.

37. IRIN report, November 15, 1999. The Hema are a group of pastoralists, closely related to the Hima of Ankole, in southern Uganda and of northern Rwanda; their cultural affinities with the Tutsi are undeniable, even though they form a group apart. The Lendu are agriculturalists and many identify with the Hutu, largely because of their anti-Hema feelings. For further details on the Hema-Lendu conflict, see "Conflit sanglant Hema-Lendu," Justice-Plus (Bunia, June 23, 1999). On the more recent clashes, in August 2000, causing 142 deaths, see *New Vision* (Kampala, August 21, 2000).

38. For an outstanding analysis, see Koen Vlassenroot, "Citizenship, Identity Formation and Conflict in South Kivu: The Case of the Banyamulenge," *Review of African Political Economy* 93–94 (September–December 2002): 499–515.

39 The issues surrounding the nationality issue are excellently discussed in ibid. and in Ruhimbika, *Les Banyamulenge*.

40. As Vlassenroot perceptively noted, the decision of the Banyamulenge to fight the rebels at the side of the Armée Nationale Conglaise (ANC) marks their entry into modernity, in large part because of the social benefits they received for having picked the "right" side: "For many young Banyamulenge, their conscription into the ANC meant the start of a military career. As a recompense for their war effort on the Haut Plateau the central government also offered them full access to education, social services and employment opportunities." Vlassenroot, "Citizenship," p. 503.

41. Unpublished document from the author's collection. For an illuminating semi-autobiographical account of the circumstances leading to the creation of the FRF, see Ruhimbika, *Les Banyamulenge*.

42. International Crisis Group (ICG), *Scramble for the Congo: Anatomy of an Ugly War* (Brussels: ICG, 2000), p. 40.

43. Ibid., p. 47.

44. Ibid., p. 40.

45. For the views in this paragraph and the next, I am indebted to Gérard Prunier; I have also drawn from Stephen Smith's insights in "Ces enfants-soldats qui ont tué Kabila," *Le Monde*, February 9, 2001.

46. Norimitsu Onishi and Ian Fisher, "Doubts on Whether Kabila's Son Can Lead the Congo," *New York Times*, January 21, 2001, p. 8.
47. David Keen, *The Economic Functions of Violence in Civil Wars*, Adelphi Paper No. 320 (London: Adelphi, 2000).
48. Fax from Groupe de Réflexion des Sans Voix, Butembo, November 28, 2000.
49. Jackson, "Making a Killing," p. 528.
50. Quoted by the Brussels-based NGO *Réseau Congolais d'Information* (Brussels: RCI, 1999).
51. United Nations, Security Council, *Report of the Panel of Experts on the Illegal Exploitation of Natural Resources and Other Forms of Wealth of the Democratic Republic of the Congo*, S/200/357, April 12, 2001. In view of the crushing evidence supplied in this document, it is with no little astonishment that one reads in a 1999 United States Institute of Peace report that among Rwanda's "direct and indirect objectives behind its continuing involvement in the Congo" are "security promotion" "nation-building, in order to leave behind a structure in the Congo that can fill the current vacuum," "economic expansion and commercial development," and "human rights promotion." John Pendergast and David Smock, *Putting Humpty Dumpty Together: Reconstructing Peace in the Congo* (Washington, D.C.: United States Institute of Peace, 1999), p. 4.
52. UN Security Council, *Report of the Panel of Experts*, p. 41. Other quotes in this paragraph are from pp. 39, 40, 41, 17, and 18.
53. Ibid., p. 17.
54. Robert Block, "Zimbabwe's Elite Turn Strife in Nearby Congo into a Quest for Riches," *Wall Street Journal*, October 12, 1998, p. 1.
55. Ibid., p. 34 COSLEG was born of a partnership between Operation Sovereign Legitimacy (OSLEG) and the Congolese Compagnie Mixte d'Import-Export (COMIEX). Among the key shareholders in OSLEG are Lieutenant General Vitalis Musungwa Zvinashe, Minister of Defense, Job Whabira, former Permanent Secretary in the Ministry of Defense, Onesimo Moyo, president of Minerals Marketing Corporation of Zimbabwe, and Isiah Rusengwe, general manager of Zimbabwe Mining Development Corporation.
56. Richard Hottelet, "The Plundering of the Congo," *Christian Science Monitor*, May 16, 2001, p. 9.
57. Quoted in Raymond Bonner, "Bulgaria Becomes a Weapons Bazaar," *New York Times*, August 3, 1998, p. 3.
58. For excellent explorations of this theme, see William Reno, *Warlord Politics and African States* (Boulder: Lynne Rienner 1998). Also, Jean-Francois Bayart, Stephen Ellis, and Béatrice Hibou, *The Criminalization of the State in Africa* (Bloomington: Indiana University Press, 1999).
59. Patrick Graham and Finbarr O'Reilly, "Victims of Their Own Wealth," *National Post*, August 21, 2000, p. D11.
60. Garreton, *Report on the Situation of Human Rights in the DCR*, p. 32. Elsewhere in the report, Garreton informs the reader that "the special rapporteur took advantage of his trip from Goma to Kinshasa during his second mission to bring copies of the 1998 examination taken by the South Kivu candidates back for correction" (p. 40).
61. Quoted in Vlassenroot, "Identity and Insecurity: Building Ethnic Agendas in South Kivu," in Ruddy Doom and Jan Gorus, eds., *Politics of Identity and Economics of Conflict in the Great Lakes Region* (Brussels: VUB University Press, 2000), p. 281.
62. Ibid., p. 282.
63. Herbst, *States and Power in Africa*, pp. 264 ff.

Chapter 15. The Tunnel at the End of the Light

1. James Coleman and Ndolamb Ngokwey, "Zaire: The State and the University," in Richard Sklar, ed., *Nationalism and Development in Africa: Selected Essays by James S. Coleman* (Berkeley: University of California Press, 1994), p. 306.
2. Colin Legum, *Congo Disaster* (Baltimore: Penguin Books, 1961), p. 1.
3. Gauthier de Villers and Jean Omasombo Tshonda, "An Intransitive Transition," *Review of African Political Economy* 93–94 (September–December 2002): 399–410.
4. Michael Schatzberg, *Mobutu or Chaos? The United States and Zaire, 1960–1990* (Lanham: University Press of America and Foreign Policy Research Institute, 1991), p. 102.
5. Michela Wrong, *In the Footsteps of Mr. Kurtz: Living on the Brink of Disaster in Mobutu's Congo* (New York: Harper Collins, 2001), p. 213.
6. Filip Reyntjens, *La Guerre des Grands Lacs: Alliances Mouvantes et Conflits Extraterritoriaux en Afrique Centrale* (Paris: L'Harmattan, 1999).
7. Michael Hirsh, "Calling All Regio-Cops: Peacekeeping's Hybrid Frame," *Foreign Affairs* 79 (November–December 2000): 2–8.
8. Richard Hottelet, "The Plundering of the Congo," *Christian Science Monitor*, May 16, 2001, p. 3.
9. Koen Vlassenroot, "Citizenship, Identity Formation and Conflict in South Kivu," *Review of African Political Economy* 93–94 (September–December 2002): 499–515.
10. Jean-Francois Bayart, *L'Etat en Afrique: La politique du ventre* (Paris: Fayard, 1989).
11. International Crisis Group (ICG), *Storm Clouds over Sun City: The Urgent Need to Recast the Congolese Peace Process* (Brussels and Nairobi: ICG 2002).
12. Crawford Young, *The Politics of Cultural Pluralism* (Madison: University of Wisconsin Press, 1976).
13. Vlassenroot, "Citizenship," p. 510.
14. Ingrid Samset, "Conflict of Interests or Interests in Conflict? Diamonds and War in the DRC," *Review of African Political Economy* 93–94 (September–December 2002): 471.
15. Ibid.
16. Stephen Jackson, "Making a Killing: Criminality and Coping in the Kivu War Economy," *Review of African Political Economy* 93–94 (September–December 2002): 519.
17. Ibid.
18. Vlassenroot, "Identity and Insecurity: The Building of Ethnic Agendas in South Kivu," in Ruddy Doom and Jan Gorus, eds., *Politics of Identity and Economics of Conflict in the Great Lakes Region* (Bruxelles: VUB Press, 2000), p. 280.
19. Jackson, "Making a Killing."
20. United Nations, *Interim Report of the Panel of Experts on the Illegal Exploitation of Natural Resources and Other Forms of Wealth in the DRC* (New York: UN, 2002), pp. 9–10.
21. Ibid., p. 11.
22. See Theodore Trefon, "The Political Economy of Sacrifice: Kinois and the State," *Review of African Political Economy* 93–94 (September–December 2002): 481–98.
23. Jean-François Ploquin, "Dialogue intercongolais: La société civile au pied du mur," *Politique Africaine* 84 (December 2001): 146.

24. Ernest Wamba dia Wamba, "La palabre comme pratique de la critique et de l'autocritique sur le plan de toute la communauté," *Journal of African Marxists* 7 (March 1984): 35.

Chapter 16. From Kabila to Kabila

1. John Le Carré, *The Mission Song* (New York: Little, Brown, 2006), p. 108.
2. This discussion leans heavily on Jean-Claude Willame's excellent analyses of electoral results, *Commentaires sur les résultats provisoires du second tour de l'élection présidentielle and Commentaires sur le résultat des élections législatives* (unpublished communications).
3. The Independent Electoral Commission (IEC) is one of five transitional institutions established by the Global and Inclusive Agreement of December 2002, along with the Truth and Reconciliation Commission (TRC), the National Human Rights Observatory, the High Authority of the Media, and the Ethics and Anti-Corruption Commission.
4. Integrated Regional Information Networks (IRIN), August 2, 2006.
5. Office of the UN High Commissioner for Refugees, MONUC Human Rights Division, Report, February 8, 2007, pp. 8 and 9.
6. Ironically, however, Bemba's father is of racially mixed origins and so is his wife, Lilia Mbombo Teixeira.
7. These include the all-powerful Société Commerciale et Industrielle Bemba (Scibe-Zaire), Scibe-Airlift (air transport), Comcell (cell phones), Lotran (car rentals), GB (supermarkets and restaurants), and Courrier Express. See Muriel Devey, "Jean-Pierre Bemba: L'enquete," *Afrique Magazine* (October 2006): 59–65.
8. On the contribution of the PSA to the rise of "rural radicalism," see Herbert Weiss, *Political Protest in the Congo* (Princeton: Princeton University Press, 1967). On Gizenga's early trajectory, see Tshitenge Lubabu, "La revanche de Gizenga," *Jeune Afrique*, no. 2397, December 17–23, 2006, pp. 54–55.
9. For a fascinating autobiographical account of her involvement in Congo politics, see Andrée Blouin, *My Country, Africa: Autobiography of the Black Pasionaria* (New York: Praeger, 1983).
10. Crawford Young, *Politics in the Congo: Decolonization and Independence* (Princeton: Princeton University Press, 1965), p. 298.
11. A partial listing includes, Kengo wa Dondo, Lunda Bululu, Gaetan Kakudji, Mulumba Tshibombo, André Futa, Roger Lumbala, Bemba Saolana, and Ramazani Baya. See *La Prosperité* (Kinshasa), January 22, 2007.
12. Christopher Clapham, "Clientelism and the State," in Clapham, ed., *Private Patronage and Public Power: Political Clientelism in the Modern State* (New York: St. Martin's Press, 1982), 22.
13. Jason Stearns, "Congo: Ia démocratie dans la ligne de mire," *Le Soir* (Brussels), p. 1.
14. *L'Avenir* (Kinshasa), March 26, 2007.
15. Jean-François Médard, "The Underdeveloped State in Tropical Africa: Political Clientelism or Neo-patrimonialism?" in Christopher Clapham, ed., *Private Patronage and Public Power*, pp. 162–92.
16. For a revisionist assessment of the "new leader" mythology, see René Lemarchand, "Foreign Policy Making in the Great Lakes Region," in Gilbert Khadiagala and Terence Lyons, eds., *African Foreign Policies: Power and Process* (Boulder: Lynne Rienner, 2001), pp. 87–106.

17. Thierry Vircoulon, "RCD: La démocratie sans démocrates," *Politique Étrangére*, no. 3 (2006): 575.

18. Michael Bratton and Nicolas van de Walle, "Neo-patrimonial Regimes and Political Transitions in Africa," Michigan State University Working Papers on Political Reforms in Africa, Working Paper No. 1, May 1993, p. 19.

19. Wolfgang Fengler, "The Power of Clientelistic Governance: Why Africa Has Not Adjusted" (Paper presented at the 2002 annual meeting of the African Studies Association, Washington, D.C.).

20. "Congo Soldiers Riot and Loot Over Pay" (Reuters), *New York Times*, January 13, 2007.

21. Office of the UN High Commissioner for Refugees (report of February 8, 2006), p. 13.

22. Arthur House, "The Congolese Security Capacity: Center of the Coalition" (Manuscript, n.d.), quoted in Crawford Young and Thomas Turner, *The Rise and Decline of the Zairian State* (Madison: University of Wisconsin Press, 1985), p. 248.

23. UN Security Council, *Twenty-Third Report of the Secretary-General on the United Nations Organization Mission in the Democratic Republic of the Congo*, March 20, 2007, New York S/2007/156, p. 7.

24. Jason Stearns and Michela Wrong, "Struggle for a Functioning Congo," *Financial Times*, August 4, 2006.

25 See Jason Stearns, "Ces invisibles assassins du Congo," *Le Soir*, November 17, 2005.

26. Patrick Chabal and Jean-Pascal Daloz, *Africa Works: Disorder as Political Instrument* (Oxford and Bloomington: The International African Institute in association with James Currey and Indiana University Press, 1999).

27. Integrated Regional Information Networks (IRIN), January 4, 2007.

28. By December 2006, however, the CONADER had overseen the disarmament of 27,821 Ituri combatants, among whom were 9,058 child soldiers, representing twice the number of combatants who surrendered their arms in North and South Kivu.

29. International Crisis Group, "Congo: Bringing Peace to North Kivu," *Africa Report*, no. 133, October 31, 2007, p. 11.

30. Ibid., p. 10.

31. Andrea Armstrong and Barnett Rubin, "The Great Lakes and South Central Asia," in Simon Chesterman, Michael Ignatieff, and Ramesh Thakur, eds., *Making States Work: State Failure and the Crisis of Governance* (Tokyo: United University Press, 2005), p. 92.

32. IRIN, January 23, 2007.

33. Cited in Fareed Zakaria, *The Future of Freedom: Illiberal Democracy at Home and Abroad* (New York: Norton, 2004), p. 17.

34. Michael Mann, *The Dark Side of Democracy: Explaining Ethnic Cleansing* (New York: Cambridge University Press, 2005), p. 3.

35. Stephen Jackson, "Sons of Which Soil? The Language of Autochtony in Eastern D.R. Congo," *African Studies Review* 49, no. 2 (September 2006): 95–123.

36. Ibid., p. 111.

37. "Is This the World's Least Effective UN Peacekeeping Force?" *The Economist*, December 4, 2004.

38. Aidan Hartley, "Congo's Election, the UN's Massacre," *International Herald Tribune*, July 29–30, 2006.

39. Francis Kpatinde, "Scandale à la MONUC," *Jeune Afrique*, no. 2264, May 3–June 5, 2004, pp. 95–123.

40. This is the subject of an excellent analysis by Severine Autesserre, "Conceptualizing Local Conflict: International Intervention in Eastern Congo" (Paper presented at the 2007 meeting of the African Studies Association, New York, November 2007).

41. See International Crisis Group, "Congo: Bringing Peace to North Kivu," p. 11.

42. The phrase is borrowed from Thierry Vircoulon, "L'État internationalisé: Nouvelle figure de la mondialisation en Afrique," *Etudes*, no. 4061 (January 2007): 9–20. For further thoughts on the same theme, see Stephen D. Krasner, "Sharing Sovereignty: New Institutions for Collapsed and Failing States," *International Security* 29, no. 2 (Fall 2004): 85–120 and James D. Fearon and David D. Laitin, "Neotrusteeships and the Problem of Weak States," *International Security* 28, no. 4 (Winter 2003): 5–43.

Index

abagererwa, 82
abahinza, 82
abakonde, 82
Acholi, 51
African Mission in Burundi (AMIB), 156
Akandwanaho, Jovia, 243
Akanyaru river, 82
Akazu, 84, 93, 113
Albright, Madeleine, 231
Alliance des Démocrates pour des Elections Libres (ADELI), 195
Alliance des Forces Démocratiques pour la Libération du Congo (AFDL), 10, 12, 16, 33, 220, 240, 252; atrocities committed by, 22, 104; Kabila and, 230; support from Rwanda, Uganda, and Angola, 21
Alliance des Forces Indépendantes pour le Changement Intégral (AFICI), 195
Alliance of Democratic Forces (ADF), 247
Alliance pour la Majorité Présidentielle (AMP), 268
Amnesty International, 201
André, Catherine, 94
Angola, 232
Annan, Kofi, 166
Apter, David, 72, 75
Arendt, Hannah, 121
Armée Nationale Congolaise (ANC), 38
Armenia, 128; genocide, 127–28
Arusha accords, 84, 123; conference (Rwanda), 84, 122, 123
Arusha Peace and Reconciliation Agreement (Burundi), 44, 142, 152, 153, 156, 161, 164

Association Coopérative des Groupements d'Eleveurs du Nord Kivu (Acogenoki), 209, 211
Association Culturelle Bahunde (Acuba), 207
Aziza Kulsum Gulamali, 243

Bababose, Mathias, 173, 175
Bagaza, Jean-Baptiste, 159
Bagogwe, 84
bahinza, 60. See also *abahinza*
Bahunde, 200
Bakajika law, 14, 212
Banande, 209. See also Nande
Bandundu, 267
Banque du Commerce et de l'Industrie (BCDI), 243
Bantu, 59; ideology, 60
Banyamulenge, 10–11, 236; confrontation with RPA, 252; early presence in South Kivu, 210; ethnogenesis, 57; exclusion of, 16; as "foreign migrants," 16; and FPR, 19; and Gatumba killings, 18; instrumentalized, 247; myth of, 66; and RCD, 22; as Tutsi in disguise, 66
Banyarwanda, 14, 60; and economic distress, 208; as foreigners, 228; immigration into Kivu, 209; and Kanyarwanda war, 13; massacre of, 200; North Kivu as home, 210; resettlement of, 14; rights of, 201; threat of domination, 13
Baramoto, General Philémon, 199, 227, 228
Barampama, Marine, 174
Barbarossa, 116

Bashi, 9; supportive of Banyarwanda, 13
Batare, 143
Batumbwira, Antoinette, 185
Bauer, Yehuda, 109, 121; on Rwanda, 118
Bayart, Jean-Francois, 253
Bemba, Jean-Pierre, 217, 236, 256; business connections, 266; campaign style, 265–66; candidate to DRC presidency, 261; corrupt behavior, 274; electoral support for, 262–64; flight to Portugal, 270
Bemba Saolana, 266
Beni-Butambo, 25
Berkeley, Bill, 111
Bezi, 143
Bidalira, Louis, 24
Birindwa, Faustin, 194
Bisengimana, Barthélémy Rwema, 14, 210
Bizimungu, Pasteur, 64, 65, 96
Blouin, Madame (Andrée), 267
Boboliko, André, 196
Bond, Karl I., 196
Boraine, Alex, 78
Bratton, Michael, 272
Brauman, Rony, 105
broadly based transitional government (BBTG), 123
Browning, Christopher, 117, 121, 125
Bruguière, Jean-Louis, xii, 102
Bubanza, 137
Bundu Dia Kongo, 269
Burundi, x; consociationalism, 171–72; costs of civil war, 162–64; demobilization of ex-combatants, 180–82; elections, 152, 158, 169–71; endangered transition, 158–88; exodus of refugees, 134, 182–84; and FNL, 142, 164; genocide, 129–39; government corruption, 174–75; heads of state assassinated, 141; and Hima clique, 138, 137; historical backdrop, 159–62; Hutu radicalism, 145, 179–80; and illiberal democracy, 157; impact of Rwanda revolution on, 143–44; influence on Rwanda, 139–40; international actors, 150–52; and *Jeunesses Révolutionnaires Rwagasore* (JRR), 135; and Kissinger, 129, 131; manufacturing of truth in, 133; and Ndadaye's assassination, 142, 145; and Richard Nixon, 129, 131; palace revolution in, 135; politics of power-sharing, 167–69; prospects for peace, 152–54; Radjabu enigma, 177–78; regroupment camps, 163–64; similarities with and differences from Rwanda, x, 133–34; social complexity, x, 133; and Tutsi-Hima, 133; and violence, 135, 159
Buyoya, Pierre, 4, 165
Bwisha, 9, 14, 201, 209

Céline, 103
Central Intelligence Agency (CIA), 250
Chikane, Frank, 77
Chrétien, Jean-Pierre, 3, 132, 133
civil war in Burundi, 160; costs, 162–64
Clapham, Christopher, 269
Clinton, Bill, 165
Coalition des Partis Politiques de l'Opposition (CPPO), 77
Coalition pour la Défense de la République (CDR), 84, 122; as spoiler at Arusha, 122
Cohen, Roger, 64, 90, 102
Coleman, James S., 249
Collectif d'Actions pour le Développement des Droits de l'Homme (CADDHOM), 237
Collectif Progressiste (CP), 195
Collier, Paul, x, 5, 7, 30, 41, 42
coltan, 255
Comité National du Kivu (CNK), 208
Commission Nationale de Réhabilitation des Sinistrés (CNRS), 153
Community Sant' Egidio, 150
Compromis Politique Global (CPG), 197
Conférence Nationale Souveraine (CNS), 191–93, 195, 201, 231; and transition to multiparty democracy, 225; exclusion of Banyamulenge from, 226
Congo, ix, x, xii; challenging received ideas, 4–7; and civil society, 258; Congo crisis, 249; Congo disaster, 250; and Cold War, 250; as geological scandal, ix; geopolitics, 3–29; object of greed, 245; social identities, 7. *See also* Democratic Republic of the Congo
Congolese Liberation Front (CLF), 236
Congolese Rally for Democracy. *See* Rassemblement Congolais pour la Démocratie (RCD)
Congrès National pour la Défense du Peuple (CNDP), 276

Conseil National pour la Défense de la Démocratie (CNDD), 76
Conseil National pour la Défense de la Démocratie-Forces pour la Défense de la Démocratie (CNDD-FDD), 76, 145, 147, 149, 152, 162, 167; and civil society, 186; and clientelism, 184; internal splits, 173–77; and security forces, 178
consociationalism, 167; unhinged, 171–72
Convention of Government, 151, 167
corruption, 172; accusations of, 173–75; and Burundi rehabilitation program, 174–75; culture of, 271; in FARDC, 274; and Office de lutte anti-fraude (OLAF), 174; and Radjabu, 177–78
crimes against humanity, 104
Crocker, Chester, 251
Cros, Marie-France, 105

Davenport, Christian, 101
demobilization, disarmament, and deinsertion program (DDR), 153
Democratic Republic of the Congo (DRC), x, 104, 231, 242; and civil society, 258; electoral commission, 261; elections, 260–80; mineral wealth, ix; parliamentary arena, 267–69; plundering of minerals, 241–42, 244–45; political exclusion, 269; post-electoral clashes, 269–70; recipe for reconstruction, 248; and survival techniques, 257. *See also* Zaire
Des Forges, Alison, 70, 88, 91, 123, 125
Destexhe, Alain, 120
D'Hertefelt, Marcel, 53
Dinka, Bernahu, 166
divisionism, 99; and critical memory, 108
Division Spéciale Présidentielle (DSP), 193, 199, 201, 202, 227
Dos Santos, Eduardo, 239
Dunia, 24
Dupaquier, Jean-Francois, 133
Durcharbeiten, 108

The Economist, 259, 279
Eltringham, Nigel, 103
Endundo, José, 272
ethnic cleansing, 200
ethnic fidelities, 207–8
ethnicity, 49–67; ban on (Rwanda), 108; ethnic memories, 119; ethnic polarization, 144; and exclusion, 35; and genocide, 99; Hamitic hypothesis, 54; and Hutu radicalism, 161; imagined, 52; invented, 51; manipulation of, 101; moral, 49; and myth-making, 50; obliteration of, 99–100; and political tribalism, 49–50

Fashoda, 87
Feierman, Stephen, 51
Fein, Helen, 79, 87, 109, 119, 121, 128; on genocide by attrition, 105; on rationality of genocide, 127; on retributive genocide, 134
Finkelkraut, Alain, 90
Finley, M. I., 53
Fizi-Baraka, 238
Forces Armées Congolaises (FAC), 232. *See also* Forces Armées Zairoises (FAZ)
Forces Armées de la République Démocratique du Congo (FARDC), 269, 273; parallel with ANC, 274
Forces Armées du Burundi (FAB), 181
Forces Armées Rwandaises (FAR), 17
Forces Armées Zairoises (FAZ), 193, 199; and ethnoregional identities, 202; appalling performance of, 226; and looting, 201, 203, 220; as political machine, 227–28; unraveling of, 228
Forces Démocratiques pour la Libération du Rwanda (FDLR), 23, 275
Forces du Changement Démocratique (FCD), 77
Forces Nationales de Libération (FNL), 142, 145, 148, 169; abuses by, 172–73; and demobilization, 181; FNL-*icanzo*, 176; and human rights violations, 172; ideology, 149, 179–80; inconclusive cease-fire negotiations, 172, 178; and Joint Verification and Monitoring Mechanism (JVMM), 180; and regroupment camps, 148; rejects peace talks, 153; as scapegoats, 172; support from peasants, 164
Forces pour la Défense de la Démocratie (FDD), 24, 44, 75; splits within, 148
Forces Républicaines Fédéralistes (FRF), 23
France, complicity in genocide, 87, 127
Freud, Sigmund, xi, 106
Front de Libération National (Frolina), 38

Front de Résistance Patriotique de l'Ituri (FRPI), 275
Front des Démocrates du Burundi (Frodebu), 72 , 153, 170, 172; split between moderates and hard-liners, 142
Front des Nationalistes et Intégrationnistes (FNI), 275
Front Patriotique Rwandais (FPR), 37, 237; as counterrevolutionary force, 82; invasion of Rwanda, 81; support of ethnic Tutsi for, 230
Front Uni de l'Opposition (FUO), 195

Gahutu, Rémi, 58
Garde Civile (GC), 199, 227
Garreton, Roberto, 22, 96, 231, 235, 245
Gasana, James, 126
Gashari, 14
Gashumba, Ildephonse, 85
Générale des Carrières et des Mines (Gécamines), 203, 244
genocide, 63, 64; Armenian, 110; blowback effects, 140; in Burundi, 71, 129–40, 141; and compliance from above, 125; controversies about, 130; credit for, 106; denial of, 73, 103; differences between Rwanda and Burundi, 144; and fear, 120; invented, 72, 129; and grass-roots killers, 124–26; judaization of, 112; and Holocaust, 91–92, 111; of Hutu and Tutsi, 63 ; ideological dimensions, 110; instrumentalization of, 105; intentionalist theory of, 117; and land hunger, 126; and mass murder, 131; and myth-making, 63; official truths about, 133; "partial," 4; as rational choice, 124; retributive, 110, 144; in Rwanda, 109–29; Rwanda and Burundi compared, 69–74; and security dilemma, 124; of Serbs, 90; strategic aims, 95
Gersony, Robert, 96; report, 104
Ghonda, Antoine, 272
Gikongoro, 115
Gisaro, Muhoza, 10
Gisenyi killings, 122
Gishari enclave,14
Gitera, Joseph, 116
Gizenga, Antoine, 267
Global and Comprehensive Peace Agreement, 17, 261, 280

Global Cease-fire Agreement, 152
Goldhagen, Daniel, 115
Gourevitch, Philip, 88, 89, 95
Great Lakes Initiative, 154
Great Lakes region, 3–5; ambivalent boundaries, 3; human losses in, 4–5; from paradise to Hobbesian universe, 4; and peace process, 154; violence evocative of Thirty Years War, 28; and *Volkgeist*, 3
greed, 5–6; and violence, 7, 24, 256. *See also* Collier, Paul
Groth, Alexander, 124

Habimana, Pasteur, 149
Habyarimana, Juvénal, 17, 69, 79, 81, 83; and army coup, 115; and integration of Tutsi, 116; and plane crash, 86, 93, 116, 124
Halpern, Benjamin, 56
Hamites, 58; as counterrevolutionaries, 81–82; and *féodalo-Hamites*, 58, 82; official label for Banyarwanda, 209; and racist propaganda, 58–62
Hamitic hypothesis, 54–56, 112; and anti-Tutsi propaganda, 59; and Bantu ideology, 60; and Christianity, 54; as frame of reference, 82; as phantasm, 57–58; stereotypes, 58–62; and Ten Commandments, 60
Hansen, Holger, xv
Hara, Fabienne, 150
Haut Conseil de la République (HCR), 191, 194, 197
Hearts Grown Bruta: Sagas of Sarajevo, 90. *See also* Cohen, Roger
Hema, 235, 254; Hema-Gerere, 25; Hema-Lendu conflict, 15, 235–36
Herbst, Jeffrey, 30, 42, 43, 221, 222, 247
Hilberg, Raul, 121
Hima, 133, 137; as distinct from Tutsi-Banyaruguru, 133
Hima empire, 61
Hitler, Adolf, 113, 117, 118. See also *Mein Kampf*
Hoffman, Eva, 106, 107
Holocaust, 91; contextual differences, 120; as frame of reference, 89; misleading parallel with Rwanda genocide, 91, 121
Holbrook, Richard, 277
Hoyt, Michael, 136

human rights violations, ix; all sides involved, 276; arbitrary arrests in Burundi, 175–76; by FNL, 172; by Nkunda, 277; and RPF, 96–98
Human Rights Watch (HRW), 69, 89, 94, 172, 236
Hunde, 201, 209; claims to Gishari enclave, 14; expulsion of, 210; and *mutuelles*, 207, 208; and Nande against Banyarwanda, 13; opposition to Banyarwanda, 208. *See also* Bahunde
Huntington, Samuel, x, 19, 20, 30, 41; and kin-country syndrome, 222
Husson, Edouard, 117
Hutu (Burundi): and Tutsi, 7; extremism, 118–19, 142, 179–80; and Congo civil war, 147–49; genocide of, 70–72, 129–41, 223; insurrection, 134, 136; and FNL, 145, 148–49; and Palipehutu, 71; and party splits, 142; and political fragmentation, 149; and power-sharing, 167–69; radicalism, 145–46, 179–80; refugees into Rwanda, 139; and regroupment camps, 148; and republican model, 139
Hutu (Congo), 7; intra-Hutu differences, 9; as "Bantu Hamites," 9; reductionist trap, 7; as Rwandophones, 12
Hutu (Rwanda): anti-Tutsi pogroms, 139; anti-Tutsi propaganda, 58–62, 115; and Arusha conference, 84–85; diasporas, 39–40; exclusion of, 35; "Hutu Power," 85, 123; impact of Ndadaye's assassination on, 85–86; impact of plane crash on, 86–87; inter-Hutu violence, 94; and mythical representations of Tutsi, 57–65; racism, 60–61, 114; RPF invasion, 58; and reductionist trap, 7; regional dimensions, 82–83; revolution, 81, 112; and Tutsi, 7. See also *inyenzi*
Hutu Power, 23, 85, 123

ibiyetso, 115
Inga, 232
inkontanyi, 101
interahamwe, 17, 24, 27, 32, 72, 88, 95, 126, 147, 223, 275
Inter-Congolese Dialogue (ICD), 253, 269, 271
interlacustrine metaphor, 3
International Committee for Support of the Transition (CIAT), 262, 279

International Crisis Group (ICG), 39, 239, 275
International Monetary Fund (IMF), 218, 219, 255
International Rescue Committee (IRC), 5, 216
inversionary discourse, 72
inyenzi, 37, 38, 60, 115
Itombwe, 65
Ituri, 24

Jackson, Stephen, 242, 255, 278
Jeunesses (youth wing of UFERI), 200, 203, 226
Jeunesses Révolutionnaires Rwagasore (JRR), 135, 136, 137
Jews, 111, 113; and Tutsi, compared, 91, 112
Jogo Baptista de Matos (general), 239
Jones, Bruce, 122

Kabarebe, Colonel James, 243
Kabila, Joseph, xiv, 240
Kabila, Laurent-Désiré, xiii, 17, 96, 104, 217, 238; assassination, 218; ineptitude, 238, 239; nepotism and cronyism, 271; rise and fall of, 230; self-proclaimed leader of AFDL, 220; stonewalling on refugee issue, 231
Kadege, Marie-Alphonse, 176
kadogos, 239, 240, 241
Kagame, Alexis, 55
Kagame, Paul, xii, 12, 38, 95, 96, 97; as hero, 95; listened to by the West, 95; Pentagon fascination for, 95; responsibility for shooting down Habyarimana's plane, xxii; and selective memory, 106; and troop airlift to Kitona, 232
Kahwa (chief), 25
Kaiser, Paul, 171
Kalehe, 9
Kalinda, André (chief), 211
Kamitatu, Cléophas, 194
Kamitatu, Olivier, 272
Kangura-Magazine, 63
Kanyarwanda war, 13
Kanza, Thomas, 194
Kapend, Eddy (colonel), 239
Kaplan, Robert, 89
Kapuscinski, Ryszard, 89
Karamira, Frodouald, 83
Karenga, Ramadan, 176

Kashala, Oscar, 266
Kataliko, Bishop, 255
Katumile Masire, 218
Kayibanda, Grégoire, 82, 114
Kayitesi, Odette, 173
Keen, David, 15, 241
Kershaw, Ian, 118
Khartoum, 22, 178
Khmer Rouge, 90
Kibeho killings, 73
Kiga, 82, 139
Kigali, 231–33, 242, 252–54, 275
Kigwe, 53
Kinshasa, 23, 232, 234, 247; slaughter of Tutsi, 234, 237
Kirere, 241, 242
Kisangani: mutiny, 18; battle for, 234
Kissinger, Henry, 129
Kolakowski, Leszek, 68
Kosovo Liberation Army (KLA), 90
kubohoza, 94
Kundera, Milan, 104
Kuper, Leo, 128
Kyungu, Gabriel, 200

The Lancet, 5. See also International Rescue Committee
land problem, 4, 13–15; land alienation in Kivu, 14; sale of native lands to Tutsi refugees, 211; and immigration, 228–29
Lanotte, Olivier, 91
Leave None to Tell the Story, 89, 95. See also Des Forges, Alison
lebensraum, 115
Legum, Colin, 250
Lendu, 254
Levene, Mark, 110, 120
Levi, Margaret, 207
Levi, Primo, 100
Ligue Iteka, 155
Lijphart, Arend, 167, 185
Linden, Ian, 54
Lizinde, Théoneste, 83
Lonsdale, John, xi, 49, 50, 51, 67
Lord's Resistance Army (LRA), 149
Loury, Glen, 206
Luba, 266
Lubanga, Thomas, 25
Lubumbashi, 148; slaughter of Tutsi in, 234
Lumumba, Patrice, 114

Lusaka accords, 46, 218, 238, 240, 245, 246, 248, 258, 280

Magrivi, 28, 208, 213, 229
Mai-Mai, 23, 229, 234, 235, 238, 241; as employment option, 245; and ethnoregional configurations, 24; and marginalization of youth, 256; and social exclusion, 24; as source of violence, 245; as warlords, 217
Malinowski, Bronislaw, 53
Malkki, Liisa, 60, 101
Malu-Malu, Apollinaire, 261
Mamdani, Mahmood, 78
Mandela, Nelson, 90, 151, 165
Mann, Michael, 4, 278
Marangara, 139
Mararo, Bucyalimwe, 28, 211, 213, 214
Martyazo, Republic of, 136
Masasu Nindaga, 239, 240
Masisi, 3, 4, 6, 13, 210; Banyarwanda immigration into, 209; killings of population in, 276; Masisi war, 8
mass murder, 121–23
Masunzu, Patrick, 23, 67, 252, 259
Matadi, 232
Mayer, Arno, 117
Mbaki Batshia, Simon, 269
Mbandaka, 104
Mbata, Operation, 13
Mbeki, Thabo, 152
Médard, Jean-Francois, 271
Mein Kampf, 115. See also Hitler, Adolf
Melson, Robert, 110, 113, 132, 135
memory, politics of, 99–108; ambivalence of ethnic, 101; thwarted, 102–3; manipulated, 103–5; enforced, 105–6; and recognition, 106; work of, 106
Memory, History and Oblivion, 102. See also Ricoeur, Paul
Mende, Lambert, 22
mercenaries, 227
Micombero, Michel (captain), 135, 144, 159
Midlarsky, Manus, 127
Miles, William, 111, 112
Ministry for the Reinsertion and Reinstallation of Displaced and Repatriated Persons (MRRDR), 154, 155, 183, 184
Ministry of National Solidarity, Human Rights and Gender (MSHRG), 183

Mishamo refugee camp, 39, 134
Mission Immigration Banyarwanda (MIB), 14, 208
Mission de l'Organisation des Nations Unies au Congo (MONUC), xiv, 246, 262, 279
Mitterrand, François, 87
Mitterand, Jean-Christophe, 87
Moanda, 232
mobilized diasporas, 36–37
Mobutu, Sese Seko, 95, 193, 217; control over FAZ, 199; as creature of CIA, 224; ethnic loyalty to, 202; exclusionary policies, 32; and kleptocracy, 218; legacy of corruption, 271; "Mobutisme sans Mobutu," 231; and prebendal rule, 224
Morgenthau, Hans, 259
Mouvance Présidentielle (MP), 191, 192, 196, 197
Mouvement de Libération du Congo (MLC), 22, 236, 243
Mouvement Démocratique Républicain (MDR), 83, 86, 94, 122
Mouvement de Réhabilitation du Citoyen (MRC), 170
Mouvement National Congolais (MNC), 114
Mouvement National pour la Révolution et le Développement (MNRD), 83, 85, 86, 94, 116, 122, 123, 126
Mouvement Populaire de la Révolution (MPR), 194
Mouvement Révolutionaire pour la Libération du Congo (RLC), 240
Mouvement Social pour le Renouveau (MSR), 268
Movimento Popular de Libertação de Angola (MPLA), 239
Muembo, Joseph, 10
Mugarabona, Alain, 76
Mugesera, Léon, 82, 92
Mugisha, Adele, 235
Muhabura, Tito, 211
Mulelistes, 37, 38, 134; Muleliste rebellion, 66, 219, 227
Mulenge, 10, 65, 210
Muller, 237. *See also* Ruhimbika, Manasse
Munanira (newspaper), 16
Murego, Donat, 83
Museveni, Yoweri, 25, 38, 70, 95, 97, 238, 240; as Tutsi, 61
Mutezintare, Damas, 103

mutualités, 198, 206, 213; tribalisation of, 213–14
Mutuelle agricole des Virunga (MAGRIVI), 28. *See also* Magrivi
myth-making, xi, 52–67; and distortion of reality, 52; and ethnicity, 52; functions, 53; and genocide, 57; and Hamitic ideology, 54, 57; and historiography, 55; and missionaries, 92; origins and transformation, 52–53

Naimark, Norman, 127
Nande, 9, 60, 208, 270; vs. Hutu and Tutsi, 13
National Army for the Liberation of Uganda (NALU), 19
National Congolese Army (NCA), 66
National Council for the Defense of Democracy, 75. *See also* Conseil National pour la Défense de la Démocratie (CNDD)
National Disarmament Commission (CONADER), 275
National Resistance Army (NRA), 38
National Security Council (NSC), 77
National Sovereign Conference, 219. *See also* Conférence Nationale Souveraine (CNS)
nationality question, 15–16; citizenship rights granted and withdrawn, 212–13; law of 1981, 229; law of 1972, 229; and national conference, 16
Ndadaye, Melchior, 12, 16, 32, 36, 59, 61, 70, 111; iconography of his execution, 59; impact on Rwanda, 85; murder of, 145–46, 160
Ndarisigaraniye, Damien (colonel), 176
Ndayikengurukiye, Jean-Bosco, 145, 148, 166
Ndayizeye, Domitien, 165, 176
Ndayiziga, Charles, 176
Ndele, Albert, 194
Ndikumana, Jean-Bosco, 175
Ndizeye, Charles (a.k.a. King Ntare), 137; killing of, 138, 141
Ndolamb Ngokwey, 249
négationisme, 102
negative forces, 246
neo-patrimonialism, 271
Newbury, Catharine, xv
Newbury, David, xv, 65

Ngbandi, 199, 200, 227; "gang of four," 228
Ngendadumwe, Pierre, 119, 145
Ngendakumana, Leonce, 173
Ngoma, Zaidi, 22
Ngwaka, 200
Nindorera, Willy, 184
Niyonzima, Deo, 176
Nixon, Richard, 129, 130
Nkubito, Alphonse, 96
Nkunda, Laurent (a.k.a. Nkundabatware), 17–19, 270; background, 277; and mixed brigades, 275; threat to Congo, 276
Nkurunziza, Pierre, 145, 148; as born-again Christian, 171; election to Burundi's presidency, 153; head of CNDD-FDD, 145
Nora, Pierre, 107
Nolte, Ernst, 117
Nsabimana, Emmanuel, 178
Nsabiyumva, Evariste, 174
Nsengiyaremye, Dismas, 83
Nshimirimana, Adolphe, 185
Ntaganza, Ladislas, 123
Ntaramyira, Cyprien, 116
Ntare (king), 138
Ntega, 139
Ntezimana, Vincent, 123
Nyamwesi, Mbusa, 22, 25, 236; head of RCD-Bunia, 233
Nyanga, 15
Nyangoma, Leonard, 75, 147, 148, 161
Nyanza-Lac, 134, 136
Nyarugabo, Moise, 232
Nyerere, Julius, 142, 164
Nzimbi, Etienne (general), 227
Nzirorera, Joseph, 84
Nzomukunda, Alice, 173

Observatoire pour l'Action Gouvernementale (OAG), 155
Office des Mines d'Or de Kilo Moto, 242
Omasombo, Jean, 250
Organization of African Unity (OAU), 202
Ould-Abdallah, Ahmedou, 142, 151, 168

Pagès, Father, 55
Palipehutu, 58, 134; birth, 71, 72; and Hutu radicalism, 145. *See also* Forces Nationales de Libération; Palipehutu-Forces Nationales pour la Libération
Palipehutu-Forces Nationales pour la Libération (Palipehutu-FNL), 44, 145; exclusion from Arusha peace talks, 149; internal rifts, 148. *See also* Forces Nationales de Libération
Parti Démocratique Social Chrétien (PDSC), 196, 199
Parti Libéral (PL), 83
Parti Lumumbiste Unifié (PALU), 267, 268
Parti Populaire pour la Reconstruction et le Développement (PPRD), 268
Parti pour la Libération du Peuple Hutu (Palipehutu). *See* Palipehutu; Palipehutu-Forces Nationales pour la Libération
Parti pour l'Unité et la Sauvegarde de l'Integrité du Congo (PUSIC), 25
Parti Social Démocrate (PSD), 83, 103
Parti Solidaire Africain (PSA), 267
patronage, 224
patron-client ties, 210, 224; clientelism of representation, 269
People's Power Committees (PPC), 231
People's Republic of China (PRC), 129
People's Self-Defense Force (PDF), 231
Platteau, Jean-Philippe, 94
Ploquin, Jean-Francois, 258
political myths, 57–68; and ethnicity, 57; and ethnogenesis, 65–66; and genocide 57–64; and Greater Rwanda, 64–65; and Hamitic hypothesis, 57–58; of origins, 92. *See also* myth-making
Power, 62, 63
power-sharing, Burundi, 168–69
premise of inequality, xi, 34, 92; in Burundi, 31
Pretoria, 145, 152, 165
Protocole de la Réconciliation Nationale entre les Rwandais, 116
Prunier, Gérard, 97
Putnam, Robert, xiii, 205, 207, 214, 215
Pweto, 240, 246

Radio Libre des Mille Collines, 82, 93, 104, 111, 118
Radjabu, Hussein, 159, 167, 173–78, 185, 187
Ranke, Leopold von, 56
Ranger, Terence, 51, 52
Rassemblement Congolais pour la Démocratie (RCD), 11, 23, 34, 67, 96, 235, 251;

clones of, 24; defections from, 252; and ethnic divisions, 25; factions, 217, 234; involvement in export of minerals, 243; RCD-Goma, 232; Rwanda dominance of, 23; sponsored by Kigali, 232
Rassemblement Congolais pour la Démocratie-Bunia (RCD-Bunia), 233, 236
Rassemblement Congolais pour la Démocratie-Goma (RCD-Goma), 232, 236, 237, 253
Rassemblement Congolais pour la Démocratie-Mouvement de Libération (RCD-ML), 25
refugees (Hutu), 182; armed by Kabila, 21; as conflict-generating factor, 20; destruction of camps, 214, 223; in eastern Zaire, 96, 230; killed by AFDL, 231; killings by RPA, 234; and land problem in Burundi, 182–83; manipulation of, 20; raids on Rwanda, 20; turning against Tutsi civilians, 135; as vectors of violence, 223
refugees (Tutsi), as "fifty-niners," 14, 228; and expropriation of native lands, 14–15; as foreigners, 13; "refugee warriors," 228
regroupment camps (Burundi), 148, 163–64
Regroupement des Nationalistes Congolais (RENACO), 268
Reporters Without Borders, 178
revolution, 113; ethnic underpinnings of, 114; exclusionary implications, 114; Hutu, 113; Hutu and Nazi revolutions, 112, 113; impact on Burudi, 148
Reyntjens, Filip, 77, 91, 106, 125, 161, 165, 170, 251
Richards, Paul, 74, 76
Ricoeur, Paul, xi, 100, 102; on memory and translaboration, 108
Rosenberg, Tina, 90
Rothchild, Donald, 124
Ruberwa, Azarias, 23, 237, 266, 270
Rubuka, Aloys, 176
Ruhengeri killings, 122
Ruhimbika, Manasse, 23, 237
Rujiro, Tibere, 243
Rumonge, 134, 136
Rutshuru, 3, 6, 9, 28; Banyarwanda immigration into, 209
Ruzibiza, Abdul Joshua, xii, 133
Rwabugiri (king; *mwami*), 64, 215
Rwabukumba, Seraphin, 84

Rwagasore (prince), 141, 145
Rwanda, ix, x; compared to Burundi, x, xi; Congo connection, 276; exports of diamonds from, 254; genocide, 79–86, 109–28; and the Holocaust, 109; Hutu revolution, 81; invasion by RPF, 81, 116; and Jews, 111; and premise of inequality, xi; plundering of mineral wealth, 254; site of genuine revolution, 135; thinly disguised dictatorship, x
Rwanda Alliance for National Unity (RANU), 38
Rwanda Defense Forces (RDF), 10; and destruction of refugee camps, 223
Rwanda Patriotic Army (RPA), 33, 66, 69, 229, 239, 242; as shield for Banyamulenge, 259
Rwanda Patriotic Front (RPF), xii, 10, 12, 37, 73, 83, 86, 91, 146; attacks on civilians, 122; invasion by, 119; invasion of Rwanda, 81; and Israel, 111–12; responsibility in genocide, 116; responsibility in killing Hutu, 133; search and destroy operations in DRC, 92, 133; targeting of IDPs by, 126. *See also* Front Patriotique Rwandais (FPR)
Rwandophone, 12, 222; allochtons and autochtons, 278
Rwasa, Agathon, 142, 145, 161; and biblical mysticism, 148
Rwigema, Fred, 38

Sachs, Jeffrey, 186
Sagatwa, Elie, 86
Salim Saleh (general), 242, 243
Samset, Ingrid, 254
Sanders, Edith, 67
Sans Défaite et Sans Echec militia, 177
Savimbi, Jonas, 233
Schatzberg, Michael, 250
Scott, James, 9
security sector reform (SSR), 187
Seeing Like a State, 9. *See also* Scott, James
Sékou Touré, 267
Seligman, C. G., 54
Sémelin, Jacques, 120, 131, 136, 137
Sendashonga, Seth, 96
Serubuga, Laurent, 85
Serufuli, Eugene, 27, 28
Service National de Renseignement (SNR), 185

Shaba insurrections, 227
Shweka, Mutabazi, 237
Simbananiye, Arthémon, 138
Simba rebellion, 24
Simon Wiesenthal Center, 112
Smith, Stephen, 104, 105
social capital: origin of concept, 206; neglected aspects, 206–7; and democratic performance, 214
Société Minière de Bakwanga (MIBA), 244
Société Minière et Industrielle du Kivu (Sominki), 242
South Africa, 154
Spitaels, R., 208
Stanley, Henry Morton, 51
Stearns, Jason, 269
Strizek, Helmut, 101
Sudan People's Liberation Army (SPLA), 22
Swing, William, 262

Tabliq, 40
Ternon, Yves, 120
Thambwe, Alexis, 22
Third Reich, 91
Tibasima, John Ateenyi, 25, 236, 243
Tilly, Charles, 26
Todorov, Tzvetan, 98
Tous pour la Paix et le Développement (TPD), 27
Transitional Constitutional Act, 192, 194
Truth and Reconciliation Commission (TRC), 77, 78, 166
Tshisekedi, Etienne, 192, 193, 194, 225, 266
Tull, Denis, 27
Tutu, Desmond, 77
Tutsi (Burundi): extremism, 144; Hima vs. Banyaruguru, 137; internal struggles, 137–38; involvement in 1972 genocide, 136–38; supremacy, 139–40
Tutsi (Rwanda): and Banyamulenge, 57; diaspora, 37; exodus, 36; extremism, 114; Hima empire, 61; killings of Hutu, 136–38; and JRR, 138; as "pastoral Europeans," 54; pre-Tutsi traditions, 56; physical markers, 253; refugees into Burundi, 143; re-imagined by Europeans, 55; roots in Kivu, 210; slaughter of, 234; second-generation diaspora, 38–39; stereotypes, 60–64; transfer of land to, 211; and UNAR, 37; women as Mataharis, 61, 62. *See also* Banyamulenge
Twagiramungu, Faustin, 83, 96

Uganda, 235, 243, 246; backing of rebel factions, 256; confrontation with Rwanda, 25; and looting of minerals, 242, 254; plunder and war effort in, 254
Uganda People's Defense Forces (UPDF), 234, 242
UMOJA, 28
Umutesi, Béatrice, 20
Uniao Nacional para a Independencia Total de Angola (UNITA), 97, 233, 239
Union Démocratique Populaire et Sociale (UDPS), 193, 196, 199, 225, 266, 270
Union des Démocrates Indépendants (UDI), 193
Union des Fédéralistes et Républicains Indépendants (UFERI), 196, 199, 200; pogroms against Kasaians, 226
Union des Forces Nationalistes et Lumumbistes (UFONAL), 196
Union Nationale des Travailleurs Zairois (UNTZ), 198
Union Nationale Rwandaise (UNAR), 38, 114
Union pour la Nation (UN), 268
Union pour le Progrès National (Uprona), 134
Union Sacrée (US), 191
Union Sacrée de l'Opposition Radicale (USOR), 195, 196
United Nations High Commission for Refugees (UNHCR), 96, 153, 183
United Nations Mission in Rwanda, 63
United States Committee for Refugees, 40, 95
USAID, xii, xv
Uvin, Peter, 93, 114
Uvira, 10, 237
Uwilingiyimana, Agathe, 103

Van Acker, Frank, 24
Vangu Commission, 16
Vansina, Jan, 56
Veyne, Paul, 57
Victoria Group, 343
Vidal Claudine, 55, 105

Villers, Gauthier de, 250
violence, ix, x; anti-Tutsi, 75, 115, 121; against Banyarwanda, 213, 229; as discourse, 74–76; effect on wildlife, 4; ethnic cleansing, 77; and greed, 256; instrumental use of, 122; rationality of, 121; and RPF invasion, 121; as subliminal text, 77; as self-fulfilling prophecy, 139
Vircoulon, Thierry, 15, 272
Virunga National Park, 8
Vlassenroot, Koen, xv, 15, 24, 245, 252, 254, 256

Wagner, Michele, 94
Walle, Nicholas van de, 272
Wamba dia Wamba, Ernest, 97, 217, 233, 236, 258
Wedgewood, C. V., 29
Weiner, Myron, 20
West Nile Liberation Front (WNLF), 40
Westerman, Diedrich, 54

We Wish to Inform You That Tomorrow We Will Be Killed with Our Families, 89. *See also* Gourevitch, Philip
Wilde, Oscar, ix
Winter, Roger 95
Wolpe, Howard, 150, 155
Woodrow Wilson Center (WWC), 155
World Bank, 255; aid to Burundi, 187–88, 218
Wrong, Michela, 251

Yav Nawesh (general), 239
Young, Crawford, 43, 51, 224, 253, 268

Zaire, 191
Zakaria, Fareed, 157
Zartman, William, 221
Zigiranyirazo, Protée, 84
Zimbabwe Defense Forces (ZDF), 244
Zimbabwe Defense Industries (ZDI), 244
Zuma, Jacob, 152, 164
Zvinavashe, Vitalis (general), 244

Acknowledgments

My immediate purpose in putting together this volume is to make readily accessible to interested scholars a selection of my recent (and not so recent) writing on former Belgian Africa. Although most of these appeared in professional journals and edited volumes, none was a source of high visibility. The themes explored in this book have incubated in a wonderfully stimulating and diverse academic environment. Following my long-awaited retirement from the University of Florida, and from the time I left USAID in 1998, after four years in Abidjan and two in Accra as Regional Advisor for Democracy and Governance, I had the opportunity to serve as visiting lecturer at Berkeley, Smith College, Concordia (Montreal), and Brown and subsequently at the universities of Bordeaux, Antwerp, Copenhagen, and Helsinki. My post-retirement gypsy-scholar career has given me plenty of occasions to bounce ideas off an array of students, colleagues, and USAID officials, who to one degree or another shared my interest in the tragic destinies of the Great Lakes region of Central Africa. Their contributions are reflected in many of the essays in this volume.

I have many people to thank, first and foremost, the students in my graduate seminars at the universities of California at Berkeley, Antwerp, and Copenhagen. Many have gently provoked me into rethinking some of the ideas developed in this book. I owe a special debt to Filip Reyntjens, my long-time friend and colleague at the University of Antwerp, whose knowledge of the politics of the Great Lakes is unsurpassed, and to Holger Hansen, Chair of the African Studies Center at the University of Copenhagen, for repeatedly inviting me to teach and lecture on Central Africa. My long-time friend and colleague Frank Chalk deserves equal thanks for iniviting me to teach at Concordia University (Montreal) in the fall of 2000. Special mention is owed to Danielle De Lame, for sharing with me her wide-ranging expertise on Rwanda, and to David and Catharine Newbury for keeping me abreast of their pioneering work on the Great Lakes and their continuing support in my efforts to challenge received ideas about the history and politics of the region. No words can properly acknowledge my indebtedness to Jan Vansina: our many phone conversations on Rwanda's complicated past have provided me with powerful adrenalin boosts when I needed them most. I am also grateful to Koen Vlassenroot, of the University of Ghent, for his patience and unfailing assistance in sharing with me his meticulous knowledge of Mai-Mai politics in eastern Congo. And I much appreciate the judicious advice proffered by Crawford Young and David Newbury while putting the finishing touch to the manuscript.

Thanks are due as well to my African friends and graduate students who, sometimes literally, went out of their way to educate me on the past and recent history of the region. Among the many names that spring to mind, those of Maurice Niwese, Deo Niyonzima, Willy Nindorera, Jean-Marie Ngendahayo, Séverin Mugangu, Bucyalimwe Mararo, Emmanuel Lubala, Bosco Mushikwa, Antoine Ghonda Mangalibi, Pierre Nzokizwanimana, Roger Bashali, and Roger Kasereka deserve special mention. None of them, to use the ritual phrase, are responsible for any errors of fact and interpretation that the reader may detect. I also owe a special debt of gratitude to Ashley Leinweber for helping me navigate the treacherous waters of electronic files when the time came to submit the manuscript to the editor.

I also wish to extend my appreciation to the editors and publishers of the following books and journals for permission to reprint—with only minor alterations in the text and titles—the materials appearing in this volume: Chapter 1 ("The Geopolitics of the Great Lakes Region") from *L'Afrique des Grands Lacs, Annuaire 2005–6*, ed. Filip Reyntjens and Stefaan Marysse (Paris: L'Harmattan, 2006), pp. 25–54; Chapter 2 ("The Road to Hell in the Great Lakes") from *Facing Ethnic Conflicts: Toward a New Realism*, ed. Andreas Wimmer et al. (New York and Oxford: Rowman and Littlefield, 2004), pp. 61–77; Chapter 3 ("Ethnicity as Myth") from *Armed Conflict in Africa*, ed. Carolyn Pumphrey and Rye Schwartz-Barcott (New York: Scarecrow Press, 2003), pp. 87–112; Chapter 4 ("Genocide in Central Africa: Which Genocide? Whose Genocide?"), *African Studies Review* 41, no. 1 (April 1998): 3–16; Chapter 5 ("The Rationality of Genocide") from *Genocide: Essays Toward Understanding Early Warning and Prevention*, ed. Roger Smith (Williamsburg: Association of Genocide Scholars, 1999), pp. 17–25; Chapter 6 ("Hate Crimes"), *Transition*, nos. 81–82 (2000): 114–33; Chapter 8 ("Rwanda and the Holocaust Reconsidered") from *The Political Economy of the Great Lakes Region in Africa* (London and New York: Palgrave, 2005), pp. 48–71, first published in *The Journal of Genocide Research* 4, no. 4 (December 2002): 499–518; Chapter 10 ("Burundi at the Cross-Roads") from *Security Dynamics in*

Africa's Great Lakes Region, ed. Gilbert Khadiagala (Boulder: Lynne Rienner, 2006), pp. 41–58; Chapter 11 ("Burundi's Endangered Transition") from *Working Paper*, Swiss Peace Foundation, 2006; Chapter 14 ("DRC: From Failure to Potential Reconstruction") from *State Failure and State Weakness in a Time of Terror*, ed. Robert Rotberg (Washington, D.C.: Brookings Institution, 2003), pp. 29–70; and Chapter 15 ("The Tunnel at the End of the Light"), *Review of Political Economy*, nos. 93–94 (2002): 389–98.

Contributions not previously published include Chapters 7 ("The Politics of Memory"), 9 ("Burundi 1972: A Forgotten Genocide"), 12 ("A Blocked Transition: Zaire in 1993"), 13 ("Ethnic Violence, Public Policies and Social Capital in North Kivu"), and 16 ("From Kabila to Kabila: What Else Is New?"). The first was presented in Copenhagen in 2002 at a conference on the Rwanda genocide organized by the Danish Center for Holocaust and Genocide Studies. The second was prepared for the 2006 colloquium "Opting for Genocide," organized by Andreas Mehler and cosponsored by the Hamburg Institute of Social Research and the Institute of African Affairs of the University of Hamburg. The third is from a lengthier report commissioned in 1993 while I served as USAID Regional Adviser on Governance and Democracy for West Africa, in Abidjan. The fourth is a communication written for the conference "Social Capital in Eastern Congo," organized at the University of Antwerp, in 2001. The final chapter was specifically written for this volume following the 2006 elections in the DRC.